PROJECTIVE
Psychology

CLINICAL APPROACHES
TO THE TOTAL PERSONALITY

▼

EDITED BY

Lawrence Edwin Abt & Leopold Bellak

GROVE PRESS, INC.   NEW YORK
John Calder, Ltd.   London

Contributors

▼

Lawrence Edwin Abt, Ph.D.
Consulting Psychologist, New York City and Larchmont, New York

Leopold Bellak, M.D.
Director of Psychiatry, City Hospital at Elmhurst, N. Y.

Daniel Brower, Ph.D.
Consulting Psychologist, New York City and Upper Montclair, New Jersey

Susan K. Deri, M.A.
Psychologist in Private Practice, New York City

Molly R. Harrower, Ph.D.
Research Professor of Clinical Psychology, Department of Psychiatry, Temple University Medical Center, Philadelphia

Asya L. Kadis
Director of Group Psychotherapy Department, Postgraduate Center for Psychotherapy, New York City

Sidney Levy, Ph.D.
Director, Research Institute for Personality, Psychotherapy, and Education, New York City

Robert M. Lindner, Ph.D.
(1914-1956)

Ruth L. Munroe, Ph.D.
Visiting Professor, Graduate Division, College of the City of New York

Harold M. Proshansky, Ph.D.
Department of Psychology, Brooklyn College

Joseph M. Sacks, Ph.D.
Chief, Clinical Psychology Service, Veterans Administration Hospital, Brockton, Mass.

Arthur Weider, Ph.D.
Research and Medical Psychologist, New York City

Fredric Wertham, M.D.
Director Lafargue Clinic, New York City

Adolf G. Woltmann, M.S.
Consulting Psychologist, New York City

Introduction

▼

THIS *Projective Psychology* is a welcome contribution to both the theory and the practice of projective methods. As the title indicates, this volume is concerned with *projective psychology*, which is emerging as a body of concepts and methods clearly to be distinguished from most of the other divisions or schools of psychology. As stated by Dr. Abt in the paper on "A Theory of Projective Psychology,"

> we may look upon perception as an active and purposeful process which involves the whole organism in relation to its field. By its nature perceptual activity has roots that extend deeply into the whole matrix of the individual's past experiences, and the perceptual activities of the individual reach out to fashion his orientation to the future.

This statement unequivocally asserts the dynamic, constitutive character of all perception, which, as Dr. Bellak says, is "apperception—defined as meaningful perception."

It is important to recognize here what seems to be essential for both the study and the diagnosis of the individual, identified personality—namely, that there is an active process going on of transforming the world of situations and people into the forms, meanings, and values which the individual has learned selectively to perceive, by imposing upon them or investing them with the meanings they have for him.

In my opinion this does not imply any subjectivism or dualism or any other of the traditional assumptions. Rather, it is a recognition of how each organism comes to terms with life, and how the human organism, becoming a personality, learns selectively to perceive and to respond to the environing world of events and people *as they appear to him* and as he feels toward them.

It is being recognized that each individual, having grown up and been educated (in the larger sense) in a cultural group, will, of necessity, perceive the world of events and of people in the traditional patterns of his culture. How each individual receives and responds to this cultural patterning and to parental care, rearing, and training will be revealed in his idiomatic perception and his individualized way of thinking, acting, and feeling, as disclosed by projective tests.

This recently developed conception of perception, coming from experimental studies and intensive clinical investigation by psychoanalysts, provides one of the major contributions to dynamic psychology, probably of equal significance with the conception of libidinal energy, instincts, and other terms indicative of striving and desiring in the organism, if not of greater significance.

For psychology, this newer orientation directly conflicts with the long accepted ideas of stimulus and response (the psychologist's version of cause and effect) and raises serious question about the validity of the assumption that the stimulus or question presented by the experimenter will mean to the subject (animal or human) what the experimenter has decided it should mean to the subject.

Thus the ideal of objectivity in psychological studies is beginning to receive critical examination as it is realized that a situation or a questionnaire, however standardized and objectively presented, will be perceived and responded to by each subject in his nearly unique way, although there will be in any large series of subjects certain regularities.

As I have suggested elsewhere,[1] there are a number of new developments in scientific thinking and procedures which depart radically from the assumptions and methodologies long accepted as "the" scientific method. Some of these new assumptions are peculiarly appropriate to the problem of personality development and the clinical task of diagnosing individual personalities.

Thus the notion of "feed back" and servo-mechanisms coming from electrical engineering is bringing into contemporary discussion the conception of circular processes whereby a machine or

---

[1] *Projective Methods* (Springfield, Ill.: C. C. Thomas; 1948).

an organism may exhibit a capacity for self-regulation, of selective awareness and even purposive striving, that do not occur as simple cause and effect or stimulus and response. Nor is it possible to deal adequately with some of these problems of individual personality development or diagnoses by recourse to the familiar statistical techniques or standardized tests that are concerned with group regularities, not idiomatic expressions. Increasingly it is being recognized that we must develop a "biological relativity" to deal with the problem of the individual organism-personality, every single measurement of which is relative to that individual and to all the other measurements or observations we make.

While it may to some appear far-fetched, it may be suggested that the rise of dynamic psychology and of projective methods is comparable to the emergence of quantum physics and the new concepts and methodologies developed for the study of identified events as contrasted with the study of statistical regularities of anonymous events or particles, as in classical physics.

While it is not necessary to approach projective psychology with this orientation, it may be helpful to recognize these newer conceptions and methodologies as offering a way of understanding projective psychology, and more especially the projective methods presented in this volume.

As indicated in the table of Contents, the papers in Part II deal with individual projective methods for clinical use, and those in Part III with the application of projective methods to industry and to action research. The ten papers in Part II present both the theory and the application of a number of projective methods for clinical work, indicating the special advantages of each method. The papers in Part III are indicative of the growing need for more dynamic concepts and methods in the study of groups and social situations where both research and practical decisions have been handicapped heretofore by the reliance on methods that could yield only limited results. While it is hazardous to prophesy, it seems clear that social psychology and sociology will increasingly face problems for which they will need these new and promising projective procedures and these recently developed understandings of perception and dynamic psychology.

Lawrence K. Frank

Preface

▼

THIS book has been prepared because of the great need that exists today to bring within the confines of one volume for easy reference the variety of projective tests and procedures that constitute the growing armamentarium of the clinical psychologist. Although virtually all clinicians are familiar with at least several projective procedures and employ them as appropriate, there is no one today who is fully in command of the vast amount of knowledge and highly developed special skills that the projective methods presented in *Projective Psychology: Clinical Approaches to the Total Personality* require in clinical use.

For this reason principally, and also because of the fact that projective psychology is a rapidly growing discipline in which many clinicians should have a voice, we have preferred to have the separate chapters on the several projective instruments and procedures prepared by leading workers whose competence with a particular technique or application in a special setting has been established. The result, we believe, is a happier one than might have occurred had we ourselves presumed to present the field of projective psychology from the background of our experience alone.

The projective methods offered have been chosen with a catholicity which grows out of our belief that projective psychology is young and vigorous, and that it is important to set forth what is actually being practiced at the present time. We have imposed no restrictions upon the contributors, urging each to express as fully as he liked his own views, and asking only that the material offered have a practical orientation which may increase its usefulness as it finds application in the hands of others. The emphasis in each instance is chiefly upon the clinical use of the various procedures rather than upon their use as research tools in personality or clinical inquiries.

To each of the contributors we wish to express our deep appreciation and thanks, and we hope that the full volume does justice to their individual labors. Unavoidable complexities of publication made it impossible to include the contributions of three authors originally scheduled to participate. They were Gerhardt Saenger, Helen Sargeant, and Howard Siple. We greatly regret not having their excellent contributions and wish to express our thanks for their good will and cooperation.

We are especially grateful to Virginia R. Abt and Sonya Sorel Bellak, who have done so much to lighten our editorial task through their own sustained efforts.

L. E. A.
L. B.

New York

Contents

▼

PART I

The Theoretical Foundations of Projective Psychology

PART II

Projective Tests in Clinical Psychology

PART III
Projective Tests in Nonclinical Areas

Figures

▼

Tables

▼

PART I

▼

The Theoretical Foundations
of Projective Psychology

The Theoretical Foundations of Projective Psychology

INTRODUCTION

Both of the papers that comprise Part I may be looked upon as an introduction to projective methods through an examination of their theoretical foundations. Since the explicit formulation of the projective hypothesis by Lawrence K. Frank[1] in 1939, not only have projective methods had increasingly wider application, but their number, scope, and purpose have become correspondingly enlarged. The almost inevitable consequence of the developments in this area during the past decade has been an ever-widening gap between the several projective test procedures and their theoretical substructures. There is a continuous interaction between theory and practice in any science or discipline, and it is becoming increasingly necessary to seek an integration between theory and practice in projective psychology as one step in the direction of continuous mutual enrichment of empiricism and construct building.

There is impressive evidence on all sides, as work goes forward feverishly in the development of new projective tests, that these methods have begun to outgrow their theoretical backgrounds and that the time for serious stock-taking of their basic theoretical foundations has long been at hand. It is in the form of consideration of such issues that the two chapters that follow concern themselves.

In common with other scientists, psychologists develop five chief kinds of materials: (1) intellectual tools and concepts; (2) descriptions of specific situation-person relationships as represented by genetic and dynamic studies of personality; (3) hypotheses; (4) physiological and psychological models; and (5) propositions of some degree of generality which have been found

---

[1] L. K. Frank: "Projective Methods for the Study of Personality," *Journal of Psychology*, Vol. 8, (1939), pp. 389–413.

to be consistent with more or less comprehensive bodies of physiological and psychological evidence.

The intellectual tools and concepts of the science of psychology consist of a multitude of definitions, distinctions, and constructs to which psychological data may be ordered. These intellectual tools and concepts, of whatever sort and degree of generality, represent the habits of thought of psychologists—the manner in which they have found it useful and rewarding to think and talk about psychological phenomena, the classifications they have found helpful, the concepts that have demonstrated their fruitfulness in the construction of hypotheses and models, and those portions of the language of mathematics and of statistical methods which have demonstrated value in psychological inquiries.

There is a growing body of genetic and dynamic studies of personality which has in recent years reached impressive proportions. These personality inquiries have suggested concepts, hypotheses, and models, and they have provided information that may be used to test the "truth" of psychological propositions. A prominent example of a concept that has helped to stimulate and guide research is that of the self which currently enjoys great vogue.

Hypotheses and models fall largely in the realm of speculation and cannot usually be sharply distinguished from each other. A hypothesis is a proposition that the investigator has some reason to believe may turn out to be "true"—that is, one which may turn out to be consistent with a substantial body of relevant evidence. An instance of such a hypothesis is the notion that personality may be looked upon as a Gestalt which runs a dynamic course in time. Models may be simply an elaborate form of hypothesis—assumptions and conclusions deduced to be consistent with a set of propositions and therefore capable of being regarded as probably "true." Such models frequently help to refine existing concepts and tools of analysis and somewhat less often play a role in the development of further hypotheses.

In psychology models have the important advantage of requiring the investigator to offer an explicit statement of his assumptions. Hence the process of model building helps to give precision to psychological thinking, contributes to forcing the investigator to recognize the limitations of the particular set of assumptions with which he is working, and may aid him in recognizing and perhaps accepting alternative possibilities which might otherwise not have come to his attention. The current conception of the ego, id, and superego, as originally developed by Freud and elaborated by many others, is of the order of a model that may possess great heuristic value in clinical psychological formulations.

There is reason to believe that during the past two decades in particular the psychology of personality has made substantial progress in adding to the store of its intellectual tools, in increasing the volume of studies concerned with the "total personality" in contrast to more segmental inquiries, in developing important and potentially far-reaching hypotheses. The projective hypothesis is an example that may be continuously put to crucial test short of actual experimentation by means of any one or a combination of the several projective methods.

The projective hypothesis, it is becoming more and more clear, has to be handled with considerable care. There is, for example, the possibility of an incautious extrapolation of the notion beyond the limits for which it was devised. Of perhaps greater current significance, however, stands an additional consideration. Behind the projective hypothesis itself stands a whole matrix of assumptions which probably differ from one projective psychologist to another and which have largely been kept implicit. If projective psychology is to grow in acceptance and validity, it is essential that these assumptions be made fully explicit and it is necessary that they be tested to ascertain whether they have established validity and generality within the area of inquiry in which they are being employed. It is clear that the conditions of their testing must be public and repeatable upon demand if the data they provide are to be admitted to the general body of concepts and propositions which will prove useful in personality study and in clinical psychological evaluation.

The question of the validity and reliability of the several projective methods is something of concern to a considerable body of professional workers, and developments in projective psychology must be in the direction of satisfying demands with respect to these matters. There is an impressive body of professional experience, however, which testifies to the need, at least as far as projective tests are concerned, for looking upon validity and reliability of projective procedures as likely to be something of a quite different order from similar notions about psychometric tests. Behind the expressed concern for validity and reliability probably exists a series of reservations about the body of propositions upon which the projective hypothesis actually rests. In the broadest sense of the expression, these propositions are derived from psychoanalysis, and their specific nature has to be set forth before new ground can be broken in projective psychology.

More important than the full statement of the propositions of psychoanalysis upon which projective psychology rests is the undertaking of a serious effort to relate analytical and non-analytical psychology more closely to what is likely to be the advantage of each. In a small way the two chapters that next follow move in this direction.

▼

In this first paper Dr. Leopold Bellak traces the historical development of the concept of projection, now so widely and loosely used. Attempting to verify experimentally Freud's original clinical description of projection, he found it necessary to redefine the perceptual processes involved in what are known as projective methods. While he prefers to use the terms "apperceptive psychology" and "apperceptive distortion" in preference to the more familiar terminology, Bellak's contribution places him quite clearly in the main stream of projective psychology. If his terminology should appear convincing and useful, it will find acceptance in due time. His attempt to restate basic psychoanalytical concepts in terms of the process of apperceptive distortion and the Gestalt theory of learning will certainly require further experimental work and exploration.

His formulation of personality theory based upon this reconceptualization should, however, help to resolve some of the problems facing the clinician using projective methods. It constitutes one span of the bridge across the schism that still separates nonanalytical from analytical psychology. The span is completed, and further supported, in the next paper.

▼

On the Problems of the Concept of Projection

A THEORY OF APPERCEPTIVE DISTORTION

Leopold Bellak

INTRODUCTION

PROJECTION is a term very much in use in present-day clinical, dynamic, and social psychology. Frank [8][1] suggests that projective methods are typical of the current general trend toward a dynamic and holistic approach in recent psychological science as

---

[1] Italic figures in brackets refer to the "References" at the end of each paper.

well as in natural science. In the context of his article he likens projective techniques to the position of spectral analysis in physical science.

The term "projection" was introduced by Freud *[9]* as early as 1894 in his paper "The Anxiety Neurosis," in which he said: "The psyche develops the neurosis of anxiety when it feels itself unequal to the task of mastering *[sexual]* excitation arising endogenously. That is to say, it acts as if it had projected this excitation into the outer world."

In 1896, in a paper "On the Defense Neuropsychoses" *[10]*, elaborating further on projection, Freud stated more explicitly that projection is a process of ascribing one's own drives, feelings, and sentiments to other people or to the outside world as a defensive process that permits one to be unaware of these "undesirable" phenomena in oneself. Further elaboration of the concept took place in his paper on the case of Schreber *[11]* in connection with paranoia. In brief, the paranoiac has certain homosexual tendencies which he transforms under the pressure of his superego from "I love him" to "I hate him," a reaction formation. This hatred he then projects onto or ascribes to the former love object, who has become the persecutor. The ascription of hatred takes place presumably because emergence into consciousness and realization of the hatred is prohibited by the superego, and because an externalized danger is more readily dealt with than is an internal one. More specifically, the superego inhibits expression of the hatred because it morally disapproves of it.

Healy, Bronner, and Bowers *[16]* define projection, similarly, as "a defensive process under the sway of the pleasure principle whereby the ego thrusts forth on the external world unconscious wishes and ideas which, if allowed to penetrate into consciousness, would be painful to the ego."

While projection thus originated in connection with psychoses and neuroses, it was later applied by Freud to other forms of behavior; for example, as the main mechanism in the formation of religious beliefs as set forth in *The Future of an Illusion [12]* and in *Totem and Taboo [13]*. Even in this cultural context, projection was still seen as a defensive process against anxiety. While Freud originally considered repression the only defense mechanism, at least ten mechanisms are at present spoken of in the psychoanalytic literature. Although projection is firmly established as one of the most important defensive processes, relatively little work has been done on it. Sears [26] says: "Probably the most inadequately defined term in all psychoanalytic theory is projection." There is a long list of papers on projection, however, particularly clinical-psychoanalytic ones and some academic ones.

The widest use of the term "projection" has been made in the field of clinical psychology in connection with so-called projective techniques. These include the Rorschach Test, the Thematic Apperception Test, the Szondi, Sentence Completion, and a great number of other procedures. The basic assumption in the use of these tests is that the subject is presented with a number of ambiguous stimuli and is then invited to respond to these stimuli. By such means it is assumed that the subject projects his own needs and press and that these will appear as responses to the ambiguous stimuli.

The definition of projection previously stated served our purposes well until a crucial point arose in connection with attempts at the experimental investigation of the phenomenon which are reported elsewhere [3, 4]. The first experiment consisted in provoking a number of subjects and giving them pictures of the Thematic Apperception Test under controlled conditions. In the second experiment the subjects were given the posthypnotic order to feel aggression (without being directly aware of it) while telling stories about the pictures. In both instances the subjects behaved according to the hypothesis of projection and produced a significant increase of aggression as compared with their responses to the pictures without having been made to feel aggressive first. Similarly, when the subjects were under posthypnotic order and were told that they were extremely depressed and unhappy, it was found that they projected these sentiments into their stories. Until this point there was no need to change the concept of projection as the ascription to the outside world of sentiments that are unacceptable to the ego.

When the experiment was varied, however, to the extent that the posthypnotic order was given to the subject that he should feel extremely elated, it was found that elation too was projected into the stories to the Thematic Apperception Test pictures. At this point it occurred to me that this could not possibly be subsumed under the concept of projection as a defense mechanism, since there obviously was no particular need for the ego to guard against the "disruptive" effects of joy. Such a case can be hypothesized, for example, as when joy is inappropriate, as in the death of a person toward whom ambivalence is felt. Such was not the case, however, in the experiment. Therefore it was necessary to examine further the concept of projective phenomena and to suggest a re-examination of underlying processes.

As so often happens, it was found on careful rereading of Freud (following a reference by Dr. Ernst Kris) that Freud had anticipated our present trend of thought. He said in *Totem and Taboo* [13], page 857

> But projection is not specially created for the purpose of defence, it also comes into being where there are no conflicts. The projection of inner perceptions to the outside is a primitive mechanism which, for instance, also influences our sense-perceptions, so that it normally has the greatest share, in shaping our outer world. Under conditions that have not yet been sufficiently determined even inner perceptions of ideational and emotional processes are projected outwardly, like sense perceptions, and are used to shape the outer world, whereas they ought to remain in the inner world.

And (on page 879):

> The thing which we, just like primitive man, project in outer reality, can hardly be anything else but the recognition of a state in which a given thing is present to the senses and to consciousness, next to which another state exists in which the thing is *latent*, but can reappear, that is to say, the co-existence of perception and memory, or, to generalize it, the existence of unconscious psychic processes next to conscious ones.

I believe that this thought of Freud's, not further elaborated upon or not systematically expressed anywhere and stated without any of the sophistication of modern semantics, contains everything necessary for a consistent theory of projection and general perception.

Freud's main assumption is that memories of percepts influence perception of contemporary stimuli. The interpretation of the Thematic Apperception Test is, indeed, based on such an assumption. I believe that the subject's past perception of his own father influences his perception of father figures in TAT pictures, and that this constitutes a valid and reliable sample of his usual perceptions of father figures. Clinical experience, as well as experimental investigation, has borne out this point. My own experiments have shown that the behavior of the experimenter can bring out sentiments that originally were probably related to the father figure. While these sentiments had a demonstrable but temporary over-all influence on the perception of stimuli, individual differences were maintained according to the genetically determined structure of the personality.

It seems, then, that percept memories influence the perception of contemporary stimuli and not only for the narrowly defined purposes of defense, as stated in the original definition of projection. We are compelled to assume that *all* present perception is influenced by past perception, and that indeed the nature of the perceptions and their interaction with each other constitutes the field of the psychology of personality.[2]

It is necessary to describe the nature of these perceptual processes and later to attempt to formulate a psychoanalytic psychology of personality based on these conceptions.

APPERCEPTION AND APPERCEPTIVE DISTORTION

To use the term "projection" for the general perceptual processes described above does not seem very useful in view of the history of the concept and its present clinical applications. On the other hand, "perception" has been so definitely linked with a system of psychology which has not been concerned with the *whole* personality that I hesitate to use it in the context of dynamic psychology any further. While terminology is certainly not a matter of primary importance here, I propose that the term "apperception" be used henceforth.[3] I define apperception as an organ-

---

[2] This theory, in its broadest implications—namely, that perception is subjective and is the primary datum of all psychology—is, of course, not original with Freud. Hume's *"Nihil est in intellectu quid non antea fuerit in sensibus"* is practically a perceptual theory of personality. Similarly, philosophical idealism, such as Schopenhauer's *Die Welt als Wille und Vorstellung* and Kant's transcendental state, represents a similar position.

[3] I prefer the following definition (from C. P. Herbart: *Psychologie als Wissenschaft*, Part III, Sect. 1, Ch. 5, p. 15, as quoted in Dagobert D. Runes, (ed.): *Dictionary of Philosophy*): "Apperception (lat. *ad* plus *percipere* to perceive). in psychology: The process by which new experience is assimilated to and transformed by the residuum of past experience of any individual to form a new whole. The residuum of past experience is called apperceptive mass."

ism's (dynamically) meaningful interpretation of a perception. This definition and the use of the term "apperception" permit us to suggest, purely for the purpose of a working hypothesis, that there can be a hypothetical process of noninterpreted perception, and that every subjective interpretation constitutes a dynamically meaningful *apperceptive distortion*. Instead, we can also establish, operationally, a condition of nearly pure cognitive "objective" perception in which a majority of subjects agree on the exact definition of a stimulus. For instance, the majority of subjects agree that Picture No. I of the TAT shows a boy playing the violin. Thus we can establish this perception as a norm, and say that anyone who, for instance, describes this picture as a boy at a lake (as one schizophrenic patient did) distorts the stimulus situation apperceptively. If we let any of our subjects go on to further description of the stimulus, however, we find that each one of them interprets the stimulus differently; for example, as a happy boy, a sad boy, an ambitious boy, a boy urged on by his parents. Therefore we must state that purely cognitive perception remains a hypothesis, and that every person distorts apperceptively, the distortions differing only in degree.

In the clinical use of the TAT it becomes quite clear that we deal with apperceptive distortions of different degrees. The subject is frequently unaware of any subjective significance in the story he tells. In clinical practice [5] it has appeared that simply asking the subject to read over his typed-out story may often give him sufficient distance from the situation to perceive that the gross aspects of it refer to himself. Only after considerable psychotherapy, however, may he see his more latent drives; yet he may never be able to "see" the least acceptable of his subjective distortions, on the presence of which any number of independent observers might agree. It may be permissible, then, to introduce a number of terms for apperceptive distortion of different degree for purposes of identification and communication.[4]

FORMS OF APPERCEPTIVE DISTORTION

Projection.—It is suggested that the term "projection" be reserved for the greatest degree of apperceptive distortion. Its

---

[4] It must be understood that these various forms of apperceptive distortions do not necessarily exist in pure form and frequently patently coexist with each other.

opposite pole would be, hypothetically, a completely objective perception. Projection was described originally in clinical psychoanalysis as pertaining to psychoses in particular and to certain neurotic defenses generally, and to some "normal" maturational processes. We may say that in the case of true projection we are dealing not only with an ascription of feelings and sentiments which remain unconscious, in the service of defense, but which are unacceptable to the ego and are therefore ascribed to objects of the outside world. We may also add that they *cannot be made conscious* except by special prolonged therapeutic techniques. This concept covers the phenomenon observed in a paranoid that can be essentially stated as the change from the unconscious "I love him" to the conscious "He hates me." True projection in this case is actually a very complex process, probably involving the following four steps:

(a) "I love him" (a homosexual object)—an unacceptable id drive;
(b) reaction formation—"I hate him";
(c) the aggression is also unacceptable and is repressed;
(d) finally, the percept is changed to "He hates me."

Only the last step usually reaches consciousness.

I suggest calling this process *inverted projection*, as contrasted with simple projection, which is discussed below. The first step in the process usually involves the operation of another defense mechanism, reaction formation. It is sufficient to say here that, in the case of the paranoid, "I hate him" is approved, while "I love him" (homosexually) is socially disapproved and was learned early by him in relation to his father as a dangerous impulse. Therefore in this case "I hate him" extinguishes and replaces the loving sentiment. Thus in inverted projection we really deal first with the process of reaction formation and then with an apperceptive distortion that results in the ascription of the subjective sentiment to the outside world as a simple projection.

Simple Projection.—This is not at all necessarily of clinical significance, is of frequent everyday occurrence, and has been well described in the following joke:

Joe Smith wants to borrow Jim Jones's lawn mower. As he walks across his own lawn he thinks of how he will ask Jones for the lawn mower. But then he thinks: "Jones will say that the last time I borrowed something from him I gave it back dirty." Then Joe answers him in fantasy by replying that it was just in the condition in which he had received it. Then Jones replies in fantasy by saying that Joe will probably damage Jim Jones's fence as he lifts the mower over. Whereupon Joe replies . . . and so the fantasy argument continues. When Joe finally arrives at Jim's house, Jim stands on the porch and says cheerily: "Hello, Joe, what can I do for you?" And Joe responds angrily: "You can keep your damn lawn mower!"

Broken down, this story means the following: Joe wants something, but recalls a previous rebuff. He has learned (from parents, siblings, etc.) that the request may not be granted. This makes him angry. He then perceives Jim as angry with him, and his response to the imagined aggression is: "I hate Jim because Jim hates me."

In greater detail this process can be seen as follows: Joe wants something from Jim. This brings up the image of asking something from another contemporary, his brother, for example, who is seen as jealous and would refuse angrily in such a situation. Thus the process might simply be: the image of Jim is apperceptively distorted by the percept memory of the brother, a case of inappropriate transfer of learning. I shall have to attempt to explain later why Joe should not relearn if reality proves his original conception wrong. The empirical fact is established that such neurotic behavior does not usually change except under psychotherapy.

Joe differs from the paranoid not only by the lesser rigidity with which he adheres to his projections but also by less frequency and less exclusiveness as well as the smaller degree of lack of awareness, or inability to become aware, in addition to how patently subjective and "absurd" the distortion is.

Certainly a not infrequent process may be the following. Someone arrives late at work on Monday morning and believes, incorrectly, that his supervisor looks angrily at him later on. This is spoken of as "a guilty conscience"; that is, he behaves as though the supervisor knew that he had come late, when actually the supervisor may not know of it. This means that he sees in the supervisor the anger that he has come to expect in such a situation. This behavior can then be understood again as a simple (associative) distortion through transfer of learning, or in more complex situations the influence of previous images on present ones.

Sensitization.—If we modify the above case of a subject's coming late to work to the degree that we have a situation in which the supervisor feels a very slight degree of anger at the latecomer, we may observe a new phenomenon. Some subjects may not at all observe the anger or react to it, while others may observe it and react to it. In the latter case we shall find that these subjects are the ones who tend to perceive anger even at times when it does not objectively exist. This is a well-known clinical fact and has been spoken of as the "sensitivity" of neurotics. Instead of the creation of an objectively nonexistent percept, we deal now with a *more sensitive perception of existing stimuli.*[5] The hypothesis of sensitization merely means that an object that fits a preformed pattern is more easily perceived than one that does not fit the preformed pattern. This is a widely accepted fact, for example, in the perceptual problems of reading, wherein previously learned words are much more easily perceived by their pattern than by their spelling.

Sensitization, I believe, is also the process that took place in the experiment by Levine, Chein, and Murphy [19]. When these experimenters first starved a number of subjects and then fleetingly showed them pictures in which, among other things, were depicted objects of food, they found two processes: (a) when starved, the subjects saw food in the fleeting pictures even if there was none, and (b) the subjects correctly perceived actual pictures of food more frequently when starved. Apparently in such a state of deprivation there is an increased cognitive efficiency of the ego in recognizing objects that might obviate its deprivation, and also a simple compensatory fantasy of wish fulfillment which the authors call autistic perception. Thus the organism is equipped for both reality adjustment and substitutive gratification where real gratification does not exist. This is really an increase in the efficiency of the ego's function in response to an emergency—a more accurate perception of food in the state of starvation. I believe that this process can also be subsumed under our concept of sensitization, since food images are recalled by

---

[5] A very similar process has been described by Edoardo Weiss as objectivation.

the starvation and real food stimuli are more easily perceived.

An experiment by Bruner and Postman [7] may possibly also follow the same principle. The authors had their subjects adjust a variable circular patch of light to match in size a circular disk held in the palm. The perceptual judgments were made under the influence of varying degrees of shock and during a recovery period. Results during shock did not vary markedly. During the post-shock period, however, the deviations of perceived size from actual size became very marked. The authors tentatively proposed a theory of selective vigilance. In terms of this theory, the organism makes its most accurate discriminations under conditions of stress. But when tensions are released, expansiveness prevails and more errors are likely to result. We may make the additional hypothesis that the tension results immediately in a greater awareness of the image in memory, and more acute judgments of equality of size between the percept memory of the disk and the light patch are made.

Whether *autistic perception*, the perception of desired food objects in the state of starvation among stimuli that do not objectively represent food objects, constitutes a form of simple projection or is a process that should be described as distinct from it depends on rather fine points. Both Sanford [24] and Levine, Chein, and Murphy [19] have demonstrated the process experimentally. We may say that the increased need for food leads to a recall of food objects, and that these percept memories distort apperceptively any contemporary percept. The only argument that I can advance for a difference from simple projection is that we deal here with simple basic drives that lead to simple gratifying distortions rather than to the more complex situations possible in simple projection.

The concept of the *mote-beam mechanism* of Ichheiser [18] may also be subsumed under the concept of sensitization. Ichheiser proposes to speak of the mote-beam mechanism in cases of distortion of social perception in such a way that one is exaggeratedly aware of the presence of an undesirable trait in a minority group although one is unaware of the trait within oneself. In other words we can say that there is a sensitization of awareness (coexistent with unawareness of the process itself and of the existence of the trait within oneself, as inherent in any defensive mechanism) owing to one's own unconsciously operating selectivity and apperceptive distortion.

Externalization.—Inverted projection, simple projection, and sensitization are processes of which the subject is ordinarily unaware, and decreasingly so in the order mentioned. It is correspondingly difficult to make anyone aware of the processes in himself. On the other hand every clinician has had the experience of a subject's telling him a story about one of the TAT pictures as follows: "This is a mother looking into the room to see if Johnny has finished his homework, and she scolds him for being tardy." On looking over the stories in the inquiry, the subject may spontaneously say: "I guess that really was the way it was with my mother and myself, though I did not realize it when I told you the story."

In psychoanalytic language one may say that the process of storytelling was preconscious; it was not conscious while it went on, but could easily have been made so. This implies that we deal with a slightly repressed pattern of images which had an organizing effect that could be easily recalled. The term "externalization" is suggested for such a phenomenon, purely for the facilitation of the clinical description of a frequently occurring process.

Purely Cognitive Perception and Other Aspects of the Stimulus Response Relationship.—Pure perception is the hypothetical process against which we measure apperceptive distortion of a subjective type, or it is the subjective operationally defined agreement on the meaning of a stimulus with which other interpretations are compared. It supplies us the end point of a continuum upon which all responses vary. Inasmuch as behavior is considered by general consent to be rational and appropriate to a given situation, we may speak of *adaptive behavior* to the "objective" stimulus, as discussed below.

In my own earlier experiments it was found that aggression could be induced in subjects and that this aggression was "projected" into their stories in accordance with the projection hypothesis. It was further found that certain pictures are more often responded to with stories of aggression, even under normal circumstances, if the experimenter does nothing but simply request a story about the pictures. Also it was found that those pictures, which by their very nature suggested aggression, lent themselves much more readily to projection of aggression than others not suggesting aggression by their content.

It is believed that the first fact—that a picture showing a huddled figure and a pistol, for example, leads to more stories of aggression than a picture of a peaceful country scene—is nothing more than what common sense would lead one to expect. In psychological language this means simply that *the response is in part a function of the stimulus*. In terms of apperceptive psychology it means that a majority of subjects agree on some basic apperception of a stimulus and that this agreement represents our operational definition of the "objective" nature of the stimulus. Behavior consistent with these "objective" reality aspects of the stimulus has been called *adaptive behavior* by Gordon W. Allport [1]. In Card No. I of the TAT, for example, the subject adapts himself to the fact that the picture shows a violin.

Several principles may be enumerated:

(a) The degree of adaptive behavior varies conversely with the degree of exactness of the definition of the stimulus. TAT pictures and the Rorschach Test ink blots are purposely relatively unstructured in order to produce as many apperceptively distorted responses as possible. On the other hand, if one of the pictures of the Stanford-Binet Test—the one depicting a fight between a white man and Indians—is presented, the situation is well enough defined to elicit the same response from the majority of children between the ages of ten and twelve.

(b) The exact degree of adaptation is determined also by the *Aufgabe* or set. If the subject is asked to describe the picture, there is more adaptive behavior than if he is asked to tell a story about it. In the latter case he tends to disregard many objective aspects of the stimulus. If an air-raid siren is sounded, the subject's behavior is likely to differ greatly if he knows about air raids, expects to hear sirens, and knows what to do in such situations. He will differ from the subject who does not know the significance of the sound and who may interpret the noise as anything from the trumpet of the Day of Judgment to the announcement of a stoppage of work and behave accordingly.

(c) The nature of the perceiving organism also determines the ratio of adaptive versus projective behavior, as previously discussed. The Levine, Chein, and Murphy experiment demonstrated sensitization, and we have found that people distort apperceptively in differing degrees. Even the same person when awakened from sleep may react altogether differently to a stimulus than when wide awake.

Other aspects of the subject's production—for example, those given in response to TAT pictures—have been more simply discussed in an earlier paper [3]. I referred there to what Allport has termed "expressive behavior."

By *expressive aspects* of behavior we mean that if a variety of artists are exposed to the same conditions, one cannot expect the same creative productions. There would be individual differences expressed in the way the artists make their strokes with their brushes or with their chisels; there would be differences in the colors they prefer and differences in arrangement and distribution of space. In other words, certain predominantly myoneural characteristics, as Mira [21] calls them, would determine some features of their product.

Expressive behavior is of a nature that differs from both adaptation and apperceptive distortion. Given a fixed ratio of adaptation and apperceptive distortion in a subject's response to either Stanford-Binet picture, persons may vary in their style and in their organization. One may use long sentences with many adjectives; another may use short sentences with pregnant phrases of strictly logical sequence. If individuals write their responses, they may vary as to upper length and lower length in spacing. If they speak, they may differ in speed, pitch, volume. All these are personal characteristics of rather stable nature for every person. Similarly, the artist may chisel in small detail and with precision or choose a less exacting form. He may arrange things either symmetrically or off-center. And again in response to the air-raid signal, someone may run, crouch, jump, walk, talk—and do each of these things in his own typical way.

If, then, adaptation and apperceptive distortion determine *what* one does and expression determines *how* one does it, it is needless to emphasize that one may always ask *how* one does *what* one does. Adaptive, apperceptive, and expressive behavior are always coexistent.

In the case of artistic production, for example, the ratio of adaptive to apperceptive material and to the expressive characteristics may vary, of course, from artist to artist and, to a certain extent, from one product to the other of the same artist. In a similar way, expressive behavior influences the TAT productions, accounting for individual differences in style, sentence structure, verb-noun ratio *[8]*, and other formal characteristics. Expressive features reveal, then, *how* one does something; adaptation, and apperceptive distortion speak of *what* one does.

AN ATTEMPT TO INTEGRATE CONCEPTS OF APPERCEPTIVE DISTORTION AND BASIC CONCEPTS OF PSYCHOANALYSIS

Apperceptive psychology and its clinical instruments are children both of psychoanalysis and of academic clinical psychology (particularly of the dynamic theories of Gestalt psychology concerning learning and perception). Nevertheless there has been a deplorable lack of integration of the two methods of approach and a lack of understanding between the exponents of psychoanalytic and those of nonanalytic psychology. A later paper by Dr. Abt presents a systematic discussion of apperceptive distortion (projective psychology) within the frame of contemporary nonanalytic psychology. Here I wish to show that the basic psychoanalytic concepts can be stated in experimentally verifiable form, as problems of learning theory, and particularly of apperceptive distortion.

I believe that such a restatement is important since the clinical psychologist using projective techniques often finds it necessary to employ a psychoanalytic approach and does so with unnecessary misgivings and insufficient clarity. At the same time, the clinical psychologist is not infrequently called upon to treat the patient he has tested. The relationship between projective testing and planning of psychotherapy is close, as further described in the chapter on the Thematic Apperception Test. With this thought in mind, the subsequent discussion is presented: problems of psychotherapy and a number of special dynamic problems seen in terms of apperception.

We believe it can be said that psychoanalysis is a theory of learning concerned especially with the life history of the acquisition of percepts, their lawful interaction with each other, and their influence upon the perception of later stimuli. This formulation is a rudimentary attempt at present and is merely designed to set the general frame of reference for the theory of apperception advanced earlier. Systematic restatement of all psychoanalytic doctrines and experimental verification must remain for the future.[6]

The learning of percepts is chiefly stated in terms of the libido theory, primarily a series of genetic propositions concerning personality. The complex constellation of the œdipal triangle and its fate constitutes a nuclear concept. The lawful interaction of percepts and the memories thereof is covertly present in what Freud has to say about parapraxes and symptom and character formation. The influence of past percepts upon the contemporary apperception is implied in the concept of defense mechanism and the genetic interpretation of contemporary behavior.

In this light the libido theory may be regarded as involving propositions concerned with the history of the perception of oral, anal, and genital stimuli, and the reaction of the significant adults (parental figures) to them. Since psychoanalysis developed as a clinical empirical science in which the beginnings of methodology are only now becoming manifest, it does not distinguish between underlying learning hypotheses and the actual results. It describes the effect of early oral frustration of an individual without stating that the law of primacy is consistent with the assumptions of the importance of early experience. It does not systematically explore, in terms of reward and punishment, the effect the mother's reaction has upon the acquisition of cleanliness, but deals nevertheless, in a manner yet to be experimentally stated, with the effect that the image of the mother will have on this individual's later perception of bodily functions. That is, the percept memory of the mother will have a determining influence on later perceptions. "The child identifies with the mother" can be stated as the fact that the child perceives the mother and retains a memory of that percept. The child learns to associate pleasure or avoidance of anhedonia with the maternal percept. It learns to behave according to the rules of the mother in order to avoid anhedonia which can derive from inorganic reality (the child might burn itself) or from the mother's disapproval, which could take the form of withdrawal of love or actual physically painful punishment. The percept memory of the mother becomes a guiding image, motivated by the wish to avoid anhedonia,

---

[6] This is not meant to be another attempt at neo-Freudianism; rather, it is an attempt to advance Freud's teachings methodologically.

which exerts a selective influence on behavior; it becomes part of the self-system of the child, or an "ego ideal," in Freud's language. Actually, of course, there is not a single percept of the mother but a whole series of percepts, as Paul Schilder has already pointed out *[25]*. There is mother giving, mother taking, mother cleaning, mother playing, and so on. The percept of the mother differs with the age of the child, and one percept becomes superimposed upon another. Thus the percept of the mother, say at age fourteen of the child, is the final outcome of all the percepts of mother up to that time. This composite, according to the concepts of Gestalt psychology, will be more than the sum total of the percepts. It will have its own configuration.

Psychoanalysis, we can say, has been particularly interested in the selective fate and organization of these memory traces. Freud had discovered that earlier learned percepts had become unrecognizable to the individual and to the outsider in the process of integration of percepts. He spoke of their having become *unconscious*. The psychoanalytic technique was designed to recognize the parts that constitute the whole which is immediately observable. Dream images and their analysis by means of free association are probably the best example. The manifest dream constitutes the final Gestalt. "Free associations" reveal the parts that went into the image and permit us to order the dream events into the continuity of the stream of thought processes. Freud's *principle of overdetermination* can then be stated as merely a demonstration of the Gestalt principle that the whole is more than the sum of the details.

If the self-system (personality) can be seen as a complex system of percepts of diverse nature, influencing behavior selectively, it makes no difference whether the organism at birth is seen as a *tabula rasa*, to be structured entirely by the later learned patterns, or whether it is thought of as born with a number of determining factors of ontogenetic, familial, or a general biological nature. Which biological drive a theory postulates, whether it speaks of sexual drive, aggression, need for security, or avoidance of anhedonia, any one alone or any number combined, is not essential for our theory. Whatever drive presents itself is modified and shaped by the various learned percepts. Furthermore, each percept is modified and integrated with every other percept.

Psychoanalysis has chosen to speak collectively of those percepts determining the behavior that is consistent with avoidance of reality difficulties and the testing of logical propositions as the ego. It has chosen further to identify those of the ego percepts which are more definitely associated with goal ideas of long-range nature, or more closely circumscribed and more definitely patterned after a particular person as the ego ideal. The percepts governing "moral" behavior are collectively called the superego. Originally, the parental images (or those of other significant adults taking the parental role) constitute the representation of society, which, of course, later becomes enlarged.

At first Freud arrived at the awareness of these perceptions by reconstruction from adults—that is, by breaking down the whole of the patient's percept of a maternal figure into its historical component parts. Later on, his reconstructions were confirmed by direct observation of children. Psychoanalysis also treats of the laws of changes of percepts by interaction among themselves into different configurations. The best example of this process is the dream work in which symbolization, condensation, and displacement are the processes leading to the final configuration of the manifest dream.

The *theory of defense mechanisms* is really a theory concerned with the selective influence of memory percepts on the perception of contemporary events. Each defense mechanism is a hypothesis concerning the lawfulness of interaction of images under certain circumstances. If, for instance, a mother has aggressive feelings toward her child along with affectionate feelings at the same time, one of the possible results of this conflict of sentiments may be described by psychoanalysis as reaction formation— the mother may be entirely unaware of her aggressive feelings and may manifest excessive affection. We can restate this by saying that the following lawfulness is implied: when a stimulus arouses percept memories that elicit both aggressive and nurturant attitudes, and the aggressive one has met with disapproval, then the disapproved one is extinguished and the approved one reinforced. This statement makes reaction formation an experimentally verifiable concept, at least in principle. Of course any number of further supplementary hypotheses may have to be made to fit the complex model of real life situations. Furthermore, Gestalt principles may possibly be better able to fit the model. It may be experimentally demonstrated that when a "good" image and a "bad" image are simultaneously exposed, the result will be a reinforced "good" image modified by some aspects of the "bad" image. Mother love as the result of reaction formation has the restrictive features of overprotectiveness; that is, some of the originally coexisting aggression manifests itself in the new guise. Reaction formation may, in fact, be adequately expressed, as for instance in Guthrie's principle of conditioned discrimination, which is stated by Hilgard as follows [17]: "If two stimuli are sufficiently distinguishable, the organism can be taught to respond to one of them and to cease responding to the other. This is done by the methods of contrast. That is, one of the stimuli is regularly reinforced, the other regularly nonreinforced. The selective extinction which results is known as conditioned discrimination because the organism has learned to react differentially to the two stimuli. . . ." As I mentioned earlier, the paranoid originally reacts to the homosexual love object with love and then with hate—as in the typical ambivalence of the boy to the father. He has an image of the loved father (as the big protector) and an image of the aggressive-sadistic father (of primal scene origin). These images may apperceptively destroy any other perception of males. By conditioned discrimination through the social mores and the fears of the father, love-response is extinguished and the hate-response remains to be projected.

Freud's theory of neurosis has always been stated as a compromise formation. That is, it is a statement of the best possible Gestalt in a given system of forces—the id, the ego, the superego, and reality. Freud's theory of the outbreak of an adult neurosis may be stated as follows: "A neurosis becomes manifest when a contemporary constellation of forces coincides with the pattern of a traumatic childhood situation." Under such circumstances the neurosis is a repetition of the earlier established reaction pattern. For example, a patient was married to a much older woman who dominated him in many ways. He had early been a partial orphan brought up by the mother. When his wife deserted him this otherwise well adjusted man broke into acute anxiety attacks. When by chance he visited the near-by city in which he was born and which he had visited frequently in the past few years, he wandered aimlessly into a department store, became uncomfortable and increasingly anxious as he approached the exit. At this point he spontaneously recalled that as a small boy he had one day been lost by his mother and had stood crying in the door of the same department store. He instantly experienced a decided relief. It appeared, on exploration, that being left by his wife had created a terror in him similar to the emotion felt when he had been lost by his mother; that is, the present situation fitted a preexisting pattern.

Freud's original contributions, which were concerned with hysterical amnesia or with the traumatic origin of neurosis, with parapraxes, and with dreams, were really hypotheses concerning learning, forgetting, and the methods of recall (hypnosis, persuasion, and free association).

SOME SPECIAL DYNAMIC PROBLEMS SEEN AS CASES OF APPER-CEPTIVE DISTORTION

Hypnosis.—Hypnosis is one of the processes in which a subject's apperception can be temporarily altered and in which major distortions can be introduced. While we cannot hope to solve the problems of this highly controversial phenomenon, we can attempt to understand it with the help of the concepts so far advanced.

The hypnotic process starts with a gradual decrease of the subject's apperceptive functions and a final limiting of these functions to the apperceptions of the hypnotist's voice (apperception it is indeed, since different subjects often give the hypnotic instructions a different meaning). This process of exclusion of apperception is similar to the one instituted by a person when he gets ready to sleep. In fact Ferenczi's theory of hypnosis suggests that the hypnotist represents the parental image that once upon a time lulled the child or ordered it into sleep. In our terms the hypnotist is apperceptively distorted by the image memories of the parent. Accordingly, if the hypnosis proceeds well, these parental images, via the hypnotist, have as highly controlling an influence upon the perception of any other stimuli as did the parents in early infancy, during which there was no differentiation between thought and reality.

Obedience to posthypnotic orders demonstrates conclusively that image memories of which the subject is not aware and of which he is unable to become aware may have a controlling influence over action. The percept memory of the subject of the hypnotist apperceptively distorts the present stimulus. When, for example, the hypnotist asks the subject how his seat feels, the subject may obediently jump up with a feeling of heat on his seat. In experiments I ordered subjects to feel angry or depressed. That is, the subject recalled a past situation of anger or depression and the memory of this situation distorted the apperception of the TAT cards in such a way as to suggest social situations involving aggression, grief, etc.

Mass Psychological Phenomena.—Mass psychological phenomena can be understood in a way very similar to hypnosis. As Freud pointed out in *Group Psychology and the Analysis of the Ego* *[14]*, each individual introjects the "mass" or group as a transitory factor into the ego and the superego. We can say that while the individual is a member of the group, he "sees the world through the eyes of the mass." The group is seen temporarily as an authoritarian figure, and, as in hypnosis, the apperception of the group gains a controlling influence over most other image-memories. Thus lynching, stampeding, and fighting come about by facilitation of primitive impulses.

Transference.—While the term "transference" is frequently used quite loosely, I wish to restrict its meaning to the emotional relationship of the patient to his psychoanalyst. An integral part of this relationship is that the analyst is at least theoretically a figure who does not enter actively into emotional relationships and refrains from punishing, praising, or in any way manifestly reacting to the patient's moods.

Transference implies that the patient transfers to the analyst sentiments that he has learned previously. He may thus expect to hear criticism, punishment, or praise from the analyst and may frequently apperceptively distort the analyst's reactions. It is part of the analytic work to show the patient at plausible points the difference between his distortions and the facts.

The analyst's lack of response has a unique effect which differentiates the transference situation from that of any other apperceptive distortion of a similar parental figure. When a patient has found that one particular way of attempting to manipulate the relationship does not succeed, another pattern of behavior emerges. For instance, one patient bluffed a great deal in a part of his analysis, showed off his considerable knowledge, and tried to amuse the analyst. When this was pointed out to him and it was clear that the analyst failed to respond to the patient's exhibitions, the patient reacted with aggression and later with plain anxiety and dependence. We can say that this patient had originally developed a number of behavior patterns for dealing with his anxiety. When his most recently learned pattern failed, he regressed to an earlier one, just as Mowrer *[22]* has demonstrated in another context, and then again to an earlier one. Eventually his relation to the analyst became similar to the one he had had with his parents when he was quite small. His apperception of the analyst was distorted by the various images of the parents at various ages. When, for instance, his œdipal fear of the father was reenacted, he was made aware of his fearful expectations. He learned that these fears are unfounded; that is, he relearned the earlier troublesome patterns by insight and conditioning in the transference situation and by "working through" in his external world.

The transference situation can then be described as one in which the patient distorts his apperception of the analyst with increasingly earlier images of the parents and other significant figures of his early life.

Psychoses.—In psychotic delusions and hallucinations we may say that the early images have emerged so strongly as to have a greater distorting influence upon the apperception of the contemporary world than in any other condition.

If we say that our current apperception is a Gestalt, a composite picture of all the previously learned apperceptions, then we can say, schematically speaking, that certain early images of a fearful nature were so strong in a given patient as to powerfully distort all later ones that might have been of a more harmless nature.

Usually the apperceptive distortion at first affects only a small group of stimuli. In the early paranoid it still involves only one individual or a very few. Sometimes the original distortion is not necessarily absurd and can keep juries busy checking for long periods. With the progress of the disease the patient's distortions usually become more marked and more nearly all-inclusive. The system formation of the paranoid becomes more and more ramified until it involves the whole world—his whole apperceptive field.

Therapy.—The psychoanalytic theory of therapy can be restated in the following steps *[6]*:

Communication: The patient communicates with the analyst by means of free associations. Through these the analyst learns of the patient's behavior in a great many situations and finds a number of common denominators in the patient's behavioral patterns.

Interpretation: When the analyst has become acquainted with a number of life situations of the patient, he may perceive a certain common denominator in the behavioral patterns and point it out to the patient in such doses as seem to him to be suitable at various times.

(a) Horizontal Study: The therapist may find a common denominator among the behavior patterns and interpersonal relations of the patient's contemporary life situation, and we may speak of this process as a horizontal study of patterns.

(b) Vertical Study: Sooner or later it will be possible to trace by free association or otherwise the historical development of these patterns in the life history of the patient, leading to a more or less definitely defined early set. We may speak of this part of the therapeutic investigation as the vertical study of life patterns. Frequently it is necessary to point out both the vertical and the horizontal common denominators of the patient's current behavior in order to lead to a solution of his problems.

(c) Relationship to the Therapist: As a special case of current life situations of the horizontal pattern in its relation to the earlier historical ones, the relationship to the therapist may be discussed specifically in what is known in psychoanalysis as *analysis of the transference situation.*

Interpretation, then, means that the therapist points out to the patient the common denominators in his behavioral patterns, horizontally, vertically, and in special relation to the therapist. In all three instances the therapist finds that the patient suffers from apperceptive distortions of life situations. Interpretation really consists in pointing out the *common denominators of the apperceptive distortions* and, in certain cases, in demonstrating the relationships of earlier life situations to percept memories in which these apperceptive distortions arose. The process involves the analysis of the present complex apperception into the parts that came to constitute the whole.

A brief example may be of help here. The patient may have appeared with the presenting problem of vague anxiety attacks. It may develop that these apparently puzzling attacks occur typically when the patient is in contact with a strict authority who produces hostility in him. After this horizontal pattern has appeared, at one time or another a vertical one may also be found —the patient had a more or less specific relationship to his father, who originally produced these feelings of hostility in him with the resulting anxiety. Further study will reveal a whole history of relationships to similar authorities prior to the current situation and a similar attitude that is expressed to the therapist.

Insight: Insight development is the next step in the therapeutic process. The term "insight" is one abused almost as much as psychotherapy itself. Frequently the term "insight" is used to mean simply that the patient is aware of being mentally ill. This is used most often in the discussion of psychotics, usually without implying any more than just that. In the context of dynamic psychotherapy insight must have this meaning—*the patient's ability to see the relationship between a given symptom and the previously unconscious apperceptive distortions underlying his symptoms.* More strictly speaking, we define insight as the patient's apperception (i.e., meaningful perception) of the common denominators of his behavior as pointed out by the therapist. The problem is seen in a new light and handled differently from then on.

This process may be analyzed into two parts:

(a) Intellectual Insight: The patient can see the interrelationship of his different horizontal and vertical patterns; he can see them as special cases of a general class, or, in Gestalt language, he learns by insight and experiences closure. The pieces of isolated happenings become a memory whole, and a repatterning and relearning takes place.

(b) Emotional Insight: The patient reproduces the affect pertaining to the intellectual insight—relief, anxiety, guilt, happiness, etc.

If the intellectual insight alone is produced, limited or no therapeutic results may be achieved because emotional repatterning is an essential of the therapeutic process, be it conceived of as a regular libidinal-metapsychologic process or as a learning process in conventional academic psychological terms. The affect must be part of the Gestalt of a therapeutic experience.

Working Through: The next step in therapy consists in the working through of the new insight:

(a) Intellectually: The patient now applies what he has learned to pertain to a few situations, as pointed out by the therapist, to a number of other situations to which the same general denominator applies. If a pattern of apperceptive distortion was pointed out to exist as applying to the patient's present employer, his teacher, his analyst, and his father, he may now remember situations involving an uncle, a superior officer in the army, an elder brother, or others as having been reacted to similarly.

(b) Therapeutically (Emotionally): In the therapeutic situation, psychoanalytically known as the transference situation, the patient originally "transfers" the emotional patterns of behavior as discussed previously and works them through.

(c) Behaviorally: Outside the therapeutic session the patient goes on meeting situations discussed and new ones similar to the ones scrutinized. While in real situations, he is aware of the insight he recently gained. Under the influence of that new "mental set" he reacts differently to a progressive extent to these situations in the corrective direction suggested by the analysis of the situation. New problems arising are re-analyzed and the problem is worked out by persistent adjustment and readjustment between mental set and reality.

While the process of insight and the purely intellectual aspects of working through are best explained by Gestalt learning theory, the therapeutic and behavioral working through are actually best seen as a matter of conditioning and reconditioning, as well as a problem in which trial and error and reward and punishment lead to the final best result.

SUMMARY

The concept of projection has been re-examined. Earlier experimental investigations of mine had shown that the definition of projection as a defense mechanism was inadequate. Instead, projection is shown to be one of a number of processes of "apperceptive distortion." These apperceptive distortions are best seen as due to the structuring influence of the memories of past apperceptions on present apperceptions. Thus the dynamic theory of the psychoanalytic psychology of personality can be seen in terms of the history of past apperceptions (e.g., of the parents, etc.) and of their influence on the individual's apperceptions of the contemporary world. Psychoanalysis can be seen as a theory of learning applied to the genesis of percept memories and their lawful interaction with each other. These are expressed in the theory of defense mechanisms, symptom formation, and character formation. The hypotheses advanced were tentatively applied to an understanding of hypnosis, group psychological phenomena, transference, psychoses, and the processes involved in psychoanalytic therapy, in an attempt to integrate concepts important for the clinician using apperceptive methods.

REFERENCES

1. ALLPORT, G. W.: "The Use of Personal Documents in Psychological Science," *Social Science Research Council Bulletin*, No. 49 (1942).
2. BALKEN, E. R., and MASSERMAN, J. H.: "The Language of Phantasy: III. The Language of the Phantasies of Patients with Conversion Hysteria, Anxiety State, and Obsessive Compulsive Neurosis," *Journal of Psychology*, Vol. 10 (1940), pp. 75–86.
3. BELLAK, L.: "The Concept of Projection," *Psychiatry*, Vol. 7 (1944), pp. 353–70.
4. ——: "A Further Experimental Investigation of Projection by means of Hypnosis," (unpublished).
5. —— et al.: "The Use of the TAT in Psychotherapy," in *Journal of Nervous and Mental Disease*, April 1949.
6. ——: "A Note of Some Basic Concepts of Psychotherapy," *Journal of Nervous and Mental Disease*, Vol. 108 (1948), pp. 137–41.
7. BRUNER, J. S., and POSTMAN, L.: "Tension and Tension-Release as Organizing Factors in Perception," *Journal of Personality*, Vol. 15 (1947), pp. 300–8.
8. FRANK, L. K.: "Projective Methods for the Study of Personality," *Journal of Psychology*, Vol. 8 (1939), pp. 389–413.
9. FREUD, S.: "The Anxiety Neurosis," in *Collected Papers*. International Psychoanalytical Library; London: Hogarth Press; Vol. I, 1940.
10. ——: *Neuropsychoses*. International Psychoanalytical Library; London: Hogarth Press; Vol. I, 1940.
11. ——: "Psychoanalytic Notes on an Autobiographical Account of a Case of Paranoia (Dementia Paranoides)," in *Collected Papers*, Vol. III, pp. 387–470.
12. ——: *The Future of an Illusion*. International Psychoanalytical Library, No. 15; London: Hogarth Press; 1940.

13.   ——: *Totem and Taboo.* In *Basic Writings of Sigmund Freud,* edited by A. A. Brill, New York: Modern Library; 1938.

14.   ——: *Group Psychology and The Analysis of the Ego.* International Psychoanalytical Library, No. 6, London: Hogarth Press; 1940.

15.   GUTHRIE, E. R., and HORTON, G. P.: *Cats in a Puzzle Box.* New York: Rinehart & Co.; 1946.

16.   HEALY, W., BRONNER, A., and BOWERS, A. M.: *The Structure and Meaning of Psychoanalysis.* New York: Alfred A. Knopf; 1930.

17.   HILGARD, E. R.: *Theories of Learning.* New York: Appleton-Century-Crofts; 1948.

18.   ICHHEISER, G.: "Projection and the Mote-beam Mechanism," *Journal of Abnormal and Social Psychology,* Vol. 42 (1947), pp. 131–3.

19.   LEVINE, R., CHEIN, I., and MURPHY, G.: "The Relationship of the Intensity of a Need to the Amount of Perceptual Distortion: A Preliminary Report," *Journal of Psychology,* Vol. 13 (1943), pp. 283–93.

20.   MILLER, N. E., and DOLLARD, J.: *Social Learning and Imitation.* New Haven: Yale University Press; 1941.

21.   MIRA, E.: "Myokinetic Psychodiagnosis," *Proceedings of the Royal Society of Medicine,* February, 1940, Vol. 35.

22.   MOWRER, O. H.: "An Experimental Analogue of 'Regression' with Incidental Observations on 'Reaction-formation'," *Journal of Abnormal and Social Psychology,* Vol. 135 (1940), pp. 56–87.

23.   ROBINSON, E. S.: *Association Theory Today.* New York: D. Appleton-Century-Crofts; 1948.

24.   SANFORD, R. N.: "The Effects of Abstinence from Food upon Imaginal Processes: A Further Experiment," *Journal of Psychology,* Vol. 3 (1936), pp. 145–59.

25.   SCHILDER, P.: *Entwurf zu einer Psychiatrie auf Psychoanalytischer Grundlage.* Internationale Psychoanalytische Bibliothek, Leipzig, Wein, Aurick, No. 17 (1925).

26.   SEARS, R. R.: "Survey of Objective Studies of Psychoanalytic Concepts." *Social Science Research Council Bulletin,* No. 51 (1943).

▼

LAWRENCE EDWIN ABT in the paper that follows attempts to proceed further in the direction of relating projective methods and projective psychological theory to the rest of the science of psychology through an examination and formulation of the entire matrix of assumptions, conceptions, and propositions that up to now have been made only covertly. There is a dilemma faced by every rising generation of psychologists: orthodoxy versus independence, loyalty versus deviation, secession, schism, apostasy. Dr. Abt finds projective psychology as presently formulated largely a psychology of protest, which impresses him as healthy independence and originality rather than an evidence of competitiveness and inability to accept the authority personified by its intellectual father, academic psychology.

Although this chapter approaches the field from a direction different from the preceding one, in a number of important ways the views of personality become identical at a majority of points. Taking projective methods as a point of departure, Abt arrives at a holistic theory of personality which seeks to integrate the genetic and dynamic field approaches in a way useful to the clinician.

▼

A Theory of Projective Psychology

Lawrence Edwin Abt

INTRODUCTION

PROJECTIVE psychology is the name that may be given to an increasingly systematic point of view developing in contemporary psychology. The term refers to a more or less common body of assumptions, hypotheses, and propositions which, although they have not as yet enjoyed formalization, are finding their specific expression in the hands of clinicians who employ projective methods of one kind or another in the study and diagnosis of personality. The conceptual matrix of the projective point of view in psychology consists of a number of concepts about personality which are both implicit and explicit, as well as a number of conceptions as to the nature and task of science in general,[1] and I regard it as unlikely at this stage of its formulation that consensus will be reached on all major theoretical issues by those who feel committed to, or identified with, the use of projective methods in the study, diagnosis, or therapy of personality.

The structure of the emerging science of projective psychology, of which only the first story has been erected, rests, I believe, upon a foundation of rather secure concepts of broad generality, theoretical importance, and wide application that have grown up in recent years principally within the behavior sciences. An examination of the movement of ideas in certain other sciences, notably biology and physics, would show, however, that a similar point of view and a similar approach to the subject matter of these sciences are beginning to make themselves manifest.[2] In this chapter I have sought to take only the first steps in the long process of developing what I hope will eventually be a fully mature projective point of view in psychology which will prove of such scope and value that it may finally attract adherents in large numbers. I take such initial steps in a preliminary way with due caution because I am sensitive to the need for the development of a consistent and fruitful theory of personality upon which the projective point of view may grow and from which it

---

[1] The entire doctrine of causality in science is in process of reformulation, and new patterns of causality are beginning to emerge. These are expressed as an increasing trend in the direction of organicism in science, and an insistence upon the principle that all legitimate forms and entities studied by scientists are to be thought of in terms of continuously evolving systems.

[2] Several significant trends in science may be discerned, and these represent the newer climate of ideas: (1) There is a diminishing need for and reliance upon absolutes. (2) Concepts such as "ultimate truth," scientific "fact," and the so-called "laws of nature" are being either discarded or fundamentally reworked. (3) "Facts" are being looked upon by scientists as constituting working hypotheses which have a kind of heuristic value rather than some established validity. (4) Science, as a system of ideas, deals not with final facts and unchanging truths, but rather with what is relative and conditional, plastic and fluid, within the flux of existence. (5) As a system, science has no reality apart from the persons who construct and operate it. (6) No question of science can have any meaning unless it involves a problem of measurement along a scale, the order of which is that of a continuum. (7) The simplest fact in science requires some judgment of value as even a first approximation.

may expect to receive the kind of encouragement that is so essential to its development. In the absence of a really useful theory of personality of the sort that projective psychology sorely needs, I can suggest only the broad outlines of a theory of projective psychology. But even the rough geography of a new terrain is worth charting.

THE ORIGINS OF PROJECTIVE PSYCHOLOGY

I find it useful to look upon projective psychology as the psychology of protest. As the psychology of protest it is peculiarly a child of the contemporary psychological scene. From both a methodological and a conceptual point of view, projective psychology may be considered to represent a strong revolt against many of the main currents of academic psychology, to which it is actually so strongly indebted. The projective point of view in psychology runs sharply counter to the American tradition of behaviorism, which still saturates so much of contemporary academic psychology. It is of course true that we live and work in a time of many sophisticated and modified behaviorisms—molar and molecular, logical and operational—so that it becomes difficult to state precisely what we mean by a tradition of behaviorism in academic American psychology. But I am of the opinion that the proponents of these more sophisticated behavioristic views all owe a large debt to their intellectual father, Watson.

In writing as I do about projective psychology and its origins, I do not believe that I have erected behaviorism, in any of its many current forms, as a straw man that the new point of view must proceed to attack with spirit. Rather, I regard it as demonstrable that behavioristic tenets and notions, in one form or another, constitute the underlying working assumptions of an overwhelming number of contemporary American psychologists.[3]

---

[3] Support for this contention may be found in K. W. Spence's paper, "The Postulates and Methods of 'Behaviorism,'" in the March 1948 issue of the *Psychological Review*. After a consideration of the various theoretical formulations that go under the name of "behaviorism," Spence suggests that there are today no proponents of the original Watsonian version of behaviorism. He writes as follows, however: "Many of the basic postulates of his formulation are to be found in the present-day varieties of behaviorism and, what is more important, probably, in the underlying working assumptions of the great majority of present-day American psychologists."

Indeed, I regard it as likely that those in whom the behavioristic strain is strongest will be among the first to deny the proposition, but I think that this can be only because they have for so long taken for granted the very behavioristic conceptions that I believe characterize their theoretical position.

We can discern within any science perhaps two different but largely complementary types of scientific inquiry that may be pursued. The first type is frankly behavioristic, and the second is principally functional. Northrop [13] has faced this issue squarely in his recent address as chairman of the Section on the History and Philosophy of Science of the American Association for the Advancement of Science:

> In a behavioristic inquiry one ignores the inner constituents of the system and their relations within it. One concentrates attention, instead, upon what happens with respect to the response of the system when, everything else being kept constant, some specific stimulus or input is brought to bear upon it.
>
> In a functional study, on the other hand, the central subject matter under investigation is the intrinsic structure and internal properties of the system itself. In such a study the input and output are used merely to throw light on the character of the system which connects one to the other.

I believe that projective psychology is concerned quite clearly with a functional study of the individual, in Northrop's sense, and that it must be fully prepared to dispense with any sort of behavioristic inquiry. It is obvious that a functional appraisal of personality must always be stated in dynamic terms, and the projective point of view in psychology is strongly committed to a dynamic rather than to a static approach to behavior. A dynamic point of view for projective psychology requires that we look upon all behavior as active and purposeful—active in the sense that the individual strives toward the development of a relationship with the world of physical and social reality, and purposive or functional in the sense that the individual's behavior is directed toward the attainment of a goal. Within the framework of projective psychology, then, behavior is always regarded as goal-directed, and it tends to lead to the elimination of or reduction in the pattern of stimulation that incited it.

To say that projective psychology insists upon a dynamic and functional analysis of personality is to suggest that it is concerned not with isolated bits of behavior but rather with the important and more complex techniques by means of which the individual seeks to organize his experience with the physical and social environments and order it to his own unique needs. Projective psychology is interested in an inquiry with respect to the role of all the psychological functions and processes that operate within the context of the total personality. Hence the projective point of view employs a holistic outlook in which behavior in a particular modality of expression is studied within the matrix of the whole personality and must be understood in relationship to all other behavioral expressions of the individual. The projective productions of individuals are therefore to be regarded merely as parts of a whole. It is this approach to the study and diagnosis of personality, more even than the specific limitations of the several projective tests, that must be held accountable for our need to employ various projective methods, as well as nonprojective techniques, in the assessment and diagnosis of a single personality. And even when a wealth of behavioral data has resulted from our insistent attempts to understand the whole of the personality process, projective psychology holds that, at most, we have achieved only a cross-section of the time-Gestalt which is the personality process.

The dynamic, functional, and holistic elements in projective psychology can be traced rather readily to certain historical developments within the behavior sciences. First, and foremost in importance, have been the development and elaboration of psychoanalytical propositions with their insistence upon the motivated character of all behavior and their dedication to a historical (genetic) and longitudinal view of personality. In the current market place of psychological ideas and conceptions, psychoanalytical thinking, of course, enjoys wide currency; and it is well known that many of its concepts and propositions have invaded even the traditionally strong retreats of academic psychology. A second historical development of great significance for projective psychology, which has been inspired largely by experimental findings and which therefore rests, for the majority of American psychologists, upon more secure and respectable foundations than those provided by the richness of clinical data alone, has been that of Gestalt psychology.

In a number of significant ways, as Brown *[3]* has pointed out, the views of psychoanalysis and Gestalt psychology represent many points of essential agreement, so that their incorporation into a developing science of projective psychology has been accomplished with a minimum of conceptual confusion. In the two theories of psychology we may discern the following important areas of rather basic agreement which become significant for projective psychology:

1. There is close agreement in general between the two theories with respect to the structure and development of personality. Freud's multiple-structured self is not essentially different conceptually from Lewin's division of the person into regions. The dynamic and economic interchanges that are postulated as occurring with respect to the id, ego, and superego in psychoanalysis find parallel expression in Lewin's system of barriers and the classes of movements across them.

2. Gestalt psychology is celebrated for its insistence upon the wholeness or totality of the organism, and for its idea that wholes enjoy a priority over parts. In an organismic way Gestalt psychology regards the individual as being a self-regulating system. According to the Gestalt point of view, the changes and modifications of the organism are achieved in accordance with economic laws. The approach of psychoanalysis to similar issues and propositions about them is basically the same and we can discern little conflict.

3. Psychoanalysis postulates an essential and intimate working relationship between psychological mechanisms and dynamisms functioning within the individual and the socioanthropological culture and milieu of which he is always a part. J. F. Brown's application of topological principles to social psychology, and the impressive contributions of Lewin and his co-workers in action research and related areas during the past decade, point to a congruence of views.

4. Both Gestalt psychology and psychoanalysis utilize an impressive number of independently derived constructs which can be employed by their proponents as powerful interpretative tools in the description of personality. Recent studies in the methodology of science suggest that the hypothetico-deductive method is likely to be the most fruitful procedure for

scientific advancement. This method, in all its variations, encourages the development and use of operationally derived constructs which are similar to the concepts of person, vector, valence, reality-dimension, and the like in Gestalt psychology, and to the concepts of ego, libido, and similar constructs employed in psychoanalytical thinking.

In each of the two systematic points of view, only the behavior of the individual is observed in a wide context of different situations. In both theoretical systems the behavioral data are ordered to the general theory of the particular point of view by means of concepts similar to those indicated above. The result, for both points of view, is usually an integration or patterning of descriptive and interpretative statements about the individual, his behavior, and the field within which it has occurred.

5. A belief in psychic determinism and in the uniformity and continuity of psychological nature is common to both Gestalt psychology and psychoanalysis. Each theoretical position holds that all psychic phenomena have a cause and a meaning as well as an economic function with respect to the psychobiology of the whole organism.

In view of the broad general areas of basic agreement between the two theoretical systems of psychology, I do not regard it as surprising that concepts arising originally from each theoretical position have found not only their way into projective psychology, but a specific application in it. Clinicians of the widest differences in psychological background and personal predilection who may be said to work within the projective framework of psychology have discovered that it is relatively easy, and usually highly rewarding, to employ concepts that have arisen quite independently in the two psychological frames of reference. In practice, however, it is well known that the utilization and integration of concepts from the two approaches to psychology have seldom been achieved without compromise. Gestalt psychology, for example, has always insisted upon the most rigorous possible definitions of its constructs, and upon the principle that their ultimate sanction should always rest upon the crucial test of experimentation.

I feel that this insistent demand for experimental validation of each concept within the larger framework of theory—a principle with which psychoanalysis has not usually found itself in sympathy—has found expression in projective psychology largely as the need to subject the data that emerge from the application of projective tests in the study and diagnosis of personality to some kind of *formal* analysis.[4] In a like way, with somewhat less methodological sophistication, psychoanalysis has required within projective psychology the development of tendencies in the direction of a *content* analysis of projective data.[5] It is perfectly obvious that there is nothing fundamentally in opposition with respect to the two types of treatment of projective data, and that basically each method of analysis tends to supplement the other. But it is a fact that the development and utilization of content analytical procedures of projective data have lagged far behind the growth and acceptance of formal analytical methods.

It is of considerable historical consequence to the present state of projective psychology that advocates and practitioners of this point of view have expressed a much stronger allegiance to the formal rather than to the content method of analysis of projective data. In part this situation has come about because much of the development, and a great deal of the utilization, of projective tests have been in the hands of psychologists who were originally saturated with the principles and techniques of experimental psychology. Originally psychologists of laboratory and brass instrument persuasion, they demanded that any application of a projective test become inevitably an experiment. As an experiment the projective test quite naturally became subject to

---

[4] A *formal* analysis of a projective test protocol is a procedure that rests basically upon a desire to mathematize the separate scoring factors in the protocol in such a way that quantitative relationships among them become apparent. The decision to quantify the scoring factors, and even to set up factors in the first place which can be quantified, rests ultimately upon the assumption that statements made about an individual subjected to the test will possess greater precision if they are stated in mathematical terms. The contributions of experimental psychology to the development and refinement of projective tests may be held accountable for the formal treatment of projective scoring determinants.

[5] The *content* analysis of the projective test record, on the other hand, is inspired largely by the psychoanalytic assumption that projective test data lend themselves to a type of symbolic interpretation essentially different from, and frequently more useful than, a consideration of the protocol in terms of its structural characteristics.

the same requirements of rigid control that other psychological experimentation demanded. I do not decry this situation, but we must recognize that it has had important and far-reaching results on the growth of projective psychology up to the present time.

Concurrently psychiatrists and psychoanalysts who began to interest themselves in considerable numbers in one or another of the developing family of projective tests were beginning to acquire both a methodological and a conceptual awareness that had not characterized their work at an earlier stage. Here was another professional group which approached the study and diagnosis of personality from a background of rich clinical data and which began to make its significant contributions to the maturing of projective methods and the projective point of view in psychology. Behind the hopes of the several professional groups that have joined forces for the advancement of projective methods has been an increasing conviction that the time has long been ripe for the emergence and development of a genuinely experimental science of psychopathology. It is clear that for many of the members of the two professional groups the projective methods represented an avenue of potentially great fruitfulness along which they might travel with speed and relative certainty in the direction of an experimental psychopathology.

As a natural consequence of the developments I have briefly outlined, much research in projective psychology has been directed along lines that Allport [1] has characterized as *nomothetic*. I suspect that such developments in projective psychology were fostered more out of respect for the prevailing American scientific temper than that they were always fully appropriate to the treatment of projective data. Just as the recent surge of interest in projective productions of whatever sort can be understood as a kind of protest against the sterility of much current laboratory psychology and its insistence upon a study of the simpler psychological processes and restriction to the investigation of problems for which techniques are already largely available, so too there has been, even in the protest attempts themselves, a strong and insistent need to keep the research work in projective psychology well within the bounds of scientific respectability required by contemporary professional prejudices. Indeed, as Allport [2] has recently suggested, the unusual interest in projective productions is itself an article of scientific irreverence offered by those who find themselves out of sympathy with the overwhelming demand for objectivity in psychology at any price.

I regard it as likely that a stronger commitment by projective psychology to an *idiographic* approach to the treatment of projective data would, among other things, have resulted in research stress being placed more on content analysis and less on formal analysis, although this point is certainly subject to disagreement. Again, it is perfectly obvious that research in projective psychology has actually been along both lines of inquiry; but it has been hampered, when oriented along idiographic lines, by the fact that only the first faltering steps in the quantification and treatment of idiographic data have been taken. Perhaps, as some have suggested, the projective tests actually lend themselves more readily to the nomothetic type of inquiry. If this is so, I believe it is only because no really thoroughgoing attempts have been made to devise projective instruments and procedures that are not based on a concern with the establishment of general laws of personality structure and function.

As Allport has somewhere suggested, a concern with the establishment of general laws of personality functioning rests ultimately upon the dubious proposition that psychological causation is somehow actuarial rather than distinctly and uniquely personal. Projective psychology is firm in its insistence that psychological causation is always and everywhere uniquely personal and never simply actuarial, and this insistence grows out of a deep conviction that there is broad theoretical justification, both within psychology and within other sciences, for studying the individual as an individual rather than as a representative of a class of individuals, all the members of which are presumed to possess a finite number of ascertainable traits in varying amounts.

CURRENT CONCEPTUAL TRENDS IN PROJECTIVE PSYCHOLOGY

If we look at the body of hypotheses and propositions that characterize the projective point of view at the present time, it is possible for us to discern a limited number of trends in conceptualization which may be regarded as important signposts along the road to a genuine science of projective psychology. These several signposts may be said to constitute the explicit climate of ideas in which projective tests and projective psychological principles find expression in the day-to-day work of clinicians. As we review the relatively small number of conceptual trends which are actually explicit rather than implicit at the present time, we can readily appreciate that a great deal more effort has been devoted to the development and application of projective tests than to a careful and thorough attempt to fashion a theory of projective psychology, which is so sorely needed.

We may discern the following significant trends in conceptualization of behavior and personality in projective psychology:

1. Personality is increasingly viewed as a process rather than as a collection or aggregation of relatively static traits which are utilized by the individual in responding to stimuli.

The essence of any process, of course, is the fact that it runs a dynamic course in time. For projective psychology the result of viewing personality as process is that the picture which emerges from the application of a group of projective tests in the study of an individual is always qualified by the injunction that the projective behavior made available for analysis can, at best, represent only a cross-section of the total personality process. It becomes only a part of the temporally extended whole which is the personality.

In the utilization of projective data for interpretation, therefore, the clinician must be prepared to go beyond the projective behavior itself, by the process of inference, to arrive at a conception of the subject that embraces some of his past life history and some of his orientations to the near future. If the clinician is to erect a structure of warranted inferences about the individual who is being studied, he must be prepared to order his data and conceptions to a theory of personality that is itself prepared to furnish dynamic concepts. The task of building such a theory of personality adequate to the organization of varied projective data is still largely to be accomplished.

2. The personality studied by means of projective procedures is regarded as a process constantly influenced by the individual's interactions with his physical and social environments, on the one hand, and by the state and intensity of his needs, on the other.

In this view, personality is the process the individual uses to organize his experiences in terms of a changing world of physical and social reality and to order such reality to his own needs and values. Both physical and social reality become changed for the individual in the direction dictated by his systems of needs and values, and what becomes important is the individual's conception of his relationship to the physical and social environments. This conception of the individual's unique relationship with the world of physical and social reality is what Frank *[8,9]* has referred to as the person's "private world." Not only the individual's needs but also his values are behavioral determinants in that they function to create the world in which the individual lives and make possible the unique ways in which he learns, through experience, to come to terms with the demands made upon him by the physical and social environments.

Such a view of the person and his relationship to the world stresses the proposition that culture and personality are continuous and that it is basically academic to demand that they be separated and be treated in other than a thoroughly interdependent fashion.

3. There is an increasing tendency within projective psychology to rely upon field theory as an adequate frame of reference to which to order projective behavioral data.[6]

Behavior is always studied as a function of person-situation relationships, and the dynamic terms used to describe such relationships are jointly derived from both Gestalt psychology and psychoanalysis. This trend in conceptualization is congruent with the proposition that culture and personality are continuous and must be treated as interdependent variables, and it insists that all projective behavioral data must be ordered to a currently existing frame of reference the nature of which must also be explored before warranted inferences about the individual may be drawn.

The several projective tests study not so much the culture part of the complex, culture-personality, as they do the highly individual ways in which the person reacts in the psychological field and adheres to or departs from the recurring patterns and practices of the cultural field in which his behavior occurs.

4. Under the influence of psychoanalytical thinking there is a

---

[6] "Field theory" in psychology refers essentially in the present context to the concept of a system of interdependent variables. The behavior of the organism is regarded at any moment of its life history as being the resultant of the totality of all the relevant variables operating both within the field and within the organism.

marked trend toward the establishment of two classes of propositions about personality: dynamic (field) and genetic (historical and developmental).

Although there is common acceptance by projective psychologists that the projective tests provide at best only a cross-sectional approach to the assessment of personality, nevertheless there is strong adherence to the notion that personality as process is a continuously developing entity that functions from birth until death. Thus there is a commitment to the study and consideration of personality as a kind of time-Gestalt, and to the need for data which are related to a longitudinal consideration of personality. The projective methods, applied at various stages in the personality process, represent cross-sectional analytical attempts to build up a more substantial series of inferences as to the significant genetic factors that have shaped the personality as it appears at any given moment of its life history.

By a process of clinical inference the projective psychologist can often utilize the subjective and objective facts made available to him, in his procedures of personality exploration, to establish a series of dynamic and genetic hypotheses about the individual which represent for the clinician a formulation of varying degrees of adequacy.

5. There is an increasing interest in the formulation of a picture of the "personality as a whole."

The picture of the "personality as a whole" that can be formulated through the utilization of projective data applies obviously only to a cross-sectional statement of the unity and integration of the personality part-processes at a given time in the life history of the individual studied.

It is clear to all but the overenthusiastic that projective techniques do not aim at a *complete* formulation of the *whole* personality, since this is actually well beyond the capacities of clinicians today, but rather that they seek to provide a series of significant descriptive statements about the personality which may prove useful with respect to a particular and often quite restricted purpose.

The process of limiting, in a realistic way, the aims and potential accomplishments of projective methods is not essentially a disillusioning one. It is simply a procedure of studying as many personality variables as possible with the instruments available, and of refraining from placing the individual in some superficial behavioral category. Murray and his co-workers in their *Assessment of Men* have struck at the heart of the matter:

> To identify a man as an introvert, for example, gives us no information as to his energy level, his fluctuations of mood, his enduring emotional attachments, his membership systems, his political ideology, the pattern of his erotic fantasies, the strength of his conscience, his major dilemmas, his intelligence, his initiative and resourcefulness, the degree of his self-confidence, his dominant aims, the level of his aspiration, his chief abilities, and a great many other important components. [14]

6. There is a marked trend in the direction of constructing a conceptual scheme in terms of which adequate formulations of different personalities can be made for clinical purposes.

Especially in projective psychology is there a conviction of the pressing need to construct an increasingly comprehensive, coherent, and usable theory of personality which will satisfy to a greater degree than is possible at the present time the twin aims of science: explanation of the past behavior of the individual and the prediction of his future behavior. Some have expressed the hope, which has grown not only out of troubles of the past but also out of the difficulties of the present, that it may be possible to arrive at some sort of common conceptual scheme of personality which will do full justice to all existing sectarian views without provoking further professional bloodletting.

A substantial number of workers in projective psychology appear convinced that the way out is the gradual building up of a logically and psychologically consistent series of concepts and variables which can be defined operationally and which can be put to the crucial test of experimentation. Until the conceptual underbrush has been thoroughly cleared away, projective psychology as a way of looking at the behavior of real persons in real situations is likely to have arrested development.

THE NATURE AND ROLE OF PERCEPTION

Because all projective methods, in one way or another, depend upon the operation of the perceptual mechanisms of the individual, it is important for projective psychology to reach some kind of tentative agreement as to the nature and function of perception. I have already suggested that the projective point of view is greatly indebted not only to Gestalt psychology, the principal experimental effort of which has been directed to a study of perceptual processes and their role in governing the organism's behavior, but also to the main body of general experimental psychology, and importantly to much recent and significant experimental work in social psychology. These several converging attacks upon the problem of perception make possible the beginning stages of development of a basic theory of perception which should prove extremely useful in projective psychology.

For our purposes the first factor of significance that emerges from the varied experimental efforts in the field of perception is the general *selectivity* of all perceptual processes. There is an imposing body of both theoretical and experimental evidence which is prepared to suggest that the selectivity of stimuli may be regarded as a function of the "frames of reference" of the individual. It has been one of the burdens of the whole trend of experimental psychology to establish clearly the principle that stimuli should be looked upon as having in and of themselves no absolute stimulus value. On the basis of years of experimental effort it has become established that each stimulus is perceived always in relation to the pattern of other stimuli among which it appears embedded in reality or to which it has become functionally related through the past experiences of the individual. Koehler has suggested in great detail, from the point of view of Gestalt psychology, in what ways and under what conditions the characteristics of a stimulus are determined by its relationship to a total configuration of which it is a part.[7]

In terms of an impressive body of evidence, which need not be cited here, we may assume that the general selectivity found in all perceptual acts of the individual is caused by, or more properly is a function of, certain *internal* and *external* factors of perception which operate in lawful ways.

Almost since its inception Gestalt psychology has directed its principal experimental attention to the investigation and discovery of the laws that govern the external factors in perception.

---

[7] The reader is referred to the 1947 revision of Koehler's *Gestalt Psychology* for a full and lucid statement of the configurational approach to the ways in which the characteristics of the stimulus are determined by its relationship to the field in which it occurs.

From years of work in this area a significant body of experimental data and a number of supportable and stable conclusions of wide generality have resulted. More recently, because of an increasingly pressing need to understand the ways in which the individual looks at himself in relationship to the real world, Rogers [18] and others who associate themselves with his nondirective point of view have begun an investigation of what they refer to as the individual's "internal frame of reference." For a number of Rogers's co-workers the internal frame of reference may be thought of in terms of the *self-concept*, which is currently enjoying both theoretical and experimental attention.

Raimy [17], who has recently sought to codify and advance the idea of the self-concept within the framework of nondirective counseling theory, offers the following hypotheses about the role of internal factors in perception, which are largely congruent with the theoretical position in projective psychology that I am advancing:

1. The self-concept is a learned perceptual system that is governed by the same principles of organization that govern perceptual objects.

2. The self-concept regulates behavior. The awareness of a different self in counseling results in changes in behavior.

3. A person's awareness of himself may bear little relation to external reality, as in the case of psychotic individuals. Logical conflicts may exist in the self-concept for the external observer, but these are not necessarily psychological conflicts for the person.

4. The self-concept is a differentiated but organized system, so that even negatively valued aspects of it may be defended by the individual in order to maintain his individuality. The self-concept may be more highly valued than the physical organism, as in the case of the soldier who sacrifices himself in battle in order to preserve the positively valued aspects of his self-concept, courage and bravery.

5. The total framework of the self-concept determines how stimuli are to be perceived, and whether old stimuli are to be remembered or forgotten. If the total framework is changed, repressed material may be recalled.

6. The self-concept is exceedingly sensitive in yielding to rapid restructuring if conditions are sufficient, yet it may also

remain unaltered under conditions which, to the external observer, are violent conditions of stress. In counseling, the counselor tries to create a permissive atmosphere in which the client
can drop his guard and look at the parts of the self-concept that
are causing difficulty.

It is evident that Raimy regards the internal factors in perception which he handles in terms of the self-concept as crucial in
affecting the behavior of the individual, and that as a result of
counseling or psychotherapy the changed conception of the self
which is brought about by these procedures may become reflected in new behavior patterns as the individual begins to perceive himself in a new relationship to the world of physical and
social reality. There can be little doubt, I think, that such subjective or internal factors in perception are often of great significance in regulating a person's behavior, and that it should be useful for our present purposes to have a succinct statement of the
conditions under which they may be presumed to function.

It is also important to reach some understanding with respect
to the circumstances responsible for the development of the self-
concept or internal perceptual factors, and it is in this area that I
have found Piaget's studies and hypotheses illuminating. Piaget
[15], who has sought to develop what amounts to a genetic
theory of perception in his work with young children, has suggested that for the child the physical world is never perceived
as unstructured, no matter how restricted the child's frame of
reference. Piaget thinks that the young child is able to invest
any stimulus field with certainty and smugness so that his perceptual acts are stable. However, as the child matures and begins
to experience various sorts of social pressures to which he must
learn to respond in an acceptable and approved fashion according
to the demands of the culture area of which he is a part, he has a
strong tendency to change his percepts to accord more and
more with those of other persons. Piaget's studies suggest that
this is the technique by means of which the thinking of the
child becomes socialized, and that the child is really incapable of
thinking in the adult sense until his percepts have become socialized.

Raimy's notion of the self-concept can, of course, be formulated in a number of other ways. Sherif [20], for example, has offered a statement of the situation in terms of the concepts of

set and psychology of attitudes, has carefully reviewed the literature in this area, and has made important experimental additions
to it. Sherif's formulation of the problem has, I believe, important
implications for projective psychology. Perhaps the most significant finding of his is the fact that the more vague and unstructured the stimulus field, the more important becomes the role of
set and the internal factors in perception in accounting for the
behavior of the individual.

The external frames of reference—the so-called autochthonous determinants of Gestalt psychology—which are instrumental
in helping the individual to organize his perceptual world are too
well known to require restatement here. But despite the admitted
importance of the internal frame of reference—the internal or subjective perceptual factors—which is of crucial significance in our
formulation of a theory of projective psychology, it is a fact that
this important conception about behavior has received considerably less attention in the literature than it has deserved.

On the basis of the experimental work that has been undertaken in studying the roles of the internal and external factors
in perception, it seems to me that it is possible to postulate some
kind of one-to-one relationship between the two frames of reference. We may, for our purposes, regard this relationship as being
a function of both the nature of the stimulus field (in which
external perceptual factors are important) and of the order and
intensity of the needs of the individual (in which internal perceptual factors are significant). Thus, as I have already suggested,
the more structured the stimulus field, the more dependent
behavior usually is upon the operation of the external factors in
perception; and, conversely, the greater the vagueness and ambiguity of the stimulus field, the greater the opportunity for and
need of internal factors in perception to operate. It is demonstrable that even in the presence of an unstructured stimulus
field the behavior of the individual is always to be regarded as
lawful; but the lawfulness of such behavior arises from needs and
values, of both a physiological and a psychological nature, which
function within the individual. Murray's [12] work with children
has suggested that the state of needs of the individual is of great
significance in perceptual behavior, and the studies of Stern and
MacDonald [23], also with children, have indicated the impor-

tance of mood in the child's perception of the appearance of other persons.

The fact that there is a shifting in the relative importance of the internal and external factors in perception in relation to the nature of various stimulus fields that can be presented to an individual constitutes the grounds on which all the projective methods ultimately rest. Indeed, if it were not possible to set up a series of situations to which the person can relate himself under reasonably controlled conditions, in which subjective perceptual factors become strong determinants of an individual's behavior, I believe that the opportunities for the investigation and analysis of personality structure which the projective tests make possible simply could not be realized.

Experimental evidence for the prepotence of internal over external factors in perception, under conditions in the laboratory in which the stimulus field has been made vague and ambiguous, may be found in the continuing experimental work of Bruner and his associates at Harvard. Bruner and Goodman [4], for instance, have studied the role of need and value as factors in perceptual distortion, developing three empirical hypotheses to be tested:

1. *The greater the social value of an object, the more will it be suspectible to organization by behavioral determinants.* It will be *selected* perceptually from among alternative perceptual objects, will become *fixated* as a perceptual response tendency, and will become perceptually *accentuated.*

2. *The greater the individual need for a socially valued object, the more marked will be the operation of behavioral determinants.*

3. *Perceptual equivocality will facilitate the operation of behavioral determinants only in so far as equivocality reduces the operation of autochthonous determinants without reducing the effectiveness of behavioral determinants.*

Their experiments are useful in suggesting rather clearly that need and value are actually organizing factors in perception; and Bruner and Goodman offer evidence which indicates that their three hypotheses can be experimentally sustained. Levine, Chein,

and Murphy [11], who had somewhat earlier studied the relationship between the intensity of a need, in this instance hunger,
and the amount of perceptual distortion that results from it,
have offered data that are largely congruent with the findings
of Bruner and Goodman. In addition to these two studies, which
have attacked the role of subjective factors in perception from
somewhat different points of view, there are a number of other
studies, of which those of Dembo [6] and Sliosberg [22] are representative, presenting evidence with respect to other dynamic
conditions and processes of the individual which affect the nature
of his perceptual acts.

As a result of the body of evidence that has been established,
and the theoretical implications of it, we may look upon perception as an active and purposeful process which involves the whole
organism in relation to its field. By its nature perceptual activity has roots that extend deeply into the whole matrix of the
individual's past experiences, and the perceptual activities of the
individual reach out to fashion his orientation to the future. Not
only are all perceptual processes, therefore, intimately bound to the
separate and discrete past experiences of the individual which
have become behaviorally organized to provide a certain meaning
and unity for him in the present, but they are also strongly tied
to his anticipation of the future, especially of the near future, of
which they may be thought to be a kind of reflection. There is
evidence to suggest that as a result of his past perceptual activities the individual tends to build up or acquire a sense of certainty with respect to the consequences of his present perceptual experiences. Percepts that in the past have been validated
by his subsequent experiences evidently tend to become fixated
as perceptual response tendencies and tend to lead to a feeling of
comfort or security. Percepts that have not enjoyed subsequent
behavioral validation tend to lead to a state of tension and become experienced as uneasiness or anxiety.

There can be little doubt that one of the chief functions of
perception, considered in the widest sense, is that of making it
possible for the organism to protect itself against situations and
circumstances which are harmful and painful to it and which do
not contribute to its welfare and survival. Perceptual acts establish
the grounds for the individual's exercising foresight with respect

to potentially harmful situations and circumstances. For this reason, among many others, each separate act of perception necessarily involves a judgment of some kind or other by the individual with respect to the consequences that a given course of behavior may involve for him.

At the present time there is a slowly developing body of rather slender evidence which is beginning to suggest to us that an important function of perception is that of acting as an *ego defense*. An example of the kind of evidence that is accumulating is offered by Postman, Bruner, and McGinnies [16], who write as follows:

"Value orientation not only contributes to the selection and accentuation of certain percepts in preference to others, it also erects barriers against percepts and hypotheses incongruent with or threatening to the individual's values. We suggest that a defense mechanism similar to repression operates in perceptual behavior."

Within the framework of projective psychology my formulation of the situation is somewhat different. I believe that perceptual processes function in such a manner that they permit the individual to maintain a state or level of anxiety for which he has, through learning, acquired an adequate amount of tolerance. The amount of anxiety that a person has learned to tolerate is undoubtedly a function of a considerable number of personality variables, all of which we assume are affected in different ways and to different degrees by the experiences of the individual. Psychoanalysis has stressed the principle that each person possesses a set of defense mechanisms which are utilized in an individual way and which operate in such a manner that his anxiety level may be kept within manageable limits. Apparently one of the functions of perception is to permit certain of the psychoanalytical defense mechanisms to operate so that the individual is able to maintain a fairly constant level of anxiety. The evidence in this field suggests, indeed, that perception plays a significant role in the process of psychological homeostasis, which is dynamically achieved through the functioning of the several defense mechanisms.

I suspect, on the basis of certain experimental findings arising both from the laboratory and from social psychology, that as the stimulus field becomes progressively more and more unstructured

—a process that forces the individual to rely increasingly upon internal or subjective factors in perception—that is a tendency for his anxiety level to increase markedly.

It is evidently not the stimulus field itself that catalyzes anxiety. Rather, I think it is the fact that the ambiguous stimulus field demands of the individual that he seek new behavioral orientations and either utilize old and inadequate behavior patterns or establish new behavior sequences. The dynamic process of ordering behavior to a new situational relationship is probably what accounts for an increase in the amount of anxiety the individual experiences. It is my conviction that, as the person's anxiety level is increased by this dynamic process of adjustment to the point beyond which the ego, through past learning, has become accustomed, there is a strong tendency for the projective mechanism to function. As the projective mechanism is called into play, it permits the ego to order itself into new and adequate relationships with both physical and social reality. As a consequence of the functioning of the projective mechanism under these conditions, the amount of anxiety being experienced by the individual tends to be lowered to the point at which the individual again feels comfortable and secure.

In formulating the process I have used as a key principle the concept of psychological homeostasis, which is certainly a construct of wide generality and application. It is reasonable to assume that projection is not the only psychological "buffer" employed by the ego to maintain a level of tolerable anxiety. Indeed, we must presume that other defense systems also are utilized; and Postman, Bruner, and McGinnies, in their contribution already cited, have suggested that their experimental data lead readily to the conclusion that repression is another defense dynamism which may be involved in the process of seeking a state or condition of psychological homeostasis. While asserting that other defense mechanisms also appear to be utilized by the individual when he is presented with a stimulus field in which the dimension of ambiguity has been increased, it is clear that for projective psychology the operation of the projective mechanism is of greatest importance. In projective psychology we are interested principally in the study of projective behavior and only secondarily in an examination and evaluation of other behavioral manifestations of the individual.

If the principle of anxiety tolerance and the need of the individual to attempt to maintain a level of anxiety to which he has become accustomed through learning are valid and of wide generality, as I believe, then we may presume that such dynamic processes as the operation of the projective mechanism occur constantly in his everyday experiences as he is forced to face all sorts of socially and physically ambiguous stimulus fields to which he is required to make some sort of adequate adjustment. In such common day-to-day situations which call upon the individual to make a series of socially relevant and appropriate adjustments, I am of the opinion that both physical and social reality become actually invested with the needs, values, wishes, fantasies, and the like, of the perceiver, and become transformed by him in such a way that he usually experiences a minimum increase in the anxiety level he is prepared to handle.

Thus it is perfectly proper to speak of perception which is wish-directed, need-directed, value-directed, fantasy-directed, and so on. In using these terms in this way I am attempting to suggest that the perceptual experiences of the individual become colored by these elements of his personality and that these elements or components of personality account for a distortion of both physical and social reality in such a manner that the felt security and integrity of the perceiver are threatened to a minimum. I believe that this process can be nicely exemplified in the application of the Rorschach Test.

In responding to the Rorschach cards, for example, the subject may offer a considerable number of productions that can be scored as F+. In terms of Rorschach theory and practice, F+ is a direct measure of ego strength or integrity, in that it signifies that the ego perceives reality, as represented by the ink blots, with optimum accuracy—that is, that most of the perceptual distortions which might have been introduced by the subject by his wishes or impulses have been either rejected or kept at a minimum. From another point of view the projective productions in the Rorschach protocol that are scored as F+ responses measure the reality-testing functions of the ego and become, therefore, an expression of the quality of the ego's contact with reality and an index of the role of extra-ego functions in perception —and, by inference, in the personality of the subject.

It may be objected that this thesis can be exemplified by the Rorschach Test but that it cannot readily be demonstrated with certain of the other projective procedures. This, I think, is not so. For example, Sliosberg [22] has shown that children develop a sense of meaning of objects and events which is more fluid in play than in nonplay situations. Homburger [10], Erikson [7], and Murray [12], with so-called play techniques and other projective methods, have made use of this greater flexibility of play to study the deeper desires and suppressed wishes of children; and some fascinating examples of projective behavior have resulted. These several experimental attempts all have in common, I think, the fact that in play situations children characteristically feel more secure and comfortable and that when they are presented with ambiguous stimulus fields they tend to produce projective data which mirror their needs, wishes, fears, etc. In accord with our formulation it appears that the projections of children in such situations result from the fact that the stimulus material presented to them causes a reorganization of their relationship to the physical and social environments.

It is a phenomenon of wide occurrence that the majority of persons appear most secure and comfortable when they are permitted to function in terms of what is old and usual in their experience, and that much insecurity, uncomfortableness, and even anxiety may result as they face situations new and strange to them. I believe it is this circumstance that must be held accountable for the frequent feelings of strain and apparent anxiety with which so many subjects seem to react as they are presented with the stimulus materials offered by the different projective tests. Frequently, and perhaps almost always, these stimulus materials are both new and strange, and they result in the person's being placed in a situation in which, as he sometimes puts it, "the usual rules of the game" do not apparently apply. Clinical experience with a number of the projective methods has established my conviction that when any psychological task is ill-defined, and when in addition the stimulus field is either quite ambiguous or new in the experience of the subject, the testee tends to react with anxiety, which may be either minimum or strong. As the quantum of anxiety becomes increased through the efforts expressed by the person to relate himself to a new and unstructured stimulus field, I believe that the projective mechanism is called into play. If this formulation of the process is correct, the function of perception, as I have suggested, is to decrease the amount of anxiety felt by the individual so that he can come to some new terms with his physical and social environments which will permit him to deal with them with maximum ease and comfort.

This is precisely the situation usually presented to a subject when a projective test is administered to him, and in terms of the formulation I have offered I do not find it difficult to understand why it so frequently happens that the individual proceeds to invest the projective materials with his own wishes, impulses, fantasies, values, and the like. In principle, almost any sort of stimulus materials may be presented to a person to effect projective behavior. What is important is the amount of structure of the stimulus field, and the essential thing is the way in which the subject's performance is interpreted. The amount of structure of the stimulus field may be considerable, but it is preferable to keep it at a minimum so that internal or subjective factors in perception may be free to function, allowing the individual to invest the stimulus situations to a maximum degree with his own needs, values, fantasies, etc.

The TAT, for example, presents the subject with a series of tasks that are new and with stimulus fields sufficiently unstructured and ambiguous to cause him to project his own emotional world, to offer his private conceptions of the physical and social worlds, and to manifest his efforts to organize his behavior and relate himself to those worlds. What emerges from these several attempts at projection and from his efforts to relate himself to the physical and social environments with which he is interacting is a kind of X-ray picture of the individual, as Frank [8] has characterized the process. The projective data suggest in what terms the person thinks of himself in relation to the physical and social environments as he seeks to mold them to his own peculiar needs and values. An examination of the TAT cards is convincing that they have been carefully chosen and designed to offer a series of unusually rich and variegated stimulus fields. Through the use of TAT data we can often build up a strong structure of inference with respect to the manner in which a given personality tries to relate itself to other personalities. Because of the nature of the stimulus fields offered by the TAT the projective data which result from the application of the cards are frequently extremely useful in getting at the interpersonal orientations of the subject and in permitting the clinician to develop supportable inferences with respect to the interpersonal attitudes and feelings of the subject toward most of the significant figures in his life.

Projective tests have, of course, been applied principally in the study and diagnosis of personality. It is a common experience, however, for the clinician to find that the application of a projective test frequently has therapeutic value for the testee.[8] If the general trend of our theory of perception is valid for projective psychology, no one need be surprised about this outcome. Indeed, we may assume that the presentation to a subject of a series of varied stimulus fields by means of projective methods may actually serve to help the individual lower his level of anxiety by offering him an opportunity for catharsis. I suppose that the stimulus materials require that the subject order himself into a new relationship with his physical and social environments. In the process of achieving a new orientation the projective mechanism is called into service and there may be a lessening of anxiety.

SOME POSTULATES ABOUT PERSONALITY

Against the background of the relative sterility of much of current academic psychology, we can discern an increasing tendency for American psychologists to look for a way out through a more intensive and serious study of personality. It is significant that within the past two decades the literature of the psychology of personality has grown to enormous dimensions. This is partly from a growing discontent with the progress of laboratory science and partly out of a realistic concern for the potential contributions that the science of psychology can make in an age of crisis. As Rosenzweig [19] has suggested, in recent years there has been a gradual convergence of theoretical views as to the nature of personality. Despite the fact that these theoretical formulations have arisen from widely different methodological and conceptual positions, for the most part they can be reduced

---

[8] As previously suggested, the individual's initial reaction is frequently an increase in anxiety. As the test procedure unfolds, however, his behavior becomes more stabilized, and tension and anxiety tend to become what they were prior to the test. It is especially in the inquiry portion of the testing procedure, where such is employed, that ventilation of feelings may occur with consequent lessening in anxiety. In principle, a similar situation may develop with any psychological test.

to a very limited number of postulates about the nature of personality which adherents of the projective point of view may find themselves able to accept, although with some reservations.

We may look upon these tentative formulations as examples of some of the least common demoninators which apparently serve, now in one way and now in another, as the working assumptions of a considerable number of clinicians who ally themselves with the projective point of view. The conceptions of personality I am tentatively formulating here should be looked upon only as hypotheses, the function of which is to guide and inspire inquiries about personality in projective psychology. The only sanction these several hypotheses may have at the present time is that they help the projective psychologist to order the data derived from the application of projective tests into meaningful patterns that may prove useful to him in interpreting projective behavior.

The several postulates as to the nature of personality which appear useful in projective psychology may be formulated as follows:

1. *Personality is a system which functions in the individual as an organization between stimulus and response which it seeks to relativize.* This postulate stresses the conditional and relative nature of a stimulus and suggests that any stimulus is effective in evoking a response only to the extent to which it has become related to a functioning organism. A stimulus acquires the capacity to become related to a functioning organism through the learning of that organism.

The stimuli to which a person may learn to react depend upon the peculiar and individual needs and values of that person. Stimuli that possess the capacity to satisfy the needs of an individual tend to become evocative of responses, and it is one of the functions of the personality, as a system functioning within the individual between stimulus and response, to select from among the myriad of stimuli constantly impinging upon the person those which lead to a reduction in the motivation level through the satisfaction of needs.

On a phenomenological level, the selection of stimuli to which the individual may react is accomplished by means of a process we may call "*selective attention*." The process of selective attention is an activity of the perceptual mechanisms. Stimuli that

evoke responses become selected as a function of their contribution to the individual's survival and welfare, considered in the
widest sense. The process of selective attention is an activity of
the personality which causes the individual to be sensitized to
stimuli that promote his welfare and integrity and to develop in
him a lack of sensitivity to stimuli that do not promote these
ends.

Just as an individual acquires selective attention with respect
to classes of stimuli in the course of his learning how to organize
and integrate his separate experiences, we may presume that he
also develops a *"selective inattention"* (Sullivan), a process not
properly a function of the perceptual mechanisms, which we assume occurs outside of the person's awareness.[9]

2. *The personality as an organization is dynamic and motivational in character. Its capacities to select and interpret stimuli, on the one hand, and to control and fixate responses, on the
other, are measures of its integrity and unity as a functioning
system.* This postulate may be considered to be a cornerstone
of Allport's [1] view of personality, and its acceptance by the
projective psychologist involves a virtual dethronement of the
stimulus and a firm introduction of the personality as a set of
"intervening variables" and relativizing system into the old
behavioristic formula, S—R.

Personality as a dynamic organization intervening between
stimulus and response is responsible for the psychological homeostasis that occurs in behavior. Behavior may be said to have
become disordered, for example, when the personality as a dynamic and motivational system or organization is unable to relativize stimulus and response. In consequence of the loss of psychological homeostasis, the individual's old perceptual response
tendencies, acquired largely through learning, are no longer functional. The person can no longer select out of physical and social
reality those stimuli to which he is accustomed to respond. The
"lawfulness" of past behavior is lost, and the person has to sub-

---

[9] In Sullivan's formulation, "selective inattention" is a technique utilized
by the self-system to control the amount of anxiety experienced. Sullivan
regards this process as occurring outside of awareness, but it would take
us too far afield to indicate in what ways his conception of parataxic distortion, important in this context, is related to the process of selective
inattention.

stitute new, and frequently inadequate, response tendencies. We assume, however, that the substitution of new response patterns is lawful and is to be understood in terms of the needs of the individual to assert his integrity and self-consistency on a new basis.

3. *Personality is a configuration.* Personality consists of a wide variety of psychological functions and processes, and we assume that the formation of personality follows the laws of Gestalt psychology which apply to the development of any other configuration.

No projective test can be considered to "measure" the total personality, and no nonprojective personality inventory can be regarded as assessing personality in all the richness of its organization and differentiation as a process. Instead, we must assume that relatively limited sectors of the personality configuration may be evaluated by a combination of all the instruments, both projective and nonprojective, which are available to us at the present time. Since personality may be regarded as a temporally extended configuration, the task of personality evaluation or assessment is an enormously complicated procedure, in which many evaluative methods are employed to obtain a series of cross-sectional pictures that may be useful in building up a series of inferences as to the longitudinal character of the personality process.

The configurational nature of personality is the justification for a multidimensional approach to analysis which the several projective procedures represent. Each aspect of the configuration called personality which any given projective method attempts to throw light on must be regarded as *only one* expression of the total personality as process and must be considered in the light of the other behavioral expressions of the individual.

4. *Personality growth and development rest upon both differentiation and integration.* This postulate asserts that personality growth and development are dependent upon two fundamental processes, learning and maturation. Learning and maturation are jointly responsible for both differentiation and integration, which characterize the personality process in varying ways at different stages in its temporal course.

5. *Personality in its growth and development is greatly influenced by environmental factors. Of the environmental factors, those which are cultural are of prime importance.* This postulate

does not deny the role and significance of hereditary factors as determinants of personality, but stresses the proposition that environmental determinants of personality are significantly influential in making it possible for the individual to organize his separate experiences and to order his behavior toward the more adequate satisfaction of his unique needs.

These five postulates as to the nature of personality are, I believe, useful in projective psychology in that they may be used as frames of reference for thinking about personality. They may even be useful in aiding the clinician to order the projective productions of his subjects in such a way that the projective data may have more meaning. It is clear that the acceptance of even some of the hypotheses about the nature of personality makes it mandatory that the projective psychologist utilize a wide variety of procedures, both projective and nonprojective, in exploring the richness of personality.

It is obvious that the several postulates that have been outlined represent only the bare beginnings of the development of a theory of personality which must be the prior concern of all in projective psychology if the projective methods currently employed are to enjoy wider acceptance by the psychological fraternity. Academic psychologists not only have a right, but possess a responsibility, to insist that the clinician make explicit and public the ideas and conceptions that guide his inquiries with projective procedures. Whatever its other characteristics, science is a human activity, the procedures and operations of which must be public and repeatable. It is not now defensible, nor has it ever been, for the psychologist as scientist to operate with concepts that are esoteric rather than public. The guiding conceptions of projective psychology must be made explicit so that they may eventually be subjected to the test of experimentation and become a group of warranted inferences.

It is, of course, true that a number of theoretical formulations about personality, of which perhaps Murray's [12] is the most comprehensive, have been offered. All of these theories of personality have in common, however, the fact that they have not enjoyed wide acceptance among those who work within the projective framework. A theory of personality is urgently needed by clinicians who work with projective tests, and their day-today experiences should offer an opportunity for testing its worth as they order their projective data to it. Such a theory is justified not alone because we require order, but rather because it can stimulate and guide a series of crucial experiments which may have as their ultimate function that of developing wholly new perspectives of and conceptions about personality.

In this chapter I have sought to suggest something of the theoretical climate in which the fledgling, projective psychology, is developing, and some of the more significant conceptions that have acted to shape it into a useful and respectable approach to the study and diagnosis of personality. Not all the influences that have fashioned the projective point of view in psychology are of equal importance, and I have stressed those as significant which square most readily with my own preconceptions. Others would very likely accentuate other and quite different trends. But whatever the formulation of the new field of projective psychology, I do not regard it premature to suggest that the projective point of view represents a different and unique approach to the area of the applied psychology of personality to which psychologists of both experimental and clinical persuasion may be attracted.

I have presented an outline theory of perception which may be useful in understanding projective psychology. Certainly other formulations of the nature and role of perceptual processes are possible and useful, but I believe that the approach to perception I have offered may be helpful in understanding why perception is a sort of *via regia* for the investigation of the needs, values, wishes, fantasies, impulses, and the like of the individual which the several projective procedures can make available to us. I have stated the conditions under which I believe perceptual processes function to maintain the level of anxiety of the individual, and I have offered a theory as to how the projective mechanism may be called into operation.

The five postulates about personality, which are to be used as hypotheses to be tested by clinical and projective data, represent only the scaffolding about which a fully useful and comprehensive theory of personality needs to be erected. They have been offered only because of my conviction that projective psychology has a responsibility for making as explicit as possible the conceptions about personality which are used. There are obviously many implicit conceptions that clinicians use in working with projective tests, but it is their responsibility to state them. It is likely that they represent rather their own theoretical predilections than points upon which some mutual agreement is readily developed.[10]

I have indicated the importance I attach to the development of a theory of personality which may be particularly useful to projective psychologists. In the absence of this it is obvious that the projective tests are likely to find it difficult to reach maturity of such a type as to permit them fully to compete, on equal grounds, with the older approaches to personality study. Projective psychologists still manifest feelings of insecurity which are engendered not by their origin so much as by the kind of blind and unwilling scorn accorded to them by academic psychologists who insist that before projective tests can be accepted into the main stream of American psychology the projective tests must demonstrate their validity and reliability in the same way as the nonprojective tests have demonstrated their value.

I am of the belief that projective tests have developed from a climate of opinion so radical and different from that which made possible other personality assessment procedures that their validity and reliability can never be established in the same ways. To demand these things of the projective methods is to require something that simply cannot be met.

The projective tests have made it quite clear that we must be prepared to abandon the spurious distinction between quantitative and qualitative data. Both sorts emerge in the study of personality and we must develop techniques of data treatment which permit us to handle both types. Fortunately for projective psychology, there is increasing recognition of the situation; and we may expect the next few years' work to provide us with

---

[10] Unless clinicians actually make their conceptions explicit and public, of course, we have no way of knowing to what extent they may become integrated into the theory of projective psychology as presently formulated. One suspects, however, that many of the implicit conceptions of clinicians who work with projective tests are not of a kind capable of ready integration into current conceptions of projective psychology.

the necessary skills to handle personality data of whatever type in a more appropriate and adequate manner.[11]

REFERENCES

1. ALLPORT, G. W.: *Personality: A Psychological Interpretation.* New York: Henry Holt & Co.; 1937.
2. ———: "The Use of Personal Documents in Psychological Science." *Social Science Research Council Bulletin*, No. 49 (1942).
3. BROWN, J. F.: "Psychoanalysis, Topological Psychology, and Experimental Psychopathology," *Psychoanalytic Quarterly*, Vol. 6 (1937), pp. 227–37.
4. BRUNER, J. S., and GOODMAN, C. C.: "Need and Value as Organizing Factors in Perception," *Journal of Abnormal and Social Psychology*, Vol. 42 (1947), pp. 33–44.
5. BRUNER, J. S., and POSTMAN, L.: "Tension and Tension-Release as Organizing Factors in Perception," *Journal of Personality*, Vol. 15 (1947), pp. 300–8.
6. DEMBO, T.: "Der Ärger als Dynamisches Problem," *Psychologische Forschung*, Vol. 15 (1931), pp. 1–144.
7. ERIKSON, E. H.: "Studies in the Interpretation of Play: I. Clinical Observation of Play Disruption in Young Children." *Genetic Psychology Monographs*, Vol. 22 (1940), pp. 556–671.
8. FRANK, L. K.: "Projective Methods for the Study of Personality," *Journal of Psychology*, Vol. 8 (1939), pp. 389–413.
9. ———: *Projective Methods.* Springfield, Ill.: Charles C. Thomas; 1948.
10. HOMBURGER, E.: "Configurations in Play: Clinical Notes," *Psychoanalytic Quarterly*, Vol. 6 (1937), pp. 139–214.
11. LEVINE, R., CHEIN, I., and MURPHY, G.: "The Relation of the Intensity of a Need to the Amount of Perceptual Distortion: A Preliminary Report," *Journal of Psychology*, Vol. 13 (1942), pp. 283–93.
12. MURRAY, H. A.: *Explorations in Personality.* New York: Oxford University Press; 1938.
13. NORTHROP, F. S. C.: "The Neurological and Behavioristic Psycho-

---

[11] Several important steps have already been taken in this direction. As an example of one, see L. J. Cronbach's "A Validation Design for Qualitative Studies of Personality" in the November-December 1948 issue of the *Journal of Consulting Psychology*.

logical Basis of the Ordering of Society by Means of Ideas," *Science*, Vol. 107 (1948), pp. 411–17.

14. OSS Assessment Staff: *Assessment of Men*. New York: Rinehart & Co.; 1948.

15. PIAGET, J.: *The Language and Thought of the Child*. New York: Harcourt, Brace & Co.; 1926.

16. POSTMAN, L., BRUNER, J. S., and McGINNIES, E.: "Personal Values as Selective Factors in Perception," *Journal of Abnormal and Social Psychology* Vol. 43 (1948), pp. 142–54.

17. RASKIN, N. J.: "The Development of Nondirective Therapy," *Journal of Consulting Psychology*, Vol 12 (1948), pp. 92–110.

18. ROGERS, C. R.: "Significant Aspects of Client-centered Therapy," *American Psychologist*, Vol. 1 (1946), pp. 415–22.

19. ROSENZWEIG, S.: "Converging Approaches to Personality," *Psychological Review*, Vol. 51 (1944), pp. 248–57.

20. SHERIF, M.: "A Study of Some Social Factors in Perception," *Archives of Psychology*, 1935, No. 187.

21. SKAGGS, E. B.: "Ten Basic Postulates of Personalistic Psychology," *Psychological Review*, Vol. 54 (1947), pp. 255–62.

22. SLIOSBERG, S.: "A Contribution to the Dynamics of Substitution in Serious and Play Situations," *Psychologisch Forschung*, Vol. 19 (1934), pp. 122–81.

23. STERN, W., and MacDONALD, J.: "Cloud Pictures: a New Method of Testing Imagination," *Character and Personality*, Vol. 6 (1937), pp. 132–47.

PART II

▼

Projective Tests in Clinical Psychology

Projective Tests in Clinical Psychology

INTRODUCTION

It is in clinical psychology, of course, that the various projective tests have enjoyed their widest application and show their greatest promise as instruments for research, personality study and diagnosis, and appraisal of the progress of psychotherapy. The several projective methods used in this applied branch of the psychology of personality represent, we believe, a significant forward step in the development of a genuine science of personality study and diagnosis. As projective test procedures have become more and more refined, and as clinicians have learned with increasing skill to apply them in the study of many different types of personality reactions, the techniques have begun to contribute importantly to an ever widening yet progressively more precise knowledge not only of behavior disorders but also of behavior dynamics.

The chapters presented as Part II are only a representative sample of the whole area of projective psychology at its present state of development. The projective procedures presented, however, are among the most widely employed and useful currently available. It is important to point out that not all of the projective methods reported on here exactly fit the definition of projection considered in its narrowest sense. Our justification for including them in our *Projective Psychology* rests upon the belief that these procedures are referred to as "projective" by the clinicians who utilize the methods in their day-to-day work of study and diagnosis of personality.

It is rare to find a clinician fully competent in the administration and interpretation of all these procedures. It is a much more common situation for clinicians to depend upon a relatively few projective methods with which they are likely to feel most secure. It is our hope that the acquaintance of clinical psychologists with projective techniques with which they are not now fully familiar or of special applications of methods long familiar may increase their diagnostic skills through providing them with additional projective instruments for their clinical armamentarium. It seems clear that for a more comprehensive appraisal of the personality *as a total process* for diagnostic purposes we must be prepared to utilize, rather than a single test, a variety of projective procedures, each of which has been carefully chosen to contribute to a configurational evaluation of the individual.

Part II includes papers on projective methods that not only are well known but also enjoy application in many clinical settings. In the selection of projective procedures for this section, we have been guided by an insistence that the methods shall have demonstrated their fruitfulness in clinical psychological work. The projective tests and techniques included here are obviously of diverse origins, and it is evident that each is in a different state of development and standardization. This fact need not disturb the reader. No responsible scientist can quarrel with the principle that any testing procedure requires both calibration and validation. We certainly do not assume the position that any of the projective methods we have chosen which have not been standardized and validated should not be subjected to the most rigorous tests of this sort that can be applied. We think, however, that the whole process of validation of projective methods requires careful and thoughtful evaluation, and that this over-all task is a prior step to the serious and painstaking attempt at standardization and validation of any specific projective method or technique.

There is a developing feeling among some clinicians that until the recent past probably too much time has been consumed in the evaluation of personality by means of the Rorschach Test. The Rorschach Test certainly stands today in a position of commanding importance in the field of personality assessment and diagnosis. Yet it is true that some of the other projective procedures—new, unstandardized, and unvalidated as they are—have begun to prove themselves enormously helpful in psychodiagnosis. As the field of projective psychology has earned greater acceptance, there has been a developing tendency for clinical psychologists to abandon the Rorschach Test for some of the newer, briefer, less well-standardized projective methods. This abandonment has been chiefly to preserve the Rorschach Test for application in those clinical situations which demand the rigor, precision, and elegance of psychodiagnostic statement which the Rorschach alone can provide. The inevitable result of this trend away from the Rorschach Test has been growing appreciation of the possibilities of some of the other projective techniques which Part II comprises.

It is, then, the changing state of affairs within clinical psychology itself that provides the justification for the amount of space in this book devoted to the newer and briefer assessment procedures. It is difficult for the practicing clinician to learn much about these projective methods in the current psychological literature, and the better-known methods like the Rorschach are ably represented by any number of fundamental source works. It is hoped that this book will help remedy the situation by providing the clinician with useful information about such projective methods as the Szondi Test, finger-painting, and figure drawing, as well as such special approaches as content analysis and the inspection method for the Rorschach. We feel that no reader has a right to expect that any chapter will provide him with *all* the information that may be necessary for the skillful use of a particular method or application in a special situation. We are persuaded that it will always be necessary for the practitioner to refer constantly to the basic literature, and this book makes no pretense that it provides a complete treatment of each projective method covered.

In the preparation of the chapters for this portion of *Projective Psychology*, contributors have been guided chiefly by the consideration that their paper should review something of the background of the particular method and then that it should usefully indicate as clearly and briefly as possible how the method may be employed as a clinical, and occasionally as a research, technique. Wherever possible, the contributor has sought to avoid presenting material elsewhere available. Thus the several chapters on particular aspects or use of the Rorschach Test make no attempt to provide instructions in the use of this method because this is available in any number of excellent books.

Examination of the contents of Part II will reveal that a number of projective methods have not been included. Chief among those to be found missing are several art techniques, psychodrama and sociodrama, play techniques, and certain others like the Picture Frustration Test. Despite the omission of these projective methods, we feel that those included represent a judicious choice of methods currently popular and useful in psychodiagnosis.

Those projective methods included are certainly of greatly different use and worth. Sometimes this situation grows out of the nature of the projective test or method itself, and often it is merely a comment on the newness, lack of formalization of the procedures of administration, scoring, and interpretation, and the relative inexperience of clinicians with the particular procedure. Without being at all hostile, one must be prepared to say that some of these techniques are largely in the divining-rod stage of development; but it is probably not accurate, as some have charged, that the average clinician needs an exceptionally clear crystal ball in addition to the projective method if he is to function effectively. We believe that, in the final analysis, less concern should be directed to the tentative nature of certain projective methods than to the serious and careful training of clinical psychologists who must use them.

The projective tests presented in this second part, although generally accepted as projective methods, vary widely in methodology and theoretical substructure. We recognize that in perhaps all the projective methods presented here there are *adaptive, expressive,* and *projective* elements, but in greatly varying amount from one procedure to the next. Thus the Rorschach Test cards contain structures with properties and characteristics to which the average subject may respond in a largely adaptive manner. This process leads quite naturally to the production of "popular" responses. In general, we believe that the adaptive behavior elicited by such stimulus materials can probably be considered as a stable index of the individual's reality orientation. It is becoming more apparent that certain of the projective tests are of greater use than others for stimulating adaptive, expressive, and projective behavior, and that, depending upon the purpose of the inquiry, the clinical psychologist will choose that procedure which in his experience has proved most useful for the particular purpose at hand.

In his discussion of the content analysis of the Rorschach Test protocol Robert M. Lindner points out to what extent the Rorschach is generally used as a form-analytic technique and a study of the expressive, organizational qualities of the individual. Lindner's position is precisely that clinicians should be concerned with *what* the subject produces as well as *how* he produces it, and it was with exactly the same notions that Leopold Bellak in Part I sought to differentiate apperceptive and expressive behavior, respectively. The papers of Ruth Munroe and Molly Harrower clearly indicate a primary interest in the structural elements of the Rorschach Test, those aspects which up to now have constituted its main usefulness.

The Thematic Apperception Test, on the other hand, is primarily based upon the process of apperceptive distortion, and specifically of that which occurs in the area of interpersonal relations. While it, too, has organizational and expressive aspects, which some authors have used as the basis for their interpretative and diagnostic schemes, it can approach the Rorschach Test as little in that sphere as the Rorschach can in turn approach the usefulness of the TAT in giving apperceptive content.

The Mosaic Test and the Bender Visual-Motor Gestalt Test are as exclusively as possible tests of expression and organization, and they appear to function primarily on a myoneural basis, being therefore chiefly useful at present in differentiating gross disturbances of a possibly organic basis from the more nearly functional disorders.

The finger-painting procedure, while similarly based on expressive characteristics, stands out by its utter need for adaptation, as Asya Kadis has pointed out. This has the important advantage of making it useful for subjects upon whom the Rorschach or the TAT would make too many demands. Finger-painting, however, need not lack apperceptive aspects, as when attempts are made by the subject to depict something definite. In this sense finger-painting becomes a first cousin of the figure-drawing procedure: apperception of the self (via the body image) and apperception of other persons stand side by side with expressions of myoneural characteristics.

Sentence Completion Tests are based primarily on apperceptive distortion and analysis of the content of the completion words, inasmuch as the incomplete sentence technique often constitutes a social or emotional situation that the subject has to be prepared to interpret in terms of his established images and memories. In a similar way the Szondi Test is chiefly concerned with the apperception of faces and with the development of judgment of hedonic tone concerning them. What factors may influence these judgments to an extent sufficient for reliable criteria for diagnosis of certain clinical syndromes as claimed for the Szondi Test so far remains unknown.

ALTHOUGH the Rorschach Test protocol is usually handled in a formal manner, it is well known that the actual practice of many Rorschach workers involves a consideration of the content features of the record as well. Robert M. Lindner has prepared in the following chapter an outline of some of the possibilities in interpretation afforded the clinician using the Rorschach Test if he adds to his consideration of the protocol the additional dimension of content.

In view of the rather novel approach to content analysis suggested by Lindner, we feel justified in adding a special word of caution to that already provided by the author. If clinicians plan to use his suggestions for interpretation, they must seek to avoid an "If . . . , then" kind of reasoning which may force the entire burden of interpretation upon the content qualities of the Rorschach protocol to the neglect or relative neglect of the record's more formal aspects. It is clear that the only safe way of using the method of content analysis which he recommends is as a supplement to the more formal analytical procedures offered in the rich Rorschach literature.

▼

The Content Analysis of the
Rorschach Protocol

Robert M. Lindner

I

THAT the Rorschach possesses still another dimension besides those usually attributed to it has been known for many years. In fact it is more than likely that Hermann Rorschach himself was denied, by his untimely death, the opportunity for investigating this aspect of his important work. Albeit obliquely, this is hinted throughout his monumental monograph. Many of the cult-bound Rorschachers tend to miss his intention in the furor of their preoccupation with the letter to the neglect of the spirit of his achievement [6].

The dimension of the Rorschach to which reference is made is that of *significance*. In three previously published papers it has been my privilege to explore the possibilities of this dimension. As the culmination of a decade of observation I have been able to isolate forty-three separate responses; each of these seems to relate specifically to and appears with regular frequency within the various diagnostic categories with which the psychiatrist, the clinical psychologist, and the psychoanalyst are concerned [2]. That this work has borne fruit is testified to by a steady interest in it on the part of the profession.

I cannot help believing that the approach to the Rorschach Test from the content side enormously enriches the value of the Rorschach protocol for diagnostic and therapeutic purposes. The added dimension of significance successfully combats the sterile structuralization of the personality under examination and permits a more intimate insight into the actual working dynamics in a given case. This addendum to clinical intuition has, so to speak, a rounding-out function which raises the instrumentality of the Rorschach Test to new heights and sharpens its edges as a clinical tool. Properly and cautiously employed, it gives the clinician a surer and firmer foothold for his task of understanding the human material presented to him for study and help.

Briefly, the thesis in work already published and in this paper is that *what* the patient under Rorschach scrutiny produces is quite as important as *how* he produces it, and that occasionally it is more so As a practicing analytical psychologist and psychological clinician, I recognize that the productions of the patient are related intimately, if often obscurely, to the dynamics of his personality. It is a *result* of the mechanics—sometimes devious—of his performing, and as such, and like all other products, it has a basic significance that we can understand, once given the clue.

The Rorschach examination is a process of continuous disclosure. Onto the raw, undifferentiated, plastic, and manipulable matter which the blots present, the examinee projects the end products of his internal performing. This material emerges in a form suitable for analysis, but only after it has passed through the refining exercises demanded of all psychological products. What the original impression of the blot stimulus is in any given case can only be discovered through patient retrogressive exploration by free association. What emerges vocally upon presentation yet connects, however tenuously, with that fundamental impress and, at the very least, conforms to a *type* at once classifiable and personal. As can be seen, this makes it possible for all responses to be arranged according to classification among diagnostic categories as long as such categories are descriptive. Moreover, in addition to the general applicability of a response for classification among diagnostic entities, each reflects a personal element in that it has been subject to the distortive and defensive manipulations especially peculiar to the individual producing it.

When faced with the reality of the Rorschach response, the psychologist until recently has been forced to examine the special ways in which it was produced from qualities inherent in the blot itself, from its purely physical features. The selection by the subject of elemental qualities and properties of the material was regarded as conforming to diagnostic patterns. But the actual images produced by the alchemical binding of such properties were largely disregarded. It is true, however, that some concern for the images and their possible *meanings* persisted. Thus certain classes and categories of images appeared meaningful on an empirical basis, and where they persisted in a record, mention was made of the possibility that through them was reflected "something more" about the patient, his personality organization, or his special conflicts. Sequence analysis of the records was another and more rewarding way in which the problem was met. Here the total and progressive orientation of the record, from image to image, was looked upon as the repository of additional information. Although being a step in the right direction, nevertheless this approach was bound to be a sterile one because only by inference and intuition was it possible to add to the traditional way of estimating the record.

Those of us who have worked in the content area have come to accept the following propositions: (a) that certain responses reflect basic processes within the personality; (b) that certain responses are characteristic of various diagnostic groupings; (c) that certain responses indicate essential motivants and dynamisms within the patient; and (d) that certain responses "act as road markers and signposts along the difficult path of clinical differentiation."

Up to the time of this writing, forty-three responses that are consistent with the above propositions have been isolated. Their isolation has been accomplished over a period of some years by a continuous recording of their appearance among cases where a specific diagnosis was achieved. The statistical techniques are admittedly poor and simple, consisting solely of frequency tabulation. The results are therefore to be regarded as merely tentative, established only by high order of frequency when checked both ways—retrogressively and prognostically—against diagnoses achieved or dynamics uncovered. In all, the records from 2,200 group administrations and the same number of individual examinations were culled in this way in the original surveys. A better statistical check is required with cases drawn from sources closer to adequate sampling requirements. It seems, however, that the pragmatic test has been withstood successfully by all of the forty-three, according to reports and communications from other clinicians.

There has been some confusion about the way in which these forty-three and perhaps other responses yet to be isolated are to be utilized. Some clinicians have persisted in regarding them as magical formulas and have viewed the appearance of one or more of them in a record as proof positive of a diagnostic impression. Others have chosen to abandon the traditional approaches to the Rorschach wholesale and have depended on content alone to yield all they require from the examination. Both of these approaches are inappropriate. It cannot be too often stressed that the approach through content is only an *additional* approach, adding another dimension to the Rorschach responses, and that it must take its proper place among other approaches. It is no excuse for avoiding, nor can it ever take the place of, routine and well-established Rorschach survey by usual methods or for the clinical experience, intuition, and other techniques in the clinician's armamentarium. These responses do little more than highlight and focus attention upon central problems, conflicts, perplexities, areas and foci of discord, hurts and places of lowered psychic resistance, within the personality of the examinee. They indicate, sometimes quite sharply but never exclusively, the best diagnosis of the personality being examined. They aid in diagnostic differentiation. They help guide in the tortuous process of diagnostic elimination. And they suggest beyond the mere statement of the spoken response.

II

The following are the responses that have so far been found to be significant and meaningful from the point of view of content analysis. Where they appear within the protocol, it appears that the examiner is justified in giving special consideration to the diagnoses attached to them or to the problems they encompass. Their appearance at least signalizes the need for an examiner to exclude their implications from his total impression of the patient by good evidence, or, if he cannot do this, to devote more than passing attention to the matters they imply. It must once again be stated as a caution that these responses are not given by *all* members of a special group, but that where they appear there is increased possibility of a patient's falling within a limited diagnostic area.[1]

1. *Card I. Lower Central D.* The normal male subject will usually give "a female torso." He will point to the feminine-like distribution of flesh on the hips and the rounded softness of the gluteal muscles. Homosexuals see this as "a male torso," it appearing to them as muscular and containing other qualities heterosexually adjusted observers do not project. Especially will this response appear among feminine-type male homosexuals. The response "a muscular mannish female" appears profusely among the masculine-type male homosexuals.

2. *Card I. Central Light-Gray Rare Detail on Midline.* Normal subjects rarely mention this area. The responses "a tomahawk" or "a hammerhead" are given chiefly by aggressive psychopaths. Obsessive character types may try to use it, will describe it, and will be very critical of themselves when they cannot assign it properly. It appears as "a tooth" among adolescents who are perturbed by guilt over masturbation and among adults who have unresolved masturbation problems. Marked depressives, in the trough of the mood cycle, when using the blot as a whole (W) for any concept, will point to it as evidence of rotting and decay.

3. *Card I. Paired White Spaces in Upper Half of Blot.* These will be seized upon by agitated depressives and negativistic personality types. They will tend to isolate them from the rest of the blot

---

[1] Although locations given here are from the usual upright position of the cards unless otherwise specified, nevertheless the interpretations apply equally to responses made when the cards are held in any other position.

and from the lower pair of white spaces. The response will usually be given together with a somatized reference such as "this is how I feel inside," and will be described as "emptiness" or "a hole." Paranoid types showing both referential and influential ideation will use the spaces as "a ghost walking" or "an invisible man." A patient suffering from amnesia as a result of concussion gave "the ghost of a man I killed overseas." The projections here of "apparitions" and "ghostly figures" or "spirits" will be found especially among individuals who believe themselves to be subject to manipulation by forces beyond their ken or control.

4. *Card I. Upper Central Portion with Clawlike Projections.* This place is convenient for the projection of oral fantasies by orally fixated individuals with marked or hidden aggressivity. The series of responses likely to appear extends from "birds with open mouths" to "a mouth." In instances where the affect is shallow or stinted, the response may be along the lines of "a disembodied mouth." Here it appears as if the response mirrors the defensive attempts of the patient to deny his essential aggressivity.

5. *Card I. Whole Blot.* The whole (W) response of "eagle," "bird," or "bat," when combined with movement of the winglike projections, forms one of the most useful diagnostic clues for the separation of the paranoid schizophrenic from the obsessive with paranoid coloring, as well as from other entities that contain paranoid elements. Always on the appearance of this whole response an examiner should question regarding the movement of the wings and the direction of such movement of the wings. For some reason paranoid schizophrenics are often unable to perceive outward movement of the wings. They report, instead, projecting movement inward only, toward themselves, from a fixed position.

6. *Card I. Densely Shaded Areas throughout Entire Blot.* The responses "blobs of dirt," "dust mice," "termites," "petrified fecal matter," and "animal droppings"—or responses of this order—are clues to obsession-compulsion with typical anal-erotic aggressive character structure.

7. *Card II. Center White Space.* So-called normal subjects ignore and disregard this area. It is chosen by negativistically inclined persons, however, by those with rigid personality structure, by elderly persons with fixed and undeviating character patterns, and finally by anxiety neurotics. The last group favor "a spinning top." The projection of movement onto this area I regard as a

prognostically hopeful sign: the inhibition and repression signified by the response, when combined with movement, are not too far below the surface, and the therapeutic possibilities are correspondingly more favorable. Inelasticity of the personality is indicated by the projection of an unmoving and static image upon this place.

8. *Card II. Large Detail.* "Two bears kissing" or "two bears (or other animals) with their paws together" are in the innocuous class of response to the whole card, exclusive of the two red-colored areas in the upper half. But responses such as "two bears fighting with blood splashed around" are often significant for the episodic kind of psychopath who entertains aggressive fantasies and is markedly hostile toward the outer world. This kind of response is similarly indicative of petit mal epilepsy, transient fugue states, hysteria, tantrum behavior in children, and the many traits and tendencies comprised within the old designation of "epileptoid personality types." Any mention of "blood" on this card must be investigated further and the categories of psychopathic personality, aggressive paranoia, excited catatonia, and ideopathic epilepsy held open until otherwise eliminated in cases of major mental involvement.

9. *Card II. Whole Blot.* The response "clowns with red faces and caps on and red feet" appears among the affect disorders and is an index to mood swing. In my experience it appears in Rorschach testing previous to a change from the depressive to a manic phase. On occasion it has served as one of many indices to successful electro-shock therapy with depressed patients and with moderately ruminative obsessive cases.

10. *Card II. Central Detail above White Spaces.* Where the responses "a pair of pliers" or "some sort of tool" are given, they usually mask the obvious phallic symbolism of the shape and denote hesitancy in coming to grips with an underlying sexual problem. Anxiety relating to genital activity can be assumed where the response from this location is accompanied by a reported strain kinesthesis. In every instance encountered I have found it in exhibitionism, acute castration anxiety, genital phobia, and inadequacy convictions regarding sex. The "tooth" response here betrays masturbating activities with guilt and conflicting feelings about masturbation.

11. *Card II. Center Lower Pink Rare Detail.* This portion of the

card is frequently seized upon by paranoid individuals with diffuse homosexual ideation and vaguely influential thought content as a channel through which they express mysterious notions of electrical influences. They tend to produce such images as "pipelines with holes through here," "an electric plug," or "a radio tube."

12. *Card III. Middle D in "Human" Form.* The average subject usually overlooks or fails to comment upon the ragged but somewhat rounded projection in the "chest" region of the manlike figures. But homosexuals, of whatever type, seem to be troubled by this feature and show hesitation regarding the sex of the figures. Apparently they are more alert and sensitive to slight sex differences in day-to-day living, and the imposition of these irregular protrusions reminds them of their own ambivalent status, evoking the confusion expressed by hesitation when they are asked about the sex of the concept. Such persons tend to solve the problem by stressing the femininity of the projected image as "it must be a couple of women"; the more open type of homosexual will meet the issue squarely with "a couple of queers," or "two fellows with breasts."

13. *Card III. Lower Central Light-Gray Detail.* Inward hostility projected upon the environment is indicated by observing movement accompanying perceptions of the class of "jaws closing" or "a mechanical scoop." Patients who yield such responses will also report phobias about crowds and busy places and avoidance reactions in connection with theaters, restaurants, and similar places. They will feel that the world is hostile and unfriendly toward them, and that the environment is crushing them and robbing them of their individual identity. When such a response to this area appears conjoined with a "blood" reaction, it testifies to latent hostility and sadistic aggressivity. Actually it demonstrates the clinical formula: sadism → projection of aggression outwardly → fear of inability to control aggression → perception of hostility from the outside, which last is aimed to prevent the fulfillment of aggressive and sadistic wishes.

14. *Card III. Red Lateral Details and Red Center Detail.* The "blood" response to any of these areas or all of them should be given the same value as the similar response in Card II. The response is commonly found among epileptics, episodic psychopaths, and hysterics with underlying aggression.

15. *Card III. "Human Figures."* Immaturity is disclosed by the testee of average intelligence who avoids the human response and substitutes therefore such concepts as "Donald Duck," "Mickey Mouse." Schizoids who feel themselves to be motivated by hostile forces beyond them, who believe that they are being directed, motivated, and manipulated by others, will respond to these parts of the blot with "puppets," "marionettes," and "mechanical dolls."

16. *Card IV. Bulbous Areas along Lateral Aspects of Bottom Center.* Average or normal subjects will form concepts such as "a horse's head" or "the head of some insect" from this area. Such subjects rarely attend in a more than passing fashion to the shading characteristics that encourage the perception of "a pair of eyes." Persons with strongly paranoidal tendencies, however, and those whose symptom-complexes include ideas of influence or reference, deliberately note the "eyes," abstracting them from the head of the insect or animal and adding the impression that "they are looking at me." Such responses appear with similar frequency from strongly inferiority-convicted persons. Among these such a response probably represents a projection of the idea of being under the close scrutiny of the examiner and the examination.

17. *Card IV. Whole Blot.* The "suicide" card is an apt name for Card IV. Responses containing such projections as "a decaying tooth," "a rotted tree trunk," "a pall of black smoke," "something rotten," "a burned and charred piece of wood" appear in severe depressive states with suicidal overtones and self-annihilative thought content. Where the response to this area frankly mentions death, however, there is a fair prospect that the patient will benefit from convulsive therapy.

18. *Card IV. Upper Central Diffuse Gray Area.* Latent homosexuals of either sex, and especially males who show that curious but frequent combination of fear of and wish for penetration, may give "a projectile" or "a ship cleaving through water." Sexually derived anxiety is expressed through a response of the order of "a bomb falling." Tension mounting to a blow-off point is indicated by answers in the class of "an explosion." This will be found among psychopaths and epileptics who are seeking a return of the homeostatic balance through a tensional discharge and among alcoholics of the "spree" and "bender" kind [3].

19. *Card IV. Midline Area.* An accurate guide to the presence in an individual of free-floating, unattached anxiety is to be found in the response "a skeleton." It apparently denotes an over-all, un-canalized, and widely diffused neurosis. It will also be observed commonly among adolescents suffering from *Weltschmerz.*

20. *Card IV. Whole Blot.* The "gorilla" relished by magazine readers, when regarded from the standpoint of the clinical psychologist in Rorschach work rather than from that of the magazine writer, signifies the projection of self in an effort to depict the baser side of the personality. It is found among depressives and ruminating obsessives who experience strong guilt reactions and self-recrimination.

21. *Card IV. Whole Blot.* The "man at stool" ranks high as a response given by compulsive characters who show the classical and expected traits of niggardliness, miserliness, misanthropy, etc. Patients who present gastrointestinal complaints, particularly constipation, and somatically deluded agitated depressives, also utilize this concept frequently.

22. *Card V. Upper and Lower Semivertical Projections.* Where these parts are seen as moving, the testee will usually show ideation concerned with being manipulated by strong forces beyond his control. Paranoid schizophrenics have a penchant for using these projections. Neurotic-type alcoholics and other oral-incorporative types combine them with the "hills," "valleys," or "breasts" that they find in the wings of the blot.

23. *Card V. Outline Silhouette of Entire Blot.* Suspicious paranoids and obsessives find the edges of this blot especially fertile for the projection of "faces" and "mouths." Schizophrenics give "a disembodied mouth" or "only a mouth." The progressive fabulation of the response beginning with "mouth" and eventually encompassing the whole blot is a major clue to serious schizoid involvement.

24. *Card VI. Whole Blot Exclusive of Upper D.* Anxiety neurotics and individuals exhibiting chaotic sexuality view the lower D here as the prospect a gynecologist would observe in the course of performing a vaginal examination. They often append "diseased" to the image. As an example, an anxious psychoneurotic gave "the diseased sex parts of a syphilitic Negress." Anxious and sexually maladjusted patients, moreover, usually refuse to acknowledge the "penis" in upper D, but are curiously ready to note lower D's resemblance to the female genitalia.

25. *Card VI. Winglike Projections in Upper Third of Blot.* Although Card VI is famous for its sexual symbolism, other significant content appears on its presentation. The "explosion" response to the upper third usually indicates mounting tension within the patient and can serve as a warning of approaching discharge of accumulated tensions among epileptics, hysterics, and psychopaths. When it appears in temporal (sequence) immediacy with a sexual construct, it points to an urgency of the sex drives that are crowding for expression and are based on hostility and aggression. It is found regularly in cases where sexuality is infantile in its aims, and where sexual misconceptions—misconceptions involving the use of sexuality for aggression—play a determining role in the formation of symptoms.

26. *Card VI. Midline Area.* "A projectile plowing through the earth," "a boat cleaving through water," "a bullet in flight," or "an arrow speeding through the air" are all in a class of responses that have value in separating paranoid-type psychopaths from other varieties. They are given also by latent homosexuals who unconsciously fear attack.

27. *Card VI. Bottom Center Edge of Blot Incorporating White Space.* The "child nursing" response is one of the most interesting of all the possible answers to this portion of the blot. To obtain it the white space is perceived as a breast inserted into the mouth of a nursing child. Usually the testee who gives such a response will comment upon the "fanged teeth" in the mouth. This reveals pronounced oral aggression and is an index of latent sadism. Patients who give this response are observed to be pessimistic in philosophy, aggressive in behavior, and independent in action. In an earlier paper I cited in connection with this response the case of the patient who saw here "two mouths biting on one breast." In his treatment it eventually developed that a strong sibling rivalry was one of the chief dynamic determinants of his neurosis.

28. *Card VI. Upper Central Darkly Shaded Area of Vertical Protrusion.* Those patients who offer "a human figure (nonliving)," "a statue," or the "silhouette of a man" in this portion of the blot are often found to be plagued by ideas of inadequacy. Sometimes they will exhibit a loss of personal identity and experience feelings of depersonalization. This is usually a reaction to an unsatisfactory body image, in Schilder's sense. Interestingly

enough, when these projections are accomplished with visible strain, it may be due to an effort to overcome scoptophilic inclinations, as can be observed with erythrophobes who strive long and hard for these images.

29. *Card VI. Whole Blot.* Secretive and suspicious paranoids are likely to project hereon images like "an overcoat on a clothes tree," "a blanket hanging over a line," or a "shroud." The rare true paranoids will dwell lengthily on the card in such terms.

30. *Card VI. Whole Blot.* "Dirt," "bird or animal droppings," and responses in this class to any portion or part of the blot have the same value here as in Card I for the obsessive-compulsive syndrome based on anal-erotism.

31. *Card VII. Bottom D.* The "hinge" response is the one usually given by relatively well-integrated examinees. Latent homosexuals often give "buttocks," and those inclined toward sodomy will stress what is probably regarded as the cloacal area. The special physical attributes of this blot region also provoke projections based upon notions of penetration which are disguised symbolically. Sometimes reliable clues to intrapsychic conflict over sexual aims are given by responses here.

32. *Card VII. Center White Space.* Lack of ability for socialization, suspicion of the motives of others, and ideas of self-insufficiency are indicated where the response to this area is "a skating pond," "an iceberg," or something similar. These responses are encountered commonly among emotionally immature individuals who present work and concentration disabilities and who tend to drift toward a dependency on alcohol and drugs as means of obtaining social ease. Such patients will also report intense loneliness and vague, diffuse anxiety.

33. *Card VII. Upper Third of Shaded Area.* "Two women with funny hair-do talking over the back fence," "two Indians looking at each other," or "children talking" are the common and innocuous responses to the stimuli provided from this area. When such images include expressions of anger and strife, however, as, for example, "women yelling at each other" or "children quarreling," it apparently betrays inner turmoil with guilt projected as hostility toward others. Because this kind of response reflects warring internal impulses, it is frequently associated with schizoid tendencies.

34. *Card VIII. Upper D, Including d of White "Bony Struc-*

tures," with Blue-Gray Interlacings. This region appears as "a head of threatening and forbidding aspect" or "a death's head" to individuals who are hysterically inclined and those who suffer from a pronounced anxiety neurosis. Emotionally well-balanced subjects rarely combine the white and color here; if they are mentioned at all they are treated discreetly. Nevertheless hysterics make exotic combinations from them and attribute awesomeness to the images they make.

35. *Card VIII. Lowered Colored D, with Blue Strands Attaching to Rest of Blot.* The connecting link between the blue middle D and the pink-and-orange bottom D is remarked by anxious neurotics but overlooked or casually treated by the average subject. With the anxious type this area becomes "a heavy, hanging object," "a guillotine blade," or "a massive piece of metal suspended by a cable." They tend to comment upon the strained aspect and tautness of the strands, fearing that they will part or break and that the object will come crashing down. Quite often they project themselves into this strainful situation with considerable and visible empathy.

36. *Card VIII. Whole Blot.* Where this card is viewed as presenting "an emblem," "a family crest," "an insignia," "a medal," or something similar, it betokens severe and marked prestige drives in individuals who are essentially inadequate. It indicates also ambition for achievement and recognition: if the "animals" are directly mentioned, the projection points toward ruthlessness in the treatment of others on the way toward achieving personal goals. Such responses are common among those who seek to dominate their environment. When combined with additional paranoid content, they are helpful in unmasking grandiose delusions.

37. *Card VIII. Blue Areas.* The responses "banners waving" and "flags flying" appear to originate from persons with high feeling tone. If they appear within an otherwise depressive clinical-Rorschach pattern, they indicate potentiality for drastic and unpredictable alteration in such a picture. Content-oriented Rorschachers note such responses among the hypomanias in affect cases just preceding a change or shift in the manic-depressive cycle, as well as among some optimistic, insight-lacking psychopaths.

38. *Card VIII. White Space between Pink and Blue Areas.* When white is used in the chromatic cards the examiner should always regard the testee with suspicion as to his psychological integrity.

It can be stated almost categorically that so few normal and even neurotic subjects use the white on Card VIII that its use is practically diagnostic of impending, remissed, or active psychosis. Serious mental disturbance is indicated where white spaces only are utilized on presentation of the colored cards. This proposition supports and correlates well with Hermann Rorschach's implication that the absence of color is more dangerous than the rejection of color. In the area considered here, excited catatonics and agitated depressives yield "a vampire," "a white bat," or "a ghost flying." Deteriorated schizophrenics and patients showing a progressive organic involvement, postencephalitics, and paretics may say "a nightmare" or "a white something."

39. *Card IX. Upper Central Light Portion.* The average testee will show little interest in this area or attend only to its outlines and project "a violin" or "a musical instrument." Personalities that include a large element of mysticism and a predilection for speculation about the supernatural will frame concepts revealing such trends. At the further end of the scale the area will be used in a more detailed fashion by patients with strong paranoidal trends and ideas of influence. Such persons will also use the sharply differentiated D region at the base of this central area as "eyes looking at me," as in Card IV, bottom D.

40. *Card IX. Whole Blot.* The function of Card IX in mobilizing anxiety is well known. Psychopaths reject it more frequently than they do any other card. Psychoneurotics, on the other hand, seize upon it as a vehicle to express their preoccupations. Agitated depressives use it to reflect somatic delusions and to localize them through self-reference. However, just because it is so potent for mobilizing anxiety, and therefore neurotics too reject it, one must exercise the greatest caution in applying content analysis to this card. The rejection of the psychopath can be distinguished from the rejection of the neurotic by the manner and tone of the refusal. The psychopath will treat the card disdainfully, tossing it aside with "it means nothing to me" or a similar comment. Neurotics will imply feeling in their rejection, noting "it's ghastly" or "it's ugly" or the like.

41. *Card X. Reverse Position, Middle Blue dd.* The response "an extracted tooth" to this small area is to be expected from chronic masturbators and patients with serious conflicts over masturbation.

42. *Card X. Reverse Position, Middle Blue D.* Anxiety neurotics and, so it seems, patients with a background of severe religious training and those who have suffered under parental tyranny give a response in the class of "two blue figures climbing up the sides of cliffs." For them the situation is a precarious one, with the figures in danger of falling. Some add that if the figures fall, they will become impaled on "the devil's fork" below (bottom D when blot is reversed). These latter show marked preoccupation with the problem of good and evil.

43. *Card X.* Despite the profusion of images this card is capable of producing, it has so far proved to be surprisingly sterile for meaningful content. On the other hand it is a useful blot for initiating free associations or for aiding a clinician in overcoming resistances of the natural reluctance order either for purposes of beginning treatment or for obtaining information of special significance in the examination. For this reason it is included here.

III

There has been some recent comment to the effect that "complex or unconscious responses, in the sense of Freud, those corresponding to Jung's association experiences, are extraordinarily rare in the Rorschach" [1]. Those who have investigated the content aspects of the test, however, find themselves in almost total disagreement with such a point of view. Considering the Rorschach response as a product of performing—and, for the most part, aligning ourselves with the orientation of dynamic psychology—we cannot subscribe to the idea that form-interpretations and the structuralization of the response pattern are the sole returns of testing or that the test is not a means for delving into the unconscious. In experiments on which I have been engaged for more than three years, and which are now in the stage of preparation for publication, I have been able to demonstrate that many responses—indeed, most responses except those which are exceptionally common and to which the blots so readily lend themselves—are produced only after a process of distortion, displacement, condensation, and, indeed, the operation of perhaps every machanism that lies behind the dream. It is my belief that there is little if any difference between the dream and the Rorschach response. They are both products of the organism's internal "work." They are both meaningful symbolically. They both come from the same or from similar psychic areas.

It cannot be too often stressed nevertheless that the conclusions from content analysis have to be treated cautiously and with scientific circumspection. An attitude of objective skepticism is the one best suited to the content analyst. The forty-three responses thus far isolated should be subjected to the severest tests—statistical and empirical—before they are accepted fully and integrated wholly into the compendium of Rorschach knowledge. Where they are used they should be employed only as faint beacons lighting the path of clinical diagnosis and, in company with his growing retinue of techniques, guiding the steps of the clinician whose task it is to understand and to help his fellow men.

REFERENCES

1. BROSIN, H.: "Clinical Aspects of Rorschach Testing" (the seventh in the Fourteenth Annual Series of Conference Talks at the Institute of Living, February 25, 1948), as abstracted in the *Digest of Neurology and Psychiatry*, Vol. 3 (1948), p. 214.

2. LINDNER, R. M.: "Some Significant Rorschach Responses," *Journal of Criminal Psychopathology*, Vol. 5 (1944), p. 775.

3. ———: "Content Analysis in Rorschach Work," *Rorschach Research Exchange*, Vol. 10 (1946), p. 121.

4. ———: "Analysis of the Rorschach Test by Content," *Journal of Clinical Psychopathology*, Vol. 8 (1947), p. 707.

5. ———: "Psychopathic Personality and the Concept of Homeostasis," *Journal of Clinical Psychopathology and Psychotherapy*, Vol. 6 (1945), p. 517.

6. RORSCHACH, H.: *Psychodiagnostik*. BERN.: Hans Huber; 1932.

▼

In the following chapter Ruth L. Munroe brings up to date her 1944 Inspection Rorschach and, we believe, greatly extends its usefulness. To anyone acquainted with the subtleties of the Rorschach Method and with the types of records which frequently result it will come as little surprise that the inspection procedure that Dr. Munroe proposes is not easy to master. Based upon some of the most competent and careful work in the whole field of research with the Rorschach Test, Munroe's Inspection Method has earned a well-deserved acceptance among projective psychologists.

We feel that its full statement here will lead to ever wider application of the procedure, a step of value not only in clinical psychological research but also in personality diagnosis and study.

▼

The Inspection Technique for the Rorschach Protocol

Ruth L. Munroe

The Inspection Rorschach consists essentially of a check list of the major variations, quantitative and qualitative, commonly used in Rorschach interpretation. An entry is made for each item on the list where the performance of the subject deviates from the normal range. The bulk of this chapter is devoted to a roughly quantitative statement of what is to be considered a significant deviation. Basic knowledge of the Rorschach method is assumed.[1]

USES OF THE INSPECTION RORSCHACH

The procedure may be used for three relatively distinct purposes:

1. *As a Recording Device*—It is a convenient recording device.

---

[1] The quantification here offered is based on the Klopfer scoring system. The principle of the Inspection Technique could apply to any scoring system, but of course different quantitative standards would have to be presented.

Because of its comprehensive nature it may serve as a guide to quick covering of the basic data for interpretation. Integration of the data, along with observation of idiosyncratic variations in sequence and content for building a personality picture, still requires the judgment of a skilled examiner.

The Inspection Rorschach Record Blank appears below with a sample case following. The Inspection Rorschach proper involves only filling out the check list. Supplementary items are added in the present format for optional use in cases where traditional material is desired beyond the inspection procedure. Plus and minus signs and letters offer a graphic indication of the direction, degree, and type of deviation.

2. *As an Instrument for Research.*—The check list has merit for quantitative research on group differences for several reasons that are set out below.

(a) The separate items listed have greater intrinsic significance than the items on the traditional psychogram. They cannot be translated into trait terms, but they have some stability in technical Rorschach terms. A strong *CF* trend, for instance, always implies a tendency toward emotional lability, no matter how it is expressed, how modified, or even if repressed by other factors. The item 3 *CF* by itself, as in the traditional tabulation, has no such secure implication. In the very short protocol with no *FC* it may represent great explosiveness. In the longer protocol with good *FC* it usually means desirable spontaneity. Rarely, in the very long protocol with much *FC*, 3 *CF* may actually suggest a weak *CF* trend. Percentages are often preferable to absolute numbers, but this generalization applies much more to some determinants than to others. F%, for instance, is fairly stable, but the chiaroscuro responses and *S, C,* etc., are important *almost* in absolute terms. Extremes in the number of responses markedly affect the significance of the percentage for most determinants. For instance, 2 *M* in ten responses are very different from 20 *M* in a hundred responses or even 10 *M* in fifty responses.

The entry on the check list represents an evaluation of the major dependencies within the protocol of the item considered. An entry for *CF* suggests a real *CF* trend in the individual; an entry for *M*, a real excess in the use of this determinant. The incidence of such trends in various groups may thus be studied independently of, let us say, a factor like intelligence, which would

INSPECTION RORSCHACH RECORD OF HIGHER L STUDENTS

Student	1	2	3	4	5	6	7	8	9	10	11	12	13	14	15	16	17	18	19	20	21	22	23	24	25	26	27	28	29	30	31	32	33	34	35	36	37	38	39	40
ACE Total Percentile	66	60	57	73	30	80	77	88	77	55	75	89	65	67	63	70	79	62	56	70	79	60	51	79	63	35	30	65	77	75	60	75	56	45	73	93	85	55	84	42
Number of R	19	22	18	38	28	19	31	28	28	21	21	33	41	42	19	25	27	18	19	39	12	20	38	30	20	30	30	16	47	50	24	20	45	68	33	24	17	20	17	15
T/R >60"<30" (+,−)																																								

not applicable to group protocol

	1	2	3	4	5	6	7	8	9	10	11	12	13	14	15	16	17	18	19	20	21	22	23	24	25	26	27	28	29	30	31	32	33	34	35	36	37	38	39	40
Refusal (√)																																								
LOCATION W (+,−,V,B)	+B	+B	+V	+(−)	+V		−V	+V	B	+				(B)	B/V	−	+	+	+	+	+V/B	+V/B	+V	+V/B	V			+	(−)	+B/V	+B	+		(V)	+	(−)	(+B)/(+)	(+B)/(+)	+V	+
Dd (+)	(+)							(+)					+									(+)	(+)													(+)				
S (+)				+	+		+	(+)						+		++	++																	+	(+)					
Suc (r,↑)			(Z)	(Z)	Z							Z							Z	Z					Z	Z							Z							
CONTENT P,Com (−)		(−)	(−)	(−)	(−)		(−)						(−)	(−)				−						−						−										(−)
O (+,B)		B	B	B	B		B	(B)	B	B			B	B(+)		B	B	B			+B/V	+B	+B						+B/V	+B/B	+B			(B)	(B)		B			
At,Sex (+)				+		+	(+)	+				(+)		+			++						(+)	+										+	(+)					
Range (+,−)	−		(−)		(−)		(−)			−		(−)	(−)			(−)												(−)				(−)	(−)	(−)		(−)	(−)	(−)		(−)
FORM F% (+,−)	+					−	(−)					+			−				−		+	−				−	(−)				−	(−)	?		−					−
F(V,B,E)		(B)		(B)										B		BB		BB	(−)		(B)	(B)/BB	BB			(−)/(+)				BV			BV							
SHADING Shading Shock (±)(√)																			?					√	√							√	√			√				
FK,Fc (+,−)				(+)						−								−		?		(−)					(−)	(−)		(−)	(−)	(+)	(+)	(+)	(+)					(−)
c (+)			+			+																	+	+	+	+				+			+	+				+	+	
C'(+)							(+)		(+)		(+)			(+)	(+)	(+)	(+)	(+)	(+)		?	+	+	(+)	(+)	+	+	(+)	(+)	+		(+)	+	(+)				.	.	+
K,k (+)							(−)	+	+	+	+	+	+	(+)	(+)/c	+	(+)	+	+	+	(+)	(+)	(+)/(+)	(+)/(+)	+	(+)/(+)	+	+	(+)		(+)		+	(+)		+	(+)	(+)		
MOVEMENT M (+,−,B,r,d)	−	(B)	+Br	r	8dr	rd	(+)/+Br	(+)/+Br	+Br/+Bg/+(B)	r			r	+B	r	++	++	(+)	r	+	− /Br/Br−B	r/Br−B	(+)/Br	(+)/Br	8dr	+		(+)	+	+B/Br/++	+B/Br/++	+/(+)r/+rd	+/(+)r/+rd	(+)r/+rd	(+)	(−)	(+)r/+(r)	(+)r/+(r)	++	+
FM,Fm:M (+,−)					+				+			+	r	(−)		−	−	(+)/(−)	L		+		(−)/(−)	(−)/(−)	−	B/V		− /+	− /+	(−)	(+)	(+)	BV	(+)	(+)/(+)	(−)	(+)		r/+(r)	
m (+)	(−)	+	+	(+)	(+)	+	+	+	++	++		(+)	+	(−)		−	++/+	+/+	+	+		++	++/++	(+)/(+)	++			++	++	+/++	++	++	+	+	+	++	+	++	++	
COLOR Total Movement (+,−)	(−)		+	+	+	+	+	+	+	++			+	(−)	(−)	+(+)	+(+)	+	+	+		++	++	(+)/(−)	+			++	++	+	++	++	+	+	+	++	+	++	++	
Color Shock (±)(√)	√				√		√																	√				√		√	√				√	√	√			
FC (−,B)	−	B	B	(B)	−	−	?	?	−	−		?		(B)	−	−	?	(B)	−			(B)	B	(−)				B		(B)	(B)	(B)		(+)	−		−			
CF,CF:FC (+,−)	(−)		(−)	(−)	?	+	+	(+)	(−)/(−)	(−)/(+)	(+)	(−)	−	(−)	+	+	+	+	++	−	− /−	++	++/++	(+)/(+)				++	+	(−)	−	−	+	(+)	−		(+)		(−)	
C>1,Cn(+)																								++	++															
Total Color (+,−)	−		+	−	−	−	+	?	−	−	?	?	−	−	−	−	−	−	+	+	+	+	+	+		−	+	++	+	+	−	−	(−)	(−)	+	−	+	+	+	+
Color: Movement (+,−)	−	−	−	−	−	−	+	−/−/−	−/−/−	−/−/−	(−)	−	−	−	−	−	−	−	−	−	−/−	−	−	−		−	−/−	−	−/−	−/−	−/−	−/−	−/−	−/(−)	+	−/−	−	−	(−)	(−)

TABLE 2

SUM OF CHECK-LIST ENTRIES

For higher L and Higher Q Students, Considering Direction of Deviation Only

	CHECK LIST	OVEREMPHASIS ON DETERMINANT (+)		UNDEREMPHASIS ON DETERMINANT (−)	
		Higher L	Higher Q	Higher L	Higher Q
Number of R	Median	26	25	−	−
T/R>60"<30" (+, −)	not applicable to group protocol				
Refusal (✓)		0	1	−	−
LOCATION	W (+,−,V,B)	19	15	5	8
	Dd (+)	7	9	−	−
	S (+)	10	17	−	−
	Suc (r, 1)	6	4	−	−
CONTENT	P, Com (−)	−	−	9	4
	O (+,B)	7	4	−	−
	At, Sex (+)	6	12	−	−
	Range (+,−)	1	1	19	15
FORM	F% (+,−)	5	23	16	5
	F(V,B,E)	see notation below			
SHADING	Shading Shock (±) (✓)	3	4	−	−
	FK, Fc (+,−)	6	4	6	10
	c (+)	7	7	−	−
	C'(+)	16	7	−	−
	K, k (+)	12	11	−	−
MOVEMENT	M (+,−,B,r,d)	23	4	4	11
	FM, FM:M (+,−)	6	7	11	13
	m (+)	14	11	−	−
	Total Movement (+,−)	29	12	1	4
COLOR	Color Shock (±) (✓)	9	15	−	−
	FC (−,B)	−	−	8	15
	CF, CF:FC (+,−)	16	14	8	11
	C>1, Cn (+)	2	0	−	−
	Total Color (+,−)	8	2	6	14
Color: Movement (+,−)		0	2	28	16
1 or more B or B/V entry		27	19	−	−
1 or more B or B/V entries disregarding entries in parentheses		16	1		
1 or more V or E entry		3	11		
Median number of checks		9	8		

tend to raise the number of responses and so throw all calculations from the psychogram out of order.

(b) In contrast to studies of isolated Rorschach *patterns*, the check list preserves the value of the fairly comprehensive survey of the personality customarily covered by the psychogram. In fact the survey is extended to include many familiar items not usually tabulated. An important advantage of the Rorschach over any other test at the present time lies in the possibility of covering in routine quantification a very wide, quasi-inclusive range of personality reactions.[2] It is possible to ask the qusetion, How do these groups differ? with the hope that major differences in personality trends along the usual lines will emerge and may be studied in their interrelationships.

(c) After enough practice to familiarize the examiner with the standards for entries on the check list, a protocol may be dealt with in about fifteen minutes. Entries may then be quickly tabulated on the research form. This form allows for rapid horizontal calculation of the incidence of the separate items in the groups considered. It also allows for consideration on the vertical axis of the constellation of scores in any individual case or small group of cases which deviate from the group trends observed.

For greater vividness the research form is presented here as filled out for a particular study: the Rorschach performance of college students classified into two groups on the basis of the constellation of their scores on the Linguistic and Quantitative subtests of the American Council on Education test. Only the group markedly higher on the "L" section is shown (Table 1, facing p. 92). Quantitative comparison with the group markedly higher on the "Q" section appears in Table 2 on opposite page. This table represents counting *on the horizontal axis*. Chi-squares are easily calculated for the group differences.[3]

Case 21, Table 1 illustrates reading *on the vertical axis;* that is, the pattern of scores for the individual student. Noteworthy is

---

[2] The standardized test is in principle standardized for a limited aim. The other projective tests afford an inclusive personality picture, but lack the quantification of the Rorschach which facilitates a survey approach.

[3] I mention a new technique just encountered in a preliminary report by another investigator. He has translated the separate entries into scales according to notations for the degree of over- or under-emphasis recorded, and then has used a product moment *r* instead of Chi-square.

the fact that Case 21 shows a reversal of the major group trends observed all along the line. Special inquiry revealed that her academic performance was also reversed. Actually it was typical for students whose abilities lie more in the "quantitative" than in the "linguistic" direction. She had a mild reading disability. She had done unusually fine work in mathematics and physics. Reconsideration of the ACE data indicated that she had been classified as markedly better on the linguistic section because her "L" score put her at the 51st percentile, and her "Q" score put her at the 3rd percentile. Surely the most likely explanation of the phenomenon of an excellent science student testing at the bottom of the group for "quantitative" ability is that something went wrong with the ACE. Since neither the Rorschach nor her college record remotely made clear why a girl majoring in mathematics could not solve at least half a dozen problems in simple arithmetic on the ACE (while doing pretty well on verbal materials), it is appropriate to suspect a simple clerical error.[4]

Special examination of the other deviant individuals appearing on Table 1 proved more instructive psychologically, but description of the apparent relationship between the patterns of Rorschach scores and special background factors would take us too far afield.

(d) The Inspection Rorschach *adjustment score*—to be discussed presently—offers a usable single quantitative measure of considerable interest for research.

3. *As a Quantitative Adjustment Measure.*—Counting up the number of entries on the check list offers a quantitative score for "adjustment" which appears to correspond well (not perfectly, of course) with the clinical evaluation of the Rorschach examiner, and also to have substantial meaning in relation to personality function when checked against external criteria.

Perhaps personality integration would be a better term than "adjustment." The definition used is very inclusive: the ability of the subject to function reasonably well relative to his capacities without serious inner tension. No distinction is made between overt maladjustment and inner distress, nor does the score offer anything like specific diagnosis and prognosis. It merely in-

---

[4] Her ACE scores were reported from her school. The original test was not available for checking.

dicates the amount of "disturbance" currently present in the personality as determined by the Rorschach Test.

In a way this inclusiveness is an advantage. We do not impose any particular social definition of adjustment upon the individual, but we can accept both the solitary poet and the active go-getter as reasonably well-integrated people. We can penetrate the front of the neurotic "leader," however successful. It seems probable that the adjustment score gets at deeper personality trends than we can formulate successfully in behavioral terms at the present time—simply because it is derived so inclusively from a huge sample of disturbances at the "deep" level tapped by the Rorschach.

As regards immediate usefulness in prediction for any given practical situation, the inclusiveness is, of course, a serious disadvantage. Personality studies of normal groups, not to mention studies of highly successful individuals in special fields, reveal that they are not always well-integrated people. On the contrary they are occasionally as tense, unhappy, driving, or difficult as many patients who bear a label of neurosis. It cannot be too strongly emphasized that the adjustment score should *never* be used by itself in any sort of adverse practical decision concerning an individual.[5]

The adjustment score can, however, be a useful item in conjunction with other materials. A good adjustment score seems to offer a fair guarantee that the assets of the person, as measured by other tests or clinical observation, will be adequately used. Naturally the person has to have qualifications for his job.

The gifted individual with a poor adjustment score may turn in a superlatively good performance or he may be a dismal flop. The history of these individuals is often quite varied—they do very badly in one situation, very well in another.

Thus while the quickly obtained adjustment score is not by itself of any great predictive value, it appears to add an important dimension to psychological studies. Special assets and liabilities may be seen in different perspective when they occur in personalities that are generally well or poorly integrated. Statistically speaking, persons with poor adjustment scores are more

---

[5] This statement applies to the vast majority of full Rorschach analyses as well, or even full test batteries.

likely to show difficulties at the time of testing, or to break down later on, but with many important exceptions. With far more confidence one may say that these persons are more vulnerable to special circumstances and that more careful study is required of the conditions under which they may flourish.

The Inspection Rorschach adjustment measure was designed for use on large "normal" populations. Without revision it would not be suitable for selecting deviant individuals in essentially atypical groups, such as children or the feeble-minded.[6] Nor is it suitable for refined differentiation in an essentially "problem" group like the ordinary clinic population. One of the validating criteria for the adjustment measure is that the vast majority of subjects tested *as patients* in clinics, hospitals, and private practice do have scores in the "problem" range. Doubtless one would find a high positive correlation between number of entries on the check list and severity of disturbance in a population ranging from the outpatient applicant to the deteriorated hospital case. Unfortunately this is not the range significant for practical clinical work. It should be emphasized that the adjustment score does *not* offer adequate discrimination between an early malignant schizophrenia in a generally well-preserved personality and a tumultuous adolescent crisis that is essentially benign. Every experienced examiner is familiar with the case where the psychogram looks normal and the disease process shows only in the content or sequence of responses. Repeated entries for poor form, for thematic preoccupation, etc., almost always bring these cases into the problem range of scores on the check list; but the gravity of the patient's condition may not be adequately represented. Conversely, the very dilated rich personality or the very constricted personality with many *dd*, high *A%*, etc., sometimes registers scores higher than the clinical prognosis warrants. Compulsive characters often do very well in our culture.

---

[6] In principle the check list may perhaps be considered to work even with these groups. The poor form-level of children and aments, for instance, certainly reflects their poor appreciation of reality, and one might call them maladjusted to adult standards. In practice, of course, we are not interested in this very obvious fact, but we need to know whether the child is maladjusted according to child standards and whether a feeble-minded person has enough emotional stability to function in a protected environment despite his intellectual handicap.

A good adjustment score in the clinic should never supersede the examiner's judgment, but it may suggest more careful consideration. We have occasionally reversed an initial impression of severe disturbance after filling out the check list because of the enforced review of the total assets of the personality. On the whole, however, the Inspection Rorschach has little to contribute to careful clinical diagnosis. Its practical value lies in the rough indication of problems not already recognized. It can be a useful adjunct to other tests in educational and vocational guidance. It should *not* be considered as a continuous scale, superior to clinical evaluation in prognosis for the definitely sick, in which the greater the number of checks, the more serious the personality disturbance.

Even within the normal range it is doubtful whether subjects with a check-list score of 2 or 3 are significantly better adjusted than those with a score of 6 or 7. In our own work we regularly enter a star (*) and an explanatory note after a check-list score that deviates from our clinical judgment, and a question mark (?) where scoring of the group protocol is so uncertain that the check-list entries are unreliable. Such qualification appears in about five per cent of college students routinely tested. This procedure mitigates error in practical evaluation of the individual case. In group studies the investigator must decide whether he prefers to include identified errors in the interest of standard procedure or whether he can afford to apply a modicum of unstandardized judgment.[7]

CONSTRUCTION OF THE CHECK LIST

The idea of making a check list came into being in 1940 [2] as a purely practical expedient for recording noteworthy items about the Rorschach protocol in the course of hasty work on large groups of normal students. In 1944 [3], following the observation that a tally of entries seemed to correspond surpris-

---

[7] The same problem arises with other tests. Case 21, referred to previously, was included despite the fact that the ACE seemed clearly erroneous.

Throwing out Rorschach scores where the examiner determines, in the process of blind evaluation, that the quantitative score is inaccurate presents important differences. Nevertheless when the Inspection Rorschach score is used as an "objective" measure in group studies, the starred scores should probably be included for most problems.

ingly well with clinical judgment, and following reflection upon the values and limitations of the check list originally devised, we introduced a systematic revision. It was felt that the mechanical tally worked primarily because of the relatively comprehensive nature of the check list. The principle of adding up signs is new neither to the Rorschach nor to the adjustment questionnaire. The novelty of the 1944 revision lay in the fact that the signs were not rigorously limited in advance. On the contrary, effort was made to allow for the recording of almost any pronounced trend, quantitative or qualitative. The definition of a pronounced trend was not determined by arithmetic, but rather by clinical judgment. The check list merely attempts to put into arithmetic the norms every examiner carries in his head.

The following analysis may clarify the role of the major experimental population, female students, in the construction of the check list. It may explain why we have been unwilling to use statistical procedures in developing the instructions, although our sample is excellent—every entering student since 1940. In our files there are large samples from other colleges, mostly with peculiar selection of cases, and we have seen many more, occasionally with good selection. In our files are also hundreds of records from secondary schools, small groups of normals from many walks in life studied for a variety of reasons, and several hundred records of individuals referred by psychiatrists, social agencies, or themselves.

Despite the bulk of this material, the problem of preparing an adequate sample for general statistical norms for the relatively refined distinctions made on the check list seems insuperable. On the contrary it is clear that variability from group to group in the use of the separate determinants is very great, even among normal groups, even within the college population. For instance entries for M and $M:FM$ 4:1 are so frequent at Sarah Lawrence College that we became uneasy about the standards set in 1944. Yet they are very infrequent in at least two other institutions from which we have seen a large, careful sample. In one, $F\%$ is very frequent; in the other, S. Yet both entries are rare at Sarah Lawrence College. Sex is clearly only one of the variables involved.

It seems highly inexpedient to base norms on any sample short of Gallup poll dimensions. Rather, we feel that the Rorschach is useful for large-scale work because it has a relatively good *clinical tradition,* so that the test builder is not forced to rely upon a limited empirical sample. The placing of items is far from perfect, but it seems preferable to using college sophomores (Bernreuter, et al.). Even the questionnaires developed during the war on larger, far more representative samples showed an unfortunate tendency to vary from one induction station to the next and even more in application to civilian populations.

At any rate, in experimental work the check-list standards were *applied to* Sarah Lawrence College students with every effort to avoid bias from our own preponderant experience. In no sense were they *derived from* the college group. In my opinion it is better to attempt to understand the nature of normal groups by applying to them the present Rorschach tradition. We shall understand the test determinants better as we observe how they operate in different groups.

It seems preferable to postpone improving the entries by statistical methods until we have more substantial data.

To return now to the measurement of adjustment, why should a recording of "pronounced trends" add up to a score for—well, really for *mal*adjustment, since the high score is the poor one? Largely, I think, because the Rorschach is based on the principle of optimal rather than maximal performance in respect to any given determinant. The textbook definitions of M and FC sound like the kinds of traits that should maximally be present: inner maturity, creative imagination, intelligence, social adaptability. Yet any clinician knows that too many M relative to FM or total R or color turns out badly. Even form accuracy, even the production of brilliant original responses, become unhealthy beyond a certain point. It is the gifted schizophrenic who reaches *maximal* performance on brilliant originals, not the successful inventor.

The natural propensity of the Rorschach method was helped along a little by a clinical weighting of trends on the same principle as the definition of pronounced trends just discussed; that is, by the exercise of clinical judgment.

The aim was to highlight trends likely to cause trouble, playing down trends that are frequently nonpathogenic or that typically represent successful cushioning of difficulties. For instance, very high $W\%$ probably always represents excessive tension or whatever, and it always receives one "bad mark" on the check list. A $W\%$ approaching 100 per cent is so common among gifted intellectuals and normal adolescents (young children are not check-listed), is so often a reflection of *constructive* tension, that it is never allowed more than one entry. A predominance of bizarre or insubstantial W's is clinically suspect. This feature is entered on the check list by letters. Thus the schizophrenic who gives mostly W, but mostly queer ones, receives three counts toward a poor score on the W item, whereas the brilliant professor with the same quantity of W receives only one bad mark.

M receives different handling because it seems that beyond a certain point increase in M becomes a progressively serious factor. The brilliant professor may give many M but if he approaches 100 per cent M the Rorschach examiner is rightfully alarmed. Even if only half of his responses are M, the examiner wants reassurance that the personality as a whole is able to handle so very pronounced an "introversive" trend. Thus increment in M is weighted on a purely quantitative basis (up to three entries), and poor quality of M receives additional entries.

Another illustration is P. Serious failure to use P and/or common responses is penalized. In interpretation we often feel that the subject who gives mainly popular and common responses is not a very interesting person, but he is likely to be all too well adjusted. Excessive P in the "problem" range is almost always a positively good indication that social adaptability is relatively well preserved. Thus a pronounced P trend never counts "against" the subject in the Inspection Rorschach score.

Furthermore, separate entries were considered so far as possible in relationship to each other. Mostly they stood up well to clinical reflection on their integration. They represented relatively stable, relatively independent trends. A high $F\%$ means something, no matter what its setting, and the entry is not covertly duplicated elsewhere. On the other hand, while "refusal" always means something, its meaning is much more contingent upon what card is refused. In preparing the instructions for the check list we observed that refusal of Card VIII or Card IV automatically involved entries for color or shading shock, whereas refusal of Card V had no such involvements. Thus a blanket entry for "refusal" on the check list would result in a covert weighting of relatively innocent refusals, and refusal of Card V, which is "clinically" the most dubious, would sail through with a single bad mark.

In constructing the standards for entries on the check list we tried very hard, *as Rorschach clinicians,* to keep in mind not only the single item but also its repercussions. We hope that test-dictated correlations operating against valid weighting (like color shock and refusal of Card VIII) have been eliminated. Personality-dictated correlations have not been eliminated—like the pedant whose high $F\%$ is necessary to control explosive CF and who is able to function mainly because his excessive dd trend is associated with an unduly low $W\%$. In other words, he is carefully not ambitious beyond his psychological status. His Inspection Rorschach score may be high—too high for most of these individuals under ordinary circumstances. This is the kind of person who often makes out for a lifetime on a complicated system of checks and balances—and who may go to a psychiatrist in an anxiety state if he is promoted to a position where a dd solution is insufficient. (See discussion above of inadequacies in the adjustment measure for practical prediction.)

A point to be emphasized, however, is that these more or less successfully weighted bad marks do not appear in a vacuum. In the first place the check list is designed to pick up a much greater variety of deviation in the negative direction than lists of "signs," or, by analogy, the adjustment questionnaire. But in the second place the positive assets of the subject are at least considered. *Absence* of entry on the check list is not a neutral matter. On the contrary it means that the subject was actually examined on these points and that his performance was definitely satisfactory. Therefore the bad marks may be seen against a *demonstrated* optimal performance on other points. The comprehensive nature of the check list allows the subject to be judged on the gamut of normal as well as deviant responses.

VALIDITY AND RELIABILITY OF THE ADJUSTMENT MEASURE

A careful study of the validity of the adjustment measure for 348 college students has been published [4]. Roughly speaking, 85 per cent of students in the lowest quartile, according to the Inspection Rorschach, were either referred to the college psychiatrist or were the subject of much discussion in a faculty committee whose task it is to review the work of each student. Only

15 per cent of the top quartile of the group met this criterion, and their problems were for the most part qualitatively less severe. The adjustment measure (a rating in this study) also showed a fair correlation with college performance and was markedly improved when combined with the ACE measurement of intelligence. Recent check indicates that the findings on students entering in 1940, 1941, and 1942 are confirmed by those entering in 1946.

Data from other colleges have not been published. We have, however, seen the distribution of Inspection Rorschach scores from several institutions. They seem approximately the same as ours. For these "normal" groups the median is about nine or ten entries. (The median for patients referred by psychiatrists runs to about fifteen entries.) We have been informed that the adjustment measure shows no correlation with academic performance at an institution that uses objective tests instead of teacher grades as a measure of performance. The adjustment score correlated .70 with students' ratings of each other on "adjustment" at the same institution, however.

Roe has published Inspection Rorschach data on a group of artists and a group of scientists *[6]*. For the most part she uses the research form for analyzing group trends, but she does comment that the adjustment score corresponded well with her impression of the men from interview, and that it correlated highly with the tendency to excessive drinking. Some experience is available with groups of engineers, lawyers, doctors, with adolescents, and with groups of patients whose illness was considered possibly psychosomatic in nature.

Reports of interexaminer reliability have not been favorable. In situations where the work of two examiners is to be used for strict comparative purposes, it is very important that several cases should be independently handled by both and differences in filling out the check list thoroughly discussed. We hope eventually to publish the results of an experiment where eight students of varying degrees of proficiency with the Rorschach filled out the check list for thirty cases independently, with intercurrent discussion of "errors." Agreement improved markedly during the course of this experiment but was never perfect. The main source of error was not so much differences in the mechanics of the check list as in the initial scoring upon which the check-list percentages were based. Such differences in scoring must, of course, affect any quantitative Rorschach studies. (See discussion of "notations to the left," borderline entries.)

Examples of the type of judgment expected in filling out the check list are given in the section on general instructions as well as under many of the specific items. In our experiment it was observed that the students fresh from a single-semester course on the Rorschach could do at least as well as the more experienced examiners. The judgment involved requires Rorschach common sense, not Rorschach subtlety. Too *literal* a following of instructions actually undermines both the reliability and the validity of the method. It should constantly be kept in mind that the arithmetic of the instructions is merely a device for recording "what everybody knows."

SUMMARY

The Inspection Rorschach consists essentially of a check list of the major items, quantitative and qualitative, commonly used in arriving at an interpretation. An entry is made whenever the performance of the subject deviates "significantly" on the item in question. Integration of the data for qualitative description or diagnosis remains the task of the skilled examiner.

The check list has merit (a) as a convenient recording device, (b) as a convenient comprehensive tabulation of relatively stable Rorschach *items*, and (c) as the basis of a quantitative measure of adjustment.

It has been emphasized that the adjustment measure does *not* offer a sophisticated diagnosis or prognosis and that it should *never* be used alone in practical prediction. It can add a very useful dimension in research on "normal" groups and in advising individuals presumed to be "normal." Persons with poor adjustment scores are by no means necessarily failures. There is evidence to suggest, however, that a favorable history is much more dependent upon favorable circumstances than is the case for persons with good adjustment scores.

Some indication of the derivation of the check-list quantification from clinical experience has been given. Discussion of validity and reliability has been in terms of experience by ourselves and others, subsequent to the careful experimental data presented in 1945 [4], and has included many unpublished studies.

INSTRUCTIONS FOR USE OF THE CHECK LIST

The protocol is first scored in approximately the usual manner and the number of responses is counted for each determinant. It is helpful to write the actual count on the Inspection Record blank (see example below). This practice takes very little time and facilitates more refined analysis of the data according to the usual tabulations, if desired. The appropriate entries are then made according to the instructions given here and are counted up for the final score.

In the final tally every entry—in fact, every part of a multiple entry—counts as one regardless of its nature. (The few exceptions are carefully indicated in the instructions.) Thus an entry for M reading "+ + B" would count as three, an entry for range reading "— —" would count as two, and an entry for W reading "V" would count as one.

General Comments.—In the following section an explanation is offered of the considerations that lie behind the many variations in type of entry presented in detail later. It is recommended that the examiner proposing to use the check list read this section carefully and that he keep in mind the *intent* of the instructions rather than attempt to apply them with arithmetical exactness.

Clinical judgment along familiar Rorschach lines was used in constructing the check list. It should also be used in its application. Subtle evaluation of idiosyncrasies in the manifestation of Rorschach trends is to be avoided. Pedantic adherence to the arithmetic of the instructions is equally undesirable. The main recommendation is such common sense as even the moderately trained examiner should possess.

Example of Oversubtlety.—The instructions read that where FC is more than one, an entry of "plus" should be made for CF when the ratio FC:CF is 1:2. A record contains 3 FC and 2 CF. The FC use only green and brown. The CF are violent: an exploding anus in Card II, a hacked-off hunk of meat oozing blood in Card X. The clinician may well feel that the CF trend in this subject definitely outweighs the FC resources for adaptive emotional response. Nevertheless such an evaluation goes beyond the purpose of the check list. The ratio 3:2 is so wide of the prescribed 1:2 that quantification becomes a mockery if a plus entry is made for CF. A "B" entry may be made for CF under such circumstances, but no quantitative entry is permissible.

Examples of Desirable Judgment.—

(a) *Borderline decisions.* If the above subject had given two very timid or dubious FC (e.g., where embryos in Card III are described as red after some probing) and three such violent CF, then an entry for CF should be made even though the ratio 2:3 does not meet the official requirement of 2:4. A fortiori, the same procedure should be followed when ratios of 3:5 or 4:7 are involved.

The problem arises most frequently with F per cents in the neighborhood of the cut-off point of 50 per cent. Decision should be made on the basis of the nature of the F responses. Where F is predominantly the sole determinant, the balance should be tipped toward a plus entry for F even if the calculated percentage is slightly below 50. It should be tipped in the other direction where the F responses often involve tendencies to M or FM, etc., or are promptly elaborated by other determinants. (E.g., "the profile of a friendly giant" for the usual lateral D of Card IV. In inquiry the subject remarks: "He is smiling under that big hairy beard.")

A special case, fairly common, is where the subject gives a string of 8 F in Card I, and then relaxes to an average number of R with average F%, or where a subject with quantity ambition tacks on a series of easy F responses after his natural vein has run out. Here, too, borderline decisions may be lenient. (Caution: Clinical evaluation of the special role of F is "oversubtle" beyond a middle range of from 47 to 53 per cent, very rarely a bit extended.)

(b) *Decisions where scoring is debatable,* especially when a very small number of responses is involved. For example, a subject saw witches in Card II plotting over a fire, a red bow in Card III, a colorful tapestry design with animals represented at the side in Card VIII, and a colorful wallpaper design for a nursery in Card X. On inquiry to Card X, the subject said there seemed to be animal forms suitable for a nursery design, but he had to hunt around to find any specific forms. The fire in Card II and the design in Card X are clearly CF, the red bow clearly FC. Several competent examiners differed on the scoring of the tapestry. Some called it FC, some CF.

By the arithmetic of the instructions on page 132, this variation in scoring the tapestry led to a rather marked difference in entries on the check list: no entry for 2 FC:2 CF, two entries for 1 FC:3 CF (a minus for FC and a plus for CF). Yet all the examiners agreed that in clinical interpretation the subject would be considered to show a definite CF preponderance, although resources for the FC type of emotional response are not seriously lacking. This would be recorded on the check list as a plus for CF and a minus to the left of the crucial column for FC.

In a later section I mention a scoring habit useful in reducing variations in check-list entries due to such differences in scoring —namely, a sprinkling of underlinings and question marks to indicate marginal scoring decisions. For instance, I would score the tapestry CF (?), and would recommend that the examiner who prefers the FC as basic score write it "FC (?)."

Weighting of Entries.—For most items on the check list provision is made for rough weighting of the degree of deviation from the normal range by entering one, two, or three checks (usually plus or minus), depending largely upon the number of responses involved. Thus in the protocol of average length, "8 M" require one entry (plus), "11 M" two entries. Very occasionally the M's reach so high a proportion of the total R that three plus entries should be made. The quality of the M's is entered as a descriptive letter when it is markedly deviant; for example, when the bulk of the human action is attributed to body parts instead of whole figures, "d" is entered; when the form accuracy of the M's is poor, the letter "B" is entered; and so on.

Comment.—Quantitative instructions are given for the weighting of entries, but again common-sense Rorschach judgment is urgently needed. It is impossible to provide for every contingency, even for the obvious contingencies resulting from variations in the length of the protocol. A statement of the philosophy behind the weighting is especially important because it is at best a rather arbitrary translation of the continuum of judgment into a few steps.

One entry for an item (or a notation to the left) should be made rather freely. This signifies only a pronounced trend in the personality, by no means necessarily of pathological dimensions. Reports from several investigators indicate that the median number of checks for "normal" groups is nine or ten. Few subjects have less than five entries. Typically, special groups show such a preponderance of entries for one or another item that the investigator feels unhappy about "penalizing" an individual for a very common type of test reaction. This feeling is inappropriate. The single entry usually characterizes rather than penalizes the subject, and it is precisely in the recurrence of some entries that normal groups differ.[8] Sarah Lawrence College students very often have an entry for M, rarely for F. Dartmouth College students show the opposite picture.

A *double entry* should signify a trend of respectworthy dimensions, but not in itself pathological. Harking back to the earlier example, 11 M in 20–30 responses will give any Rorschach examiner pause, though we can all cite many examples of good or superior function with such a protocol. Quite severe color shock may appear in the records of subjects who are normal by any social definition. An F% over 75 (Klopfer scoring) is a serious finding in our experience, but it is reported by other investigators as frequent (up to 15 per cent of a sizable group) not only among the feeble-minded and criminals but among college students and mature scientists.

A *triple entry*, plus or minus, should be entered only for trends of pathological dimensions. The examiner should avoid following the instructions scrupulously in the rare cases where the percentages stated call for three checks and where the trend involved does not seem to be genuinely extreme. (Entries involving two plus signs and one or more descriptive letters are not uncommon and are not considered "pathological.")

The Descriptive Nature of the Entries.—The following symbols are used in order to make the check list as graphic as possible for purposes of quick interpretation, but mainly to record outstanding data for research purposes. Details are given under each item on the pages that follow.

It is a measure of the complexity of the Rorschach method that practically the whole alphabet is already in active use, as well as plus and minus signs, arrows, underlinings, parentheses, and brackets. We have tried to follow the usual procedure in applying the initial letter of a reasonably appropriate word as

---

[8] A very high number of these moderate deviations becomes significant. The subject has too few areas of optimal integration to cope with so many mild deviations from the norm.

descriptive of the concept intended; e.g., Rapaport's "m" for miniature M is better than the "l" for little or Lilliputian M here employed, but small "m" is impossible for the movement area within the Klopfer system. Confusion with "l" for loose succession is unlikely because of the very different position on the check list and the very different manner of arriving at the entry.

+....... The plus sign indicates that the determinant in question was used to excess.
−....... The minus sign indicates that the determinant was not used to the extent usually considered desirable.
B .... This is a roving entry. It may be made *whenever* a given proportion[9] of the responses using the determinant in question is "bad"; that is, either poor in form or strange in content. It corresponds to the usual F−, but also includes fabulized responses that are not, strictly speaking, inaccurate. E.g., the thin white line in Card VI as a "raging torrent."

It may be repeated for the same responses. E.g., if the subject gives many poor original movement responses, the B may appear both under O and under M. Almost always this practice appears to offer a desirable weighting of especially important responses.
B^1, B^2, etc. Where a very limited number of responses are *extremely* "bad," the B may be entered regardless of percentage, but writing in the number of such responses serves to distinguish this problem from the usual run of B entries—which *approximate* a low F+%.

This entry appears *mainly* in schizophrenia, though not exclusively. It is useful in recording quantitatively those relatively isolated breaks in logic which are sometimes the only indication of the disease in a "normal" psychogram. Rorschach's example of the "grass bear" applies. A college student sees Card VIII as "robbers attacking a stagecoach." She explains that the top D looks like the covering they used to have on covered

---

[9] "A given proportion" is described under the most significant items below. The examiner may, at his discretion, add a "B" in any extreme case, wherever appropriate. The two violent CF in the example cited above illustrate this liberty.

wagons, and robbers wear red masks, so the lateral D's suggested robbers because they are red.

V .... This is entered for the *vague* responses, almost exclusively for vague W responses, which are essentially formless. Clouds, mud, modern painting, spring, underwater scene without specification, medical diagrams without specification, etc. In fact the first W impression is usually "V" even when the subject finds a crab or picks out the ribs later on.

These responses are, of course, quite common, and the "V" entry is made only when they are very numerous. Formless responses in D areas (rocks for the bottom D in Card VIII, a splash of ink for the blue laterals in Card X, etc.) seem less significant and are counted as only in the rare cases where practically the whole protocol is marked by vagueness. (See page 124, F (B, V, E).)

t .... This may be entered under "range" to indicate a strong thematic perseveration. E.g., noteworthy *repetition* of creatures going after food, people falling or being pushed down, quarreling, fighting, etc. It may also be used for striking perseveration in content or for stereotyped comments that seem to have meaning for the subject.

H .... Not more than 1% of Total R has human content of any kind.

U .... This entry is used under certain circumstances for F% and the color: movement ratio. It means essentially that "control" by the more refined methods implied in M, FC, and to some extent Fc or FK is *unsatisfactory*. It is entered when F% is low, not necessarily to a significant degree quantitatively, and the other scores indicative of rational control are also low. Or when a subject whose responses are very strongly concentrated in either the movement or the color area shows weakness in the more mature forms of these responses; i.e., M and FC.

l and r.... are used for loose and rigid succession by the usual definitions.

The following letters apply *only* to the movement responses, mainly to M, although they may be entered for *very striking* trends in FM and m. They may be used alone or in combination with each other if the less desirable M are of two or more types. Or a check sign (√) may be entered instead.

√ . . . . In situations where qualitative notation is time-consuming to no purpose, variations in quality of movement of any sort may be entered by a simple √. *The only exception is the B entry, which should always be entered when the M are "bad."* The adjustment score does not require the differentiated notation described in the following letters. They are useful only for qualitative interpretation and some types of research problems.

d . . . . This entry is used when action is ascribed *predominantly* to parts rather than to the whole person; e.g., kicking feet in Card IV, pointing hands in Card III or Card VII, the heads of two creatures yapping at each other or arguing in Card X. (Very faint indication of human action is better scored as → M^d or, m.)

r . . . . When action is ascribed mainly to remote or unreal personages; e.g., to Disney characters, gnomes, angels, Buddhas, marionettes, statues, caricatures, grotesques. Also to animals in human action. (Score the latter M^r → FM.)

t . . . . As under "range," this entry refers to recurrent content, here of the movement responses, which seems to be of special significance. It involves type of movement, however, rather than particular themes. The most common entry is for a predominance of very passive, indefinite, or restricted movement; e.g., looking at each other, leaning, reclining, bending, or indications of hampered movement. In *refined work* such predominance may be entered as (t p) (thematic passive), though to be counted as only one entry. The single responses may be scored M^p for convenience in later tally.

More latitude should be allowed for extensor, assertive movement, but occasionally violence and destructiveness are predominant. It may be entered as (t v) (thematic violent).

Many of the M or FM may suggest head-on conflict;

e.g., buffaloes charging with horns locked in Card V, a tug of war in Card III. May be entered as (t c) (thematic conflict).

There may be ambivalence of attitude; e.g., the arms of the central figure in Card I raised as if reaching for something, in inquiry as if waiting for something; as the threatening stance of a warrior corrected to the supplicating stance of a priest in prayer. May be entered as (t a) (thematic ambivalent).

In short, the entry "t" is a catchall for those characteristic variations in quality which (like the "B" entry) are sometimes almost the only indication of severe disturbance. They occur mainly in character neuroses, though not exclusively. *The refinements of the "t" entry are useful only in certain types of research and need not be generally observed.*

l . . . . When the action is seen mainly in very little areas—as if it were Lilliput M's (to justify the "l"); e.g., the Eskimo between the usual worms in Card X, the acrobatic lady in the top orange projections of Card IX, or the oasis scene on the outside prong of the blue lateral in Card X.

o . . . . When the usual M's in Cards I, II, III, IV, V, VII, and IX are *not* given or are very sparsely represented and a number of "original" (or relatively unusual) M's appear. Proportions depend so much on the number and distribution of the M's that exact instructions are impossible. One fairly common example is M as first response in Card I, followed by failure to see the usual figures in Cards II, III, and VII. The subject may, however, see "acrobats" in the red laterals of Card III, may see the large figures in the pink of Card X, the reclining men in the laterals of Card V, or the two rather exiguous ladies in the center of the same card, etc. Or the subject may see the figures in Card III, often as skeletons, marionettes, or otherwise "r," and otherwise only unusual M. I recall a case where, apart from Card III, the only M's were the last three responses: a devil horseman in the blue lateral, an angel with arms outflung for the inner yellow, and a saint in brown robe walking along praying for the outer orange.

Comment.—Readers familiar with the earlier form of the check list will note in this revision both a loosening and a refinement of the qualitative ("letter") entries. The loosening appears mainly in the *option* of entering a simple $\sqrt{}$ for any type of qualitative variation in the movement responses except B. *Optionally*, they may be recorded in a more refined manner than previously suggested.

Up to now only the B entry has proved statistically differentiating in a series of group studies. The failure of the previous "r" entry may have been due to the merging of "remote" and unduly passive responses. At least "r," as more narrowly defined in the present revision, has been successfully differentiating in two studies, whereas the previous "r" was not.

The entry "d" and probably the new entries "t," "l," and "o" tend to fall down in *group* studies because they are too infrequent in normal populations. Probably they will often have to be merged or omitted in statistical work comparing qualitative trends in normal groups. Review of a series of cases suggests, however, that they desirably raise the adjustment *score* in the individual case, whether entered by letter or by $\sqrt{}$. The cases cited under "o" illustrate the point. By the previous instructions the M's described rate at most one entry, quantitative or qualitative ("r" for the angels and devils). The M's are in themselves too good for the "B" entry. It is the peculiar distribution that makes them clinically significant.

Factors Considered in Determining When a Quantitative $+$ or $-$ Entry Is to be Made.—The first consideration here was sheer number of responses of a given type, in absolute number or percentage, as seemed more expedient. Recurrent throughout the instructions is a rough indication of the adjustment to be made for the very long or very short protocol. The former is defined as over fifty and the latter as under fifteen responses, but the examiner is expected to use common sense in adjusting standards to protocols that approach either extreme.

Under many items some provision is made for consideration of qualitative factors in determining the significance of any given *number* of responses. Arithmetical instructions are offered as guides, but are intended to express the following general principles. The examiner will find specific instructions easier to remember if he grasps the general principles. He may occasionally apply the principles in cases not specifically mentioned below:

(a) Original or unusual responses using a particular determinant are as a rule more significant than responses very commonly seen and are therefore more heavily weighted. E.g., two ladies reclining in a harem for the white areas at the bottom of Card V are more significant for the S trend than a top in the white area of Card II or a skull in Card VIII.

(b) Responses occurring first on a card atypically, or otherwise unusual in setting, are as a rule more significant. E.g., the white center of Card II as a top, or a temple, or the opening of a cave, or a ballerina, or whatever is much more significant as regards the function of S for the subject when it occurs as the first response to Card II than when it occurs incidentally later on.

(c) Responses are usually considered "stronger" when they involve the whole or large areas of the blots than when the location is D or d. E.g., "a floral display . . . because it's so colorful" for the whole of Card X carries a somewhat heavier CF weight than "some sort of flower . . . because flowers often have that shade of yellow" for the lateral D alone.

(d) Affect-laden responses are weighted somewhat more heavily. Affect load may be indicated by the subject (e.g., the bat is ominous because it is so black, the mud is disgusting) or it may be implicit in the content (e.g., blood, fire, flesh, putrescence, etc.).

Additional Responses.—

(a) *Secondary determinants of responses given during the main test.* Unless otherwise specified such additional responses should be counted as one half in calculating percentages. The major exception is the "strong" additional determinant. It is often difficult to decide which determinant in a complex response is the most important. Experience with the scoring habits of many students and well-qualified examiners indicates that this decision is the most frequent source of variation in scoring. The problem is of no great importance in interpretation because the examiner deals qualitatively with an additional response according to its merits. For the check list, additional responses that seem about as important as the main response are underlined in scoring and are treated almost like main responses. Of course, by this procedure none of the check-list figures add up to 100 per cent, but it has seemed more useful to enter pronounced trends with some accuracy rather than to preserve arithmetical integrity.

E.g., Card IV as ominous black storm clouds driven by the wind. This response involves C′ K, and m. No matter which one chooses as the main score, the other determinants are very significant. Or green inchworms crawling along inchworm fashion for the center bottom D of Card X. Here again color and movement are both vividly seen. Whichever determinant is considered "main," the additional is "strong." In contrast is "a bat pouncing on its prey," with later explanation of lifted wings and open claws—"and the blackness also made it seem like a bat." In this response the FC′ is definitely secondary to a vivid sense of movement and is weighted one half.

(b) *Responses given during the inquiry.* Such responses are infrequent in the group Rorschach, and they received no special consideration in the 1944 version of the check list. They present a serious problem in a few individually administered protocols, a problem to which no satisfactory solution has been found. With some reluctance we recommend that they be *omitted in calculations for the check list, except as they may influence a borderline decision.*

Comment.—The merit of omitting responses added in inquiry is a relatively standard administrative approach. The demerit lies in deliberate renouncement of data that are often of obvious clinical importance. Up to now the check list has renounced subtleties, but the aim has been to register the "obvious" comprehensively. If a test-shy artist *[Roe's data, 5, 6]* reveals himself mainly in the more informal atmosphere of the inquiry, no examiner will like confining quantification to the initial inhibited performance. A strong CF trend may emerge clearly during the inquiry, whereas the main test shows only color shock and a high F%. The later addition of many meticulous form responses may suggest a larger amount of compulsiveness than was originally demonstrated. The spontaneous appearance of good M in inquiry may mitigate the interpretation in cases where M was initially inhibited by color shock. Psychotic elaborations may come out, as when a patient remarked in the inquiry to Card VIII: "I didn't want to tell you before that I caught on to the reason for all the sex things," (he had given no sex responses), "but now I see that you meant me to see how spirituality" (top blue areas) "overcomes man's lower nature" (fusion of blue and red color with animal content; previously he had given only the popular animals after what looked like ordinary delay due to color shock).

Roe introduced the device of increasing the *Number of R* used in calculating percentages throughout the check list by one half the number of responses added in inquiry, and then handling these responses like any other additionals. Thus a subject giving fifteen responses in the main test and ten more in inquiry would receive a *Number of R* of twenty as a basis for all calculations. In our experience this device is helpful in the majority of cases, but not in all. At times it leads to distortion rather than clarification of the clinical picture, depending upon the nature of added responses.

The reason for the difficulty in quantification here is that adding responses in the inquiry has no *general* clinical significance. The meaning of this behavior is contingent upon a great variety of factors and must be differently weighted in each case. We have toyed with the idea of listing the major types of cases and recommending differential treatment for each type. Such procedure becomes hopelessly cumbersome. Furthermore, the listing would depend too much upon the clinician's judgment in a very personal sense because there is no substantial clinical tradition for the handling of these responses.

In contrast to the defense of judgment as a basis for establishing the check-list standards, we feel that experimental-statistical investigation alone can decide whether Roe's procedure is preferable to omitting these responses altogether. The problem is one of *expediency* in quantifying an item essentially unquantifiable on the basis of current methods.

Scoring Procedures.—Scoring is essentially the same as in any Rorschach work.[10] It is useful to note the qualitative items required for the check list as one scores each response. For instance

---

[10] Earlier versions of check-list instructions stressed items to be omitted, convenient format, etc. With increased interest in the research value of the separate entries on the check list as against rapid practical judgment, we have come to score more carefully. Discussion with other persons using the check list has made it seem advisable to leave the format entirely to the discretion of the examiner. Individuals differ as to what they find convenient.

a formless W response is scored W^v; unreal characters in action M^r. Poor form is recorded by the usual minus, or plus-minus, or minus-plus for less marked inaccuracy. Fabulized responses are given the usual scoring with a "b" added, "B" if extreme. (The various minuses and b's are lumped together for the B entry.) Color and shading shock are noted as they appear: (CS) if mild, *CS* if pronounced. "Strong" additionals are underlined. Doubtful scores are followed by a question mark. It is helpful to write "note" or some descriptive word after any response of qualitative importance which either does not fall in the check-list categories or deserves special attention. The scored case given below will serve as an example.

These frills are not offered as further refinements of a refined scoring system, but merely as a convenience. The examiner should be warned that if he attempts to fill out the check list on a long protocol scored and laboriously tabulated in the usual way, he will not find it a simple task. He will have to hunt out the W's, M's, etc., in order to determine their quality, review the protocol for color and shading shock, and all the other data not routinely tabulated. In our experience the routine introduction of major qualitative notes on the scoring sheet is helpful even for full interpretation, especially in long complicated protocols.

Notations "to the Left."—It was suggested from the start that for purposes of qualitative interpretation performance that approached but did not quite meet the standards set for entry on the check list should be recorded by an appropriate sign to the left of the "entry column." Experience has shown that these notations to the left also have quantitative value, and it is now suggested that they be made routinely. Standards are left loose —whatever seems almost but not quite worth a main entry.

Evidence for the value of these notations has come from three sources. The first has been statistical comparison of normal groups. In Table 1, notations to the left are presented in parentheses. In almost all group studies, Chi-square calculations of qualitative group trends have been improved by inclusion of these notations. Of course, in such studies we are not concerned so much with potential trouble spots (as in the total adjustment score) as with the nature of the reaction pattern characteristic for the group.

Secondly, consideration of routine *re*test of students in the senior year at Sarah Lawrence College cogently suggests that notations move from the left to the main column or vice versa far more often than main entries simply appear and disappear without qualifying notation. Doubtless this fluctuation is due in part to inaccuracies of the Inspection Rorschach, but it also seems due in considerable part to genuine change in the student.

Thirdly, in the small experiment with students learning the Inspection technique, an adjustment score calculated as "main entries plus notations to the left" showed better interexaminer correlation than the main entries alone. Especially in the early stages of teaching, students could agree more easily that the subject showed a trend than upon the exact entry.

We do not at this point recommend that the notations to the left be routinely counted in the adjustment score. Experience with students has suggested that the reliability of the check list would be improved by more emphasis on common-sense Rorschach judgment and less emphasis on arithmetical sanctity, a suggestion incorporated in the present instructions. We think, however, that the entries described are the most significant for "adjustment." Certainly they are the only ones that have had experimental validation to date.

SPECIFIC INSTRUCTIONS FOR THE CHECK LIST

1. Number of R. Strict accuracy is not essential, but error in counting the number of responses should not exceed 10 per cent of the total. In cases where it is difficult to decide what is a response (e.g., many loose combinatorial wholes), an approximate figure intermediate between strict and loose interpretation may be entered quickly with the notation ($\pm$). The significance of later percentages should then rest slightly more heavily on qualitative considerations.

2. T/R> 60" or <30" ($+$, $-$). Not applicable to the group protocol. Enter only 1 check ($+$) for excessive time or ($-$) for unusually quick reaction.

3. Refusal ($\sqrt{}$).

$\sqrt{}$....... Initial refusal of any card or cards, with adequate response given after encouragement but *before inquiry* in individual test, during inquiry in group protocol.[11]

Flippancy is not necessarily a serious handicap. E.g., a student's response to Card X is: "Dali's version of the last moments of an undernourished sea horse." But in inquiry he duly locates the sea horse in the bottom green, and adds: "impression of silly unconnected forms—mostly fellow sea creatures (crabs, oysters, etc.) with disconnected colors."

√√..... (a) Refusal of any cards if adequate response is spontaneously given in inquiry or in testing the limits in individual administration.

(b) Refusal of 1 or 2 cards (except Cards I, III, and V) without later recovery *if* subject gives evidence of unusual timidity, antagonism, or flippancy.

(c) Refusal of 1 card (except Cards I, III, and V) without later recovery in a completely and conscientiously executed group protocol.

√√√... (a) Refusal of any card after prolonged co-operative effort in inquiry and limit testing.

(b) Refusal of 2 cards in a conscientiously executed group protocol.

(c) Refusal of 3 cards without recovery under any conditions.

(d) Refusal of Card I, III, or V without recovery under any conditions.

Discussion.—Inability to find any way of dealing with the cards is always a serious sign unless the subject recovers himself quickly (√) or at least before the test is over (√√). The standard of ability to recover is relaxed somewhat for the group protocol, since the personal encouragement of the examiner is lacking. The general attitude of the subject modifies evaluation of refusal somewhat—failure after proper effort is more serious (√√√) than refusal to come to grips with the problem (√√)

---

[11] Refusal is almost nonexistent in group administration *in our experience*, but has apparently been a major problem in some instances of army experience, etc. Where antagonistic or flippant attitudes involve many refusals and/or unscorable responses, the check-list procedure is not suitable for the group as a whole. Individual cases may have to be discarded even when group co-operation is relatively good.

in most cases. Refusal of Card I, III, or V is penalized most heavily, partly because it seems clinically more indicative of disturbance and partly because refusal of the other cards is likely to be associated with special difficulties; e.g., color or shading shock. Since refusal of the other cards contributes toward the entering of checks later on, it should not be too heavily penalized here.

4. W ($+$, $-$, B, V).

$(+)$ . . . . . $W\%$ over 50%. Enter a *second* plus ($+$) *to the left* of the notation column (a) when $W\%$ is over 75%, (b) when a strong W compulsion is clear regardless of percentage. Two plus signs ($++$) should be entered *to the left* when $W\%$ is over 90%.

$(-)$ . . . . . $W\%$ under 15%.

$(--)$ . . . W represented by not more than one popular W or 2 W vague or poor in quality. (3 or 4 W in a very long protocol.)

Note: The practice of scoring several almost independent D's separately and bracketing them together for a single additional W not infrequently reduces $W\%$ out of all proportion to the W intention of the subject. There are protocols with upwards of 20 R and barely 10 W, main and additional, where the subject's aim was to give one whole response per card. E.g., Card IV as a vase made in the shape of boots with snakes as handles and a sort of fountain arrangement at the top, with a pedestal like a piano stool at the center bottom. This subject certainly has a capacity to see details, but also there is no doubt about his need for W. Protocols in which this kind of W predominates should have a plus entry regardless of the official $W\%$, and often warrant an extra entry to the left. (We note the official number of W and add ($\rightarrow$ 100%) in the scoring section.) W for such bracketed responses should be counted as main W.

B . . . . Over 25% of all W poor form, though not *very* bad (e.g., W butterfly in Card II, W clown's face in Card VIII).

B^1, B^2, etc. A few *very* bad forms among the W (e.g., Card VII as a herd of stampeding buffaloes). In fact, even one

really bizarre form should rate a B entry if the examiner is sure of its quality.

V . . . . Over 50% of the W vague.

B
V . . . . Enter if the sum of V responses, plus the number of B
responses *counted double*, is over 50% of all W. In the
final tally this notation should count as only one entry.

                           B
NOTE: B, V, and V may be entered *alone* if W% is normal or may
be entered in addition to a plus or minus sign. Bracketed W count
as main W.

DISCUSSION: W:M ratio is not included on the check list because it
so often seems unreliable as a numerical expression of a stable trend.
M:FM, FC:CF do seem to belong together "dynamically." The
trouble with the W:M ratio is that it expresses the relationship of
broad trends which are very imperfectly represented by either W
or M as isolated scores. If W represents striving and M represents
capacity, then a high W:M ratio shows striving beyond capacity.
Unfortunately the "if" is too large. Each member of the ratio
may be affected by other factors independently to the point where
the ratio becomes merely absurd.

5. Dd (+) (*i.e., dd, di, de, dr*).

(+) . . . . . 10% to 25% of total R.

(++) . . . 25% to 50% of total R.

(+++) . (*a*) Over 50% of total R.

        (*b*) Over 25% of total R if stereotyped; i.e., if more
than half of Dd or di or de or dr or the same type
of dd in a protocol longer than thirty R.

6. S (+).

(+) . . . . . (*a*) 2 to 4 common space responses, except where
R >50 (e.g., spinning top in Card II, vase in Card
VII). Count additional S as one half.

        (*b*) 2 or 3 original space responses.

(++) . . . (*a*) 5 to 7 common space responses.

        (*b*) 4 or 5 original space responses.

(+++) . (*a*) More than 8 common space responses.

        (*b*) More than 6 original space responses.

NOTE: When common and original space responses both appear,
follow proportions given under (*a*) but count originals double.
When R is greater than 50, enter "(++)" as (+); "(+++)" as
(++).

7. *Succession* (r, l).

r .... Enter only for definitely rigid succession where there is evidence of a clear need to follow a plan.

l .... Loose succession as usually defined in the Rorschach literature.

ll .... Confused succession.

8. P, Com $(-)$.

$(-)$..... (*a*) 3 populars or less.

(*b*) Very few common responses (e.g., figures in Card VII, Eiffel Tower in Card X) even though populars are normal.

$(--)$... (*a*) Only one P.

(*b*) Not over 10% common responses, even though P is only moderately reduced; i.e., up to 3 P.

$(---)$. No P, less than 3 common responses.

9. O $(+, B)$.

$(+)$..... Over 35% of total R are original responses.

$(++)$... Over 50% of total R are original responses.

B .... Over 50% of original responses definitely poor form but not *very* bad.

B^1, B^2, etc. A few very bad originals, even one original that is really bizarre. This judgment may refer to extreme inappropriateness of content as well as to poor form.

NOTE: B may be entered alone if the number of original responses is not excessive but their quality is poor, or it may be added to the notation of numerical excess.

Original additions should be counted as l, but scoring of minor variations should be lenient.

Strongly fabulized responses and very unusual vague responses are scored as original, a policy that deviates from Klopfer's recommendation.

10. At and Sex $(+)$.

$(+)$..... (*a*) 2 anatomy or sex responses in especially significant locations (e. g., lungs as first response in Card II, organs in Card VIII).

(*b*) 3 or 4 moderately "significant" responses (e. g., stomach for red in Card III, sex organs not commonly seen, etc.).

(*c*) 4 to 6 vague or very common responses, such as pelvic bones, skeletons, skulls, etc., sex organs in Card VI, unless there is evidence of conflict.

(++)... (*a*) 3 or 4 responses as above.

(*b*) 5 to 7 responses as above.

(*c*) 7 to 10 responses as above.

(+++). (*a*) More than 5 responses as above.

(*b*) More than 7 responses as above.

(*c*) More than 11 responses as above.

NOTE: When "significant" and "moderately significant" or "common" responses occur in the same protocol, follow instructions given under (*b*), but count "significant" responses double.

In a short protocol these figures become qualitatively more important, but since with a small number of R an entry for restriction in *range* of content will also appear, no special provision need be made here.

Allow considerable latitude for special study in the field of biology or "sophistication" about sex in some groups. Refined *At* and *Sex* responses, given without evidence of conflict, should be circled in scoring and penalized only when an excessive number entails restriction in range as above. (Examples of conflict are deterioration in form level or giving a sex response first in any card except Card VI.) Good sex responses are likely to be dd or dr. If even moderately excessive, they will contribute toward a check for Dd, an appropriate penalty for a preoccupation with special content to such an extent that the natural spatial configuration of the blots is sacrificed.

11. Range (+, −, *t*).

(+)..... Enter only if the range of content categories is extremely wide and scattered. To be determined by inspection. Not a common entry.

(−)..... (*a*) Ad plus Hd 25% to 50% of total R; 15% to 35% if few A and H are given.

(*b*) Animal responses 50% to 75% of total R.

(*c*) Animal plus human responses 75% to 90% of total R.

(− −)... (*a*) Ad plus Hd 50% to 75%; 35% to 50% if few H and A are given.

(*b*) Animal responses 75% to 90%.

(*c*) Animal plus human responses 90% to 95%.

(———). (*a*) Over 75% Hd plus Ad; over 50% if few H and A are given.

(*b*) A% over 90%.

(*c*) Animal and human responses given almost exclusively.

H....... Not more than 1% of Total R has human content of any kind.

t........ (*a*) Over 25% of any other response category. (Usually at or sex. Occasionally other categories are overused by normals with a strong professional preoccupation, by schizophrenics, and a few neurotics.)

(*b*) Perseveration in content with poor form. At least three *inappropriate* repetitions of a concept (usually adequate on first appearance—e.g., the stereotyped butterflies given by patients with organic brain damage).

(*c*) Thematic perseveration, even when form is used adaptively, though not necessarily correctly. Three or more repetitions of idiosyncratic concepts.

NOTE: Both minus signs and t may be entered if necessary; e.g., a girl gave 55 A% with many repetitions of hen and chick, swan and cygnet, pig and piglet, etc. Her entry read "—t." The t entry may be doubled or tripled for very marked perseveration of any type. Rare except in severe pathology.

12. F% (+, —).

(+)..... 50% to 75%.

(++)... 75% to 90%.

(+++). Over 90%.

(—)..... Below 15%.

(——)... Below 10% if less than two thirds of the responses are Fc, FK, FC, or good movement responses.

U....... Below 25% if minus (—) or B signs have been entered for M, FC, *and* Fc, or where any two of these items are definitely (—) or B and the third is questionable.

DISCUSSION: Lack of pure form responses is not a serious hazard to adjustment, *provided* the element of rational control is strongly represented in the manner of using the more "emotional" determinants. Even moderate diminution of pure form responses is a hazard where other resources for control are either absent or markedly poor in quality.

13. F (B, V, E).

NOTE: This entry refers to the form level *of all responses;* i.e., of the total R, not merely those scored F. It is a rare entry, far less common than B or V for specific determinants like W, O, and M.

B . . . .   30% to 50% moderately poor forms.[12]

BB . . . . . .   More than 50% moderately poor forms.

B[1], B[2], etc.   A few *very* bad forms.

V . . . .   40% to 60% of total R of the vague, formless variety.

VV . . . . .   More than 60% vague.

E[13] . . . . . .   (*a*) More than 40% finicking F responses.

(*b*) Almost no F— or V responses, even if form is not markedly overexact.

B

V . . . .   As described under W, enter if the sum of V responses plus twice that of B responses lies between 40% and 60% of total R. Count as only one entry in the final tally.

VVE, VEE. This entry is characteristic of compulsiveness with explosive trends or a tendency to "evaporate." The degree of the condition and the preponderance of compulsive control are suggested by the combination of V and E.

BBE. . . . .   This entry should be reserved for the variability in form level suggestive of early schizophrenia.

---

[12] Percentages required have been raised somewhat over previous instructions to make the instructions conform to our own practice. The intent was to catch cases where the poor forms are scattered among several determinants, including F, and to give extra weight if concentrated in one determinant used to great excess.

[13] E stands for exact—that is, overexact. It is entered when much attention is paid to finicking evidence for the response, or where the search for accuracy limits response to the meticulous dd or both. It is also entered where practically every response is average or above in accuracy, or where the subject *regularly* insists upon the two-ness of his observations or *repeatedly* examines the symmetry of the blots, etc.

In scoring the group protocol we rarely enter E because the accuracy of the form and the intent of the subject are hard to determine to the point of judging *over*exactness. Perhaps the entry should be dropped.

NOTE: Any two letters may be entered and counted separately if the criteria for both are fulfilled.

14. Shading Shock ($\sqrt{}$). See criteria for color shock, Item 23.

15. FK, Fc ($+, -$).

($+$)..... If over 50% of R fall into either or both of these categories in any combination. For qualitative purposes enter FK and/or Fc to the left of the scoring column if over 25%.

($-$)..... If not more than one Fc is present. (Exception, one really good Fc, main or strong additional, is sufficient in a protocol of less than 15R.) No penalty for omission of FK.

($--$)... If FC is also entered as minus ($-$).

NOTE: It is rarely possible to score *absence* of Fc with certainty in the group protocol. If at least two responses are present, which are often seen as Fc, the ($-$) entry should not be made even when there is no positive evidence that the shading was used.

DISCUSSION: FK and Fc are usually favorable signs and are therefore entered only if so excessive as to suggest a sort of stereotyping of this type of response. Qualitatively they are important indicators of the *kind* of adjustment. When excessive, or even when moderately overemphasized in the absence of FC, they usually represent a compensatory adaptation, but one that usually works fairly well. Absence of both Fc and FC suggests a serious lack in tempered social relations.

16. c ($+$).

($+$)..... (*a*) 2 or 3 wholly undifferentiated c. (1 if R $<$ 15; 3 or 4 if R $>$ 50); e.g., mud, dirt, stone, spilled ink, fur. Count strong additionals as 1, others as 1/2.

(*b*) 4 or 5 poorly differentiated cF. [14] (2 if R $<$ 15; 5 or 6 if R is $>$ 50); e.g., surface of the moon; fur if animal is specified; stones if contours contribute to concept.

($++$)... (*a*) 4 or 5 undifferentiated c. (Adjust to number of R.)

---

[14] Klopfer scores some of these Fc. We prefer to think of the distinction between Fc and cF as analogous to Fc and CF in the Klopfer system, scoring Fc only when the form of the object is considered, regardless of refinements in the use of texture.

     (*b*) 7 or 8 poorly differentiated cF. (Adjust to number of R.)

(+++). (*a*) Over 6 undifferentiated c. (Adjust to number of R.)

     (*b*) Over 9 poorly differentiated cF. (Adjust to number of R.)

NOTE: When both types of c occur, follow proportions given under (*a*) but count the (*b*) type of response at 1/2.

Additional c is almost always strong or equivalent to main c except as an incidental completion to a good form; e.g., figures standing on rocks in Card VII.

17. K, k (+).

(+)..... 2 or 3 K or k, KF, or kF in any combination. (1 or 2 if R <15; 3 or 4 if R> 50.) Count strong additionals as 1, other additionals as 1/2.

(++)... 4 or 5 such responses, adjusted to length of protocol.

(+++). More than 6 such responses adjusted to length of protocol.

18. C' (+).

(+)..... (*a*) 2 or 3 undifferentiated C' responses or emotionally toned FC'; e.g., the bat is *ominous* because it is so dark. (1 if R<15, 3 or 4 if R>50.)

     (*b*) 4 or 5 FC' (2 or 3 if R <15, 5 or 6 if R> 50). Count additionals as 1 unless given for small portion of response; e.g., black snouts on animals in Card VII. In such cases count 1/2.

(++)... (*a*) 4 or 5 C', as above. Adjust for length. Count +++ if color is (−).

     (*b*) 6 to 8 FC', as above. Count as +++ if total color is (−).

(+++). (*a*) More than 6 FC'.

     (*b*) More than 9 FC'.

     (*c*) See also (*a*) and (*b*) above for case where color is (−).

NOTE: When both types of C' response occur, follow proportions given under (*a*), but count the (*b*) type of response as 1/2.

19. M (+, −, B, √, *etc.*).

(+)..... 30% to 40%. (5 or 6 M if R <15, 8 to 10 M if R> 50.)

(++)... 40% to 60%. (7 to 10 M if R <15, 11 to 13 M if R >50.)

(+++). Over 60%. (More than above.)

(−)..... 2 M. (1 M if R <15, 2 or 3 if R> 50.

(− −)... 1 M or no M. (No M if R<15.)

NOTE: B, √, etc., may be entered alone or in combination with any of the signs above.

B .... If over half of the M are definitely loose in form, but not very bad; e.g., girl taking a nose dive (red lateral blots in Card III) is at the top level of B.

B^1, B^2, etc. If several M responses (or even one) are extremely poor in form; e.g., top center of Card X interpreted as a "man with white apron and blue bedroom slippers walking between pink clouds."

(√) or d,
r, t, l..... Enter when more than half of the M are of the quality described on pages 126 and 127.

(√) or o . Enter at discretion as described above when distribution of M is genuinely peculiar, the usual M being either absent or seriously reduced in a protocol with many M.

NOTE: When 50% to 65% of the M are d, r, t, or l in any combination and the rest are definitely sound, the entry may be made as √ or as r, t, d, l, whatever letters seem most descriptive. In this event the entry counts as 1 in the final tally.

When over 65% (two thirds) of the M are d, r, t, l, a double entry should be made, √√, or any appropriate combination of letters; e.g., rd or rt. The entry oo may be made, ot, ol, whatever is appropriate for specialized trends within a peculiar distribution of M.

EXCEPTION: Where only 1, 2, or 3 M are given, the quality should be very striking to warrant arithmetical application of the percentages given above. E.g., a single, definitely bizarre M in a long protocol may warrant the entry "− − Bo" or even duplication of B or o. A somewhat overcareful scientist whose only M is "butlers" in Card III, "caricatures because they're not accurate, of course," may be let off more leniently with an r to the left of the main column of entries. Arithmetically, *Macbeth* witches in Card II, a cartoon of Alphonse and Gaston in Card III, and the usual gossiping women in Card VII would require the entry "rr," an entry that seems excessive. The extra "r" in these common instances should be placed to the left. Four common "r" in 6 M, however, do warrant the double entry.

20. FM, FM:M $(+, -)$.

$(+)$..... (*a*) FM$>$ 3 or 4, where M is one or zero.

       (*b*) FM:M$>$ 2:1, where M is more than one.

$(++)$... (*a*) FM$>$ 5 to 8, where M is one or zero.

       (*b*) FM:M$>$ 3:1, where M is more than one.

$(+++)$. (*a*) FM$>$ 9, where M is one or zero.

       (*b*) FM:M$>$ 4:1, where M is more than one.

$(-)$..... (*a*) Not more than one common FM or 2 additional or faint FM. (Examples of common FM are spontaneous flying bats, walking or climbing animals in Card VIII, etc.)

       (*b*) M:FM$>$ 4:1, where FM is more than one.

$(--)$... FM $(-)$ if there is overemphasis on m.

NOTE: Count ½ for additional FM and faint FM such as "flying" bat, elicited with difficulty in inquiry, moderate action of stuffed animals, book ends. Any of the letters proposed for M or a $\sqrt{}$ may be added in the event of *very striking* qualitative peculiarities in FM. Not a common entry.

21. m $(+)$.

$(+)$..... If 2 or 3 main m are present, or 10% to 20% of total R when R$>$ 30. Count additional m as ½.

$(++)$... 4 or 5 main m, or 20% to 40% when R$>$ 30.

$(+++)$. More than 6 m, or over 40% when R$>$ 30.

NOTE: Additional m for facial expression are not included here, since in the absence of M they usually suggest a mitigation of the lack rather than a further indication of trouble and they never represent a real hazard to adjustment. They are circled in the scoring and are included in the tally of "total movement." Their mitigating effect may sometimes prevent the entering of a check there if movement is little used. They rightfully emphasize the tendency to excessive movement in the subject with many M and FM who can see nothing with static objectivity.

The letters proposed for M or a $\sqrt{}$ may be entered here for *striking* qualitative peculiarities in other types of m. E.g., predominance of things disintegrating, oozing away, or in violent eruption.

22. Total Movement (+, —).

(+)..... 60% to 75%.

(++)... Over 75%.

(—)..... 5% to 10%. (2 movement responses if R <15.)

(——)... 1% to 5%. (1 movement response if R <15.)

(———). Total absence of movement.

NOTE: In this entry *every response involving movement is counted: M, FM, m, and additionals*, except where the response is additional to a primary movement score. E.g., women picking up a basket in Card III, their skirts blown by the wind, counts only one toward total movement, although scored M, Fm. The additional m *is* counted, however, for a radio tower sending out sound waves in Card VI, scored F, Fm.

DISCUSSION: The purpose of this entry is an estimation of the extent to which the subject tends to "empathize," to project movement into the blots, regardless of the quality of his projections or even whether they are blocked or healthily subordinated to other considerations.

This summary of all movement responses is one of the very few personal innovations used in building the check list. It seems somewhat different from the problem of handling additional responses given in inquiry, in that it has a clinical rationale. It certainly should have empirical statistical investigation in a variety of groups. Total absence of movement still seems to warrant three entries, especially since standards for absence of M and FM are relatively generous. The subject who gives no movement responses whatever can otherwise receive only three entries (for M and FM), a manifestly insufficient weighting for a clinically serious reaction pattern.

23. Color Shock (√). Previous instructions (1944) allowed the use of the simple check (√) for color and shading shock, but suggested a more complicated notation dependent upon whether shock was shown primarily in excessive or blocked reaction to the color. The complicated notation has proved troublesome beyond its positive contribution and is now abandoned. The change does not affect the quantitative score for these items.

Color and shading shock is considered operative whenever the quality of the subject's performance seems to be markedly influenced by the introduction of color or shading. Indices commonly encountered follow. The examiner should endeavor to make sure that the factors observed (for instance, poor form level or comments on the blots) are specifically characteristic for the colored or shaded blots, rather than characteristic for the subject generally.

Two or three entries for color or shading shock may be made at the discretion of the examiner. One entry may be made rather freely. The majority of subjects show *some* special reaction to the appearance of color. In normal groups one entry may be expected in about 50 per cent of all subjects. As a rule, absence of any particular color shock may be considered a positively good sign.[15] Two entries may be expected in about 15 per cent of normal groups. Three entries are very rare. These indications are intended merely as suggestive for the general emphasis placed on color shock. (Shading shock is far less frequent in most groups studied.)

The following factors should be considered:

(a) Delayed response. Not available for the group protocol, but the best single indicator in individual administration.

(b) Comments by the subject, laughing, blushing, etc., if specific to colored (or shaded) cards.

(c) Refusal of colored or shaded cards. (A few very sick individuals may gradually peter out on the test and refuse the last three cards because they are last rather than because they are colored. As a rule refusal is much more specifically determined and regularly rates at least two entries when occasioned by color or shading.)

(d) Marked increase or decrease in number of responses to the colored (or shaded) cards. Rates one entry if responses to Cards VIII, IX, and X fall below 15% or above 60% without other signs of shock, or if less marked quantitative differences are accompanied by other relatively minor indications.

(e) Deterioration in form accuracy for colored (or shaded) cards. This is usually seen in the first response to the cards, but sometimes the general level is markedly less good than is typical for the subject, even though the first responses are not strikingly poor. (This is the most common indication of shock in the Group Rorschach.)

---

[15] A sad exception is presented by some psychotic records. In some very serious cases the *absence* of color shock may be a damaging sign.

(f) Marked shift in approach, even without severe deterioration in accuracy. Caution: Increase in D and FM may occur in the last three cards, especially in Card X, irrespective of special reaction to the color. Color shock should be considered only if the increase is very extreme or takes a less common form.

24. FC (−, B).

(−)..... (a) Only one main FC *or* one strong additional. (E.g., crawling green worms in Card X.)

        (b) Only two incidental additional FC, 2 F/C, 2 F ⟷ C, or two doubtful FC (CF verging on FC, or responses frequently seen as FC with no positive evidence for the score in the group protocol).

(−−)... (a) Definitely no main FC and not more than one mild additional or doubtful FC.

(B) ..... (a) Form definitely poor but not very bad in three or more of the FC responses (e.g., blue-eyed face in Card X).

        (b) One or more responses showing clear FC effort and very bad form; inappropriate or contaminated color responses.

NOTE: B may be entered alone or added to a minus sign.

As in the case of Fc, FC should be handled leniently *in the group protocol*. We score "pos FC" any response where color is *possibly* involved. The bow in Card III *may* involve an FC even if the subject has not overtly mentioned color. "Performing seals" for the top red of Card II is a concept that clearly excludes color.

Where all the color scores are merely "pos," one minus sign may be entered for FC (and for CF if suitable on similar grounds). The question mark seems preferable to a heavy weighting by minuses in the color area which is possibly unfounded. As regards total color, only three "pos" color responses rate a minus; in any event, one or two clear color answers and three "pos" rate a question mark. As regards color:movement, the entry is often clear no matter how color is scored. A notation of 15 to 17 movement responses rates minuses even if the color responses range from two clear to a possible five. On the other hand, with moderately high total movement and only doubtful color, the examiner should very carefully reconsider the total picture clinically, and should almost always be conservative in entering the necessary minus checks.

25. *CF, FC:CF* (+, −).

(+)..... (*a*) When FC is (−) as defined above, two or three strong CF or whole CF responses (e.g., fire, blood, sunset, vague anatomical drawing, colored fountain, etc.). Count ½ for additional CF (unless strong), CF verging on FC, and doubtful scorings.

(*b*) If FC is more than 1 counting strong additionals (FC or CF) as 1, ordinary additionals, the minor variants, and doubtful scores as ½.

(++)... (*a*) FC (−), 4 or 5 strong CF or equivalent.

(*b*) FC:CF = 1:3, (FC:CF = 1:3) if FC is more than 1.

(+++). (*a*) FC (−), 6 or more strong CF or equivalent.

(*b*) FC:CF < 1:4, (FC:CF = 1:4) if FC is more than 1.

(−)..... (*a*) No main CF, not more than 1 additional CF, whether FC is present or not.

(*b*) FC:CF > 4:1, if CF is more than 1 additional.

26. *C* (+).

NOTE: C includes color description and color symbolism as well as the undifferentiated color response. Primary C or Cn practically never occurs in normal protocols. Count double when they appear. Count additional and doubtful responses as ½, as above.

(+)..... 2 differentiated color responses (C des or C sym) or one pure color.

(++)... 3 differentiated color responses, or 2 pure color, or one true Cn.

(+++). 4 or more differentiated color responses, or 3 or more pure color responses, or 2 or more color naming.

27. *Total Color* (+, −).

(+)..... 30% to 40% of total R.

(++)... 40% to 60% of total R.

(+++). More than 60%.

(−)..... Less than 10% of total R, except in a very short protocol.

(−−)... Not more than 1 response using color.

DISCUSSION: No distinction is made as to main or additional responses or quality of color response. Like Total Movement (+, −) this item is a measure of the tendency to respond to the determinant, regardless of how the responsiveness is controlled.

Over- and under-responsiveness is in itself an indication of some disequilibrium. The subject who is merely highly extroversive in a controlled and balanced way will receive only one check for the whole color area; i.e., for this item. For subjects who show much poor use of color, the checks serve as a further weighting. (See discussion of Total Movement for a critique.)

28. Color:Movement $(+, -, U)$.

$(+)$ ..... Total color equal to total movement. (See Items 22 and 27.)

$(++)$ ... Total color twice as great as total movement.

U .... Absence of FC or $(CF + C):FC > 3:1$, *if* any of the foregoing plus entries is made.

$(-)$ ..... Total movement 3 times as great as total color.

$(--)$ ... Total movement 4 times as great as total color.

$(---)$. Total movement 6 times or more as great as total color.

U .... Absence of M or $(FM + m):M > 3:1$, *if* any of the foregoing minus entries is made.

DISCUSSION: These criteria are still offered with hesitation. It may be that the usual M:sum C would be preferable to *total color:total movement*. Yet the less developed forms of movement and color often seem to serve quite well as representatives of the determinant. 2 M, 6 FM, 2m : 2FC, 5CF can suggest no more than some immaturity in a girl with lively, essentially well-balanced emotional resources. By our criteria she rates approximately ambiequal, but would be heavily extroverted by the M:sum C standard. On the other hand, the girl with many M and a number of CF or C may rate close to ambiequal by the latter standard, whereas by our criteria plentiful FM, m, and additionals may indicate an extreme introversive trend, very imperfectly balanced by several explosive color responses. Very often in such cases many of the M are O—, indicative of narcissistic attitudes rather than inner stability and maturity. In our experience the greatest hazard to adjustment lies in a marked imbalance between the general responsiveness to movement and color rather than in the type of responsiveness.

It has seemed desirable, however, to record and penalize serious lack of the more developed forms of responsiveness in the emphasized area. Absence of M or FC may not be particularly important if movement or color plays a relatively subsidiary role in the personality structure. Instability in the major line of reaction is always serious. Hence the addition of (U) for excessive proportion of unsatisfactory responses on the overemphasized side.

This entry has the least substantiation of any on the check list and is the only one where standards have been *markedly* changed over the 1944 instructions. The change is in the direction of lesser weight, with more allowance for excess of movement.

CASE A.
Male—Psychiatric Diagnosis: Alcoholism with Psychoneurosis

CARD I.

(59″)　　1″:　A bat wing—or a bat, I guess.

Looking at it from above —as if you were in a tree, the bat below flying or about to take off.

CARD II.

(61″)　　17″:　Looks like two elephants —kissing each other. I don't know what the red would be—the heat from their kiss. (Laughs.)

Whole animals—standing up.

CARD III.

(58″):　Is this red supposed to mean something?

25″:　Looks like two birds— the red means nothing.

Usual figures—no movement. "Silly expression as in a Peter Arno cartoon."

CARD IV.

(62″)　　15″:　Doesn't look like anything.

45″:　Could be two lions fighting over a piece of meat—or a fish—only I don't think lions eat fish.

Meat is whole center area, fish from tail at top. The lions are the two sides with the top lateral d as mane, heads in the shading, legs vaguely indicated in the usual "boots."

CARD V.
(60″)   13″:   Animals with humps in their backs—two rhinoceroses fighting—meeting head-on.   Legs in back and horns hitting in center—"usual" lateral figures.

CARD VI.
(59″):   Can't see anything in that one.

         42″:   A skinned animal, I guess.   Rejects idea of shading as contributing factor—would look same if traced. Describes paws, head, etc.

CARD VII.
(30″)   20″:   Looks like an atoll—a reefed atoll.   Island points and bay in the middle—an aerial map showing high cliffs, etc.

CARD VIII.
(30″)   10″:   Modernistic painting. (Lays card down, picks it up, lays it down again.)   "Just that silly" (i.e., as modern painting). They make a color combination with no contours to it.

CARD IX.
(120″)   35″:   Looks like two witches up on top. (Continues to study a long time.)   Long fingernails, peaked caps—seen from waist up. (Usual figures in orange, no indication of movement even in limit testing.)

CARD X.
(61″)   28″:   A couple of bugs of some kind, fighting over something.   Usual top gray.

A couple of—all that color! That looks like what a drunk sees at times—DT's. (*E.* "What a drunk sees?") "Yes."

Lizards; that is, green snakes.   P.

Pink elephants—face of a puppy, pink puppies I mean.   Usual profile in the pink.

Blue crabs, etc.   P. Bugs and lizards are going for something, some food, between them—the crabs are eating something.

SCORING

Card i:	$W \longrightarrow do$	FM	A	P
Card ii:	(CS) $\left.\begin{array}{l} W \\ D \end{array}\right\} W^b$	$M^r \longrightarrow FM$ Csym	A "Kiss"	$\longrightarrow P$ O^b
Card iii:	(CS) W	F, ⓜ	A	$\longrightarrow P$
Card iv:	$SS \left.\begin{array}{l} D \\ D \end{array}\right\} W^b$	$FM \mp$ F—	A Food $\longrightarrow$ A	$O \mp$
Card v:	W	FM	A	
Card vi:	SS W	F	Aobj	$\longrightarrow P$
Card vii:	W^v, S	kF	Geo	
Card viii:	CS W^v	C/F	Art	
Card ix:	(CS) D	F	(Hd)	

CARD X:	D		FM		A	
	(CS) W^v⎤		CF		A → (DT's)	O^v
	D ⎟		FC,	*FM*	A	P
	D ⎟		F ↔ C^b		Ad	O^b
	D ⎦		F ↔ C,	*FM*	A	P

DISCUSSION OF ENTRIES ON CHECK LIST FOR CASE A

W ...... Over 50% warrants a plus entry. Counting the bracketed W as main R helps both in the weighting of the quantitative W striving and in evaluation of the qualitative compromise the subject is prepared to make. (See Cards II and IV.) Actually this subject gives spontaneously only two fully independent D, in Cards IX and X, and is obviously dissatisfied with those. The examiner forced somewhat the specification in Card X. Thus an extra plus to the left is justified. By the formula, V plus twice B greater than 50%, the subject's record shows seven poor to eleven adequate W, definitely V. The entry is made the more confidently because none of the W is strikingly good, and even the popular W's are somewhat dubious. This comment is made because one might hesitate to consider the kissing elephants in Card II especially bad as *W*, whatever other reservations one might have about them. Without this b scoring, the subject would not quite rate a full entry.

P .... The subject's P responses are at the borderline. Indeed, of the three definite P, two were given after some slight forcing by the examiner in Card X, and one started out as a do. However, the tendencies to P suggest that the subject's difficulty does not lie in any basic inability to think along usual lines but in idiosyncratic modifications. Hence no entry for P.

O .... Scoring of O is dependent not only on experience but on type of experience. Doubtless other examiners would quarrel with our scoring here. The rather obvious O's (including vague but highly idiosyncratic responses like "DT's") are entered with the naïve remark 4"up." Up has the merit of being short. The

INSPECTION RORSCHACH RECORD BLANK

Name . *Case. A.* . . . . Date. *9/4/47.*

Sex. M .Age. 36 .Occupation . . *none.* . . . .

. . . . , ...

. . . .

Tabulation and Checklist. . . . .   Personality Description

Number of R		:	16
T/R		:	
Refusal		:	
LOCATION	W 11 (3∨2ℓ → 100%)	: +	+ ℬ
	Dd, d	:	
	S 0,1	:	
	Suc	:	
CONTENT	P, Com 3 P3 → P	:	
	O 4 up (2ℓ IV 1F)	:	B
	At, Sex O, 1? (heat from kiss)	:	
	Range O H/ d1OA/ d	:	
	struggle for food, eating	:	−Ht
FORM	F% 4 (1−)	:	U
	F (V,B,E)	:	
SHADING	S. Shock *delay − near refusal in*	:	
	IV, VI; IV ℓ −; VII k map	:	✓✓
	FK,Fc O	:	− −
	c	:	
	C'	:	
	K,k 1 k	:	
MOVEMENT	M 1 Mᵏ → FM	:	− r
	FM,M: FM 4 2	:	+ +
	m 1 (m)	:	
	Total M't 8	:	
COLOR	C. Shock *red II, III; vague +*	:	
	derogatory VIII, X, delay IX, 43% c.c.	:	✓✓
	FC 1FC 2F ↔ C (1ℓ)	:	−
	CF,FC: CF 1 c/F 1 CF	:	+
	C 1 c sym	:	
	Total C'r 6	:	+
Color: Movement 6 : 8		: +	
Total Number of checks		: 2	20

M:Sum C= 1:5
FM+m = 5:0
Fc+c+C'
R%(8,9,10)= 43

W%	D%	d%	DdS%
70	30		

W:M= 11:1
F%= 25%
Ref, F%= 25%
A%= 70%
A +H= 10:2
Ad + Hd

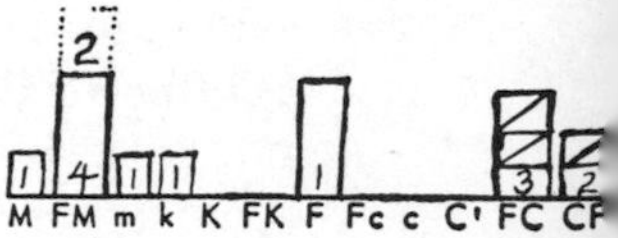

FIGURE 1. Rorschach Record filled in for Case A

conventional signs for greater than and less than ("$>$," "$<$,") seem to be confusing to many people; plus and minus have already been used in other connotations. For convenience we use the notation "up" or "dn" (i.e., "down") to indicate the direction of uncertainty.

The quality of this subject's originality is definitely poor, albeit often rather clever. (Caution: Where judgment of O is made so inclusive [i.e., including vague and peculiar concepts as well as clear O—], it has little relation to intelligence per se. We are skeptical about calculating intelligence from any listing of quantitative Rorschach data.)

Range ... A% a bit under 70 per cent warrants one minus (maybe one to the left if that were the outstanding problem). Only one (Hd) warrants another entry:H. Struggle for food (and eating, kissing) occurs in several responses and in significant places (Cards II, IV, DT's). A pronounced and quite characteristic oral theme (t) is suggested.

F% ...... By the scoring, F% is 25 per cent, too far above the cut-off point of 15 per cent to warrant even a minus to the left. An example of potential "oversubtlety" may be seen here. Actually the F in Cards III, VI, and IX appears to represent an active inhibition of the determinants usually involved in the responses given, rather than a primary interest in form such as underlies a genuine *F*. The F in Card IV is almost completely subservient to the fighting lions. On analysis it seems clear that the F trend is *very* weak, even taken in isolation. Nevertheless such analysis of the probable meaning of the specific F responses goes beyond "Rorschach common sense" into the realm of more subtle clinical appreciation—and as such may *not* determine relaxing standards as much as 10 points.

The U entry, however, is entirely justified. F% is on the low side, and other types of control (Fc, M, FC) all have minus entries. One may well wonder from the Rorschach how the subject manages any sort of effective adjustment, a question reinforced by the U entry. (The clinical history of this patient suggests that his adjustment is largely monetary. He can buy his way out of most jams and get "dried out" in decorous sanatoria.)

Shading
Shock ... Indicated on scoring sheet as *SS* in Cards IV and VI. Two near refusals with long delay and disturbed final responses, with an aerial map in Card VII, suggest very marked reaction ($\sqrt{}/\sqrt{}$).

Fc, FK... No response scorable as Fc, explicit rejection of the usual shading determinant in Card VI, no FK. (FK may sometimes be used in *borderline decisions* as a mitigating factor.) Since FC is also dubious, the double minus ($--$) is clearly warranted.

k........ By the instructions a single prominent k or K response warants a plus entry *in a very short protocol.*
    A full entry for a single relatively innocuous response has made us uneasy. Nevertheless we let it stand. In this case, as in practically all others we have encountered, anxiety of the "k" type is easily observable in other tests and/or in the clinical history. Doubtless this observation is due in part to the general prevalence of anxiety. Case A obviously tries to run away from anxiety, but there is a good deal of evidence that he does not altogether succeed and that he pushes anxiety off in a "k" manner.

M....... Subject does give one M, and therefore in a record so close to 15 R receives only one minus entry as regards quantity. Kissing elephants are a definitely poor version of human action. The entry "r" is conservative. Since absence of good H has already been entered, it seems sufficient in this case. (As mentioned above, a single poor M *may* be penalized more heavily.)

FM ..... Since M is only one, the absolute figures for FM apply. Four main and two "strong" additionals fall easily between the 5–8 FM classification. Hence the double plus entry ($++$).

Color
Shock ... The double entry here is not quite so clear as fo Shading Shock. In some instances several minor entries

(CS) on the scoring sheet may warrant only one entry. For this patient their regular recurrence, his open botheration, his failure to see the animals in Card VIII, the continuously forced or vague use of color, the moderate increase of responses in Card X, using color, all point to a quite intense and unsuccessful reactivity.

FC...... Only one FC is given (and that after slight forcing by E). Blue crabs and pink puppies, in fact even the green snakes, seem so secondary to the comment "All that color!" the order of determinants could so easily be reversed, turning the color scores into rather casual additions, that slight stretching of instructions is advisable. Hence a minus.

CF and C. Here again the protocol offers a good example of "desirable" judgment. If FC is entered as minus, a plus entry is routine. There are two W where color is clearly the main determinant. In this event the single Csym is merely confirmatory.

If, however, the examiner (let us say working "cold" from the scoring sheet) had decided to consider one FC and two F $\leftarrow$ $\rightarrow$ C as equivalent to two FC, then he would have the ratio 2CF:2FC—no entry. One C requires no entry. In such instances CF and C should at least be combined, so that total uncontrolled color would be three. Three such responses, coupled with the dubious look of the FC on the scoring sheet, would immediately suggest a review of the quality of the color answers. We think no one would argue that green lizard-snakes, even supported by blue crabs and pink elephant-puppies, offer enough evidence of adaptive emotional responsiveness to counterbalance the fact that as FC they are all part of DT's, plus silly modern art and the heat of an elephant's kiss as more direct evidence of uncontrolled use of color.

As in the example cited previously, the qualification for FC and CF *might* vary from zero to two entries, especially if the initial scoring were a bit pedantic and if the check list were handled on a purely arithmetical basis. From the angle of "Rorschach common sense" there is no problem at all.

Total

Color.... Where 37% of the responses use color one way or another, the plus entry is mandatory.

Color

Movement 6:8 does not meet the criterion of color equal to movement, hence no main entry. It is close enough to suggest an entry to the left.

USE OF THE CHECK LIST IN THE INTERPRETATION OF CASE A

1. The total score suggests serious psychopathology. The score should *never* supersede the judgment of the examiner in interpretation. When it is so high, however, the examiner should review his evidence carefully before discounting psychopathology.

2. For illustrative purposes let us simply read down the check list. It is noted that the patient's responses are meager in number, and that he has a strong W drive, although his W are often of poor quality. His original contributions are poor, although he shows adequate capacity to think along commonly accepted lines. He shows further a high A%, virtual absence of H, and marked themata (fight for food). F% (U) suggests definitely insufficient control. Pronounced shading and color shock suggest deep-seated neurotic trends. M is low and of poor quality, FM and CF are high with very poor resources of the Fc and FC variety. With a plus for color and no entry for movement, and a marginal plus for color: movement, the general picture is extratensive. High FM, no shading, and low, poor M (a) confirm the picture of a person likely to act out his problems and (b) suggest that his introversial capacities are likely to be at a pretty immature level. W:M ratio is obviously badly disturbed even if one merely considers the entries plus for W and minus for M, but the scores 11 W to 1 M are easily visible. There is some k.

These are the items which probably any examiner would pull out of the tabulation or psychogram, plus a quick look at essential qualitative data. In full interpretation, of course, the examiner on the one hand considers much more carefully the interrelationships among these items. He also studies the content and sequence of responses for finer shades of meaning and for such idiosyncratic performance as may occasionally escape quantification along the usual lines altogether. The check list offers some guarantee that important general data have not been overlooked.

INSPECTION RORSCHACH RECORD BLANK

Name. . . . . .Date. . . . . . .

Sex. . .Age. . . .Occupation . . . .

. . . .

. . . .

Tabulation and Checklist. . . . .   **Personality Description**

		:	
Number of R		:	
T/R		:	
Refusal		:	
LOCATION	W	:	
	Dd, d	:	
	S	:	
	Suc	:	
CONTENT	P, Com	:	
	O	:	
	At, Sex	:	
	Range H d A d	:	
		:	
FORM	F%	:	
	F (V,B,E)	:	
SHADING	S. Shock	:	
		:	
	FK,Fc	:	
	c	:	
	C'	:	
	K,k	:	
MOVEMENT	M	:	
	FM,M: FM	:	
	m	:	
	Total M't	:	
COLOR	C. Shock	:	
		:	
	FC	:	
	CF,FC: CF	:	
	C	:	
	Total C'r	:	
Color: Movement		:	
Total Number of checks		:	

M:Sum C=
FM + m =
$\overline{Fc+c+C'}$
R%(8,9,10)=

W%	D%	d%	DdS%

W:M =
F% =
Ref, F% =
A% =
$\dfrac{A+H=}{Ad+Hd}$

M FM m k K FK F Fc c C' FC CF C

FIGURE 2. Inspection Rorschach Record Blank

EXPLANATORY NOTE FOR THE RECORD BLANK

The principal aim of this record sheet is flexibility in serving the multiple purposes of the Inspection Rorschach. The layout of the page has been designed to permit systematic recording in blank areas of any material, quantitative or qualitative, with which the examiner may wish to supplement the codified data.

Printed instructions have been kept to a minimum on the assumption that anyone using the record sheet is thoroughly familiar both with the Inspection Rorschach instructions and with the Klopfer-Davidson Individual Record Blank.

(a) The Inspection Rorschach proper consists only of the check list. Formal entries are to be made according to the Instructions in the column to the right of the check-list box, marginal entries within the dotted line just to the left of this column.

(b) Tabulation of scores in detail according to usual Rorschach practice may be made in the space between the scoring categories and the column for entries. The only major omission is for content, here represented only by H, Hd, A, Ad, At, and Sex. Write-in space has been allowed under "Range" for other noteworthy items.

(c) Items from the Klopfer-Davidson blank not clearly visible on the check list are appended for the convenience of examiners who may wish to supplement check list and tabulation with these further data.

No special format for a scoring sheet is supplied. A blank sheet of paper seems on the whole more convenient, with the scores arranged by eye in the usual columns. The experienced examiner will space the common initial score WFAP so as to allow for possible additional determinants in later responses. For the more detailed scoring recommended for the check list, extra space should be allowed between the main scoring items so that these may appear in easily distinguishable columns.

REFERENCES

1. DAVIDSON, H.: *Personality and Economic Background: A Study of Highly Intelligent Children.* New York: King's Crown Press; 1943.
2. MUNROE, R.: "An Experiment in Large-scale Testing by a Modifi-

cation of the Rorschach Method," *Journal of Psychology*, Vol. 13 (1942), pp. 229–630.

3. ——: "The Inspection Technique," *Rorschach Research Exchange*, Vol. 8 (1944), pp. 46–70.

4. ——: "Prediction of Adjustment and Academic Performance of College Students by a Modification of the Rorschach Method," *Applied Psychology Monographs*, No. 7 (1945).

5. ROE, A.: "Painting and Personality," *Rorschach Research Exchange*, Vol. 10 (1946), pp. 86–100.

6. ——: "A Rorschach Study of a Group of Scientists and Technicians," *Journal of Consulting Psychology*, Vol. 10 (1946), pp. 317–27.

THIS chapter makes available to us an important body of information relative to the application of the Group Rorschach Test and the Multiple-Choice Rorschach Test in a variety of testing situations. Dr. M. R. Harrower's paper suggests quite clearly the extent to which the Rorschach Test, as a group procedure, finds application in clinical, military, educational, personnel, and industrial settings. In addition she provides a critical review of the value and limitations not only of the Group Rorschach Test but also of the more controversial Multiple-Choice Rorschach Test.

Just as there has been a trend in recent years toward the development of group psychotherapy as the need for such a service has greatly increased, so too the development and applications of the Rorschach Test or some modification for use with groups represent a growing conviction that there are many situations in which the employment of the Group Rorschach Test or the Multiple-Choice Rorschach Test is fully justified.

▼

Group Techniques for the Rorschach Test

M. R. Harrower

DESCRIPTION OF GROUP METHODS: GROUP RORSCHACH TEST AND MULTIPLE-CHOICE TEST

IT IS almost ten years now since the first tentative tampering with the sacrosanct Rorschach Method resulted in the Group Rorschach Techniques. In the course of these years group administration has become an orthodox and accepted procedure so that it is hard to recapture the skepticism, and in some cases hostility, which greeted its appearance, or to realize the atmosphere that made necessary the punctiliously detailed and careful accounting for every step taken in its development, together with the rather rigid standardization of instructions and procedure.

As is now common knowledge, the Group Rorschach Technique involves presentation of the Rorschach blots in the form of slides in a semidarkened room, which may accommodate, provided all seats are centrally located, as many as several hundred persons. A three-minute time interval is allotted for presentation of each slide, and the subjects write down a full description of the things they see in the blot. Following the initial presentation the slides are repeated to allow for various types of inquiries, depending on the preferences of the examiner.

As might be expected, the types of response vary from those which are monosyllabic and without amplification to full-page descriptions of a single percept. Further, these responses exhibit good and poor form, rich and expressive movement, as well as blatant and unrestricted use of color and the various reactions to shading. And while many investigators have embarked on this new method with some feelings of misgiving and even skepticism, they have found that in this respect the Rorschach is foolproof. If the test is properly conducted, material for diagnostic evaluation will be available.

A detailed account of the instructions for administration, together with those for the inquiry, will be found in my original publication *Large Scale Rorschach Techniques [13]*. In the light of many years' experience, however, I now feel that stereotyped instructions are of very little use, and anyone well acquainted with the Rorschach method who has frequently administered it individually will find that in presenting it to different groups he will do much better to address the group spontaneously, explaining the procedure without reference to any published or "correct" instructions. To a large extent the successful presentation of the group method, as indeed of the individual method, depends upon a proper rapport between the experimenter and his subjects, between the psychologist and his patients. The handling of groups is different from the handling of an individual, and any administrator of the Group Technique should think primarily in terms of establishing a good group relationship.

While at this stage it seems clear that considerable leeway should be allowed in terms of the instructions, and also, to my way of thinking, in the type of inquiry pursued, a rather rigid standardization has been maintained in regard to the slides that have been available for group presentation. For the last seven years these slides have been made by an expert photographer, Dr. M. E. Diemer. Considering the great difficulties that arose in getting reliable film during the war years, the uniformity and excellence of his production have been extraordinary. With a few exceptions the sets of slides have not differed one from the other to a greater degree than various editions of the Rorschach cards differ from one another.

While the question of uniformity in the type of booklet used by subjects for writing their responses is obviously of much less importance than the standardized slides, we have for the last five years utilized a booklet which had, as perhaps its main feature, rather unusually detailed and carefully shaded black-white representations of the blots for locating the responses. For convenience, Munroe's excellent check list [22] is included on the back page of this booklet.[1]

Essentially the same material, then, is available to the examiner as the result of the Group Method of presentation as is available to him through the individual method if he has conducted his group procedure successfully. With this material he may proceed as with gross screening by merely scanning the record for the most obviously disturbed performances [1, 13]. Or, as Munroe has so ably demonstrated, with her check list he can introduce an intermediate type of scanning and scoring whereby certain outstanding features of the performance can be rapidly assessed without the mechanics of the complete evaluation. But there is nothing to prevent the examiner from scoring the record in the traditional manner, whatever his orientation, and proceeding with the differentiated evaluation on the basis of the detailed scoring.

If the Group Rorschach procedure was greeted with raised eyebrows, the introduction of the Multiple-Choice Test [13] met with an even colder reception. It is well, therefore, to emphasize here that this test is not described as a variation of the Rorschach technique but as a different type of test. Clearly it would have been better for all concerned if this test could have been put out as a new procedure with an alternative set of ink blots. This, however, was not possible at that time. The Multiple-Choice Test can be given in group form or individually. Since our concern here,

---

[1] To avoid confusion, which still occurs, it might be well to state that I am not concerned with the sale of the slides or booklets, nor is Dr. Diemer. These are handled exclusively by the Psychological Corporation, New York City.

however, is with group techniques, it will be described as though presented in a group situation. In this case, therefore, the Rorschach slides are thrown on a screen, but the subject, instead of writing down his various impressions, chooses from a list of thirty possible choices those three which most nearly approximate his own perception of the particular blot. While we have freely admitted that this is not Rorschach's procedure, and while the final form of this test has probably not yet been devised, it none the less has certain undeniable advantages, not over and against the Rorschach but as a procedure in its own right.

The obvious difference here between the checking of answers and the recording of spontaneous impressions is to eliminate all detailed Rorschach and psychological knowledge on the part of the mechanical scorer so that the assessing of several hundred or even several thousand records becomes a technical possibility that can be accomplished in a relatively short time. As will be discussed later, various investigators have now reached the point where the Multiple-Choice answers have been transposed to IBM scoring sheets, so that we are on the verge of the time when statistically valid handling of age levels, of professional groups, and of various psychopathological entities can be collected. It was, of course, under precisely the pressure of screening demands in wartime that this particular test procedure was devised. There was a need for a machine-scored variant of Rorschach's method, and the Multiple Choice, for better or for worse, was offered in this capacity. Time did not allow the selection of responses by statistical means. A survey of the records obtained by me over a period of several years was utilized to select, for every given card, fifteen answers occurring with noticeable frequency in the records of well-adjusted individuals and fifteen answers drawn from the records of individuals with various types of psychopathology. Thus an individual's score on the test is assessed in terms of the number of times he spontaneously picks choices that have been drawn from "normal" records and the number of times he picks answers that have been drawn from the psychopathological group.

I have suggested as an appropriate "cutting point" those cases in which more than forty per cent of responses are equated with those which have been given by various types of disturbed individuals.

It is highly probable that the least valuable aspect of the test is its amenability to machine scoring. As the examiner himself becomes more immersed in the whole principle underlying projective techniques, he becomes able to utilize at its face value the meaning and significance of any answer or constellation of answers.

To illustrate this, the thirty answers to Rorschach's well-known Card II are listed below:

A

A bug somebody stepped on
Nothing at all
Two Scotty dogs
Little faces on the sides
A bloody spinal column
A white top
A bursting bomb
Two elephants
Two clowns
Red and black ink

B

An animal skin
Two bears rubbing noses
Faces of Indians on the side
Blood
Nothing at all
A white lamp
An exploding firecracker
A red butterfly
Two people playing pat-a-cake
Red and black splotches

C

Two witches
Black and red paint
Bears' heads
An empty hole
Faces carved in stone
Lungs and blood
A white sting ray
A little temple in the center
Nothing at all
An erupting volcano

Let us look at three very different choices made by individuals, A, B, and C. These choices are as follows. A's are given first:

A bursting bomb
Red and black ink
Blood
Black and red paint
An empty hole
Lungs and blood
An erupting volcano

B's choices run as follows:

Nothing at all
Two bears rubbing noses
Two witches

C's choices run thus:

Two clowns
Two bears rubbing noses
Two people playing pat-a-cake
Two witches
A red butterfly

Subject A was tested by four other psychological techniques, including the full Rorschach, a drawing of human figures, an analysis of handwriting, and the Wechsler-Bellevue Test. A full study of this material indicated an acute psychotic episode. The subject was diagnosed both through the test battery and by psychiatric interview as having an acute schizophrenia, paranoid type. On detailed testing, subject B showed initial color shock on the full Rorschach and some neurotic anxiety, which, however, was in no way incapacitating. Subject C was a "normal" worker in the clinic with superior scores on the Wechsler-Bellevue and an all-round personality rating on detailed psychological testing of "excellent."

Due, Wright, and Wright, in their sections in *Large Scale Rorschach Techniques* [13], have given ample evidence of the extent to which the Multiple-Choice Test can be used for differential diagnosis.

A description of the two group techniques having been given, let us now turn to a survey of their various uses in different fields.

THE USE OF GROUP TECHNIQUES IN INDUSTRY

The following quotation from Steiner *[24]* may serve as an introduction to this section:

> During the last ten years industry has become increasingly interested in psychological testing. Though countless opinions, both pro and con, have been expressed concerning the value of such programs, those experimenting with tests have considered results helpful in supplementing information derived from the interview, the application blank, and other sources. For the most part industrial testing programs have included personality tests of the questionnaire type, possibly because they are easily administered, quickly scored, and require little specialized training for interpretation. At this time, however, when personnel workers are becoming aware of the shortcomings of most personality tests of the questionnaire type, when periodicals are lauding results obtained by the use of the Rorschach method, and when more psychologists are receiving Rorschach training, occupational investigations utilizing this projective technique comparable in number to those in the clinical field will undoubtedly be forthcoming.

As representative of accomplishments in this field, the conclusions of Steiner *[25]*, after a four-year period of experimentation and investigation in the General Electric Company, and that of Cox *[8]* in Canada, will be presented.

Steiner's most recent findings, based upon an investigation of 920 Group Rorschach records, allow for some interesting comparisons to be made between the different occupational groups that she was able to test: contrasting engineers, clerical personnel, advertising copywriters, and commercial artists. She draws the following conclusions from her very adequate sample:

"*Engineers.*—The group records show a high W% emphasizing the more abstract forms of thinking and indicating good synthetic ability. There is also evidenced good analytic ability, and in some instances concern with the more routine features of the task. In general, human movement responses are few, although with the more recent graduates a greater incidence of M responses has been found. The F% is high though normal, indicating good refined control. Although there are few color answers, the FC to CF ratio is in favor of the form-color type of response, as is found in the college-age group of subjects previously investigated.

"*Clerical Personnel.*—The records for the clerical personnel show a low W%, a high D and d, and dd plus S. There is a decrease (as compared with the other group) in the use of human movement responses. FM responses are twice as frequently given as are the M's. Control is high but normal, and there is good emotional responsiveness, FC being equal to CF.

"*Advertising Copywriters.*—Copywriters show an emphasis on the abstract and an average concern with the practical. The most striking characteristic of this group is the high incidence of M's. The originality of the responses, the high productivity, the sensitivity, the tendency toward introspection, and the considerable tension are other features that differentiate this group. The F% is lower for this group than for all other occupational groups. There is average responsiveness to the environment.

"*Commercial Artists.*—The outstanding features in the records of the commercial artists are: the great number of responses, many of them original; an emphasis on the W (though not an overemphasis, as found by other investigators); an average concern with large details, but an overemphasis on rare details. The F% is high but normal; the M's outnumber the FM's; Fc and c responses are plentiful, while—and this is an important deviation from the other groups—CF responses are twice as frequently given as are FC's."

In my opinion such studies emphasize the most valuable use of the Group Rorschach Technique. Where group characteristics are to be elicited, where a minimum disruption in a program is important, and where sufficiently large numbers must be handled in order to give significance to the results, group presentation becomes almost a necessity.

Steiner's general conclusions in regard to industrial personnel are summarized as follows:

A general over-all comparison of industrial personnel with non-industrial personnel leads to the conclusion that the former show a strikingly higher level of tension.

Steiner's earlier published findings [24] also deserve comment at this point. Group records obtained from 144 subjects and follow-up investigations a year later provide evidence for the type of predictive hypotheses that are possible through the group procedure. On the basis of group records with both the Rorschach and Harrower blots *[12]*, these subjects were assigned an over-all personality rating ranging from excellent to poor. Table 3 exemplifies the findings in this instance. The tetrachoric coefficient of correlation, not published by Steiner, is .93.

TABLE 3
Personality Ratings of Industrial Workers

PERSONALITY RATING	NUMBER	SATISFACTORY ADJUSTMENT TO WORK	POOR ADJUSTMENT TO WORK
Excellent			
Above average	109	97% (106)	3% (3)
Average			
Poor	35	29% (10)	71% (25)

Tetrachoric coefficient of correlation = .93

Steiner has also utilized the Multiple-Choice Test in the industrial situation with similar kinds of predictive reports and followup studies a year later to determine the degree of adjustment. Her findings in this instance are epitomized in Table 4. She finds the tendency of a Multiple-Choice Test score with less than 50 per cent of poor answers to be associated with satisfactory adjustment to work, and a Multiple-Choice Test of more than 50 per cent of poor responses to be associated with poor adjustment to work. The tetrachoric coefficient of correlation in this instance is .89.

TABLE 4
Multiple-Choice Rorschach Responses of Industrial Workers

PERCENTAGE OF POOR RESPONSES	NUMBER	SATISFACTORY ADJUSTMENT	POOR ADJUSTMENT
Less than 50% of poor responses	201	95% (191)	5% (10)
50% or more of poor responses	29	34% (10)	66% (19)

Tetrachoric coefficient of correlation = .89

In a recent paper *[8]*, K. A. Cox writes of the use of the Multiple-Choice Test with department-store sales personnel:

"It is our belief that the Harrower Multiple-Choice Test could be used industrially if criteria were established which would divide employees into the high-rating and low-rating groups, against which an item analysis could be carried out to discover the items that differentiate. When these items are discovered, one can then build up personality pictures based upon the responses as to what type of personalities the high-raters and low-raters possess. Such data should be obtained in terms of local situations, as even within another branch of the same company such test items may not differentiate, since it has been found that questionnaires may work very well in one branch and will not work in another. This leads one to believe that tests must be set up in terms of a specific branch of the company, a phenomenon that warrants further investigation by those trained in social psychology and familiar with the industrial setting."

As will be discussed in another section, some of the discrepancy in the findings of investigators who have used the Multiple-Choice Test in its original form may be related to this factor. Lawshe and Forster [18], for example, have called attention to the fact that significant sex differences in score distribution and item selection reveal the need for different male and female scoring keys.

The use of projective techniques in industry is quite clearly only in its infancy. The studies of Steiner and Cox are undoubtedly the forerunners of many and extensive investigations. The challenge that industry offers is enormous. Some of the areas of much-needed research have been highlighted by Williams [26] in the following statement:

> Personalities are more complicated than materials and products, more intricate than the most complex machine ever constructed. To discover how that complicated personality, with its delicate interplay of intellectual and emotional factors, will react to a given job situation with its unique strains and stresses requires much serious research.

THE USE OF GROUP TECHNIQUES IN THE HOSPITAL OR CLINICAL SETTING

The average hospital or clinical setting affords fewer opportunities for group administration of projective techniques than does, for example, the industrial or educational field. None the less, it has seemed pertinent to include here the results of large-scale investigations, particularly that of Wittman [28], for while in this instance the patients were tested individually, the number of her subjects, 4,305, renders her results highly significant.

Wittman's study is based on 3,150 psychotic patients, 883 attendants, 172 professional adults, and 100 teen-age Girl Scouts. A brief summary of her findings is given in Table 5.

TABLE 5

Mean Scores on Multiple-Choice Rorschach for Different Types of Subject

TYPE OF SUBJECT	NO. OF CASES	NO. OF PATHOLOGICAL RESPONSES MEAN SCORES
1. Extramural controls	1,156	2.5
2. Paranoid behavior reactions	307	3.1
3. Patients without psychosis	386	3.6
4. Organic behavior reactions	450	3.8
5. Affective behavior reactions	264	4.0
6. Constitutional behavior reactions	86	4.2
7. Schizophrenic behavior reactions	641	5.8

A more detailed analysis, with a breakdown for each subgroup, is given in Table 6.

TABLE 6

Percentage of Subjects in Each Subgroup with Pathologically Significant Scores

	NO. OF CASES	PERCENTAGE PATHOLOGICALLY SIGNIFICANT
Schizophrenic behavior reactions:		
Hebephrenia	111	91.5
Simple	63	84.0
Catatonic	136	71.5
Undetermined	331	65.3
Paranoid behavior reactions:		
Paranoid (dementia præcox)	197	34.1
Paranoid state	110	31.3
Affective behavior reactions:		
Manic	112	46.9
Depressive	98	56.3
Mixed	54	73.7

TABLE 6 *(cont.)*

	NO. OF CASES	PERCENTAGE PATHOLOGICALLY SIGNIFICANT
Organic behavior reactions:		
Syphilitic meningo-encephalitic	193	55.6
Senile and cerebral arteriosclerotics	143	29.2
Organic brain diseases	78	46.7
Epileptics	36	71.9
Primary constitutional behavior reactions:		
Feeble-minded	24	81.9
Psychopathic personalities	62	54.0
Patients classified without psychosis:		
Psychoneurotics	217	58.9
Adult maladjustments	57	61.3
Chronic alcoholics	72	26.6
Extramural controls:		
Hospital attendants	883	27.1
High-school Girl Scouts	100	25.0
Professional adults	172	16.6

Discussing Table 5, Wittman says:

The schizophrenic patients have the poorest showing, and hence rank at the bottom of the list. Then come the constitutional and affective behavior reactions, followed by the organic and the patients without psychosis, the paranoid, and the extramural subjects in that order. Certainly the most significant finding is the position of one of the psychotic groups, the paranoid, ranking in one of the top positions and superior to the group of patients diagnosed as those without psychosis. Another important finding is the definitely poor level of the schizophrenic group. We have found these extremely different types of reactions for the schizophrenic and paranoid groups to be of definite value in diagnostic aid.

Concerning Table 6, Wittman writes:

The hebephrenic præcox do by far the poorest of any of the groups, with 91.5 per cent answers of pathological significance. The simple præcox also do poorly as a group. The catatonic and undetermined types have relatively poor scores, although not so poor as the feeble-minded cases that are classified in the group of constitutional behavior reactions . . . these rather inconclusive findings for the catatonic and undetermined types are possibly merely a reflection of the lack of homogeneity among the cases so classified, resulting from the indefiniteness and looseness of these diagnostic concepts. The so-called paranoid schizophrenics stand out from the other schizophrenics in dramatic fashion.

Wittman's discussion and conclusions in relation to this large study are perhaps the most thoughtful contribution to the whole problem of what it is that actually is measured by the Multiple-Choice Test. Her suggestion is that the test measures "a type of inner adjustment which might be labeled personality integration." Her suggestions are given below in full.

There are differences shown on the Multiple-Choice Test[2] between psychotic and nonpsychotic subjects, but even more between certain psychotic types. This suggests that the scale does measure some psychological factor or component. Since there are greater differences between psychotic types than the difference between psychotic and "normal" noninstitutionalized controls, however, the primary factor differentiated by the scale is not the presence or absence of psychopathology. But analysis of the data does give evidence that the scale may be a valid instrument for measuring type rather than degree of adjustment. Those patients with a passive or regressive type of adjustment extreme enough to be considered pathological do very poorly. On the other hand, those subjects making psychologically a compensatory type of adjustment are not differentiated from the "normal" or nonpsychotic subject on the basis of the scale results. Observation of the present levels of adjustment of both intra- and extra-mural groups, and study of social-service histories of the intramural groups, have suggested that this type of inner adjustment evaluated by the Multiple-Choice Test is something that might be labeled "personality integration."

The term "personality integration" as I use it implies an intrapersonal harmony of those components making up the personality as it affects the inner adjustments of the individual—that is, the degree to which the individual accepts and relates together his motivations, interests, attitudes, and all the other compo-

---

[2] Wittman has referred to the Multiple-Choice Test in her article as the "Harrower-Erickson Rorschach." To avoid confusion, however, I have substituted "Multiple-Choice Test" in quoting her.

nents making up the concept of personality. With this understanding of the term I should say that the typical paranoid patient has a good personality integration, since his lack of adjustment is not within himself but between his well-integrated self and other individuals. The schizophrenic, on the other hand, is poorly integrated, since his conflict is not between himself and others but rather between the various components of his own personality. These explanations fit into the concept of schizophrenic behavior reaction as a regressive mechanism and the paranoid as a compensatory type of reaction.

I empirically interpret the Multiple-Choice Test findings to indicate the degree of personality for the following reasons:

1. Degree of personality integration is the most significant trait that differentiates those schizophrenic groups that do very poorly on the Multiple-Choice Test from the other groups.

2. Dissociation and lack of contact with reality are also factors affecting personality integration, and these factors also differentiate the groups at either extreme of test results.

3. A negative argument to thinking of the Multiple-Choice Test scale results as a measure of emotional adjustment or stability is obtained from the data for the cases diagnosed psychoneurotic or adult maladjustment. Certainly these are very poorly adjusted emotionally as a group—so poorly, in fact, that they have become inmates of a state hospital. The scale findings, however, do not classify the majority of cases as poor. Although emotional stability for psychoneurotic and maladjustment cases would be expected to be poor, their test results are variable.

4. If we postulate differences in type as well as differences in degree of personality integration, this will explain the extreme differences in test results found among psychoneurotic and the psychopathic groups.

It is possible that certain psychoneurotic and psychopathic behavior reactions may be best understood as active compensatory reactions, while others are of a passive, regressive nature. A preliminary study of the psychoneurotic and psychopathic cases at either extreme, so far as their Multiple-Choice Test results are concerned, appears to support this hypothesis. That is, those individuals with good scores present a type of behavior reaction that is compensatory, while those with poor scores show a regressive type of behavior. It would seem that the neurotic or psychopathic patient whose behavior reaction is mediated by a type of compensation is unable to adjust to his external environment. He projects conflicts out onto other people, or onto the mores of the group, but he does not experience inner conflict. In other words, he does not lack personality integration, although it is not a "normal" type of integration but a compensating type. He has integrated his drives and their underlying motivations to his own satisfaction, but not in a manner conducive to adjustment or conformity with the group.

The psychoneurotics and psychopaths who have definitely poor Multiple-Choice Test scores seem in general to lack personality integration. They are not able to co-ordinate their drives and methods of expressing these drives, and the resultant conflict within themselves may produce a type of maladaptive behavior of either a neurotic or a psychopathic type. Instead of rationalizing their own conflicts and projecting them outward upon others in a compensatory way, they develop a passive and regressive type of behavior reactions.

Thus it may be possible to differentiate the psychoneurotic or psychotic individual whose difficulties in adjusting are due to inner conflicts and a lack of personality integration resulting in asocial, passive, and avoiding reactions from those whose behavior reactions are associated with a compensatory, defensive mechanism that expresses itself outwardly in an active, antisocial way.

5. If the Multiple-Choice Rorschach can be considered a projective technique, then we might expect that the individual with a regressive type of behavior reaction who is poorly integrated and out of touch with reality would be unable to see the well-organized, good-form responses to the Rorschach cards. On the other hand, the compensatingly well-integrated person, being both in contact with reality and without dissociation, picks out a proportion of movement and good form responses, and popular responses that yield a satisfactory score on the Multiple-Choice Test.

A second published study on the Multiple-Choice Test, done in conjunction with members of the department of student health at a university clinic [15], is included for the light that it throws on several factors. The 308 entering students at a university summer school were examined as part of the routine medical examination by the Multiple-Choice Test. Five or more poor answers, when appearing as first choices, were considered the criterion for screening.

Using this "cutting point," seventy-nine students, or 26 per cent of the total group, fell into this category. These seventy-nine students were called in for a psychiatric interview, and during this interview the Multiple-Choice Test was repeated.

As a result of the repetition a very clear distinction was found between persons who continued to give poor answers and those whose records improved on the second presentation. The duplication of a poor score was shown to correlate highly with a diagnosis based on the psychiatric interview. Of the twenty-two individuals who repeated a poor score, twenty-one (or 95 per cent) were rated by a psychiatrist as having some significant psychopathology. These twenty-one were taken for treatment during the course of the semester. Psychiatric diagnoses are listed below:

Incipient schizophrenia	3
Anxiety tension state	5
Narcissistic regression pattern	1
Adolescent reaction	3
Psychopathic personality (schizoid)	1
Psychopathic personality (paranoid)	2
Menopausal syndrome	1
Compulsive obsessive neurosis	1
Diagnosis deferred	3
Mentally dull	1
Total	21
Normal	1

From among these students, fifty-eight improved on the repeat test. Of these, thirty-nine (or 67 per cent) were considered normal on psychiatric interview. However, 33 per cent were diagnosed as having some psychopathology.

The screening-out of these individuals at the beginning of the semester was felt by the psychiatric staff to have been ample justification for the experimental study, in that difficulties were caught early in the session and systematic therapy could be initiated.

In addition to this practical contribution the program raised some questions of theoretical interest.

1. "False positives" were found to occur in individuals who had recently experienced serious physical illness, or, let us say, a somewhat legitimate preoccupation with the body. This, giving rise to frequent anatomical answers, was found to result from recent invalidism.

2. The menstrual period brought unsuspected and challenging findings. Administered at a different time of the month, the test indicates that many anatomical answers disappear from the records.

3. What might be called "situational anxiety"—that is, the fear that the medical examination per se might disqualify them for some reason—was found to be reflected in the initial records, but was absent in the repeat performances.

The most important findings of this study are clearly that it is possible in situations where time and psychiatric help are limited to isolate persons with serious psychological disturbances in order that their problems may be handled as efficaciously as possible and without undue delay.

The need to repeat the Multiple-Choice Test is not only of practical importance; it also raises the whole issue of whether or not the findings of any projective technique are significant if they occur at an isolated instance in time. It is highly significant that Szondi, whose test is one of rapid administration and scoring, has insisted that it is the pattern of ten test performances that can be considered diagnostic, whereas a single presentation may be highly misleading. It has seemed to me that largely because of the cumbersomeness of the original Rorschach Test the assumption has grown up that the personality picture of an individual, John Doe, on January 1, 1950 is for better or for worse the picture of John Doe into eternity. Longitudinal studies rather than cross-sectional studies are possible, however, with such an instrument as the Multiple-Choice Test and may, in the last analysis, prove to be its particular contribution to the study of personality.

Use of the Group Rorschach Test in medical research may be exemplified by the work of Brozek, Guetzkow, and Ancel Keys [4]. In the "Study of Personality of Normal Young Men Maintained on Restricted Intakes of Vitamins of the B Complex," the Group Rorschach records along with the Minnesota Multiphasic Personality Inventory, self-ratings, man-to-man ratings, and the Cattell Cursive Miniature Situations Test were utilized. The procedure employed and the results obtained were as follows:

The Group Rorschach Test was given three times: at the beginning of the partial restriction, at its end, and at the termination of the acute deficiency. The procedure for group testing was employed; instead of using photographic reproductions, however, actual Rorschach cards were used. The responses were recorded by the subjects on the Group Rorschach blanks, which later were sent to me for analysis. The records were scored according to the system utilized by Klopfer, and the usual calculations were made in full for each record. Personality descriptions of the individuals, based on the three successive records, were then written. In the Results below, passages taken from these original descriptions are italicized. At no time did I have personal contact with the subjects, nor was their nutritional status known to me when the original reports were made.

RESULTS

Work has been done on the effect of repeating the Rorschach which enables us to distinguish the effects due to repetition as contrasted with changes due to other causes. For example, repetition produces almost invariably an increase in the total number of responses. Therefore it is not surprising to find that all eight subjects, regardless of their nutritional status, had a larger number of responses in their second record. Taking into account the uniform changes, we may ask whether successive records indicate alterations in personality. The records will be discussed in pairs with the men grouped according to their nutritional status.

Jo and *N* (supplemented-supplemented): The subjects who were supplemented during both the partial restriction and the acute deficiency had different personality structures, as reflected in the initial Rorschach. *Jo's record was relatively good; N's* record was poor. The three tests of *N* showed no essential change. In this case the personality pattern did not improve during the six-months period of relatively good nutrition. The second record of *Jo*, on the other hand, improved slightly, the original tenseness and lack of spontaneity being lessened. In the third record a still more positive attitude toward the environment appeared.

Ja and *S* (supplemented-deficient): In both *Ja* and *S* the second record showed an improvement, while the third record of subject *S* indicated that the twenty-two days of adverse nutritional conditions did not introduce any significant change in the Rorschach responses. The third record of subject *Ja* could not be obtained.

Wa and *T* (restricted-supplemented): These men presented very different personality patterns at the start. *Wa's* first record was not a very satisfactory one; the record of *T* was better. In the case of *Wa*, a negative change occurred in the period of partial restriction. In the second record *he was driving himself with a tight rein, being more puntilious and paying greater attention to detail, showing more anxiety and less spontaneity.* The third record showed some relaxation of the tension. The same does not hold for subject *T*, whose three records were similar.

Wi and *G* (restricted-deficient): In the case of *Wi* there was a change between the initial and final records. The third record indicated *considerably more constriction, as though the individual were having to watch his step more carefully or were combating some difficult situation.* This tendency was already indicated in *Wi's* second record. The second and third records of *G* also reflected negative change, conscious control having been slightly increased. In *G's* second and third records an *increased preoccupation with bodily sensations* appeared.

The Rorschach test provided evidence of slight changes, paralleling the slight increases in the resting level of pyruvate acid, which was taken as a specific indication of borderline dietary deficiency in the group on low vitamin intake. The fact that the Rorschach analyses were made "blindly," without knowledge of the subjects' nutritional status, increases confidence in the results. It is methodologically important that these slight changes did not have a counterpart in the data obtained by the questionnaire-type procedures—that is, the Multiphasic and the self-ratings, which demand awareness of the changes.

SUMMARY

1. Various aspects of personality were studied in eight normal young men maintained 161 days on a partially restricted intake of B-complex vitamins, which was followed by twenty-three days of acute deficiency and ten days of thiamine supplementation.

2. Self-ratings and man-to-man ratings gave no evidence of change in the status of well-being and adjustment during the partial restriction, but indicated consistent and striking deterioration during the acute deficiency. Supplementation of the diet by thiamine' alone produced rapid recovery.

3. The Minnesota Multiphasic Personality Inventory also gave no evidence of change in the partial restriction. During the acute deficiency significant changes were obtained in the scores on the three psychoneurotic scales—depression, hysteria, and hypochondriasis.

4. In the Rorschach Test records made at the end of the partial restriction, slight deteriorative changes were indicated in three out of the four experimental subjects. These changes increased in magnitude in the pair of subjects placed subsequently on the acutely deficient diet. The nature of this deterioration was loss of spontaneity with an increase in tension. The Rorschach findings suggested that individuals with "better" initial personality were better able to resist the dietary stress.

5. During the partial restriction Cattell's Cursive Miniature Situations Test indicated a very slight and statistically *not* significant increase in the number of lines erroneously crossed ("emotionality" score). During the acute deficiency there were evidences of further increased "emotionality" and "timidity." On the other hand, those indices which have distinguished psychotics from normals showed no change in our deficient subjects.

6. The personality changes were among the earliest symptoms of the experimentally produced borderline and acute deficiencies.

THE USE OF GROUP TECHNIQUES IN EDUCATION

My original studies with the group test [13], although embarked on primarily with a view to establishing procedures and norms for a new method, netted in addition some information in regard to the students who were subjects when a comparison of their test records, academic performance, and general adjustment in college was obtainable. Utilizing general over-all personality ratings of the type subsequently employed by Steiner and Abt and previously used for the individual method by Munroe, I examined 108 students who were estimated in terms of a scale including excellent, above average, average, just below average, poor, and very poor personality resources. Table 7 epitomizes my original prediction in regard to academic success or failure.

TABLE 7

Predictions of Academic Success and Failure

PERSONALITY RATING	NUMBER	WORK GOOD OR SATISFACTORY	POOR WORK SEVERAL FAILURES DROPPED
Excellent			
Above average	94	86% (81)	14% (13)
Average			
Just below average			
Poor and very poor	14	7% (1)	93% (13)

Munroe's initial findings at Sarah Lawrence College [21, 22], also based on over-all personality estimates, achieved approximately the same figures of correspondence between academic failures predicted by personality resources.

Munroe's contribution of the Inspection Technique whereby group Rorschach records can be scored rapidly allows a much greater degree of uniformity between the findings of different investigators. Her findings, which are presented in another chapter in this volume, indicate a nice interplay of experimental modification of the original Rorschach. Despite the importance of Munroe's work in the field of education, however, I shall not elaborate on it here, since this would lead to inevitable duplication of material.[3]

---

[3] Although in my own large-scale studies I have never used the Inspection Technique, I feel that it is to be recommended in the majority of cases except where the examiner happens to have had an unusual amount of experience with any one type of subject or patient and where he does not intend to make direct comparisons between his own findings and those of others. Munroe's check list, moreover, has been incorporated as part of the standardized Group Rorschach Technique in that it is included in the Group Rorschach blanks that I have prepared.

In an article entitled "The Application of the Group Rorschach Technique to the Problem of Achievement in College" [20], Montalto has made a very interesting study in relation to achievement in college. Her subjects were ninety women students in various colleges and universities in Cincinnati. These students were divided into achievers and nonachievers on the basis of their grade-point average in the two or three years of college residence. The achievers were those who had maintained an average of 1.5 or better; the nonachievers, those whose average fell below. Montalto studied the Group Rorschach records with a view to "signs of adjustment" which she describes as "a measure of quantitative features of the Rorschach protocol based on the interrelationship of certain factors." Her fourteen signs of adjustment, together with the frequency of their occurrence in achievers and nonachievers, are recorded in Table 8.

TABLE 8

Frequency of Occurrence of Rorschach Scoring Signs

SIGNS	SIGN CATEGORY	ACHIEVERS PER CENT	NON-ACHIEVERS PER CENT	DIFFERENCE* PER CENT
1	$M > FM$ or $M = FM$	83	80	3
2	$M = 3$ or more	85	82	3
3	$W/M = 2/1$ (approx.)	24	43	−19
4	$F\% = 50\%$ or less	76	66	10
5	$F+\% = 75\%$ or higher	59	55	4
6	$FK + Fc = 2$ or more	87	80	7
7	$Dd + S = 10\%$ or less	52	55	− 3
8	Sum $C > Fc + c + C'$	35	30	5
9	$FC > CF$ or $FC = CF$	91	86	5
10	$FC = 2$ or more	87	89	− 2
11	No pure C	74	73	1
12	$A\% = 50\%$ or less	91	82	9
13	$P = 4$ or more and 30%	65	68	− 3
14	$\%R$ on VIII–X 40%–60%	24	41	−17

* All differences are plus in favor of the achievers except those with the minus sign, which favor the nonachievers.

Two signs were outstanding in distinguishing the groups, in that they occurred more frequently in the nonachieving group. These signs, the ratio of W:M, W to M being approximately 2 to 1, and the percentages of responses on the last three color cards being between 40 per cent and 60 per cent.

Eliminating some of the signs and scoring the absence of two others as positive resulted in a "pattern of signs by which to make a quantitative attack on the problem of achievement in college through the instrumentality of the Group Rorschach. These signs consist of the following: F% = 50% or less, FK +Fc = 2 or more, A% = 50% or less; in addition, these signs as 'negative ones,' namely: W/M = 2/1, and % of response to the last three cards 40% to 70%. These signs, then, would assign to the achiever (woman) a personality which has good intellectual control without rigidity, possesses a sense of tactfulness and social awareness, and is relatively free from stereotyped modes of thinking, but one which does not reveal the best balance between drive and creative capacity nor react in the optimal degree to environmental influences."

Montalto's findings are summarized as follows:

The study is a purely quantitative one, and the data were subjected to analysis using primarily the methods of correlation and partial correlation. On the basis of these results the following conclusions were reached:

1. Achievers possess more signs of adjustment than non-achievers.

2. Achievers have a neurotic trend in their personality make-up which seems to be a pertinent factor contributing to their academic success.

3. A pattern of signs of academic achievement was evolved which correlated highly with grade points when intelligence scores were held constant. This consisted of five signs, three of which are "positive" and two of which are "negative" with reference to norms of healthy adjustment.

4. It is suggested that the method be subjected to further experiment in order to see if the "pattern" would work with other groups.

I consider isolation of these two "neurotic" factors in achievement to be one of the most important contributions in this study. The achievers "tend to overreach themselves in their intellectual pursuits or to have more nearly an unhealthy amount of drive. This would seem to be comparable with striving for college grades." The achievers show less response to environmental stimuli, "which may mean less than average distractibility to external influence and hence more controlled concentration on self-imposed goals such as academic attainment." These might be seen as leading to emotional disturbances.

Turning now to the use of the Multiple-Choice Test as a means of screening in the educational set-up, I mention two as yet unpublished studies. I introduced a screening program on an experimental basis with the students at Cooper Union for the Advancement of Science and Art. This screening program included the Multiple-Choice Test; the drawing of human figures, man and woman; a story or description of the figures drawn; and analysis of the graphological specimens obtained. The tests were administered by me and scored by another worker, the work of correlating the findings between the tests and those students who had sought psychiatric aid being done entirely through the Department of Admissions. The following summary of the findings comes from the Admissions office:

The psychological tests located a group of fifty-nine students with potential emotional or personality difficulties in a total of 632 students tested. Of this group of fifty-nine, *fifty-four had been previously referred to the school psychiatrist.* The other five were then interviewed. Two of these were felt to need further help. On the other hand, only one student who had not been isolated by the psychological tests was referred to the psychiatrist by the customary avenues. Such agreement between test and counseling case-finding procedures is definitely encouraging.

There is a research problem involved in this particular project over and above the screening; it relates to an attempt to find certain patterns of response typical of each group,[4] much as the interest inventories disclose such patterns. We also propose to study the response patterns of selected deviates with each school —that is, differences between very able artists, as rated by instructors, and unimaginative conformists or disorganized personalities. In the engineering school we hope to select from instructor-rated students who have taken the tests two groups

---

[4] The four groups of students referred to are art students who study by day; art students who study in the evening; engineering students who study by day; engineering students who study in the evening.

differing in personality characteristics required of those in the engineering profession. We will also study the personality patterns of a group of engineers who equal or exceed their predicted grade averages, based on academic entrance tests, compared with those of high predicted grades but who fall low on achievement, it having been felt at the impressionistic or hunch level by the instructors that there were very definitely different personality types involved in each of these groups.

In view of some of the disappointing findings in regard to the Multiple-Choice Test when utilized as a screening method for acceptable recruits, the fact that fifty-four of the fifty-nine students screened out by the tests had already sought psychiatric help or been referred to the psychiatrist is somewhat startling. My suggestion is that this group approximates more closely to those subjects who were utilized originally in the construction of the tests, since it would appear that more than we have realized the test must be altered in terms of the characteristics of the group to be screened.

Utilization of a battery of tests, among which the Multiple-Choice Test is included, is also the procedure at Keuka College.[5] Among eight students screened out by the Multiple-Choice Test for further consideration of the other test findings is the record of a student whom I shall designate as X. This student had an I.Q. of 119 on the Wechsler-Bellevue. Her performance on the Multiple-Choice Test, however, indicated very obvious emotional difficulties. Quantitatively, fifty per cent of her choices were poor answers, but a consideration of the actual choices is also of interest. On Card I, for instance, she twice sees "an X-ray of the chest," ignoring on all three groups of choices the popular "bat." On Card II there is overemphasis on the explosive type of emotional answer, "an erupting volcano," "an exploding firecracker," and "blood" being selected. The human-movement figures are seen on Card III, but on Card IV the choices of "a nasty, dirty mess," "a burnt mass," are highly significant. A very poor F— answer, "the lungs and the chest," is chosen for Card V; "gushing oil" on Cards VI and VII reinforce the traumatic picture. "Fire and ice," "a medical picture," "the inside of

---

[5] I am greatly indebted to Dr. Donald R. Gorham for allowing the utilization of the following material.

the mouth," and "storm clouds at sunset" are among her choices on the last three cards.

If there is anything at all to the principle of projection, it must be clear that this individual is psychologically disturbed. Regardless of whether or not we speak of "good" or "poor" answers, it is clear that this girl finds an affinity with, chooses, endorses, considers acceptable, answers that reflect unstable, violent, and explosive inner emotional dynamics, that the whole area is fraught with guilt ("a nasty, dirty mess"), and that she is insecure and anxious ("X-rays of the chest," "fog," and "mist"). A blind analysis of her TAT by Dr. Magda Arnold gives the additional corroborative evidence:

This is the record of a seriously disturbed girl on the verge of psychotic incoherence. She has literally been "shocked into incoherence" by life. Life has been too much for her for a long time; she still feels like a child, ill, lost in a strange land; has always felt "differently"; was able to find security only at home, protected by her mother. She suffers from her inability to cope with the world and desperately hopes for a helper who will rescue her.

She is quite sure that she will eventually find security in marriage if only a helper will come. In the meantime she is afraid of life, for men to her are weak, degenerate strangers who depend on women for their rescue. It is possible that there may have been a sexual trauma of some kind after adolescence, but that would seem to be the result rather than the cause of her attitude toward men and what they stand for. Her conviction that women have to help men by showing them the true vision might get her into all kinds of scrapes, for she has no feeling of relatedness either to men or to women and would be quite incapable of judging what the effect of her actions would be on others, except that she recognizes that she is a source of worry, without, however, quite knowing why.

Unless she can be helped she might even decide to withdraw altogether into detachment so she can be amused at the antics of people instead of frightened, and into a haven of peace where wishes count instead of actions. In this record religion is used as an escapist instead of a constructive solution, and it therefore reinforces the danger of psychotic withdrawal.

The only hopeful feature is the fact that she recognizes she needs help and, in fact, is looking for it.

Turning now to the clinical data in regard to this particular girl, one finds the following comments:

She first came to the notice of the counselor as being completely irresponsible. Could not seem to realize college had rules, and could not seem to remember them overnight when told. Began excessive dating . . . changed major . . . confused about requirements in new course. Developed acute psychotic episode . . . paranoid ideas . . . actively hallucinated.

THE USE OF GROUP TECHNIQUES IN THE ARMED FORCES

With the noted exception of the study by Abt [1], to be reported in detail below, it must be stated that the findings by several investigators are frankly disappointing. Wittson, Hunt, and Older [29], Jensen and Rotter [16], Winfield [27], and Springer [23] utilized the Mulitple-Choice Test with various groups. Wittson and Hunt [29], for example, contrasting "normal" navy personnel with those who had been discharged for various neuropsychiatric reasons, found that whereas 59 per cent of the dischargees gave more than four poor answers, as many as 44 per cent of the "normal" group fell into this category also. Springer [23] reports that "no reliable differentiation was found between those that were making a good adjustment in the service and those who were chronic offenders to naval discipline." Winfield [27], using the test with women in the Marines, concludes that "the Multiple-Choice Test differentiates something other than it purports to do, and that further research and standardization are necessary before the test can be used on a similarly selected sample for the screening of maladjusted individuals." Jensen and Rotter [16] found that 45 per cent of their officers and 36 per cent of the officer candidates had four or more responses, and they naturally conclude that the test was unsuitable for these groups.

It is quite clear, therefore, that the Multiple-Choice Test in its original form, with only ten choices for each card, administered once only under group conditions, could not in any sense be considered a sufficiently reliable diagnostic tool to be of value in military screening. As I shall discuss in a later section, however, these unsatisfactory findings have not led to the discarding of the whole idea, but rather have stimulated modifications and refinements in the test itself and so forced certain investigators to think with greater clarity about the whole question of underlying emotional disturbances in relation to the successful performance of a task.

Studies with the Rorschach administered under the usual individual conditions, on the other hand, and utilization of the group form with the results examined by experts, have both resulted in negative reports if one is to judge by the findings of Guilford [11]. He makes the following statement:

"The test was administered experimentally to several hundred students individually, according to the prescribed procedure, by members of the Rorschach Institute in one of the psychological units. Two methods of group administration were also tried, the Harrower and our own version. The results were almost entirely negative. From the individual administration of the test neither the 25 indicators, taken separately or collectively, nor the intuitive prediction of the examiner based upon the data he had from the administration of the tests gave significant indications of validity against the pass-fail criterion. There were two samples, one of nearly 300 and the other of nearly 200. The Harrower Group Administration Form also gave no evidence of being valid for pilot selection."

The actual reports [2, 3] from which Guilford takes his material are, however, somewhat more cautious in their conclusions. Referring in particular to an experimental situation in which aviation students were contrasted with patients with diagnoses of severe anxiety, by means of the individual method, the authors state: "Generalizations based on these findings are not warranted, since the samples are small and the statistical tests of significance were not applied."

An unpublished study by Gluck, Harrower, and Steiner would support these negative findings, or perhaps one may say would throw light on the problem from a slightly different angle. In this study no attempt was made to predict success, but the records of some 300 members of the Eighth Air Force, which had been taken in England during the war, were subsequently analyzed by Dr. Meta Steiner and me. The records of thirty aviators who had been decorated and had completed over thirty missions successfully were contrasted with those who had failed to complete more than five missions. No differences on any of the

Rorschach findings or significant ratios were discovered. Moreover, among this group of highly decorated individuals were records that in the normal course of evaluation would have been termed those of frankly unstable or psychopathic personalities. Such records occurred with equal frequency in the two groups. Dr. Gluck's comment, made independently, was to the effect that in psychiatric examination of these men there were among the highly successful and decorated group as many psychopathic personalities as there were in the unsuccessful. Psychopathic personalities, that is, judged by our peacetime standards. Quite clearly that which makes a successful pilot is not at present clearly envisaged in Rorschach terms. The too naïve assumption that the well-balanced Rorschach personality in normal conditions must be the personality best adapted to an environment of severe strain may be an erroneous and dangerous one. Conversely, our concept that lack of balance within a stable peacetime framework is a poor prognostic sign may again be misleading where environmental conditions are highly abnormal. We may well raise the question whether adjustment to one type of environment and condition of living, in and of itself, predicts adjustment under totally different conditions.

These negative findings have been emphasized, for it has seemed to me that only by emphasizing what a test cannot do and where it is not relevant can one come to a realistic appraisal of its merits and assets. That the Group Rorschach Test in contrast to the Multiple-Choice Test was an efficient instrument for one type of psychiatric screening—namely, for the Marine Corps recruits—can be seen by the excellent article of Abt [1] in which 1,000 subjects were investigated. In this instance the Group Rorschach Test made up part of a battery which also included the Wilkins-Miles Self-Description Inventory and the Kent Directions A Test, together with a personal information sheet. In this study Abt divided the records after an inspection rating into three groups classified as "okay," "suspicious," and "bad." Abt checked his over-all performance rating against a similar rating performed by another experienced Rorschach worker and obtained a mean square contingency coefficient of .80. He also checked his method against 141 records chosen at random, which had been scored in detail, and found here a mean square contingency coefficient of .91.

A breakdown of the thirty subjects who were discharged because of neuropsychiatric disabilities by a Recruit Aptitude Board showed that the test battery had already picked twenty-six, or 86.6 per cent. A combination of the Self-Description Inventory plus the Group Rorschach Test had detected twenty-five, or 83.3 per cent. Only four of the thirty subjects were not identified at all.

Abt found that "the most striking characteristic of the group records of the dischargees is the large amount of constriction or rigidity of personality." He feels that this suggests that the dischargees have personalities which are too colorless, with mental lives too meager, and emotional responsiveness too poor, to enable them to respond to the Rorschach slides in any other way than by form-dominated response. In short, there appeared to be a general impoverishment of personality among the dischargees.

Among the important features of this paper is the fact that the Group Rorschach Test was not expected to carry the full diagnostic load in and of itself. As the Group Test identified 56.6 per cent of all dischargees, in combination with the Self-Description Inventory, the diagnostic strength of these combined instruments jumps to 83.3 per cent. One of the fallacies too readily assumed by many enthusiasts is that any one testing technique is all-sufficient. It is my belief that had more Rorschach programs been integrated properly with other types of tests, there would have been fewer negative findings in this field.

Abt's conclusion, therefore, "that the use of the Group Rorschach Test has been shown to identify neuropsychiatric misfits missed by a typical paper and pencil inventory" is justified. It is also his statement that the Group Rorschach Test is practical for use in the psychiatric screening of Marine Corps recruits, and that when combined in a test battery with a psychometric test and a paper-and-pencil inventory it leads to the identification of over 86 per cent of those neuropsychiatrically unfit.

SUGGESTED MODIFICATIONS IN TEST PROCEDURES

As pointed out previously, a number of investigators were challenged by the discrepancy that appeared in the findings of various authors in regard to the Multiple-Choice Test. Different types of alterations of procedure and scoring methods have been suggested here.

I made one major alteration as soon as the Multiple-Choice Test in its original form appeared to be clearly inadequate. This was the introduction of 20 additional responses for each of the ten cards, making a total of 30 instead of 10 responses to be chosen from a total of 300. Moreover, by dividing the choices into three groups of ten and forcing a choice from each group, an attempt was made to see to what extent any given idea or type of response was perseverated throughout the three groups, or, in contrast, to what extent the individual could reflect a wider range of "psychic reactivity," to use Piotrowski's term, in altering his choices from group to group. Into this additional list were added certain responses found to be particularly significant by other workers, notably Due, Wright, and Wright [9].

A second modification I made lay in an attempt to give weighted scores. The suggestion was made that the response "Nothing at all" receive the score of 2, whereas responses 6 and 7, the anatomical and X-ray answers, appeared so frequently in normal subjects that they should be considered as ½ point. A suggestion in terms of modification of procedure has already been mentioned—namely, that the test should be repeated at least twice wherever possible. While these modifications are certainly no final solution, and though they do not represent the highest degree of refinement of the test, they are unquestionably a step forward over the initial procedure and short list of choices.

A modification of the procedure which has been called the Rorschach Ranking Test was initiated by Eysenck [10]. It is described as following in his own words:

> The Rorschach Ranking Test is a modification of the Harrower Multiple-Choice Test. We found that the Multiple-Choice Test had too low a reliability to be used as a screening test, and accordingly we modified the procedure so as to increase its reliability. This was done by presenting the subjects with nine alternative responses to each ink blot, asking them to rank these in order of applicability, i.e., putting a 1 after the response most like the ink blot, a 2 after the second most likely response, etc., down through a number 9 after the response least like the ink blot. The actual responses used were taken from Harrower's list. Slight verbal modifications were introduced in some cases to

suit the wording to English audiences. Four neurotic and five normal responses were offered for each blot, and the numbers of the position assigned the four neurotic responses by the subject constitute his score for that blot. The best score for each blot is therefore 30 (9 plus 8 plus 7 plus 6), and the worst score is 10 (1 plus 2 plus 3 plus 4). Scores for the ten blots are added, giving a range for the whole task of between 100 neurotic N and 300 normal N. The method of scoring increases the reliability to $r = +0.84$. This test does not correlate highly with intelligence, $r = +0.08$, but shows a slight correlation with vocabulary, $r = +0.27$. The critical level is at the score of 220; 74 per cent of neurotics and 42 per cent of normals score below this level.

In this study Eysenck then utilized four tests, Suggestibility, Dark Vision, Ranking Rorschach, and a questionnaire. He found the following:

> . . . while no one test by itself reaches a high level of prediction, a combination of the tests would considerably enhance their discriminative value.
>
> In clinical studies we have found that while the Dark-Vision test is particularly discriminative with respect to anxiety states, the Ranking Rorschach Test is particularly discriminative with regard to hysterics. Differences in selectivity of this kind may account for the fact that such correlations as we have found between the various tests have usually been rather small. They also argue in favor of the use of several tests in combination. We therefore put forward the whole battery as a useful measuring instrument for the general personality trait of neuroticism.

A study with constructive suggestions is that by Malamud and Malamud [19]. These authors state that, despite the lack of agreement on the findings in regard to the Multiple-Choice Test, it represents "an important methodological advance in projective testing." Their study "attempts to determine possible shortcomings of this test's scoring system in the light of an item analysis of its individual responses."

Utilizing the records of 488 normals as compared with 215 abnormal subjects, they made a breakdown of the scores in terms of the number of times any given response category was chosen. The following significant findings were obtained:

1. Using a critical ratio of 2.00 or over as the criterion,

twenty-one good responses are found to be discriminative in the normal direction, twenty-five are neutral, and four discriminate in the abnormal direction. Good answers classified in the same category often vary in degree or direction of discrimination from card to card. For example, Response 4 discriminates in the normal on Card IV, is neutral on Card VII, and discriminates in the abnormal direction on Card VI.

This is a very interesting finding, and is closely allied to the recent work of Cox, reported above.

2. In the abnormal direction 33 poor responses are discriminative, 14 are neutral, and 3 discriminate in the normal direction. Poor answers classified in the same category vary in degree or direction of discrimination from card to card. For example, Response 8 discriminates in the abnormal direction on Card VII, is neutral on Card IV, and discriminates in a normal direction on Card VI.

All in all, a total of 62 individual responses discriminate between normals and abnormals to the extent of a critical ratio of 2.00 or more. Of these responses, 35 discriminate to the extent of a critical ratio of 3.00 or more.

In their discussion the authors point out that the "appropriateness of assigning uniform weights to categories of responses is seriously questioned, since much depends on the type of response and the card on which it appears. Responses falling in the same category may deserve increased weights on some cards, decreased or even no weights on other cards. This would appear to be consistent with practice in the free Rorschach situation where the same response may vary in significance, depending on the properties of the card to which it is given."

The authors feel further that "weighting in the normal as well as the abnormal direction seems desirable." They further conclude that "the conditions affecting the choice of different responses vary significantly from one normal or abnormal group to another, a fact that may indicate that the test with a single scoring system cannot be applied universally with the expectation of getting consistently good results."

Challman [6] investigated three different scoring methods in a comparative study of the records of patients in a state hospital and of student nurses. A considerable difference in the discriminative power of the same set of responses could be obtained by a change of method. Thus, according to Method I, 66 per cent of the patients and 39 per cent of the nurses were screened out; in Method II, 61 per cent of the patients and 31 per cent of the nurses; in Method III, 57 per cent of the patients and 19 per cent of the nurses. Challman considered this last the most effective, and makes as his conclusion the following statement:

> With the methods of scoring recommended by Harrower for the amplified Multiple-Choice Test (not for the present one), and with a critical score of 35, the test appears to have some usefulness as a screening device. The number of false positives would probably be reduced if the test were repeated, and only those scoring over the critical score both times screened out. Also, where it is feasible, using it with a personality inventory, as Mittelmann[6] has done, appears to reduce the number of misclassifications.

Lawshe and Forster [18] utilized seven modifications of scoring in an endeavor "to raise the reliability of the test." "These modifications were aimed at the scoring of only the most discriminative items and the development of separate scoring keys for males and females." The findings are as follows:

1. The low reliability coefficients obtained from sources of college students on the Multiple-Choice Test strongly indicate the unreliability of the standard scoring and reflect the weakness of the test as a screening instrument. In cases where a low selection ratio can be used, however—that is, when the object is to select a few individuals from a large number of candidates, assuming validity to the obtained reliability—the test might be effectively used for selection.

2. Significant sex differences in score distribution and item selection reveal the need for separate male and female scoring keys.

3. For the restricted population studies, the intelligence factor does not seem to contribute significantly to the variability of the score on the Multiple-Choice Test. (Compare Eysenck.)

4. The reversal of the intended discriminate power in some

---

[6] The reference to Mittelmann's work is found in "Proceedings of the Military Session, American Society for Research in Psychosomatic Problems," *Psychosomatic Medicine*, Vol. 5 (1943), pp. 36-7.

answers indicates a need for a review of the original classification of items. (Compare Malamud and Malamud.)

5. The insufficient number of strongly discriminative items in this test does not permit a significant raising of the reliability through the elimination of weak items. The suggestion is advanced that an increase in the number of ink blots might render the test more useful in individual application.

Several investigators (Watson, Gorham, and Zuckerman) have suggested the modification of scoring the 300 items of the Multiple-Choice Test on an IBM scoring sheet. This type of study, however, has been most fully developed by Samuel Kellman, of the Detroit Civil Service Commission, who has combined this technical modification with several other important ones, including the development of what I originally termed the "Expanded Multiple-Choice Rorschach" [13].

Kellman [17] has added to the Multiple-Choice Key three additional numbers: No. 11 represents animal-movement responses, which were formerly considered under Key No. II, which leaves Key No. II for animal responses without movement. He has added a No. 12 of form-color responses, extracting from my original classification of No. III. He has added a No. 13—namely, shading responses with good form, Fc, also extracted from No. III. This leaves the original Key III for good-form responses given relatively frequently by unselected normals.

A breakdown of the 300 responses in terms of Kellman's thirteen key numbers reads as follows:

Key Number	Number of Responses in All Cards
1	27
2	23
3	24
4	23
5	5
6	29
7	24
8	29
9	41
10	30

Key Number	Number of Responses in All Cards
11	12
12	27
13	6
Total	300

Kellman's major contribution, however, lies in his elaborate sheets for machine scoring, which permit the maximum amount of information to be tabulated. This type of scoring paves the way for large-scale investigations of an impressive kind.

CONCLUDING REMARKS

In conclusion let me sketch some of the developments that may be expected to take place. At the same time I may formulate some of the dangers that should be avoided and some of the prerequisites that may safeguard the most effective use of these group devices. Let us look into the future and make the assumption that there will be an ever increasing rapprochement between the field of the physician and the field of the psychologist, where the physician will become more aware of the kind of information it would be helpful for him to have with patients, and where the psychologist, on the other hand, has cast off his academic seclusion and has oriented himself in the field of medicine sufficiently to take the responsibility of bridging the gap and making his findings intelligible to the nonpsychologically trained individual. Given this state of affairs, might it not be possible in large outpatient clinics, where persons may wait for several hours before being seen by the doctor, for certain types of group screening of the roughest kind to be conducted for the purpose of highlighting very obvious emotional disturbances?

It is certainly not beyond the realm of possibility that all colleges will require some kind of appraisal of the individual's emotional status at the time of entrance, over and above his academic achievement and acceptability on interview. As this is done with noteworthy success in several institutions once the student has entered, the possibilities of utilizing rapid and accurate screening devices prior to entering may, I think, be envisaged.

Although still at the level of research, the emergence of vocational characteristics, as seen in the work of Steiner, may be expected in the future to play a greater and greater part in the actual placement of the individual in industry.

Statistical norms for age levels, educational levels, and the like should be compiled by some central research bureau. While admittedly much remains to the experimentalist so far as concerns perfecting his own tools, it is even more important that he take the time and trouble to explain the relevance and significance of his tools in fields outside his own.

REFERENCES

1. ABT, L. E.: "The Efficiency of the Group Rorschach Test in the Psychiatric Screening of Marine Corps Recruits," *Journal of Psychology,* Vol. 23 (1947), pp. 205–17.

2. ARMY Air Forces Aviation Psychology Program Research Reports. *Printed Classification Tests,* Vol. 5, pp. 625–37. Washington: Government Printing Office; 1947.

3. ARMY Air Forces Aviation Psychology Program Research Reports. *The Psychological Program in the AAF Convalescent Hospitals.* Vol. 15, pp. 145–9. Washington: Government Printing Office; 1947.

4. BROZEK, J., GUETZKOW, H., and KEYS, A.: "Study of Personality of Normal Young Men Maintained on Restricted Intakes of Vitamins of the B Complex," *Psychosomatic Medicine,* Vol. 8 (1946), pp. 98–109.

5. CHALKE, F. R. C.: "The Harrower Stress Tolerance Test," *Psychosomatic Medicine,* Vol. 8 (1946), pp. 215–16.

6. CHALLMAN, R. G.: "Validity of Harrower Multiple-Choice Test as a Screening Device," *Journal of Psychology,* Vol. 20, (1945), pp. 41–8.

7. Cooper Union for the Advancement of Sciences and Art. *Report from the Office of Admissions.*

8. Cox, K.: "The Use of the Harrower Multiple-Choice Rorschach in a Selection of Sales Personnel for a Department Store." (A manuscript to be published shortly.)

9. DUE, F., WRIGHT, M. E., and WRIGHT, B. A.: "The Multiple-Choice Rorschach Test in Military Psychiatric Differentiation," in Harrower, M. R., and Steiner, M. E.: *Large Scale Rorschach Techniques.* Springfield, Ill.: Charles C. Thomas; 1945.

10. EYSENCK, H. J.: "A Comparative Study of Four Screening Tests for Neurotics," *Psychological Bulletin*, Vol. 42 (1945), pp. 659–62.

11. GUILFORD, J. P.: "Some Lessons from Aviation Psychology," *American Journal of Psychology*, Vol. 3 (1948), pp. 3–11.

12. HARROWER, M. R., and GRINKER, R. R.: "Preliminary Experiments with a New Projective Technique Utilizing Both Meaningful and Meaningless Stimuli," *Psychosomatic Medicine*, Vol. 8 (1946), pp. 3–15.

13. HARROWER, M. R., and STEINER, M. E.: *Large Scale Rorschach Techniques*. Springfield, Ill.: Charles C. Thomas; 1945.

14. HARROWER, M. R. and STEINER, M. E.: *Manual for Psychodiagnostic Ink Blots*. New York: Grune & Stratton; 1946.

15. HARROWER, M. R., WASHBURNE, A. C., and JACOBS, J. S. L.: "A Preliminary Screening Test for Disturbance in Personality," *Bulletin of the Canadian Psychological Association*, Vol. 4 (1944), pp. 4–6.

16. JENSEN, M. B., and ROTTER, J. B.: "The Validity of the Multiple-Choice Rorschach Test in Officer Candidate Selection," *Psychological Bulletin*, Vol. 42 (1945), pp. 182–5.

17. KELLMAN, S.: "The Proposed Revision of the Expanded Multiple-Choice Rorschach." (A manuscript to be published shortly.)

18. LAWSHE, C. H., and FORSTER, M. H.: "Studies in Projective Techniques: the Reliability of a Multiple-Choice Group Rorschach Test," *Journal of Applied Psychology*, Vol. 31 (1937), pp. 199–211.

19. MALAMUD, R. F., and MALAMUD, D. I.: "The Multiple-Choice Rorschach: a Critical Explanation of Its Scoring System," *Journal of Psychology*, (1946), pp. 237–42.

20. MONTALTO, F. D.: "An Application of the Group Rorschach Technique to the Problem of Achievement in College," *Journal of Clinical Psychology*, Vol. 2 (1946), pp. 254–60.

21. MUNROE, R. L.: "Prediction of the Adjustment and Academic Performance of College Students by a Modification of the Rorschach Method," *Applied Psychology Monographs*, No. 7, Stanford University: Stanford University Press; 1945.

22. ——: "The Inspection Technique: a Method of Rapid Evaluation of the Rorschach Protocol," *Rorschach Research Exchange*, Vol. 8 (1944), pp. 46–70.

23. SPRINGER, N. N.: "The Validity of the Multiple-Choice Group Rorschach Test in the Screening of Naval Personnel," *Journal of General Psychology*, Vol. 35 (1946), pp. 27–32.

24. STEINER, M. E.: "The Use of the Rorschach Method in Industry," *Rorschach Research Exchange* and *Journal of Projective Techniques*, Vol. 11 (1947), pp. 46–52.

25. ———: "The Psychologist in Industry," *American Lecture Series Monographs*. Springfield, Ill.: Charles Thomas (to be published shortly).

26. WILLIAMS, G.: "The Possibilities of the Rorschach Technique in Industry," *Personality*, Vol. 24 (1947), pp. 224–31.

27. WINFIELD, M. C.: "The Use of the Harrower Multiple-Choice Rorschach Test with a Selected Group of Women in Military Service," *Journal of Applied Psychology*, Vol. 30 (1946), pp. 481–7.

28. WITTMAN, P.: "The Use of the Multiple-Choice Rorschach as a Differential Diagnostic Tool," *Journal of Clinical Psychology*, Vol. 1 (1945), pp. 281–7.

29. WITTSON, C. L., HUNT, W. A., and OLDER, H. J., "The Use of the Multiple-Choice Group Rorschach Test in Military Screening," *Journal of Psychology*, Vol. 17 (1944), pp. 91–4.

Within recent years there has been an enormous increase in the number of papers on the Thematic Apperception Test. Although there are many methods of interpretation, Dr. Bellak's contribution stresses the clinical usefulness of the test in giving us information about the subject's apperceptive distortions in his interpersonal relations. Bellak is interested in presenting a method of interpretation of the test protocols which is relatively simple and economical of time, since the Thematic Apperception Test has suffered much in the past from the very cumbersome approaches to its use and interpretation. This chapter presents Bellak's own system of interpretation, which he has found not only particularly helpful in teaching the test but also exceptionally useful in employing the method as a vehicle to move psychotherapy forward.

▼

The Thematic Apperception Test in Clinical Use

Leopold Bellak

The Thematic Apperception Test, hereafter referred to as the TAT, is a technique for the investigation of the dynamics of personality as it manifests itself in interpersonal relations and in the apperception or meaningful interpretation of the environment. It consists, in its present form, of a series of thirty-one pictures. Testees are asked to tell stories about some of these pictures, thereby presumably revealing their personal, individual apperception of purposely ambiguous stimuli.

The TAT was originally described by Morgan and Murray [46] in 1935. Tomkins [80] shows that there were earlier attempts by psychologists and psychiatrists to elicit meaningful responses of subjects to pictures. Here belong workers like Brittain [18] who published such an attempt in 1907, Libby [40] who used such a procedure, like Brittain, with children in 1908, and finally Schwartz [72] who used his Social Situation Test in 1932. None of these forerunners, however, has attained the popularity of the TAT, which at present ranks with the Rorschach Test.

The TAT and the Rorschach can hardly be considered competitive or mutually exclusive techniques. The Rorschach Test is invaluable as a formal, perceptanalytic technique; it reveals better than any other tests available the formal, expressive nature of thought processes and those of emotional organization. By this token, it reveals patterns that are more or less typical for certain psychiatric disease entities or disease processes. The content analysis of the Rorschach Test, even though it has its natural limitations, has not been utilized to the extent it deserves in the majority of present methods of interpretation.

The TAT supplies the content. It gives primarily, and more so than any other test in use at present, the actual dynamics of interpersonal relationships. By the very nature of the pictures it gives basic data on the testee's relationship to male or female authority figures, to contemporaries of both sexes, and frequently it shows the genesis in terms of family relations. It may not so clearly indicate the intensity of fears as does the Rorschach, but it tells one the nature of them—fear of lack of support or fear of attack by males in specific situations—and it shows the hierarchy of needs and the structure of the compromises between id, ego, and superego. The TAT is only incidentally, and not particularly successfully, a diagnostic tool, if diagnosis means the identification of a given patient's disorder with a definite nosological group. This is better done by the clinical interview, the Rorschach, and other techniques.

The present TAT pictures are the third set to be used since 1935. Aside from additions and omissions made since the first series was issued, the second and third series distinguish themselves by being twice the original size, a fact that probably facilitates the testee's rapport with the pictures.

BASIC ASSUMPTIONS UNDERLYING THE TAT

The TAT is at present regarded as a projective test in that the stories which subjects tell about each of the pictures are considered to be projections—that is, ascriptions of feelings and sentiments, needs or drives—of the individual, which are elicited by the stimulus materials of the pictures. According to the projective hypothesis, the mechanism of projection is utilized by the ego as a defense against unacceptable forces and is, in part at least, unconscious.

Productions of the subject in response to the TAT pictures can be only partially subsumed under this somewhat restrictive definition of projection, and experimental and clinical experience has compelled us to re-examine the whole concept of projection. I have pointed out elsewhere that it may indeed be both more accurate and useful to use the term "apperception" to embrace all sorts of perception that in one manner or another are influenced by selective, personal drives and thus suffer some distortion from the hypothetically purely cognitive percept. I propose the notion that there are various processes of widely differing degrees of complexity which distort the original percept.

Projection, in the new sense in which I use it, refers to the most extreme distortion of reality only; and the definition offered above applies to it. Not only is it a largely unconscious process, but it also cannot be made conscious except when brought into awareness through prolonged psychotherapy. We may also speak of sensitization and autistic perception as types of less complex apperceptive distortions, which do not need to be examined in detail here. I reserve the term "externalization" for those apperceptive processes which function on a preconscious level and can therefor readily be made conscious. Externalization is a phenomenon that characterizes many of the responses to the TAT; for example, a subject at the time of inquiry often recognizes at least partially that he was speaking of himself in the stories recently told, although he reports that he was unaware of this fact while he told the stories. We may presume that much preconscious material of this kind also has unconscious determinants.

Psychological determinism is another assumption that is absolutely essential to the interpretation of TAT productions. The hypothesis of psychological determinism is regarded as a special case of the law of causality; namely, that everything said or written as a response to some stimulus situation, like all other psychological productions, has a dynamic cause and meaning. The principle of overdetermination must be taken into account in this context since it insists that each part of the projected material may have more than one meaning, corresponding to different levels of personality organization. It is useful to recall, by way of example, that a story may be taken quite consciously from a movie recently seen and yet may be reported only because it reflects an important conflict of the subject on a preconscious level and also because it may, at the same time, have significant symbolic meaning on an unconscious level. In a like manner a given act may have several different unconscious meanings, each of them valid in relation to the whole personality.

Startling as this principle may appear at first to behaviorists, it must be pointed out that it holds in the physical sciences also. In physics, for instance, the flight of an object through the atmosphere is the resultant of a number of factors such as its size, weight, and shape and the wind velocity. In our present language, its final path is overdetermined. And in a quite similar manner a psychological act is the resultant of a number of different psychological processes. Saying that a psychological event may have several meanings simply indicates that it may be viewed as causally related to a number of different factors.

THE ADMINISTRATION OF THE TAT

As in every testing situation, the subject should be put at ease and a proper non-committal rapport established. The subject may either be seated in a chair or lie on a couch. Usually it is desirable to have the test administrator seated behind the subject. It cannot be emphasized enough that the position should be *behind and to the side* of the subject in either case so that he cannot see the examiner but so that the examiner may have full view of the patient's facial expressions. This position may have to be modified with suspicious and otherwise disturbed patients and children.

The instructions for administration of the TAT are those which are applicable only in a clinical setting, and they are purposely less formal than some have advocated. It is clear that these procedures would not prove useful in research work, in which more rigorous rules would have to be laid down and carefully followed.

The subject may be given the instruction in an informal statement such as: "I am going to show you some pictures, and I should like you to tell me stories about what is going on in each picture, what led up to it, and what the outcome will be. I want you to make it lively and full of drama and to let yourself go freely." Then one may have to parry, in a nondirective way, any questions the subject may ask. It is entirely permissible to make some encouraging remark to the patient after the first story. Whenever necessary, one is entitled to remind the subject that what we want is a story about what goes on, what leads up to it, and what the outcome will be.

The standard procedure has been for the subject to tell his story orally and for the administrator to record the responses by hand, by means of a recording device or through the use of a hidden stenographer. It is economical in many cases to give the selected cards to the subject with written or oral instructions, emphasizing that he should look at only one picture at a time, and then to let him write the stories on plain paper in the office or at home or even as a member of the group to which the TAT pictures may possibly be shown on a screen. It is helpful to let the subject know that he is expected to write about three hundred words per story as spontaneously as possible. The following instructions may be typed on the front inside cover of the set that is given to the subject for self-administration.

INSTRUCTIONS FOR SELF-ADMINISTRATION

1. Please write a story about each picture in this folder.

2. Do not look at the pictures before you are ready to write.

3. Look at one picture at a time only, in the order given, and write a story about what is going on in the picture, what led up to it, and what the outcome will be. Let yourself go freely, putting down things spontaneously as soon as they come to your mind and without any regard for literary beauty. Be dramatic as though you were writing a script for a movie.

4. It should not be necessary to spend more than about seven minutes per story, although you may spend more time if you wish.

5. Write about 300 words per story, or about one typing-paper page if you write in longhand. If at all possible, please type the longhand story later, without changes, in duplicate, double spaced, one story per page.

6. Please number the stories as you go along, and then put your name on the front sheet.

The obvious advantage of this time-saving procedure is somewhat offset by such disadvantages as a possible loss of spontaneity by the subject, the inability to control the length of the stories, and the lack of opportunity to intervene if the subject begins to show lack of co-operation in responding. Nevertheless, in psychiatric and psychological office practice, the self-administration method has proved quite satisfactory.

Again, for practical reasons it has become more and more the custom to give only ten or twelve pictures. These may be either the first ten or preferably such a selection as may seem most indicated, most likely to illuminate the details of presumably existent problems of the patient. (A discussion of the special usefulness of each picture and the special features of personality it is likely to bring out is offered below.) This matter holds particularly true when the use of the TAT is part of a clinical practice where one is likely to know a few things about the subject prior to testing and the practitioner can permit himself as much flexibility as he wishes in obtaining material for his own use [9].

An inquiry into the stories after they are completed is most helpful. It is particularly useful after one has had some experience in interpretation and knows what to ask for. As a routine, one would inquire for free associations or thoughts concerning all places, dates, proper names of persons, and any other specific or unusual information given by the subject.

THE INTERPRETATION OF THE TAT

If we accept the hypothesis of determinism of psychological behavior, it follows that deductions concerning the personality of an individual can be based on any kind of performance. It is this fact that allows nearly anyone to design a test and to be able to demonstrate some usefulness for it. One could ask subjects to stand on their heads and base fairly good judgments upon their reaction to and the execution of this request. Similarly nearly any test can be analyzed for a great many different aspects, and since each dimension is by necessity a function of the testee's personality, one is bound to have some results. The crux of the matter, of course, is to have such tests as combine maximum usefulness with maximum validity, reliability, and economy. By the same token, we need those analytical variables or scoring categories which will offer the most information with the least effort. The TAT has been interpreted in many ways. The simplest procedure is the inspection technique. Frequently it is helpful simply to read through the stories, treating them as meaningful psychological communications; one simply underlines anything that seems significant, specific, or unique. When an experienced examiner rereads the stories a second time, he can, almost without effort, find a repetitive pattern running through them, or he can find facts of different stories falling together into a meaningful whole. This method becomes easier the more experience one has with the TAT or the more clinical, particularly psychoanalytical, experience one has.

In psychiatric practice, as pointed out in one paper [9] it may be particularly helpful to have the patient hold one carbon copy of the TAT stories while the psychotherapist has another one, and then have the patient free-associate generally to the stories and make his own attempts at interpretation.

As a frame of reference for the method of interpretation for TAT protocols which I advocate, I review briefly characteristics of the major methods of interpretation which other workers have recommended. It is essential, for full information, that the reader consult the original sources in each instance for the complete system of interpretation that has been developed.

The original technique used by Murray and his co-workers depended on an analysis of the stories by the Need-Press Method. While it is best to consult Murray's book [48] on the details of the need-press concept, it may suffice here to say that every sentence was analyzed as to the needs of the hero and the environmental forces (press) he is exposed to. To choose a very simple example, he (the hero) loves her, but she hates him: need (for) love met by (press) hate.

Every story was so analyzed according to all needs and press, and each need and press received a weighted score. A rank-order system of the needs and press could then be tabulated. At the same time the hierarchical relationships of the needs to each other was investigated, with such concepts of Murray's as need-conflict, need-subsidiation, and need-fusion, which are described below. One of nearly a dozen possible schemes of categories, as developed by Murray and Bellak in 1941 at the Harvard Psychological Clinic, is here reproduced (Figure 3). A test manual [11] and a

QUANTITATIVE DATA

Picture No.

NEEDS	n	On	Weight Score	PRESS	p	Op	Weight Score
Abasement: Submission				**Personal Press**			
Intragg: Verbal				Acquisition: Social			
Physical				Asocial			
Achievement				Affiliation: Associative			
Acquisition: Social				Emotional			
Asocial				Aggression: Verbal			
Affiliation: Associative				Physical: Social			
Emotional				Asocial			
Aggression: Verbal				Curiosity			
Physical: Social				Deference: Compliance			
Asocial				Respect			
Destruction				Dominance: Coercion			
Autonomy: Freedom				Restraint			
Negativism				Exposition			
Asocial				Gratuity			
Blamavoidance				Nurturance			
Change				Punishment			
Cognizance				Rejection			
Counteraction				Retention			
Deference: Compliance				Sex			
Respect				Succorance			
Dominance				**Impersonal Press**			
Excitance				Affliction: Mental			
Exhibition				Physical			
Harmavoidance				Claustrum			
Infavoidance				Death			
Nurturance				Imposed Task			
Nutriance				Insupport			
Organization				Physical Danger: Active			
Passivity				Insupport			
Playmirth				Physical Injury			
Recognition				Lack			
Rejection				Loss			
Retention				Luck: Good			
Seclusion				Bad			
Sentience: Epicurean				Monotony			
Æsthetic							
Sex				Failure			
Succorance				Accomplishment			

Persons	Allied		Opposing	
	M	F	M	F
Superior				
Parent				
Gov't				
Equal				
Sibling				
Spouse				
Lover				
Group				
Inferior				
Offspring				

FIGURE 3. Murray and Bellak Interpretation Categories for the TAT

guide to the interpretation were designed and were based on an earlier one by Sanford and White *[65]*. The On and Op in the blank refer to "Object needs" and "Object press;" such needs and press as were ascribed not to the hero himself, but to another figure, who was presumably a second identification figure for the storyteller, but farther removed. Aside from a page for the recording of the quantitative need-press data there was also a page for the recording of more molar qualitative data, not unlike some of the categories described in the recommendations for interpretation that are indicated below.

The need-press scheme of interpretation still has many advantages for use in experiments in which detail is most important and time is no object. The method has not become at all popular clinically, however, since it is not easy to master the need concept, and it takes four to five hours on the average for twenty stories. Therefore a great number of attempts to interpret the TAT have sprung up. Wyatt *[85]* in an excellent review of the scoring and analysis of the TAT speaks specifically of Rapaport's, Henry's, Rotter's, Tomkins's, and his own method, aside from the need-press analysis.

Rotter's suggestions for the interpretation of the TAT are presented in three steps, of which the first refers to eleven aspects of responses to be utilized for interpretation. These are as follows:

I. Autobiographical quality, coherence, predominant mood, handling of sex; endings and their relationship to the story, repetition of themes, unusual wording, attitude toward the world, characteristics of central figure, typical methods of solving problems, characters that can be identified with mother, father, son, etc.

II. In the second step five principles of interpretation are proposed: frequency of occurrence of an idea, unusualness (regarding plot, language, misrecognitions), determination of identification, determination of clichés, selecting alternate interpretations (decision between two possible interpretations).

III. The third step contains qualitative suggestions for the analysis of personality trends as the final step of interpretation.

Rapaport's interpretation, according to Wyatt, is an examination of the cliche quality of responses, and the subject's deviation from cliches serves as a baseline for orientation. In his "points of view" for scoring, Rapaport suggests two major classes:

A. Formal characteristics of story structure, of which there are three aspects:
   1. *Compliance with instructions* (omissions and distortions; misplacing of emphasis; dwelling on picture rather than on situation; introduction of figures and objects not pictured).
   2. *Consistency within the testee's production.* (Interindividual consistency, as shown by deviation in expressive and aggressive qualities; deviation from the usual significance of a particular picture, and deviation concerning language and narrative form; and intraindividual consistency.)
   3. *Characteristics of verbalization.*
B. Formal characteristics of story content.
   1. Tone of narrative.
   2. Figures of story-identifications and memory representations.
   3. Strivings and attitudes.
   4. Obstacles.

Henry, in the most extensive and detailed scheme for analysis next to Murray's, distinguishes (A) form characteristics from (B) content characteristics.

A. Form characteristics are divided into six major categories, each of which has several subclasses.
   1. Amount and kind of imaginal production. (Length of story, amount and kind of introduced content; vividness, originality; rhythm and smoothness; variation in the consistency of all these factors.)
   2. Organizational qualities. (Presence or absence of antecedents of story and of outcome; level of organization; coherence and logic; manner of approach to central concept; contribution of elaborations and of details; variation in the consistency of all these.)
   3. Acuity of concepts, observations, and their integration.
   4. Language structure (movement, action, qualifying, descriptive words, etc.).
   5. Intraception-extraception.
   6. Relation of story told to total thought content (condensed, suppressed).
B. Content characteristics.

1. General tone (positive and negative tone of language; passivity or aggressiveness of language; expressed or implied conflict; expressed or implied interpersonal harmonies or affiliative action and thought).
2. Positive content (characters described in the story; interpersonal relations; action core of story).
3. Negative content (what subject failed to say; what he might have been expected to say).
4. Dynamic structure of content (symbols, associations). In the relation of the form and content characteristics eight areas are considered: mental approach; creativity and imagination; behavioral approach; family dynamics; inner adjustment; emotional reactivity; sexual adjustment; descriptive and interpretive summary.

Tomkins, in a systematic attempt at a logically consistent analysis of fantasy, distinguishes four major categories:

1. Vectors, comprising needs, or the quality of strivings "for," "against," "under," "by," "away," "from," "of."
2. Levels, such as those of wish, daydreams.
3. Conditions that may be either external forces (Murray's press) or inner states, such as anxiety or depression. Conditions do not refer to the goals of strivings but to given states the individual finds outside or inside himself.
4. Qualities, such as intensity, contingency (certainty), temporal considerations.

The principle underlying this system of analysis is that each class can be related to any other class. One vector can be the object of any other vector (for example, the wish to act).

Wyatt himself uses fifteen variables for the analysis of the TAT: (1) story description, (2) stimulus perception, (3) deviations from typical response, (4) deviation from self, (5) time trend, (6) level of interpretation, (7) tone of story, (8) quality of telling, (9) focal figure, (10) other figures, (11) personal relationships, (12) strivings, avoidances, (13) press, (14) outcome, (15) thema.

RECOMMENDED METHOD FOR THE INTERPRETATION OF THE TAT

Since I believe that the strength of the TAT lies in its ability to elicit the content and dynamics of interpersonal relationships and the psychodynamic patterns, my method of interpretation and my scoring categories are primarily concerned with these dimensions and only to a small extent with the formal characteristics.

The main thing to remember in the interpretation of the TAT is the following: the TAT pictures are best seen psychologically as a series of social situations and interpersonal relations. Instead of responding to real people in real situations, the subject is responding to people in the pictures, which he imagines as certain social situations. Since he is under less constraint of conventionality or reality, his responses are more likely to depict his inner feelings. By this means we get at the contemporary patterns of his social behavior and may be able to infer the genesis of these patterns. Interpretation is the process of finding a common denominator in the contemporary and genetic behavior patterns of a person [14].

Among other things, this definition of interpretation implies what cannot be emphasized too much, particularly for the beginner: hardly ever should a diagnostic statement be made on a datum revealed in only one story. Impressions gleaned in one instance can be considered a very tentative inference only, for which one must try to find corroboration in other stories of some source of information external to the TAT. *A repetitive pattern is the best assurance that one does not deal with an artifact.*

To give a more definite frame of reference for scoring and a more objectively comparable scheme of interpretation, I have designed the system that the Psychological Corporation has published as the Bellak TAT Blank and Analysis Sheet [1] (Figure 4). I believe that it is a system simple enough to be most easily mastered, to serve as a guide and frame of reference, and to make it possible to glean the most important data of a complete ten-story TAT in about half an hour.

HOW TO USE THE TAT BLANK

The Bellak TAT Blank consists of a six-page folder plus separate Recording and Analysis Sheets of which one page from the folder is duplicated. On the cover of the folder one records the personal

---

[1] I am indebted to the Psychological Corporation of New York City for permitting me to reproduce here material that the Corporation originally published as the *Bellak TAT Blank, Analysis Sheets, and Guide to the Interpretation of the TAT.*

Name_____ Story No._____ (TAT Picture No._____

1. Main Theme:

2. Main hero (heroine): age_____ sex_____ vocation_____
   interests_____
   traits_____
   abilities_____
   adequacy (√, √√, √√√)_____

3. Attitudes to superior (parental) figures, or to society: (√, √√, √√√)
   autonomous_____   compliant_____   respectful_____   devoted_____
   grateful_____   dependent_____   remorseful_____   competitive_____
   resistant_____   aggressive_____   abasive_____   fearful_____
   _____   _____   _____   _____

4. Figures introduced: (√)
   punisher_____   pursuer_____   benefactor_____   teacher_____
   friend_____   reformer_____   lover_____   supporter_____
   enemy_____   '_____   _____   _____

5. Objects introduced (symbols?):

6. Objects omitted:

7. Attribution of blame: (√, √√, √√√)
   injustice_____   indifference_____   deception_____
   severity_____   deprivation_____   unfortunate influence_____
   _____   _____   _____

8. Significant conflicts: (√, √√, √√√)
   Superego-id_____   passivity-counteraction_____
   compliance-autonomy_____   achievement-pleasure_____
   _____

9. Punishment -- for crime: (√, √√, √√√)
   just_____   too severe_____   lenient_____
   immediate_____   delayed_____   none_____

10. Attitude to hero: (√, √√, √√√)
   detached and objective_____
   critical and abusive_____   _____
   involved and empathic_____   _____

11. Signs of inhibition at aggression, sex, etc.: (√, √√, √√√)
   pauses_____   change of trend_____   stammer_____   _____

12. Outcome: (√, √√, √√√)
   happy_____   unhappy_____   realistic_____   unrealistic_____

13. Pattern of need gratification: (√)   **14. Plot: (√, √√, √√√)**
   need-conflict_____   structured_____   unstructured_____
   need-fusion_____   realistic_____   bizarre_____
   need-subsidiation_____   complete_____   incomplete_____
   _____   _____   _____

Analysis Sheet for Use with the Bellak TAT Blank.

47-226AS The Psychological Corporation

FIGURE 4. Analysis Sheet for Use with the Bellak TAT Blank

data of the client and, when the analysis is complete, one writes a Final Report.

Let us assume that the examiner wishes to secure ten stories from a client and that he is going to take down these stories himself as the client tells them. The first story will be written on page 2 of the TAT Blank, the second story will be written on the back of an Analysis Sheet. Story 3 is recorded on the back of another Analysis Sheet, etc., until the ten have been recorded. The examiner now has the ten stories recorded, one on the inside cover of the Blank and nine on the back of separate Analysis Sheets. If these are placed in order, printed-side up, and laid on top of page 3 in the TAT Blank, the examiner will note that when each sheet is turned over he has an Analysis Sheet opposite the corresponding story. The Analysis Sheet for story 1 is on the front side of the paper on which story 2 is written, the Analysis Sheet for story 2 is on the front side of the sheet on which story 3 is written, etc. The analysis of story 10 (or the last story, if more or fewer stories are used) will be made on the Analysis Sheet that is printed as page 3 of the six-page Blank.

The instructions for using the Analysis Sheets are given in the next section of this paper.

After the stories have been analyzed in this fashion, the examiner can write a Summary of each of the stories in the space provided on page 4. (If more than ten stories are used, more summaries can be written on the back of page 4.) It is best to write these summaries after all the stories have been analyzed because the summary is one of the stages in formally integrating the content of the analysis of each separate story. When the Summary sheet has been completed on page 4, one is prepared to write the Final Report. It will be noted that by folding the Blank, the space for the Final Report and the Summary page may be exposed side by side.

When the task is done, the loose sheets may be stapled in the folder for safekeeping, and the Final Report is on the cover for convenient reference.

As noted above, some examiners prefer to have their patients write the stories themselves. Since the patients should not have access to the outline on the Analysis Sheet, they should write their stories on plain 8½″ by 11″ paper. If the stories are so short that there are several on a sheet, they can be cut up and either pasted or clipped to the back of separate Analysis Sheets so that the final arrangement will be the same as if the examiner himself had written on the back of the Analysis Sheets. If a separate sheet is used for each story, the folder will naturally be a little bulkier unless a typist is available to copy the stories on the backs of Analysis Sheets.

For some items on the Analysis Sheet, appropriate information from the story must be written in, using whatever short phrase or key word will most facilitate the analytic process. For others, indicated on the Blank by (√), a system of checks is suggested. A single check (√) may be used to indicate the mere presence of a given attitude, conflict, or the like. A double check (√ √) or triple check (√ √ √) may be used to indicate increasing levels of importance to be assigned to the given item in summarizing the story. It is hoped that this approach to quantification will further research studies of interexaminer reliability of interpretation in addition to increasing the flexibility of the analysis form. Blank spaces are provided for adding categories or ideas not given in the outline.

SCORING CATEGORIES

The following suggestions for the use and interpretation of the individual scoring categories of the TAT Blank may be helpful.

1. The Main Theme. The main theme is best understood as an attempt to restate the gist of the story. (It must be remembered that one TAT story may actually have more than one basic theme.) Since beginners in the use of the test go off on a tangent most often in an interpretation of the main theme, a breakdown of the main theme into five levels is recommended:[2]

    (a) The *descriptive* level: on this level the theme should be a plain restatement of the summarized meaning of the story, a finding of the common trend restated in an abbreviated form and simple words.

    (b) The *interpretive* level.

---

[2] For the beginner it is most helpful to force himself to go through all five levels. However, it may not be necessary to put them all down in writing. Particularly, the descriptive level is a crutch; it may suffice just to state the theme at this level in one's mind. The interpretive level might be recorded on each analysis sheet, and the diagnostic, or higher, level may be the basis for the summary statement.

(c) The *diagnostic* level.

(d) The *symbolic* level.

(e) The *elaborative* level.

The example of the following story may help (6BM).

"This is a young successful engineer. He is the only son in his family; his father is dead, and his mother is very close to him. He is in the oil business and he has been offered a contract to go overseas to the East Indies. He has signed the contract and is about to leave. He obtains her farewell and they part heartbroken. After a while she feels very lonesome and decides to follow her son to the East Indies. It is wartime and somehow she obtains passage on a ship to the island on which her son is. An enemy submarine sinks her ship and she perishes. Her son had not heard about her intentions but had independently planned to visit her as a surprise. He decides to return home for a surprise. The ship on which he had obtained passage is taking the same route his mother had taken. At the exact spot where his mother perishes, another enemy submarine attacks and he perishes also."

The theme on a *descriptive level* could be briefly restated as: a son lives alone with his beloved mother and leaves her—when they both try to rejoin each other they die on the same spot. On an *interpretive level* one may go a step farther and put the meaning in a generalized form, assuming a meaning beyond this story: the patient believes that if one[3] permits oneself (incestual) fantasies, such as living with the mother, then both parties die. On a *diagnostic level* one transforms these impressions into a definitive statement: this man has incestuous problems and œdipal conflicts that cause him severe guilt feelings. On a *symbolic level* one may choose to interpret symbols according to psychoanalytic hypotheses; extreme parsimony and caution must be strongly recommended since this takes one relatively farthest away from hard facts. In our example one might, for instance, possibly want to interpret the torpedoes as paternal phallic symbols which endanger and destroy both mother and son for their illicit attempted get-together.

On an *elaborative level* one must get the subjects elaborations and free associations to such specific data as: "East Indies," "en-

---

[3] The interpretive level can nearly always be stated as a generalized conditional clause introduced by "If one   "

gineer," to any proper names or dates and any other associations he can give.

2. The Main Hero.[4] The main hero of the story is the one who is most spoken of, whose feelings and subjective notions are most discussed, and, in general, the figure with whom the narrator seems to identify himself. In case of doubt the figure resembling the patient most closely in age, sex, and other characteristics should be considered the main hero. At times a man may identify himself with a female "main hero"; if this occurs repeatedly, it might be considered a sign of latent homosexuality. While practically all young men identify in Picture 2 with the young girl in the foreground, only a minority consider the figure Picture 3BM a female. Vocation, interests, traits, abilities, and adequacy of the main hero frequently depict qualities or desired qualities of the patient.

By the adequacy of the hero we mean his ability to carry through tasks under external and internal difficulties in a socially, morally, intellectually, and emotionally acceptable manner. The adequacy of the hero frequently conforms to a pattern throughout the stories and is often in a direct relationship to the ego strength of the patient.

It should also be mentioned here that at times there may be more than one hero in a story. The patient may use a second figure with whom to identify himself, aside from the clearly recognizable main hero. This happens rather rarely; usually it involves a figure introduced but not present in the picture itself, and concerns drives and sentiments that are even more objectionable to the patient than the ones pertaining to the main hero. (Other devices for emphatically trying to dissociate oneself from a story are to place it far away geographically and/or temporally; e.g., placing a story in Russia in the Middle Ages.)

3. Attitudes to Superior (Parental) Figures or to Society.

---

[4] Many of the following variables were used by me in an earlier, mimeographed Scoring Blank I designed while at the Harvard Psychological Clinic, 1940-2. Thus a great and not easily specified extent of information and stimulation concerning these variables was received from Dr. H. A. Murray, Dr. R. W. White, and indirectly from Dr. R. N. Sanford, who, with Dr. White, had written a mimeographed guide to the TAT that served as the major stimulus for systematic attempts of interpretation. I wish to express my gratitude to these and other members of the staff of the Harvard Psychological Clinic.

These attitudes are usually quite clearly brought out in TAT stories. They appear particularly in response to the pictures of people with obvious age differences. but also frequently in response to the boy with the violin. The subcategories suggested are self-explanatory, and a pattern of behavior from story to story will usually become clear.

4. Figures Introduced. If a figure is not present in the picture, and the subject introduces it into his story, we can be doubly sure that it must be a figure of great significance for him and that it constitutes an exponent of an outstanding need or fear. One might note the role which that figure plays dynamically (e.g., punisher, supporter), and at the same time note whether it appears in the form of a male or female, parent or contemporary, etc.

5. Objects Introduced. Again, because these objects are supplied strictly by the subject's mind and not at all by the picture, they deserve special notice. Frequently one class of objects, such as books, objects of art, weapons, or money, appears consistently in the stories of a subject, and must be interpreted accordingly.

6. Objects Omitted. This category is concerned with meaningful failure to include in the stories objects that are quite apparent in the pictures. Sometimes the rifle in 8BM is omitted, and at other times the pistol in 3BM, or the background of a half-dressed woman in Picture 4, etc. Under such circumstances one must look for other indications as to what problems the subject might have concerning aggression or sexual matters that cause him to exclude these or other objects from apperception.

7. Attribution of Blame. The qualities or forces that the subject blames as causing misfortune or tragedy in his story frequently constitute important clues to his conception of the outside world in relation to himself. The variables listed on the Blank are the ones most frequently met with; others may have to be written in.

8. Significant Conflicts. The superego-id variable is really more inclusive than the other items under this heading; it indicates a general class of conflicts, while the other three items give a more specific indication of the main divergent tendencies. Nevertheless, all these items deal with the more molar level of major conflictual themes, while need-conflicts, under Category 13, are concerned with the more molecular patterns of any number of needs occurring in the story.

9. Punishment for Crime. The relationship of the nature of the punishment to the severity of the offense gives us an excellent insight into the severity of the superego; a psychopath's hero may consistently get away in stories of murder with not more than a notion that he has learned a lesson for later life, while a neurotic may have stories in which the hero is accidentally or intentionally killed or mangled or dies of illness following the slightest infractions or expression of aggression.

10. Attitude to Hero. A subject will frequently depict his own conflicts by having the hero say or do things in the story and then stepping outside the narrative to criticize these actions severely. At times cynical remarks concerning his own story are simple defensive processes against real emotional involvement. Obsessive-compulsive intellectuals will frequently maintain a detached attitude, offering several possible themes with doubt pertaining to them all. Hysterics and manics or hypomanics will frequently get dramatically involved in stories full of affectivity.

11. Signs of Inhibition at Aggression, Sex, etc. Pauses are sometimes so significant that it may even pay to time them occasionally to get a notion of the severity of the inhibition in the subject. Changes of trends of the story or turning to an entirely new story are excellent indications that conflictual material was becoming too difficult to handle. Stammering, crossing out, omitting parts of the picture, rejection of all or part of a picture, or severe criticism of it are similarly points worth noticing in this context.

12. Outcome. The outcome will often make manifest the basic mood or adjustment of the patient and indicate his ego-strength. It is interesting to note whether the subject (hero) arrives at a satisfactory solution after a continuous realistic struggle or uses a *deus ex machina* device to arrive at a simple gratification which is obviously on the level of a fantasy wish-fulfillment and has little relation to an overt, manifest achievement drive. If there is a failure to arrive at an acceptable outcome altogether, it probably results from very significant, nearly insurmountable problems of the patient, and should be scored under the variables of the plot structure, Category 14.

13. Pattern of Need Gratification. The concept of conflict between various needs does not require any explanation. One

story may actually show whole clusters of conflicts between various drives of varying importance.

Murray's concepts of *need-fusion* and *need-subsidiation* are very helpful for the understanding of motivational systems in a given personality. For example, if a hero wants to buy a restaurant with the notion of giving people better and more healthful food and at the same time enriching himself by means of this public service, we would speak of a *fusion* of the hero's need for nurturance and his need for acquisition. On the other hand the hero may want to buy the restaurant because he expects it to be a good source of income which he needs to take care of his family. In this case we would say that his need for acquisition (of money) is *subsidiary* to his need for nurturance; namely, he wants to acquire money *in order to* be able to take care of his family. By means of these two concepts, whole hierarchies of motivation can be recognized in the TAT.

14. Plot. The form-analysis of the TAT stories may be helpful to a certain extent.

While such authors as Balken et al. *[5]* and Wyatt *[84]* have made an intensive form-analysis of the TAT stories, it is my belief that there is a quickly diminishing return in this approach, and this is more strictly in the province of the Rorschach Test. The categories of structure, bizarreness, and completeness, however, probably permit a fairly good appraisal of the intactness of the thought processes and the ego's ability to master the emotional material produced.

THE SUMMARY AND FINAL REPORT

After having analyzed each of the stories according to the categories, one quickly goes back over them and summarizes the main features of each on the page provided for it in the Blank. The Blank is so constructed that this summary page remains in full view as one runs through all the stories. By this process the repetitive pattern of the stories emerges almost automatically.

The form of the final report will, of course, depend on the person to whom it is addressed. As a routine, it is suggested that it be in two parts, one of which consists mostly of molar data of general description of the personality and its outstanding features. In the second part a concerted attempt must be made to be concretely descriptive. One may illustrate the molar characteristics described above by factual material from the stories to make it more meaningful to the person receiving the report and to protect oneself against flights of fancy. There should never be any statement of data that cannot be concretely supported by specific reference to story material. Apperceptive distortion is not a unique quality of testees, but can, *horribile dictu,* be found among interpreters! One may also run through the stories systematically, tying up the repetitive themes and bringing out the minor features and more tentative hypotheses.

If a diagnosis has to be offered, or if one wishes to state one, I suggest that the following formula be used: "The data represented in the TAT are consistent with the diagnosis of . . ." This expresses my belief that the TAT is not primarily a diagnostic test and also that preferably no diagnosis should ever be made on the basis of a single test. Even better, never on test evidence alone without additional information provided by a clinical interview.

SELECTION OF PICTURES FOR INDIVIDUAL TAT'S

Since I prefer to have only a single session for the administration of the TAT, both for time-saving in administration and in interpretation and also because I believe that usually an optimum of material is obtained from about ten or twelve pictures, some word must be said about the criteria of selecting pictures for a given case. Below is a description of the responses I have usually obtained in each of the pictures in this series.

Aside from the age and sex of the subject, the other factors that may play a role are the determining criteria for selecting one or the other picture. For instance, siblings, if any, will be one factor; if a member of the family is dead, that is still another factor; if there is information on clinical problems, such pictures may be selected as might show heterosexual problems or those relative to childhood, and so on.

No experimentally derived performance standards for "normals" or even for various diagnostic groups have as yet been fully established, although much work is currently being carried on to provide evidence of modal performance for members of various groups. The remarks made below, although not grounded in experimental evidence, do possess a strong background of empirical sanction.

PICTURE NO. I

This picture usually leads to an identification of the subject with the boy and brings out the *relationship toward the parental figures*. That is, it usually becomes quite apparent whether the parents were perceived as aggressive, domineering, helpful, understanding, or protective. Aside from learning about the subject's relationship to his parents, we also find out to which parent a certain kind of relationship existed. Frequently we get themes on the conflict between autonomy and compliance with authority in all its wide variations and different patterns. For example, one subject may try to escape the parental commands to practice the violin by playing in the street, but then he finally feels that he ought to go in and play the violin; or he may run away from home; or the hero might be described as not obeying his parents and doing what he wants. Later on he experiences failure because he did not obey them. Thus one subject may display guilt feelings about his autonomy while in other cases all may go well after he has broken away. Therefore this card is successfully employed especially with adolescents.

Another need this card frequently brings out is the one of *achievement*. It is particularly important to watch how the success is achieved, whether just on a fantasy level or on a reality level. Finally, we find that subjects give *symbolic sexual responses* to this card. The play on the strings of the violin, the play with the fiddle, frequently becomes a symbolic story of masturbation, and castration fears are often brought in when the subject insists that the strings have been broken. I wish to say again that extreme caution must be employed to avoid reading symbols into stories and in overrating their importance even when they are stressed.

PICTURE NO. 2

This picture of a country scene usually offers excellent indications of the subject's *family relations*. Even males usually identify with the central figure of the young girl because it is so definitely the figure in the foreground. Again, varying themes of *autonomy* from the family versus *compliance* with the conservative, backward existence are extremely frequent. These themes show the type of divergence between the subject and the family.

Most useful for our purposes is the subject's handling of the woman leaning against the tree, who is a figure often seen as pregnant. A great deal of information can be obtained from the manner in which the subject handles apperception of *pregnancy*. It may be completely ignored or it may lead to highly informative notions about it in all ages.

In this picture, which is one of those having a relatively large number of objects in it, obsessive-compulsive subjects will comment on small details such as the lake in the background and the tiny figure in the background, in addition to other objects, in a way that practically permits the diagnosis of *compulsive tendencies*. The way in which the relationship of the two women to the man in the relative foreground is discussed—whether as a farmhand run by the woman, or as a father, husband, or brother —adds a good deal of information about the *role of the sexes*.

PICTURE NO. 3BM

This also belongs among the most useful. Most males see the huddled figure as a man; if it is seen by men as a female figure, this may be considered a point to keep in mind—not to make the diagnosis, but to keep in mind factors of possible *latent homosexuality* which may be confirmed if more suggestive evidence appears in other pictures. How the object to the left is perceived often gives a great deal of information of the problems concerning *aggression*. Officially this object is described as a gun. Some subjects may recognize it as a gun; it is interesting to observe the manner of handling the aggression—whether it is used as extra-aggression (e.g., somebody else is being shot by the hero, or whether it is used as intra-aggression (the hero is being shot or he commits suicide). If it leads to extra-aggression, it will be interesting to notice what happens to the hero. Whether he is punished severely or whether he escapes is a kind of protocol that gives us a notion of the strength of the superego of the subject. On the other hand we want to get some clue as to what leads to the depressive pattern that results finally in suicide. It is obvious that this picture is a must with *depressed patients*. Sometimes the pistol may be turned into a toy pistol and thus rendered harmless. It is important to find out by checking the consistency with other stories whether it is a superficial escape from really entering into the story or whether this corresponds to the fact that the subject is simply healthy and has neither excessive intra- or extra-aggression. Again, a subject who has to repress his latent aggressiveness may completely deny the presence of the gun by simply omitting reference to it, seeing it as a hole in the floor, as a cigarette case, or not at all. Sometimes a great conflict around aggression, particularly when it has led to a compulsive pattern, will manifest itself by the subject's hemming and hawing for a considerable time over what the object might be.

PICTURE NO. 3GF

This is a picture that may also bring out *depressive feelings*. Frequently, though, it is found more useful with females to use No. 3BM, with which they can easily identify.

PICTURE NO. 4

The picture of a man's being held back by a woman brings out a great variety of needs and sentiments in regard to *male-female relationships*. Themes of infidelity are often struck, and the male attitude toward the role of women may appear. She may be a protector who tries to keep him from rushing into something poorly thought out or one who tries to hold onto him for evil purposes. Similarly, a woman's attitude toward men as persons who may have been aggressive toward her becomes apparent.

Since the woman looks somewhat unusual, she is often made the member of a *minority group*, and sentiments concerning these are displayed.

Another object of interest is the picture of the semi-nude in the background, which is perceived by more than two thirds of the subjects. If it is not perceived or discussed at all, it may be a clue to the fact that there is a *sexual problem*. On the other hand it may be seen as a poster or as an actual figure in the background, prompting themes of *triangular jealousy*. Whether the difference in depth perception, seeing it as a poster or as a live person, can be considered a differential criterion of any value is not clear thus far.

PICTURE NO. 5

A middle-aged woman looking through a half-open door is often interpreted as the *mother who may be watching* different activities. At times this becomes a symbolic story of fear of observed *masturbation*, or the mother figure appears as benevolently interested in how the child is, or she may be seen as reprimanding the subject for being up late. *Voyeuristic material* is quite frequent and may actually lead to disguised stories of the *primal scene*. Again, *fear of attack*, particularly in female subjects, is often reflected in a story of burglary, while in males it may lead to "*rescue phantasies,*" in the psychoanalytic sense.

PICTURE NO. 6BM

This is an indispensable picture for males, reflecting all the problems of *mother-son relationships* and all their derivatives in relation to wives and other women. Œdipal themes are frequent. The stories given to this picture run such a complete range of this fundamental problem that only a monograph could do it justice.

PICTURE NO. 6GF

This is really meant to be a counterpart of No. 6BM to reflect the *relationship of females to the father.* Probably because of the apparently relatively slight age difference, however, the man is usually, at least manifestly, not seen as the father image but rather as a contemporary who may thereupon be invested with any number of qualities, from those of an aggressor, a seducer, to someone who proposes marriage. Frequently this man is made into an uncle who probably represents the picture of an idealized father, as is so often done in folklore. For instance, Uncle Sam and Uncle Czar. All in all, the picture is not a very useful one.

PICTURE NO. 7BM

This picture of an old man and a young man is indispensable in bringing out the *father-son relationship* and all its derivatives (in males) in the form of attitudes to male authority.

PICTURE NO. 7GF

This picture will bring out the relationship between *mother and child in females.* It seems to encourage negative attitudes toward the mother because of the fact that the girl is looking off into the distance rather than at the mother. In turn, again, the doll may reflect relationship toward the subject's *expectancy of children.*

PICTURE NO. 8BM

This is a very useful picture. Usually male subjects identify with the boy in the foreground. The essential themes that may be developed are centered on either *aggression*—somebody was shot and is now being operated upon in the background—or upon stories of ambition—the dream of a boy to become a doctor, for example. Whether the rifle at the left is recognized or not, and what is made of it, are problems similar to that of the pistol in No. 3BM. The way in which the figures are described—for example, the attitude toward the doctor as an older person or toward the person being operated upon—if seen as a paternal figure, frequently gives clues as to the œdipal relationship.

PICTURE NO. 8GF

Nearly any theme may be produced to this picture, usually of a shallow, contemplative nature. I rarely find it useful.

PICTURE NO. 9BM

This is another indispensable picture for disclosing *contemporary, man-to-man relationships*. It may, for one thing, offer a general indication of social relationships—namely, which of the figures the subject identifies with. In extremes the subject may identify with someone outside the group who looks askance at the group, or he may be part of it or even the center. Again, *homosexual drives and fears* may become quite apparent in stories to this picture. Also, *social prejudices* may be brought to light here; for example, stories of hoboes.

PICTURE NO. 9GF

This is an invaluable picture in getting a notion of the woman-to-woman feeling, particularly for bringing out sister rivalry or daughter-mother hostility. It is very important in cases in which one suspects *depression* and *suicidal tendencies*, since not infrequently in such circumstances the girl below is made into someone who, in a panic, runs into the sea. Again, at least suspiciousness may be brought out by the fact that stories sometimes raise discussions of how this one person is watching the other maliciously.

PICTURE NO. 10

This will bring out much about the *relation of men to women*. If this is interpreted as an embrace between males by a male subject, it is a strong clue to *latent homosexuality* or even manifest problems of this nature. If it is described as a man and a woman by either males or females, it will be interesting to observe whether it is made a story of departure or arrival, reflecting in the departure theme latent hostile needs.

PICTURE NO. 11

Here are brought out *many infantile or primitive fears*, since the animals permit projection of such emotions. If a patient has *fears of attack*, this is a most useful picture since it will expose the fine features of the fears of being attacked—for example, by the phallic symbol of the dragon. Stories of *oral aggression* are frequent, and this picture offers good clues to the mood of the patient, whether or not they escape and, if so, how.

PICTURE NO. 12M

This is a most important picture for indicating the qualities of the *relationship of a younger man to an older man*, particularly as regards *passive homosexual fears* and fears of being under the domination of superior figures.

PICTURE NO. 12F

This may bring out *conceptions of mother figures*, but, all in all, it is not a picture that I have found to be notably useful.

PICTURE NO. 12BG

This also has not been found too useful in any specific case except in *suicidal* or very *depressed subjects*. It will often, however, elicit stories of someone's having jumped or fallen out of the boat.

PICTURE NO. 13MF

This is an excellent picture for disclosing *sexual conflicts in both men and women*. In very inhibited subjects this may practically lead to a "sex shock," which will find expression in the stories. In females it may elicit fears of being raped, attacked, or otherwise abused by men. In males it will often bring out guilt feelings about sexual activity and will easily show the disgust of homosexuals. Feeling between husband and wife may be projected. Not unusual are stories of *economic deprivation* in response to this picture, and *oral tendencies* will frequently appear in discussion of the breasts. Again, since this is one of the pictures containing relatively much detail, *obsessive-compulsives* will easily be recognized by their concern with details.

PICTURE NO. 13B

To a lesser degree, this is not unlike the violin picture in prompting *stories of childhood* and is of some use with young boys, though not markedly.

PICTURE NO. 13G

This picture has not been found to be especially useful in my experience thus far.

PICTURE NO. 14

This silhouette of a man can be a most useful figure. For one thing, it will be interesting to note the *sexual identification* of the object. It will often bring out childhood *fears in relation to darkness*. Again, it is an absolute must when one suspects *suicidal tendencies*, which may be expressed in a story of jumping out of the window. Frequently it will induce themes of simple contemplation and reveal much of the philosophical rationalization in the subject. Sometimes it may reveal *æsthetic interests* and offer wish-fulfillment stories. It may result in burglary stories if someone is perceived as coming into the window.

PICTURE NO. 15

Especially important is this picture of a figure in a graveyard if the subject has had a *death in the immediate family* and the clinician wants to get his sentiments regarding that death. It is a very useful picture also in that it may disclose notions and *fears of death* in any subject. *Depressive tendencies* manifest themselves clearly.

PICTURE NO. 16

The blank card is of extreme value in verbally gifted subjects, who may really let loose and project freely. If the subject has given previous indications that he has difficulty in expressing fantasy material, however, the blank card is often of no value.

PICTURE NO. 17BM

There are many useful aspects to this picture. There may be revelations of fears in stories of escape from physical trauma, such as fire, or fleeing from man. The latter often leads to disclosures concerning *œdipal fears*, particularly in children, where this picture may actually be seen as someone fleeing from the "king" or the "prince." Again, *homosexual feelings* are easily brought out even by descriptive details. Not unusual are stories of a competitive nature, making this an athletic meet or the like. In males there will often be an indication of their *body image*—whether or not they feel themselves to be muscular, etc.

PICTURE NO. 17GF

Here is another worth-while card when one suspects *suicidal tendencies in women* since it opens the way for stories about jumping from a bridge. Otherwise a great variety of stories may be told to No. 17GF, which I do not consider one of the more useful cards except for the one purpose just stated.

PICTURE NO. 18BM

This is another of the more important pictures for learning about, or verifying, any *anxiety in males*. Fears of attack, particularly of a homosexual nature, become most apparent. If anyone has anxiety at all, it is bound to come in response to this picture. On the other hand, it can be made into something innocuous, such as a story of support, for example, of a man in an intoxicated condition being brought home by his friends. How the problem of supernumerary hands is handled is frequently of great interest so far as the thought processes of the subject are concerned.

PICTURE NO. 18GF

This picture gives an excellent indication of how *aggression is being handled by women*. It may be completely evaded by the denial that any aggressive act is taking place. Sometimes stories of how one woman is helping another up the stairs or up from the floor are told in attempts to evade aggressive implications. *Mother-daughter conflicts* may appear here clearly.

PICTURE NO. 19

A picture sometimes useful with children, but otherwise not notable.

PICTURE NO. 20

The figure against the lamppost may be seen either as a man or as a woman. We do not have any definite indication of the differential implications of such sexual identification. Females may present stories of fear of men or of the dark. Otherwise fears may be brought out by either sex by making it a gangster story. Again, It may be made an entirely innocuous theme by a story of an evening's date.

THE PROBLEM OF OVERT AND LATENT NEEDS IN THE TAT

The interpreter of TAT stories is frequently presented with the necessity of deciding whether or not a need expressed pertains strictly to the fantasy level or might be expressed in reality; for example, the need for aggression or for achievement. The psychologist should have available a maximum of clinical and biographical data about the patient. It must be remembered that the clinical situation is not one concerned with testing the validity of the instrument. Problems of the validity of the TAT are dealt with in experiments and must be decided there. If one has sufficient information on the patient, then the TAT stories must be seen as complementary to the behavioral data obtained. For example, if the subject is unduly shy and retiring and the stories are full of aggression and guilt feelings about the figures, the dynamic implications are obvious.

On the other hand there are certain indications from intratest situations which permit us to make assumptions about the manifest or latent needs expressed in the TAT. For instance, in stories of achievement it is extremely important to notice whether they follow the *deus ex machina* mechanism or are actually done piece by piece and suggest much more that they correspond to a behavioral need for achievement.

It was R. N. Sanford who pointed out some important rules concerning the relationship between fantasy needs and behavioral needs. He suggested that there are certain needs that usually are high in fantasy and low in behavior: namely, those needs which are usually prohibited and inhibited by cultural pressure from overt manifestation. These are mainly the needs of acquisition, aggression, autonomy, and sexual activity, the wish to be taken care of, and the need for harm avoidance, the last two suffering more cultural repression in men. On the other hand, some needs may find little manifest expression in fantasy but may find much expression in manifest behavior because of reality demands, such as the need for order, for avoiding social blame, for learning. Again there is a class of needs which may be high both in fantasy and in behavior, indicating that while these needs are permitted and encouraged socially, they may yet be sufficiently frustrated to need particular gratification on the fantasy level. To these belong especially the needs for achievement, for friendship, and for dominance.

SPECIAL STUDIES ON THE VALIDITY AND RELIABILITY OF THE TAT

It is not my intention in this chapter to review the studies on the validity and reliability of the TAT for the purpose of evaluating them. There have been numerous attempts to establish the test's validity and reliability, although, in my judgment, by no means a sufficient number to answer satisfactorily even some of the basic questions in this area. I must refer the reader who is concerned with the serious issues and problems in connection with validity and reliability to suitable references in the bibliography and especially to Tomkins's book *[80]*, which inquires carefully into this whole area.

I do wish to refer here only to one specific problem on the validity of the TAT: namely, the potential effect of current episodes and moods on the validity of the TAT stories. Some of my earlier experiments were concerned with artificially introducing aggression in the subjects by provoking them or giving them posthypnotic orders to feel aggressive. Thereafter when these subjects were asked to give stories to the TAT pictures, it became clear that they would project some of the aggression into the stories. Split-half comparisons between five stories told under these circumstances, and five stories told without induced aggression, however, showed that the main personality characteristics persisted despite the artificial situation that was introduced. To a large extent the subjects would differ in their manner of handling the problem of aggression, either expressing it as extra-aggression or intra-aggression or reacting with guilt feelings, etc. On another occasion I studied in a similar manner depressive feelings and joyfulness. Again the effect on the TAT stories was such as still to leave the essential personality structure intact.

The effect of current experience on TAT stories was studied in the case of Julius Streicher and Alfred Rosenberg [13] who were given TAT's by Dr. G. M. Gilbert in Nuremberg at the time of their trials. In this paper I pointed out that in spite of the fact that both were certainly experiencing failure in their major objectives in life and were confronted with imminent execution, widely different personality factors appeared.

A FEW REMARKS ON SPECIAL DIAGNOSTIC GROUPS IN THE TAT

Although it has been pointed out before that I do not believe that the main strength or function of the TAT lies in its ability to diagnose specific nosological groups, it can be of use for such diagnostic indications. If I give a few stories as examples below, I do so with misgivings since I firmly believe that the pattern of a number of stories is most important and dislike giving single stories as evidence of any trend. The space available makes it undesirable to reproduce whole TAT protocols; therefore I am making a minimal use of this unhappy compromise of picking out a specific story, and I caution the reader against it.

Not infrequently one will notice that *obsessive-compulsives* give their attention to small details in the pictures, and frequently they will respond with more than one story to one picture. We may often find that the storyteller stays distant and expresses sarcastic attitudes toward the hero, remaining emotionally isolated himself. In *hysterics and hypomanics*, on the other hand, we find a great deal of affect and a lively identification with the hero.

In *manifest homosexuals* I have noticed a tendency toward frequent manifest sexual references and a recurrent shift of identification not only from males to females but also within one sex. The result is that these stories are rather difficult to score.

Manics will often indicate strong tendencies of oral incorporation; very many references to food and getting things may be apparent (though this is, of course, not pathognomic at all). Again, in *depressed patients*, suicidal themes, a depressed over-all mood, and self-depreciation, along with other signs of a very strong superego, may be apparent.

Below is the story of a manic-depressive girl in remission, illustrating the oral tendencies with three references to eating in a brief story. The picture rarely elicits any reference to food; stories of attack are more frequent.

PROTOCOL—PICTURE NO. 11

"This picture takes place in Texas about 5,000 years from now. Civilization is extinct. An atom bomb had killed everyone, and the whole earth is beginning again.

"The remains of civilization are the Spanish arch in the right lower corner. On the top are a few birds looking for *food*. There's a mountain on the left side, and from a cave a sort of snake-bodied, duck-footed animal is wiggling out. He's going to strike the birds, *eat* them, and then go merrily on his way looking for more *food*."

I do not believe that it is generally useful to give TAT's to frankly psychotic subjects, particularly schizophrenic patients, since in that case their unconscious motives are surfaced anyhow. In incipient cases, however, it may be quite useful for discovering trends. More often than not, thought disturbances will become apparent in the sentence structure and in the lack of construction in the plot. The bizarreness of theme and of fears, a general helplessness of the hero, which suggests little ego strength, are also consistent with a schizophrenic pattern. Similarly a conspicuous absence of emotional warmth and a not infrequent notion that the hero feels dead inside occur in this syndrome. Below is the story to No. 17BM of an ambulatory schizophrenic patient sent by a psychiatrist for diagnosis.

PROTOCOL—PICTURE NO. 17BM

"The man is climbing up the rope. There is a crowd chasing him. He is viewing something. Might be looking out to sea. Looking for a boat to come in. He'd be one of the men to bring in the cargo. He's alongside of the building. People are chasing him because he is on the side of a building. He is in a hurry; he is in a funny position. People are mad at him—has no clothes on. Walking around the streets naked. He is some character in history. Brutus. He wouldn't be looking for a boat after all—just fleeing from the crowd. They are after him. He took their money. He wants to get rich all of a sudden and return. He gets away—does not look worried. Gets on top of the building. Gets on the road and gets away. He has no money with him—so he gets away somehow, without money."

Children's TAT's tend to be most rewarding since they are usually so much more transparent than the stories of adults. In this respect they compare with children's dreams, particularly in their free use of simple symbolism and obviously wish-fulfilling tendencies. Below is the narrative of a bright boy, six years and seven months old, who related a plain œdipal story.

PROTOCOL —PICTURE NO. 16M

"Once upon a time there was a prince who lived in a fine kingdom in France. He had a favorite servant whose name was Roderigo. One day his servant said: 'I have traveled far and wide, Your Majesty, and at last I have seen a princess who is fit for you to marry.' 'Bring her here at once,' said the prince. He brought the lady. She was very ugly. She had black hair all around and she had pimples all around and then the prince said: 'How dare you bring me such an ugly woman!' The poor Roderigo said: 'Your Majesty, when I saw her she was very pretty.' 'I don't believe any of your brazen lies,' said the prince. 'Make him climb down the rope from the gallows or he shall be hung.' (That was the punishment he gave anyone who was wicked and slothful.) Now it happened that Roderigo was very strong. In fact, he was the strongest man in the kingdom. This princess was really very pretty. She had made an agreement with Roderigo to marry him if he would bring her to the kingdom and overthrow the king and Roderigo would run away with her. She had given him a magical scent which, if he threw it upon anybody, they would drop dead. The prince made Roderigo climb down the rope and Roderigo could do it very well because he was accustomed to those kind of rough things. As soon as he got to the bottom, he took out the bottle from his pocket and threw it upon the king. Immediately the king fell dead. Roderigo seized the princess and ran off with her to the woods. There they built a log cabin in the midst of a clearing which was surrounded by bushes so thick that no one could get through them but Roderigo. There he married the princess, who by that time had taken on her true form again, and they lived happily ever after."

The œdipal theme is clearly reflected: the king (father); the princess (mother); who by some magical means is wafted away from the father figure.

In the TAT stories of *psychopaths*, there usually appears little punishment for any aggressive act engaged in by the hero in the story, an evidence of a weakly integrated superego.

SPECIAL USES OF THE TAT

The Use of the TAT in Psychotherapy.—I believe that dynamic psychotherapy can be conceived of as a process consisting of four basic steps [14]: communication (from patient to therapist); interpretation; insight; and working through.

The patient may communicate with the therapist by free association, play, or projective methods, etc.

Interpretation means that the therapist points out common denominators that he has perceived in the patient's behavioral patterns. It is called *insight* if the patient can "see" these common denominators himself, even though he was not aware of them before. *Working through* is the term used if the patient then goes on intellectually and behaviorally to find some more examples where the same common denominator holds, and modifies his behavior according to a more rational pattern.

A variety of situations is discussed below wherein the patient is unable to communicate at all or in which he communicates in such a way that the therapist is unable to see any common denominators. In these cases I believe that the TAT is an ideal therapeutic aid. Since the TAT consists of a variety of pictures that elicit the patient's reactions to a variety of life situations, it gives the clinician a chance to see the common denominators. If the TAT material is then used in the interview situation as if it were free-association material, it may be interpreted to the patient in proper doses at proper times. At the same time the patient can experience insight and some working through with this material, as pointed out below.

Indication: First, the TAT can be used as the general basis of short psychotherapy. In cases in which it is necessary to proceed as rapidly as possible, the usual psychotherapeutic procedure of learning about the patient's behavioral patterns, conflicts, etc., may be a serious problem for the therapist since it is so time-consuming. By using the TAT the therapist becomes acquainted with the dynamics of the patient's thoughts and behavior in a very short time and can thus proceed immediately to the point of acquainting the patient with the patterns underlying his behavior and the more specifically therapeutic phases of the process. It is necessary to stress the importance of exercising extreme caution in this procedure. A case in point, illustrative of many such, is that of a veteran who came greatly disturbed because he felt nearly irrepressible aggressive impulses. He had slain his cat in anger that morning and was afraid he might injure his wife or child. With the help of the TAT it was possible for him to see much sooner than would otherwise have been possible that his aggression was really meant for his mother. This interpretation quickly relieved him of his great emotional pressure while it took much longer detailed work actually to change the dynamic structure of the situation.

Second, the TAT can be used in cases, or in particular episodes of cases, in which the patient had difficulty in free associating or in cases in which there is a dearth of associations. Instead of spending a great deal of time and effort in waiting for the patient to overcome the block or in trying to prod him into further associations, the therapist can use the TAT, in whole or in part, for productions to which the patient can associate or which can in themselves reveal as much to the patient and to the therapist as the associations that may be evoked through the more lengthy process.

Third, the TAT can be used in cases where the patient shows marked resistance to the interpretations given by the therapist. The TAT provides a situation that seems totally objective to the patient at the time he is asked to tell the stories; the patient will often be able to understand and accept the interpretation of his TAT story as it relates to himself since it is so undeniably a product of his own projected thoughts and yet can be seen more objectively while he may have found it impossible to accept the interpretations of his associations, the patterns of which may well remain hidden to him. In his free associations the interpretation is given on the basis of thoughts and behavior made known to the analyst during many sessions, associations that the patient may not be able or willing to relate to each other for many reasons. When presented with his TAT story, however, he usually accepts it as his own production and can be made to see the thoughts and underlying behavior processes that were projected into the story.

Fourth, the TAT can be used in cases where the patient feels the need for protectiveness and produces associations that are completely superficial and harmless. In such instances, since the TAT is considered an objective situation, the patient is not immediately aware of the fact that his stories are the products of his own thought and therefore are as personal as his associations. Once the stories have been told, however, he can easily be made to see the stories as projections. Often in such cases the TAT will serve to break down the patient's protective shell and he will be able to continue psychotherapy on the basis of free association, if that is desirable. Should protectiveness appear again in the course of therapy, another TAT story can be taken up.

Fifth, the TAT can be used in cases where the subject is depressed and speaks little or not at all. In such cases the TAT provides one of the few methods for getting into contact with the patient for psychotherapy. In connection with depressed cases, a TAT administered during a sodium-amytal interview often proves of particular value, especially if the patient has been unable to respond to either the TAT or sodium-amytal administered separately. Oral administration of one and a half grains of nembutal a half hour before the session has also been used in this connection [15].

Administration of the TAT for Psychotherapy.—When used as an instrument in psychotherapy, the TAT may be administered in a variety of ways. In situations in which the patient has been given a battery of psychological tests including the TAT before coming to the therapist, the orthodox procedure probably will have been used. Even under such circumstances one session, using ten pictures, usually will be sufficient for most purposes.

When given after therapeutic sessions have begun, and in cases indicated in the foregoing section, the TAT may be used with orthodox procedure or there may be one of a number of variations in the technique of presentation. If it has been decided beforehand that a TAT is desirable, all or part of one session may be devoted to getting the record. Usually only ten cards need be presented. This can be done at the therapist's office, with the examiner taking down the stories in the usual manner, or the patient can be given the pictures to take home and told to write stories himself. There are advantages and disadvantages in both procedures, as was discussed previously.

If the TAT is given only to overcome a temporary block that seems to be associated with a particular situation or pattern, the examiner may select one or several pictures which seem to be most appropriate and present them at that moment. The therapist should have no difficulty in finding the one picture or the few pictures which may permit the patient to project the thoughts that he could not express otherwise.

A variation of this last use of the TAT is to ask the patient to look at the ceiling and project a picture onto it. Some patients consider this situation as objective as the TAT and can enter into it with little difficulty. Since this is completely unstructured, it may have certain advantages over the TAT in particular instances. If the block cannot be overcome by this means, a TAT picture can be used in the usual fashion or in combination with the procedure just discussed. That is, the patient can be shown a picture and then asked to look at the ceiling and project that picture onto it, describe the picture he has projected, and tell a story about it. The changes he makes in the process of projecting the picture onto the ceiling will be quite significant for analysis and interpretation and should yield additional information.

Though I have outlined several possible ways of administering the TAT, most therapists will find additional variations as they use the test in therapy.

Interpretation and Use in Therapy.—Analysis and interpretation of the TAT usually are considered a lengthy and involved procedure. For psychotherapeutic use, however, a brief reading of the stories will provide the therapist with as much detailed information as he is likely to need before the stories are discussed with the patient.

When using the TAT in the actual psychotherapeutic session, it is good to wait a few minutes at the beginning of the session before presenting the story or stories to the patient. In that time one may find out whether there is anything more acute and specific the patient may have on his mind and that is more urgent than the material in the TAT. But if there is nothing acute, and particularly if the patient has difficulty in starting or quickly runs out of material, it is time to take up the TAT. Again, it is wise to stop with the interpretations of the TAT several minutes before the end of the session so that the patient may still have a chance either to bring up more distantly related material than was evoked or to discuss current problems that he did not remember before.

The technique of analyzing and interpreting the stories for the patient is almost as varied as the procedure for administering the test. If the TAT has been administered in toto or in slightly abbreviated form, it is best to have two copies of each story so that the patient will have one to read at the time it is being used in a therapeutic session. The method of choice in handling each story is to let the patient read it and elaborate on it if he can, then to discuss it and free-associate. After all associations have been made, the therapist steps in and discusses all the material again with analysis and interpretation. One or several stories may thus be taken up during each session. In this way therapy proceeds according to patterns revealed in the TAT stories.

Another method again, if the stories have been written in advance, is to use them only when one or several of the stories treat of the problem currently occupying the patient's attention. There too the patient should be allowed to read a copy of his stories, and often he will see the pattern of his own accord and be able to interpret the story and his own revelations, thus acquiring insight in a most desirable manner. If he fails to do this, the therapist can try to help him do so, merely to read back to the subject a story or stories and let him associate to it, without presenting an analysis until some future date, which procedure will, of course, have to be gauged.

The therapist should consider the material as he would a dream or fantasy and analyze it on that basis; sometimes it can be taken up as an almost direct statement of biographical material or to show emotional content connected with behavior patterns. In situations in which the subject has been asked to project a picture onto the ceiling, the similarity to a dream or fantasy is even more marked, so that it would naturally be interpreted in that fashion.

REFERENCES

1. ABEL, T. M.: "Responses of Negro and White Morons to the Thematic Apperception Test," *American Journal of Mental Deficiency*, Vol. 49 (1945), pp. 463–8.
2. AMEN, E. W.: "Individual Difference in Apperceptive Reaction: a Study of the Response of Preschool Children to Pictures," *Genetic Psychology Monographs*, Vol. 23 (1941), pp. 319–85.
3. BALKEN, E. R.: "A Delineation of Schizophrenic Language and Thought in a Test of Imagination," *Journal of Psychology*, Vol. 16 (1943), pp. 239–71.
4. ——: "Thematic Apperception," *Journal of Psychology*, Vol. 20 (1945), pp. 189–97.
5. —— and MASSERMAN, J. H.: "The Language of Phantasy: III. The Language of the Phantasies of Patients with Conversion Hysteria, Anxiety State, and Obsessive-Compulsive Neuroses," *Journal of Psychology*, Vol. 10 (1940), pp. 75–86.
6. —— and VANDER VEER, A. H.: "The Clinical Application of the Thematic Apperception Test to Neurotic Children," *American Journal of Orthopsychiatry*, Vol. 12 (1942), pp. 68–80; Vol. 14 (1944), pp. 421–40.
7. BELLAK, L.: "An Experimental Investigation of Projection," *Psychological Bulletin*, Vol. 39 (1942), 489–90 (abstract).
8. ——: "The Concept of Projection: an Experimental Investigation and Study of the Concept," *Psychiatry*, Vol. 7 (1944), pp. 353–70.
9. ——, BRAVERMAN, S., and PASQUARELLI, B.: "The Use of the TAT in Psychotherapy," *Journal of Nervous and Mental Diseases*, Vol. 101 (1949), pp. 51–65.
10. —— and MURRAY, H. A.: *Thematic Apperception Test Blank*. Cambridge: Harvard Psychological Clinic; 1941. (Mimeographed and privately distributed.)
11. —— and MURRAY, H. A.: *Manual of Instructions for the TAT*. Cambridge: Harvard Psychological Clinic; 1941. (Privately distributed.)
12. ——: *Bellak TAT Blank, Analysis Sheets, and Guide to the In-*

terpretation of the TAT. New York: Psychological Corporation; 1948.

13. ——: *The TAT's of Two Nazi Leaders* (to be published).

14. ——: "The Basic Concepts of Psychotherapy," *Journal of Nervous and Mental Disease,* Vol. 108 (1948), pp. 137–41.

15. ——: "The Use of Oral Barbiturates in Psychotherapy," *American Journal of Psychiatry,* Vol. 105 (1949), pp. 849–50.

16. ——, LEVINGER, L., and LIPSKY, R.: "The Reflection of an Adolescent Problem in the TAT." Presented at the meeting of the Eastern Psychological Association in Philadelphia in 1948. (To be published.)

17. BETTELHEIM, B.: "Self-Interpretation of Fantasy: the Thematic Apperception Test as an Educational and Therapeutic Device," *American Journal of Orthopsychiatry,* Vol. 17 (1947), pp. 80–100.

18. BRITTAIN, H. L.; "A Study in Imagination," *Pedagogical Seminary* (1907), Vol. 14, pp. 137–207.

19. CHRISTENSON, J. A., JR.: "Clinical Application of the Thematic Apperception Test," *Journal of Abnormal and Social Psychology,* Vol. 38 (1943), pp. 104–6.

20. CLARK, R. M.: "A Method of Administering and Evaluating the Thematic Apperception Test in Group Situations," *Genetic Psychology Monographs,* Vol. 30 (1947), pp. 257–64.

21. COLEMAN, W.: "The Thematic Apperception Test: I. Effect of Recent Experience. II. Some Quantitative Observations," *Journal of Clinical Psychology,* Vol. 3 (1947), pp. 257–64.

22. COMBS, A. W.: "A Comparative Study of Motivations as Revealed in Thematic Apperception Stories and Autobiography," *Journal of Clinical Psychology,* Vol. 3 (1947), pp. 65–75.

23. ——: "The Use of Personal Experience in Thematic Apperception Test Story Plots," *Journal of Clinical Psychology,* Vol. 2 (1946), pp. 357–63.

24. ——: "A Method of Analysis for the Thematic Apperception Test and Autobiography," *Journal of Clinical Psychology,* Vol. 2 (1946), pp. 167–74.

25. ——: "The Validity and Reliability of Interpretation from Autobiography and the Thematic Apperception Test," *Journal of Clinical Psychology,* Vol. 2 (1946), pp. 240–7.

26. DEABLER, H. L.: "The Psychotherapeutic Use of the Thematic Apperception Test," *Journal of Clinical Psychology,* Vol. 3 (1947), pp. 246–52.

27. DESPERT, J. L., and POTTER, H. W.: "Technical Approaches Used

in the Study and Treatment of Emotional Problems in Children. Part I: The Story, a Form of Directed Phantasy," *Psychiatric Quarterly*, Vol. 10 (1936), p. 619–38.

28. FREED, H., and ECCKER, W. F.: "The Thematic Apperception Test: Its Value in Routine Psychiatric Practice," *Diseases of the Nervous System*, Vol. 7 (1946), pp. 1–7.

29. FRENKEL-BRUNSWIK, E.: "I. Dynamic and Cognitive Categorization of Qualitative Material. II. Application to interviews with the Ethnically Prejudiced," *Journal of Psychology*, Vol. 25 (1948), pp. 261–77.

30. HARRISON, R.: "I. Studies in the Use and Validity of the Thematic Apperception Test with Mentally Disordered Patients. II. A Quantitative Validity Study. III. Validation by the Method of 'Blind Analysis'," *Character and Personality*, Vol. 9 (1940), pp. 122–38.

31. ——: "The Thematic Apperception and Rorschach Methods of Personality Investigation in Clinical Practice," *Journal of Psychology*, Vol. 15 (1943), pp. 49–74.

32. ——, and ROTTER, J. B.: "A Note on the Reliability of the Thematic Apperception Test," *Journal of Abnormal and Social Psychology*, Vol. 40 (1945), pp. 97–9.

33. HENRY, W. E.: "The Thematic Apperception Technique in the Study of Culture-Personality Relations," *Genetic Psychology Monographs*, Vol. 35 (1947), pp. 3–315.

34. ——: *Thematic Apperception Test: a Method of Analysis*. Chicago: University of Chicago Committee on Human Development; 1945. (Privately distributed.)

35. HUTT, M. L.: "The Use of Projective Methods of Personality Measurement in Army Medical Installations," *Journal of Clinical Psychology*, Vol. 1 (1945), pp. 135–40.

36. JAQUES, E.: "The Clinical Use of the Thematic Apperception Test with Soldiers," *Journal of Abnormal and Social Psychology*, Vol. 40 (1945), pp. 363–75.

37. KUTASH, S. B.: "Performance of Psychopathic Defective Criminals on the Thematic Apperception Test," *Journal of Criminal Psychopathology*, Vol. 5 (1943), pp. 319–40.

38. LUSAGA Y TRAVIESO, J. I., and MARTINEZ-ARANGO, C.: "Some Suggestions Concerning the Administration and Interpretation of the TAT," *Journal of Psychology*, Vol. 22 (1946), pp. 117–63.

39. LEITCH, M., and SCHAFER, S.: "A Study of the Thematic Apperception Tests of Psychotic Children," *American Journal of Orthopsychiatry*, Vol. 17 (1947), pp. 337–42.

40. LIBBY, W.: "The Imagination of Adolescents," *American Journal of Psychology*, Vol. 19 (1908), pp. 249–52.

41. LOEBLOWITZ, LENNARD H., and RIESSMAN, F., JR.: "Recall in the Thematic Apperception Test: an Experimental Investigation into the Meaning of Recall of Phantasy with Reference to Personality Diagnosis," *Journal of Personality*, Vol. 14 (1945), pp. 41–6.

42. MARTINEZ-ARANGO, C.: "Psychotherapy Based on the Thematic Apperception Test," *Digest of Neurology and Psychiatry*, Vol. 15 (1947), p. 80.

43. MASSERMAN, J. H., and BALKEN, E. R.: "The Clinical Application of Fantasy Studies," *Journal of Psychology*, Vol. 6 (1938), pp. 81–8.

44. ——, and BALKEN, E. R.; "The Psychoanalytic and Psychiatric Significance of Phantasy. Part I," *Psychoanalytic Review*, Vol. 26 (1939), pp. 343–79. Part II. The Psychiatric Significance of the Phantasy Material," *Psychoanalytic Review*, Vol. 26 (1939), pp. 535–49.

45. MEADOW, A.: "An analysis of Japanese Character Structure Based on Japanese Film Plots and Thematic Apperception Tests on Japanese-Americans," New York: Institute for Intercultural Studies; 1944. (Mimeographed and privately distributed.)

46. MORGAN, C. D., and MURRAY, H. A.: "A Method for Investigating Fantasies: the Thematic Apperception Test," *Archives of Neurology and Psychiatry*, Vol. 34 (1935), pp. 289–306.

47. MURRAY, H. A.: *Thematic Apperception Test*. Cambridge: Harvard University Press; 1943.

48. ——, et al.: *Explorations in Personality*. New York: Oxford University Press, 1938.

49. ——: "Techniques for a Systematic Investigation of Fantasies," *Journal of Psychology*, Vol. 3 (1937), pp. 115–43.

50. ——, and STEIN, M.: "Note on the Selection of Combat Officers," *Psychosomatic Medicine*, Vol. 5 (1943), pp. 386–91.

51. RAPAPORT, D.: "The Clinical Application of the Thematic Apperception Test," *Bulletin of the Menninger Clinic*, Vol. 7 (1943), pp. 106–13.

52. ——: "The Thematic Apperception Test," Vol. II, Chap. 1 of *Diagnostic Psychological Testing*. Chicago: Year Book Publishers; 1946.

53. ——, SCHAFER, R., and GILL, M.: *Manual of Diagnostic Psychological Testing: II Diagnostic Testing of Personality and Ideational Content*. Publications of the Josiah Macy Jr. Foundation (Revised Series), Vol. 3, No. 1 (1946).

55. RENAUD, H.: "Group Differences in Fantasies: Head Injuries, Psychoneurotics, and Brain Diseases," *Journal of Psychology,* Vol. 21 (1946), pp. 327–46.

56. RODNICK, E. H., and KLEBANOFF, S.: "Projective Reactions to Induced Frustration as a Measure of Social Adjustment," *Psychological Bulletin,* Vol. 39 (1942), p. 489 (abstract).

57. ROE, A.: "Alcohol and Creative Work: Part I. Painters," *Quarterly Journal of Studies on Alcohol,* Vol. 6 (1946), pp. 415–67.

58. ———: "Artists and Their Work," *Journal of Personality,* Vol. 15 (1946), pp. 1–40.

59. ROSENZWEIG, S.: "Fantasy in Personality and its Study by Test Procedure," *Journal of Abnormal and Social Psychology,* Vol. 37 (1942), pp. 40–51.

60. ———: "The Ghost of Henry James; a Study of Thematic Apperception," *Character and Personality,* Vol. 12 (1943), pp. 79–100.

61. ———, and ISHAM, A. C.: "Complementary Thematic Apperception Test Patterns in Close Kin," *American Journal of Orthopsychiatry,* Vol. 17 (1947), pp. 129–42.

62. ROTTER, J. B.: "Studies in the Use and Validity of the Thematic Apperception Test with Mentally Disordered Patients. I. Methods of Analysis and Clinical Problems," *Character and Personality,* Vol. 9 (1940), pp. 18–34.

63. ———: "Thematic Apperception Tests: Suggestions for administration and interpretation," *Journal of Personality,* Vol. 15 (1946), pp. 70–92.

64. SAENGER, G. and PROSHANSKY, H.: "Projective Techniques in Attitude and Opinion Research," in L. E. Abt and L. Bellak: *Projective Psychology.* New York: Alfred A. Knopf; 1950.

65. SANFORD, R. N.: *Procedure for Scoring the Thematic Apperception Test.* Cambridge: Harvard Psychological Clinic, 1939. (Mimeographed and privately distributed.)

66. ———: "Some Quantitative Results from the Analysis of Children's Stories," *Psychological Bulletin,* Vol. 38 (1941), p. 749 (abstract).

67. ———, ADKINS, M. M., MILLER, R. B., COBB, E. A., et al.: "Physique, Personality, and Scholarships: a Cooperative Study of School Children," *Monogr. Soc. Res. Child. Develop.,* Vol. 8, No. 1 (1943).

68. SARASON, S. B.: "Dreams and Thematic Apperception Test Stories," *Journal of Abnormal and Social Psychology,* Vol. 39 (1944), pp. 486–92.

69. ———: "The Use of the Thematic Apperception Test with Mentally Deficient Children. I. Study of High-Grade Girls," *American Journal of Mental Deficiency,* Vol. 47 (1943), pp. 414–21. "II. Study of High-Grade Boys," *American Journal of Mental Deficiency,* Vol. 48 (1943), pp. 169–73.

70. ———, and ROSENZWEIG, S.: "An Experimental Study of the Triadic Hypothesis: I. Reaction to Frustration, Ego-Defense, and Hypnotizability. II. Thematic Apperception Approach," *Character and Personality,* Vol. 11 (1942), pp. 1–19.

71. SARGENT, H.: "Projective Methods: Their Origins, Theory, and Applications in Personality Research," *Psychological Bulletin,* Vol. 42 (1945), pp. 257–93.

72. SCHWARTZ, L. A.: "Social-Situation Pictures in the Psychiatric Interview," *American Journal of Orthopsychiatry,* Vol. 2 (1932), pp. 124–33.

73. SISK, H. L.: "A Clinical Case Study Utilizing the Rorschach and the Murray Thematic Apperception Tests," *Journal of Clinical Psychology,* Vol. 3 (1947), pp. 293–8.

74. SLUTZ, M.: "The Unique Contribution of the Thematic Apperception Test to a Developmental Study," *Psychological Bulletin,* Vol. 38 (1941), p. 704.

75. SYMONDS, P. M.: "Adolescent Phantasy," *Psychological Bulletin,* Vol. 38 (1941), pp. 590–7.

76. ———: "Criteria for the Selection of Pictures for the Investigation of Adolescent Phantasies," *Journal of Abnormal and Social Psychology,* Vol. 34 (1939), pp. 271–4.

77. ———: "Projective Techniques," in *Encyclopedia of Psychology* (Harriman, P. L., editor). New York: Philosophical Library; 1946.

78. ———, and KRUGMAN, M.: "Projective Methods in the Study of Personality," *Review of Educational Research,* Vol. 11 (1941), pp. 80–93.

79. TOMKINS, S. S.: "The Limits of Material Obtainable in a Single Case Study by Daily Administration of the Thematic Apperception Test," *Psychological Bulletin,* Vol. 39 (1942), p. 490 (abstract).

80. ———: *The Thematic Apperception Test.* New York: Grune & Stratton; 1947.

81. WELLS, H.: "Differences between Delinquent and Nondelinquent Boys as Indicated by the Thematic Apperception Test," *Psychological Bulletin,* Vol. 42 (1945), p. 534 (abstract).

82. WHITE, R. W.: "The Personality of Joseph Kidd," *Character and Personality,* Vol. 11 (1943), pp. 183–208.

83.   ——: "Interpretation of Imaginative Productions," J. McV. Hunt (ed.): in *Personality and the Behavior Disorders*. New York: Ronald Press Co.; 1944.

84.   WYATT, F.: "Formal Aspects of the Thematic Apperception Test," *Psychological Bulletin*, Vol. 39 (1942), p. 491.

85.   ——: "The Interpretation of the TAT," *Rorschach Research Exchange and Journal of Projective Technique*, Vol. 11 (1947), pp. 21–6.

86.   ——: "The Scoring and Analysis of the Thematic Apperception Test," *Journal of Psychology*, Vol. 24 (1947), pp. 319–30.

Dr. Fredric Wertham's excellent chapter on the Mosaic Test is virtually the first full statement on the test which has been offered in American psychological literature. The following material will be welcomed especially by clinicians who have been intrigued by the test and by the possibilities of using it in projective test batteries. Dr. Wertham provides an authoritative statement of the theory behind the test and suggests the conditions that his experience has indicated when it may be fruitfully used.

From the rich background of his experience in psychopathology Wertham makes available what we regard as significant comments of value to the whole field of projective psychology, and it is likely that henceforth the Mosaic Test will enjoy wider application by American clinicians.

▼

The Mosaic Test

TECHNIQUE AND PSYCHOPATHOLOGICAL DEDUCTIONS

Fredric Wertham

Read all the pedants' screeds and strictures,
But don't believe in anything
That can't be told in colored pictures.

HISTORY

Not only drawings and paintings but also productions with mosaic pieces and colored blocks have been used in an unsystematic way for a long time in the observation of children. Mosaics have the advantage that they combine fixity of the materials used and flexibility of the design.

Using a set of colored wooden mosaic pieces, Margaret Lowenfeld found that the designs made with them constituted "a valuable aid in estimating emotional stability," and that it was possible "to distinguish between educational and intellectual retardation due to emotional blocking, and educational and intellectual retardation which arose from inherent mental defects." The main diagnostic uses were restricted to emotional disturbances, temperamental difficulties, formal psychological attitudes, and intellectual deficiencies.

Out of these somewhat primitive formal observations I developed an entirely new method of analyzing and interpreting mosaics by correlating in very large numbers of cases the mosaic designs made by adults and children with definite diagnostic clinical reaction types. The case material included practically every type of case to be seen in a psychiatric hospital, in patients in a general hospital needing psychiatric consultation, and in large outpatient clinics: psychoses, neuroses, somatic and neurological conditions, behavior disorders, criminals, juvenile delinquents, drug addicts, domestic-relations court cases, and normal controls.

TEST MATERIAL

With almost any kind of set of colored pieces a measure of significant results may be obtained. The mother of a young boy confined in a mental institution in Canada, having heard of this work with mosaics, gave him brightly colored small pieces of paper and asked him to make designs out of them. She pasted them securely to a large piece of paper in the patterns he had laid out, and sent them along with her letter about his case. Of course it was not possible to give an opinion on this basis, but nevertheless it was possible to make a definite diagnosis of schizophrenia from it, which was later verified. In this continuing research many different toy mosaic and experimental sets have been used.

The most satisfactory test set is one used by Margaret Lowenfeld and originally obtained by her from Czechoslovakia, to which I have added one new piece. Without this new piece the set is at present commercially available through the Psychological Corporation. One disadvantage of this set is that it is made of thin plastic material barely adequate for practical purposes and not fully suitable for research. Having had difficulty in finding the proper wood, I have had sets constructed out of aluminum with the color baked on in an enamel finish. The pieces are light in weight, sturdy, easily handled, and unbreakable and they do not wear out. The only disadvantage is their expense.

The pieces are 4/32 of an inch thick. There are six colors: black, blue, red, green, yellow, and off-white or eggshell. Each color is represented in six shapes, as follows:

Squares: 1⅛ inches on each side. Four pieces of each color.

Diamond-shaped pieces: 1⅛ inches on each side. Eight pieces of each color.

Equilateral triangles: 1½ inches on each side. Six pieces of each color.

Triangles: 1⅝ inches on the base, 1⅛ inches on each of the other two sides. Eight pieces of each color.

Triangles: 2/3 of an inch on one side, 1½ inches on the second side, 1⅜ inches on the third side. Twelve pieces of each color.

Oblongs: 1½ inches by ¼ inch. Twelve pieces of each color.

These pieces are used on a tray that measures 16 inches by 10½ inches, having a raised margin about half an inch wide to keep the blanks from sliding off as they are used.

PROCEDURE

The test should be explained to the subject in a friendly manner, first in general and then specifically. Children usually like to do the test, but sometimes they think that it is too childish for them—that they are too old to play with blocks. It has to be explained to them that they can do it as a sort of game, but that the examiner is serious about seeing and using the result. Adults, too, sometimes feel that such a simple test is beneath them. It has to be explained to them that this is a test that looks simple but is really a very useful help in arriving at a proper diagnosis of the individual's real trouble. In other words, it is important to have the subject start out in as good a frame of mind as possible, on the one hand taking it not too lightly, on the other not too fearfully.

The subject is shown the pieces in a box. The examiner takes out a sample of each shape and shows it to the subject, and then a sample of each color, explaining that all the shapes come in every color, and every color in each shape. The examiner should not state specifically that there are six shapes and six colors but should just show a sample of each. He should also not name the shapes or the colors.

After the subject has been shown what material he can work

with, he is asked to make anything he wants to on the board before which he is sitting in a comfortable position. He is told that he may take any number of pieces that he wants, of any shape or any color, and that he may make anything he wants. When he has made something, he should tell the examiner that he has finished. He should be reassured that he may take as much time as he wants, that there is no great hurry, although of course he must finish within a reasonable time. Most subjects catch on very quickly if the instructions are given clearly, fully, and in a friendly, encouraging spirit.

The examiner should look on while the subject makes the design, but his watching should be very unobtrusive; and he should do something else (like reading) at the same time, so the patient can feel free. The verbal responses of the patient while he is making the design—at least the significant ones—should be taken down and entered on the chart.

Sometimes subjects want to destroy a half-finished or almost completely finished design. The examiner should not permit the individual to obliterate his original design completely. He can, however, permit him to change the design and to add to it.

When the subject has finished his design, the examiner should ask in general terms what he was thinking of when he was making it: What does it represent? What did he want to make? What does it look like? What was in his mind? Does he like it? What does he think of it? For example, a person may make a seemingly abstract design composed of five triangles with their points touching at the center of the figure. If he says that he wanted to make a cross, or if, perhaps, he actually says: "This is a cross," then the design indicates a very serious disorder in achieving a configuration or Gestalt. (Diagnostically, this suggests an organic brain disease of cortical type.) Children often tell elaborate stories of what goes on in a design they have made: "boats floating on the water," "smoke coming out of a chimney," "people in a house," and so on.

When the design is completed, a life-size record is made of it on paper. This can easily be accomplished in the following manner: A sheet of white paper the size of the tray is placed on a table directly in front of the tray that contains the subject's design. The design itself is not touched. A corresponding block is taken out of the box and placed on the paper with exactly the same margin at the side as in the design. A ruler can be used to determine the exact measurements. The block is then traced with a thin pencil point, and the name of the color written lightly (so that it can be erased easily) in that area. The same procedure is used for the remaining blocks in the design and when completed the entire design is colored with crayon as indicated. Always write on the reproduction which side is the top of the picture, and the name of the picture as given by the subject.

Often, and especially in doubtful cases, the test should be repeated in a few days or a few weeks. Therefore when giving a test the examiner should never explain to the subject what signs and aspects are of importance for the interpretation.

ANALYSIS OF RESULTS

The interpretation of the mosaics can be made either immediately, from the original tray, or later from the reproduction recorded on paper.

The Mosaic Test does not give a picture of the dynamic structure of a personality. In this way it is to be distinguished from the Rorschach Test, which gives a description of personality expressed in the terminology of the test itself, and which is more or less independent of simple diagnostic clinical labels. To attempt something like that seems to have been Margaret Lowenfeld's original intent.

My method of interpreting mosaics is far more limited and at the same time felt to be more valid. In thousands of cases it has been found that mosaics represent certain basic or dominant processes corresponding to definite clinical entities or reaction types. Certain mental diseases are clearly and definitely revealed by the Mosaic Test. This has been verified in schizophrenia, for example, in hundreds of cases. I have never seen a patient suffering from a clear-cut case of schizophrenia make a normal design, nor have I ever seen a definitely normal person make a clear-cut schizophrenic design. Diamond and Schmale [1] have confirmed the great validity of these criteria of schizophrenia in a relatively small but evidently very well-studied number of cases, making use of a slightly different set of mosaics. After the exclusion of doubtful cases they tabulated their results in "definitely schizophrenic mosaics."

FIGURE 5. Pieces Placed on Tray by Schizophrenic Subject

Definitely Schizophrenic Mosaics

Nonschizophrenia	0
Schizophrenia	24

This diagnostic correlation does not cover the whole range of classifiable mental disorders. It is very clear in schizophrenia or in mental deficiency, less clear in the varieties of psychoneuroses and in certain types of personality. In reflecting basic or predominant psychological constellations the mosaics evidently show different levels of the complex structure of the personality. The Rorschach Test is much more useful and revealing in the study of the normal and neurotic personality. In my experience with it the Rorschach Test is often—on account of its very finesse—inconclusive, unreliable, or even misleading for the determination of the differential-diagnostic question: is this a schizophrenic process or not? This is also confirmed by Diamond and Schmale [1], who state: "Particularly in schizophrenic disorders, significant abnormalities in the mosaic may appear before any single diagnostic or psychological test is reliably and consistently abnormal."

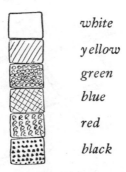

FIGURE 6. Key to the Mosaic Test Designs

OUTLINE OF CHARACTERISTICS

Despite the limitation of means, the possible variety in mosaic designs is very great. Empirically, certain characteristics have been singled out that one should have in mind when evaluating a design. It is of no value, however, to chart these characteristics separately and make statistical computations. The designs are to be evaluated as a whole. That is the way to realize their diagnostic significance in relation to typical, formal, clinical-reaction types.

The examiner will do well to accumulate a fairly large amount of case material for himself. This can be done easily and relatively quickly wherever case material is available. He can then interpret against the background of the many cases he himself has seen.

In order to learn the method fully the examiner should not limit his own experience only to children, as he may be tempted to do if he works in a child-guidance clinic. To become expert in the method it is indispensable that from the beginning one also interpret the designs made by adults because they are so much simpler to interpret, especially in cases with psychoses.

The enumeration of the following characteristics is intended as a scheme which the examiner should have in mind so that he can give an objective description of the designs. It should be used in

FIGURE 7. Normal Abstract Design

conjunction with the differential diagnostic criteria outlined later under the heading of different clinical conditions.

Some designs are very clear-cut and their diagnostic significance is easily realized. But there is, of course, a large area where the designs are not so clear. The same is also true of clinical conditions. While it often happens that a mosaic test makes a decisive contribution to the diagnosis of a clinically difficult case, it also often happens that clinically unclear cases reflect their complex structure in a diagnostically unclear mosaic design.

It is important to realize that what is involved in this test is not merely a question of the discovery of defects or a question of normality or abnormality, but the finding of qualitatively different designs correlated with qualitatively different reaction types. Even normal persons make designs that permit interpretation of certain dominant personality features, although they are far more difficult to define clearly.

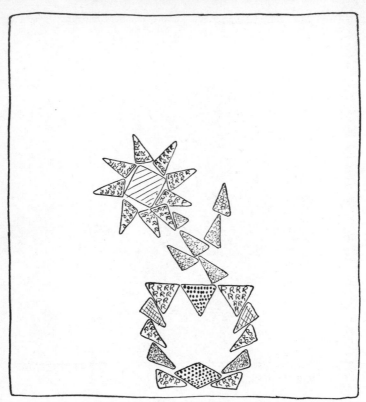

FIGURE 8. Normal Representational Design

1. *Number of designs.* Is there just one large one or are there several small ones? Generally speaking, the making of several very small simple designs is an indication of abnormality.

2. *Coherence or incoherence of design.* A child of three makes an incoherent, unorganized "all-over pattern" that more or less fills the whole board. In older children and in adults incoherence is an indication of abnormality. In delirium tremens, for example, if the subject can be induced to make a design, he may make an incoherent one. The same may happen in deteriorated cases of schizophrenia or in advanced cases of dementia.

3. *Is the design representational or abstract?* A representational design is one that represents a definite, concrete object, or at any rate is intended to represent one. As a general rule the mosaics lend themselves more easily to abstract designs than to

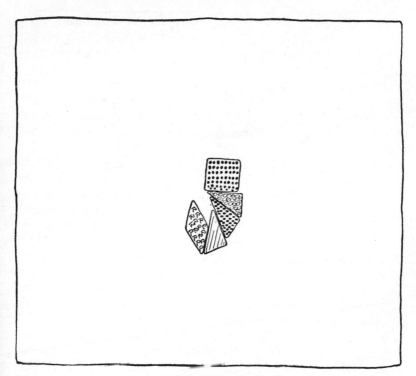

FIGURE 9. Simple Agglutination

concrete ones. Both abstract and representational designs occur in normals.

4. *Harmony of the design as a whole.* The design, whatever it may be, should hang together and should have no outstanding discrepancies or discordant features. There is, of course, a matter of degree involved.

5. *Completeness or incompleteness of design.* Even without the subject's saying so, one can sometimes see that the design is not complete. This may be due to various reasons that can be deduced from the design itself, from the behavior of the subject, or from his verbal responses.

6. *Meaningfulness or emptiness of design.* Some designs give one the impression that they are empty, that nothing has been achieved. This emptiness is of great diagnostic significance, especially if the design is otherwise well made, punctiliously and

exactly executed, and if it uses many means. Emptiness often occurs in schizophrenia. It is characteristic that the clinician often uses the term "empty" when describing schizophrenic subjects.

7. *Simple or complex design.* The mosaics of the average normal, well-integrated person have a certain complexity. Designs that are too simple are suspect of some deviation, which may be due to an intellectual defect or to a more or less severe disturbance.

8. *Compactness or looseness of design.* In compact designs all the pieces touch one another. In loose designs space is left between the pieces. Both adults and children sometimes distribute these spaces skillfully, but of course an equal amount of perspicacity is necessary to fit very different shapes and colors tightly together. Among normal people, with some exceptions, "loose" designs are more likely to be made by impressionistic, imaginative types and compact ones by matter-of-fact people.

9. *Distinctness of configuration.* Lack of achievement of a configuration or Gestalt is always a very important sign. From this point of view the Mosaic Test is a sensitive Gestalt test.

10. *Relation of design to object.* This relationship may be realistic, schematic, faulty, or completely lost and merely intended. The schematic or overschematic relationship to an object, such as a house, for example, occurs in schizophrenic psychoses or in schizoid personalities. There is of course a good deal of overlapping between these different characteristics. Schematic designs often are made of only black and white and leave out all other colors. This lack of color is in itself a sign.

11. *"Static" or "dynamic" designs.* The term "dynamic design," as used here, means a design in which some movement is indicated; for example, "smoke coming out of a window" as shown by a black piece placed adjacent to the window. These are useful in suggesting different ways in which perceptual reality is organized.

12. *Expression of configuration.* This may be achieved by means of the pieces themselves or by the empty space they enclose. The latter is far more frequent among children. For example, they may put four diamond-shaped pieces together and see the configuration of a star, which is the form of the space left

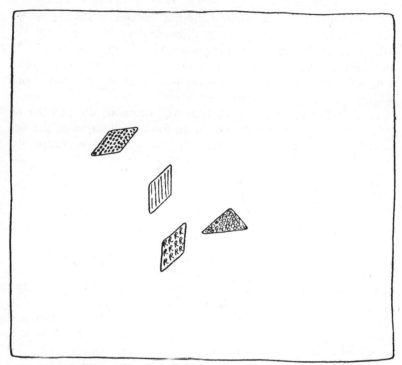

FIGURE 10. Four Scattered Pieces without any Pattern

in the middle. In adults this may indicate emotional abnormality (opposition to self or to the environment).

13. *Position of design within the frame of the tray, general distribution, etc.* Most important here is the relationship to the margin. Individuals with fear and anxiety, however well concealed, compensated for, or guarded against, tend to make designs that come into contact with the raised rim of the tray. Obsessive-compulsive subjects, for example, make what may be called "margin-bound" designs. Such a design may be so constructed that all its pieces come into contact with the margin on all four sides of the tray. Or a design may be built from the lower margin upward, from the upper margin downward, or on one of the margins on the side. In some designs all the pieces come into contact with the margin, in others there is a smaller design in the center with "margin-bound" pieces all around. The sim-

plest formulation of a "margin-bound" design is that it represents a defense against anxiety. The anxiety may come from totally different sources. "Margin-bound" designs may occur in all kinds of anxiety states, in anxious personalities (who make otherwise normal designs), in organic neurological conditions such as spastic paraplegia, or in epilepsy.

14. *Number of pieces used*. It is well to count the number of pieces used and indicate the count on the reproduction of the design. For practical purposes one may distinguish four groups:

(a) Very few, isolated pieces;
(b) Small number of pieces;
(c) Moderate number of pieces;
(d) Very many pieces.

The average normal lies between (c) and (d). Psychotic subjects use fewer pieces than do normal controls.

15. *Choice of color*. Designs may be very colorful or colorless. Colorful designs include red, blue, green, and yellow. Colorless designs may use only white or only white and black. White and yellow sometimes go together as indicating a certain "colorlessness." Blue and black sometimes go together as indicating an emotional darkness, in the sense of depression. That agrees with the statement made many years ago by Vassily Kandinsky, the originator of abstract art, that blue-black may stand for grief. This has often been seen in mild reactive depressions and in depressive personalities.

A normal, fairly large design, generally speaking, should include some red unless the design depicts a concrete object the nature of which would exclude that color. If one goes to an art museum and inspects, for example, a large number of landscapes by different masters and different schools, in different styles, one finds that they nearly all contain at least some red, even when the nature of the objects depicted does not make this imperative.

The use of colors may be harmonious or disharmonious. One color or two related colors may be preferred. Colors may be used to indicate the natural hue of an object, such as a green tree or a red roof, or they may be used merely as a decorative ornamentation of an object without regard to its natural colors. A child, for example, may make an airplane ornamented by an elaborate color scheme. Some subjects use color indiscriminately, as though it did not exist.

16. *Choice of shapes.* Is only one shape used, or several, or all? The use of only one shape indicates a certain monotony and rigidity and intellectual or emotional inability to make use of the means readily at hand.

17. *Emphasis on form or on color.* The Mosaic Test bears out what is known from other experiments in type-psychology: namely, that cyclothymic and schizothymic types differ in their sensitiveness to color as opposed to form. Tachistoscopic exposure of colored figures has shown that cyclothymic types are more sensitive to color, and that schizothymic types are more sensitive to form.

18. *Simple geometric designs.* Restriction to very simple geometric forms, often coupled with failure to achieve them, is typical of cortical organic brain disease. Schizophrenic patients may make such simple geometric forms too, but they usually achieve a good configuration in them and make several rather than only one.

19. *Appropriate choice of shapes for intended representation.* On a different level this corresponds to the realistic use of color in the representational mosaic. The use of an inappropriate shape for a simple geometric design often occurs in organic brain disease and in dementia. For example, the patient wishes to make a simple circle, which he could achieve best with oblongs or diamonds; but if among these oblongs or diamonds he uses one equilateral triangle or one square, the configuration of the circle becomes definitely impaired.

20. *"Stone-bound" designs.* We speak of "stone-bound" designs when there is evidence of fixation in form, and usually also in color, on the individual piece after it is once put down. The subject is influenced by the shape of that piece, and this tendency to fixation dominates the direction and arrangement of the entire design. Of course it disturbs the configuration intended.

21. *"All-over patterns."* The essential principle of orientation in all mosaics is the relation of the pieces to the tray, of the figure to the background. At the earliest stage when children can make mosaics at all the only principle of organization discernible is to spread the pieces over the whole tray. Very young children do

that in an unorganized way. All-over patterns in an organized manner are also made by adults. In them this compulsion to fill all available space and cover the whole background represents a primitive factor.

Mosaics with all-over patterns have an interesting analogy in art. It was only in the later stages of the classical period of Greek vase painting that figures stood out clearly against a uniform background. On the early, primitive vases of the Dipylon style of about 900 B.C. the geometric ornaments covered the whole surface of the vase. Making use of archaic mechanisms for modern purposes, modern painters sometimes make all-over patterns too. A good example is Miro's *Formes sur fond noir* (1935).

22. *Symmetry.* Symmetry may be completely absent, it may be merely indicated, or it may be present and integrated harmoniously with other principles of organization. It may be expressed in form or in color, or, as usually, in both. In almost any good design symmetry is present in some degree as a constructive factor of organization. The principle of symmetry may be so exaggerated as to stand out above all other principles of organization. When there is a marked contrast between a very pronounced symmetry and a meagerness or even emptiness of the design as a whole, we speak of this as "supersymmetry." Supersymmetry is a formalistic, rigid, external symmetry.

23. *Repetition.* Some subjects make the same small design several times with only certain variations in color. This may amount to stereotypy. It is interesting that patients with whom clinically we use the term "stereotypy"—namely, schizophrenic patients—are most likely to make stereotyped designs.

24. *Content.* The content of designs—that is, the nature of the object chosen and its direct or symbolic significance—is of secondary importance in the Mosaic Test. Some subjects make abstract designs with indications of sexual significance; for example, an oblong structure with a red triangle on top representing a phallic symbol.

25. *Relation of design to verbal utterances of the subject.* What the subject says is most important in children, but with adults it may also be necessary to take this into account. The subject's words help an examiner to understand the nature of a design if it has a realistic connotation, and they will also tell him the relationship between the intention and the finished product.

DIFFERENCES BETWEEN CHILDREN AND ADULTS

Studies in eidetic imagery have shown that in the psychosensory sphere a metamorphosis takes place in human development between childhood and maturity. My studies of the differences between children and adults in the Mosaic Test throw further light on this psychological phenomenon.

Young children may display in the Mosaic Test a sovereign facility in depicting concrete objects with such limited means as the mosaic pieces. They play reality where the adult gets stumped by it. Since there are no round pieces, an adult would find it next to impossible to represent a small wheel. But an eight-year-old boy had no trouble making a bicycle whose wheels were represented by square pieces.

Children are better able to abstract from the literalness of the shape of the pieces and to use them freely for realistic purposes. They are more daring and expressionistic in making representational designs, while adults are likely to be more academic and impressionistic.

Color as a device for ornamentation is much more frequent in children. When making a representational design they may use color decoratively rather than realistically. Such decorative color schemes occur in normal adults chiefly in abstract designs. In general, children's mosaics reflect a vivid perception of color.

Much more frequently than adults, children make dynamic designs—for instance, the moving parts of a motor. In their whole attitude toward their designs, both in making them and in speaking about them, children have a tendency to dramatize and animate them. In young children a simple design may become the starting-point for a whole story or even for elaborate fantasies.

Using the empty space as the Gestalt is much more frequent in children than in adults. All-over patterns become progressively less frequent from the very young child to the mature person. Children like to use many pieces.

DIAGNOSTIC INTERPRETATIONS

Normals.—Normal mosaics are easily recognized. The number of pieces used is fairly large, and the material, both shapes and colors, is freely used. The configuration is clear, the designs are full and harmonious. They may be representational or abstract.

Schizophrenics.—We have found that the Mosaic Test reveals with great clarity a fundamental psychological aspect of the schizophrenic process. There is a dissociation between content and form. This is a typical splitting of psychic functions, a phenomenon that made Bleuler give the disease the name "schizophrenia." (The phrase "splitting of the personality," much abused by laymen and unfortunately also by many psychiatrists, has nothing to do with Bleuler's conception of schizophrenia. Long ago Freud also warned against the wrong use of such expressions as "splitting of the personality.") The interpretation of the mosaics made by schizophrenics shows that two tendencies that should form a unity are no longer properly integrated: the tendency to the expression of content, and the tendency to formal organization. The formal tendency that is expressed, for example, in supersymmetry gains the ascendancy and emancipates itself from the whole sense or content of the design.

Supersymmetry is an almost pathognomonic sign of schizophrenia. Its diagnostic significance becomes the greater the more inadequate and emptier the design is otherwise. It is merely one expression of the general overemphasis on the formal principles of organization in schizophrenia. Other signs are repetition, exaggerated formal schematization, and stereotypy. Some schizophrenic subjects make a more or less empty central design, with the principle of symmetry expressing itself in two wings protruding from the sides.

Schizophrenic designs are usually abstract and not representational. When patients with a schizophrenic psychosis attempt to make a concrete object, the relationship of the design to the object is likely to be unsatisfactory. It may be very unrealistic, or vague, or excessively schematized.

Typical is the unrealistic use of color. Often schizophrenics limit their designs to black and white. Sometimes color is entirely disregarded, or it may be used only as a formal element to achieve a rigid symmetry. Frequently schizophrenics use only one color for a design. This may be yellow or white or green, but it is hardly ever red and never black. On the whole, schizophrenic patients use form more than color. These signs are often present in the very earliest stages of the disease that the clinician has a chance to see. In advanced cases of schizophrenia with deterioration, the mosaics show only rudiments of organization, such as two pieces of the same shape or color placed together. They may be scattered incoherent jumbles composed of isolated pieces.

I have had occasion to study many cases of schizophrenia in remission—both spontaneous remissions and remissions following the various kinds of shock therapy. In all these remissions the schizophrenic process is still readily capable of diagnosis in the mosaics. Despite the disappearance of the clinically conspicuous symptoms, the mosaics may show all the signs of a definite process. This indicates clearly that the Mosaic Test reaches fundamental levels of the personality independent of the varying symptomatic manifestations. Sometimes in remissions the mosaics show an improvement—that is to say, an attenuation—of the schizophrenic mosaic signs and an indication of a more healthy organization. For example, there may be more color, less rigidity, and an increase in the number of pieces used. I have found these improvements far more in the spontaneous remissions than in those after the various insulin and shock therapies. This may be a very important criticism of these modern violent methods.

The clinical diagnosis of childhood schizophrenia (which more often than not is wrongly made) should be considered scientifically only if it is validated by the specific productions in mosaics.

Paraphrenic group.—This term is used here in the Freudian sense to include paranoid psychoses, paranoia, the paraphrenia of Kraepelin, and the more strictly so-called schizophrenic paranoid psychoses. It is often a dramatic occurrence in a clinic that one can at a glance make a specific and reliable diagnosis of a severe psychosis in cases that have presented innumerable social and clinical difficulties before. For example, we have often seen cases from the domestic-relations court where there was a question of jealousy and a mutual array of accusations. Often enough such jealousy may be harmless; sometimes it is morbid but not definitely psychotic. If one sees many such cases, every once in a while one finds that one of the partners is psychotic. The Mosaic Test may indicate quickly and conclusively the presence or absence of a psychosis. This type of design is a compact small mass composed of a few closely placed pieces. It has no discernible organization either in form or color, except that the pieces touch one another. We have called this "simple agglutination."

A simple agglutination indicates a severe functional psychosis

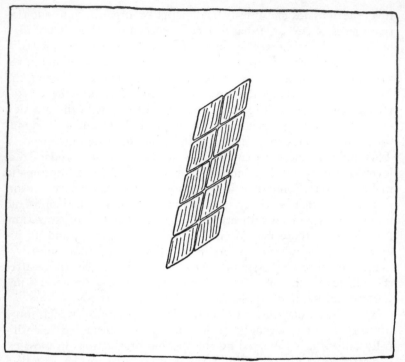

<small>FIGURE 11.</small> Cerebral Arteriosclerosis with Subcortical Symptoms

of paraphrenic stamp. It has never been seen in a healthy person. One often sees cases of simple schizophrenia in postadolescents. If these patients make a simple agglutination, it clinches the diagnosis of a severe psychotic process and rules out the other possibilities that so often come up in differential diagnosis, such as reactive or psychopathic states or emotional disorders in individuals with inferior intelligence. Simple agglutinations are as pathognomonic for severe chronic functional psychoses as the Wassermann test is for syphilis.

Organic brain disease.—Conditions with organic brain disease are characterized by a disorder in the organization of the designs. In the Mosaic Test it is possible to distinguish two kinds of lesions.

The "cortical pattern."—Patients with senile dementia, severe cerebral arteriosclerosis, dementia paralytica, Korsakov's psychosis, or severe encephalopathy following trauma express their cortical defect in an inability to achieve a good configuration. There is a dismemberment and dissolution of the Gestalt.

Patients with dementia use very few pieces, and they like to represent very simple, elementary geometric forms such as a circle or a star. They are likely to use shapes inappropriate for their goal and they tend to use color indiscriminately. The combination of choosing a very simple pattern and of being unable to achieve a good configuration is typical. Sometimes subjects with diffuse cortical brain disease make a number of very small incomplete designs. In the most advanced conditions of dementia, patients merely place a few scattered pieces on the board.

Contrary to the remissions in schizophrenia, where even in clinically fairly good remissions the designs still express the full schizophrenic process, the remissions in dementia paralytica following malaria treatment reflect the improvement. The patients in good remissions will use more pieces, do not restrict themselves to simple forms, and achieve better configurations. This difference in mosaics indicates that whereas malaria treatment affects the fundamental process of dementia paralytica, no known form of treatment affects the fundamental disease process in schizophrenia.

The "subcortical pattern."—The "subcortical pattern" is characterized by "stone-bound" designs. At the expense of an inner plan the patient follows the impetus inherent in the shape and color of the pieces put down so that the whole response becomes reduced to a more mechanical or automatic level.

In the normal brain there is a plastic utilization of inner and outer stimuli. The patient with impaired brain function becomes excessively dependent on outer stimuli at the expense of his inner goal. If one follows the successive utilization of the stimulus of each new piece as the patient makes the "stone-bound design," the "bondage to the stimulus" (*Reizgebundenheit*, as Goldstein called it) becomes apparent. "Stone-bound" designs may be seen in such diverse clinical conditions as postencephalitic Parkinsonism, cerebral arteriosclerosis, congenital spastic paraplegia, and Jacksonian epilepsy.

Mental deficiency.—The mosaics of mental defectives are so characteristic that in the practical use of the clinic we speak of them as "mental-defective designs." As a rule they show not a disorganization but a good organization at a low organizational level. These patients usually make a number of very small, simple, compact, and completed designs. Each design is made up of pieces of only one shape. The color scheme is often enumerative, with one piece of each available color. The same patterns occur over and over in all kinds of mental defectives, young and old, quiet or disturbed. In the lowest I.Q. range, subjects cannot achieve these elementary patterns. They make incoherent, scattered, and fragmentary mosaics.

Mosaics are a valuable adjunct to quantitative psychometric tests. Not every difference in intellectual functioning can be truly expressed in terms of a little more or less: an I.Q. or a mental age that is higher or lower. At certain nodal points there is a qualitative change in the organization of the use of intellectual resources. The Mosaic Test is a realistic indicator of the functioning level of intelligence. Very frequently when psy-

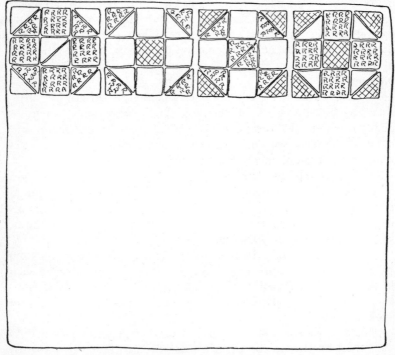

FIGURE 12. Obsessive State in a Severe Obsessive-Compulsive Neurosis on a Schizoid Basis

chometric tests indicate various degrees of borderline intelligence, mosaics show plainly whether or not the individual actually functions at a mental-defective level.

I have found an important exception to the specific diagnostic significance of "mental-defective designs." Ocassionally adult patients make these designs, although on psychometric tests they may make very high scores. Such a discrepancy almost invariably indicates the presence of a severe psychosis. It is to be understood that in both practice and research the Mosaic Test is to be used in connection with clinical examinations and other standard mental tests.

Manic-depressive psychosis. Manic states.—Manic patients, like other psychotics, use fewer pieces than normal people. Their designs are relatively simple. Typical are massed and jutting red

FIGURE 13. Obsessive State on an Affective Basis with Depression

pieces. The emphasis of the whole design is on color rather than on form.

Depressive states.—On account of their lack of initative and concentration, patients with severe depression cannot usually be induced to make designs. In milder depressive states black and dark blue are characteristic of subdued and depressive moods and attitudes. This significance of black and blue is valid only when other colors are also used in the design. Designs using only black or black and white have a different meaning. The former sometimes occurs in epileptic states; the latter is a typically schizoid feature.

Disorders of consciousness.—Patients with delirium—in contrast to severe depressions—can be aroused to make a design. They do not achieve any meaningful configuration, and their mosaics are incoherent, without any order or organization. In another disorder of consciousness, the epileptic twilight state, the patients make characteristic designs showing the clinical difference between the un-co-ordinated behavior of the delirious patient and the usually formally well-co-ordinated behavior of a patient in an epileptic fugue or twilight state. These subjects often make small, peculiar, and weird designs. They are not incoherent, but on the contrary are well co-ordinated.

Epilepsy.—Although the mosaics of epileptics show no uniformity, they are not healthy designs. Epileptics often make small, simple patterns, similar to "mental-defective designs," although on psychometric tests they may show average intelligence. Sometimes they make "stone-bound" designs. Often the insecurity, fear, and anxiety of the epileptic mentality, even if clinically not apparent, are expressed by the placing of the design close to the edges of the tray.

OTHER CONDITIONS

Psychopathic personalities.—Psychopathic personalities approach the normal in the number of pieces used. Schizoid personalities may show the characteristics of the schizophrenic mosaic pattern in very attenuated form and in larger designs. Their production may be clear and expressive, but they may show rigidity, monotony, repetition, or exaggerated stylization. Often they avoid the color red. In their organization the emphasis is on form rather than on color. The mosaics of psychopathic personalities

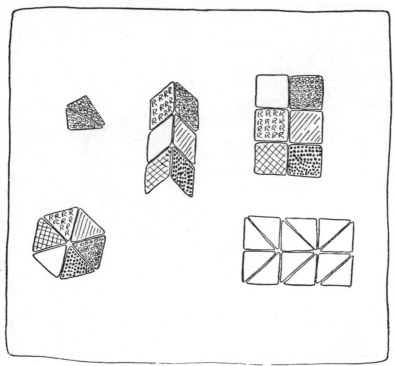

FIGURE 14. Typical Mental Defective Pattern

with pathological lying (pseudologia fantastica) do not reflect the superficial productivity shown in their fabrications, but the underlying inadequacy is expressed in somewhat inadequate designs. It is possible to infer general personality characteristics from mosaics, but these criteria are less clear-cut and classifiable.

Psychoneurosis.—In general there is no clear-cut distinction between the mosaics of psychopathic personalities and those of neurotics. Depressive features in neuroses may be reflected in a preponderance of black and blue. Anxiety may be expressed by clinging to the margin or by designs that take the form of a picture frame. This may be coupled with an avoidance of the open area of the central space, or there may be a small design in the middle which the frame encloses. It is interesting that the same kind of complete or incomplete frame occurs in the Navajo sand paintings in which the central picture is "tied in," as the Indians express it, "to keep out evil." Sometimes there is a marked dis-

FIGURE 15. Catathymic Crisis, Suicidal Attempt

crepancy in the style of the inner or central design and the outer or framing design. This indicates a severe emotional conflict to be found in cases of psychoneurosis or catathymic crisis. Conspicuous use of red generally indicates impulsiveness, excitability, or stimulation in the emotional or sexual sphere. In obsessive-compulsive states mosaics reveal whether the condition is on a schizoid basis, implying a guarded prognosis, or on an affective basis, implying a good prognosis. Sometimes they indicate a certain relationship to organic factors.

Simulation.—Subjects who consciously simulate mental symptoms make revealing designs. They use many shapes and colors but their designs are so meaningless and inconsistent that they could be genuine only in a patient in profound confusion or with the severest type of intellectual deterioration. During the war, when I examined many patients for draft boards, and after the war, when I examined many veterans, the Mosaic Test was an invaluable aid in the diagnosis of simulators, who are not so infrequent as is generally assumed.

Some of the main diagnostic characterizations of pathological processes may be expressed in a simplified formula:

Organic cortical brain disease: disorganization;
Organic subcortical brain disease: organization interfered with by automatism;
Mental deficiency: good, compact organization on a very simple level;
Schizophrenia: primitive, loose, overorganization;
Paraphrenia: pseudo-organization, only by contact;
Simulation: deliberate lack of organization;
Delirium: absence of organization.
Depressive psychosis: inability to initiate organization.

The Mosaic Test can be used to special advantage in conjunction with the Rorschach test. While the Rorschach test functions predominantly within the sphere of the study of the structure of the personality and of Freudian categories, the Mosaic Test is operative primarily in the sphere of pathological processes and of Kraepelinian categories. Its sensitiveness is notable in cases of lobotomy and topectomy. Whereas the Rorschach test in these cases does not give conclusive results (Piotrowski, 1948), the Mosaic Test indicates in every case—regardless of clinical improvements or results in other tests—a defect. Thus the Mosaic Test fills a gap not only in practice but also in theory and research.

REFERENCES

1. DIAMOND, B. L., and SCHMALE, H. T.: "The Mosaic Test. I. An Evaluation of its Clinical Application," *American Journal of Orthopsychiatry*, Vol. 14 (1944), p. 237.
2. GOLDSTEIN, KURT: "Zur Theorie der Funktion des Nervensystems," *Archiv für Psychiatrie*, Vol. 74 (1925), p. 370.
3. ———: *Organism: A Holistic Approach to Biology Derived from Pathological Data in Man*. New York: American Book Co.; 1939.
4. LOWENFELD, MARGARET: "A New Approach to the Problem of Psychoneurosis in Childhood," *British Journal of Medical Psychology*, Vol. 11 (1931), p. 194.
5. ———: *Play in Childhood*. London: Gollancz; 1935.
6. ———: "The World Pictures of Children," *British Journal of Medical Psychology*, Vol. 18 (1939), p. 65.

7. MALEVICH, KASIMIR: *Die gegenstandslose Welt*. Munich; 1927.

8. WERTHAM, FREDRIC: "A New Sign of Organic Brain Disease: Stone-Bound Mosaic Patterns," *Transactions of the American Neurological Association*, 1939.

9. ——: "The Relationship of Psychogenic and of Constitutional Factors," *Archives of Neurology and Psychiatry*, Vol. 22, (1929), p. 1201.

10. ——: "Experimental Type Psychology," *Archives of Neurology and Psychiatry*, Vol. 24 (1930), p. 605.

11. ——: "Eidetic Phenomena and Psychopathology," *Archives of Neurology and Psychiatry*, Vol. 24 (1930), p. 809.

12. ——: "The Catathymic Crisis," *Archives of Neurology*, Vol. 37 (1937), *Journal of Nervous and Mental Diseases*, Vol. 86 (1937), p. 346.

13. ——: *Dark Legend: a Study in Murder*. New York: Duell, Sloan & Pearce; 1941.

14. ——, and BLEULER, M.: "Inconstancy of the Formal Structure of the Personality. Experimental Study of the Influence of Mescaline on the Rorschach Test," *Archives of Neurology and Psychiatry*, Vol. 28 (1932), p. 52.

15. ——, and GOLDEN, LILI: "A Differential-Diagnostic Method of Interpreting Mosaics and Colored Block Designs," *American Journal of Psychiatry*, Vol. 98 (1941), pp. 124.

16. ——, and WERTHAM, F. E.: *The Brain as an Organ: Its Post-Mortem Study and Interpretation*. Chapter IX, "Correlation of Lesions with Psychopathological Phenomena," New York: The Macmillan Co.; 1934.

▼

In the next contribution Sidney Levy sets forth the possibilities of using figure drawings of the human form as projective productions worthy of interpretation along with other projective and psychometric data.

Figure drawing is clearly only in its infancy and lacks even that degree of standardization which may be said to characterize certain of the other projective methods. Nevertheless, as Dr. Levy indicates, figure drawings in the hands of the skilled clinician provide a rich source for personality study and evaluation. In his approach to interpretation Levy stresses the importance of the notion of body image and of the distortions that occur in it as significant psychological constructs around which to organize certain kinds of clinical data of frequent occurrence in personality investigation.

There seems little question that in the period which lies immediately ahead figure drawing as a projective procedure will come to earn greater acceptance among clinicians who seek an additional basis for their inferences about personality.

▼

Figure Drawing as a Projective Test

Sidney Levy[1]

INTRODUCTION

"The profession of psychology is much like living, which has been defined by Samuel Butler as 'the art of drawing sufficient conclusions from insufficient premises.' Sufficient premises are not to be found, and he who, lacking them, will not draw tentative conclusions, cannot advance." [116, page 22]

The clinical psychologist who analyzes drawings is in the challenging situation of arriving at sufficient conclusions from insufficient premises. In order to avert cynicism and disillusion it is well to emphasize that the technique of analyzing drawings is

---

[1] Although the author assumes sole responsibility for the contents of this chapter, many individuals have contributed to this work both directly and indirectly. Chief among them are Karen Machover, whose name is pre-

257

without sufficient experimental validation, rarely yields unequivocal information, and frequently misleads the unwary into plausible misstatements about the personality of the person whose drawings are being studied. Many of these statements are similarly true of the Rorschach Test and other projective techniques, but drawing analysis is especially vulnerable to misuse for a number of reasons. Since there is no complicated scoring system to master and no long apprenticeship to serve, the drawing test is an especially attractive instrument for the impulsive or reckless individual.

Notwithstanding all these negative statements, I regard drawing analysis as so fruitful and economical a source of information about personality that I believe the practice of prefacing other more complicated techniques of personality assessment with the "drawing-a-person" technique is a defensible clinical practice.

The amount of information that can be secured from this projective technique varies with the skill and experience of the psychologist and from subject to subject. As for the reliability and validity of judgments based upon drawing analysis, there is inadequate information available. The incomplete and inadequate experimentation in this area by myself and others, however, is promising enough to warrant continued exploration of the merits and limitations of drawing analysis. What is more, the lack of adequate information about validity does not negate the clinical utility of this technique. We are concerned here with a phenomenon that has been skillfully exploited by psychologists in the area of intelligence and aptitude testing where a number of tests, each with a low or undetermined index of validity, when combined with other tests of insufficient validity, yield acceptably valid results. For example, in the Army Air Force, selection of student pilots was made on the basis of a battery of eighteen tests, the validity of any one of which was so low that selection made on

eminently associated with this technique and whose word-of-mouth influence has been basic and pervasive; Murray Krim has contributed substantially to a review of related research; Dr. Herbert Zucker, who in personal discussions presented a penetrating analysis of basic assumptions and limitations of the technique; Dr. David Wechsler, who during the course of case presentations contributed illuminating insights; Dr. Elsie Toller, who checked the author's diagnostic statements against much of her clinical material; and Professor Brian E. Tomlinson, who supplied the original stimulus to clinical research.

the basis of a single test gave results which were little better than chance [66]. But when the eighteen tests were combined into a single battery, the validity of the total battery was .60. When information yielded by the drawing test is congruent with the results secured from other techniques, the clinician's confidence is fortified.

The drawing procedure may be regarded as a situational test in which the subject is presented with a problem, and in his efforts to solve it he engages in verbal, expressive, and motor behavior. This behavior, as well as the drawing itself, is observed by the clinician, and hypotheses are then tested against other available information.

ASSUMPTIONS

The material presented in this chapter has been empirically derived. Those interested in theoretical concepts and rationale will find it necessary to seek elsewhere [102]. There are certain basic assumptions about figure drawing, however, which may be made explicit. It is assumed that every aspect of behavior has some significance. Gestures, facial expressions, doodling, seemingly adventitious motor movements, all have meanings that may or may not be accessible to interpretation. While the drawing study is in progress, the subject is behaving as well as drawing. He makes verbal comments, indulges in facial expression, may play with the paper or pencil, shake his legs, bite his fingernails, and so on. Any observable behavior is appropriate material for the clinical psychologist. As Hutt says, "One has only to recall the recent studies of Allport and Sherif, the unique work of Werner, the ever-widening research program in graphology, the new approach through autokinetic and myokinetic tests supplied by such researchers as Sexton and Mira, and the complex phenomena observed in the Mosaic Test by Kerr and Wertham to realize that behavioral processes offer significant leads to the enrichment of personality theory and personality diagnosis." [79].

Some clinicians have said to me that "it is not cricket" to use the behavior of the subject as part of the drawing analysis. The drawing test is not a parlor game or a stunt, but a serious procedure, the purpose of which is to arrive at an understanding of the individual being studied. The clinician, however, is interested in the patient, not in the drawing per se. It is therefore entirely reasonable to use whatever data emerge form the experiment which are helpful in describing and understanding the subject's personality.

Some observers believe that each drawing is largely a matter of chance, training, or skill. This is one possible point of view, but projective psychology assumes that no behavior is accidental; all behavior is determined. The determinants, however, are usually multiple and of varying degrees of accessibility, thus complicating the task of analysis.

Some clinicians interpret each drawing as a projection of the body image or self-concept. While this is frequently the case, it is not necessarily so. I have concluded that a drawing may be a projection of self-concept, a projection of attitudes toward someone else in the environment, a projection of ideal self-image, a result of external circumstance, an expression of habit patterns, an expression of emotional tone, a projection of the subject's attitudes toward the examiner and the situation, an expression of his attitudes toward life and society in general. It is usually a combination of all of these. Furthermore, the drawing may be a conscious expression or it may include deeply disguised symbols expressive of unconscious phenomena. The only definitive statement that can be made is that the clinician must avoid an arbitrary, naïve, or dogmatic approach to the "draw-a-person" technique.

THE BASIC PROCEDURE

Equipment.—The basic procedure consists in presenting the subject with a moderately soft pencil and blank paper approximately 8½ by 11 inches in size. The paper should be placed in a pile within arm's reach so that the subject may select the sheet and place it in any position he prefers. There should be an adequate flat desk surface and sufficient illumination. The individual must be comfortably seated, with sufficient room for arms and legs. At this point it seems appropriate to caution against the frequently observed practice of permitting the subject to be seated along the side of a desk so that it becomes necessary for him to twist his body and shoulders. It is also undesirable to use a surface area so limited that the subject cannot rest his arms upon it. It is desirable to permit the subject to assume his usual state of relaxation so that any physical tensions may be assumed to be endogenous.

Directions.—The examiner says: "Will you please draw a person." This will usually result in a number of questions, such as "The whole person?" "What kind of person?" and in many protestations about the artistic ineptitude of the subject. In response to the class of questions relating to the kind of drawing, the examiner should limit himself to a very general statement, such as "Draw whatever you like in any way you like." This may be repeated in an effort to encourage and stimulate the subject, but no more specific directions should be given. In response to expressions of doubt about the artistic competence of the subject, the examiner may say: "That's all right; we're not interested in how well you draw as long as you draw a person." This may be repeated and rephrased, but may not be made more specific.

At this point the subject may respond in any one of a number of ways. For example, he may draw a complete person, an incomplete person, a cartoon, a "stick" figure, a stereotype, or an abstract representation of a person. Or he may express continuing reluctance. Each of these kinds of behavior yields information about the individual and is not to be regarded as wasteful of time. The clinician is just as much interested in the subject's behavior preliminary to and during the drawing as he is in the resulting artistic production. If the subject continues to be reluctant, the examiner may use whatever skills, techniques, or persuasion are available to him without giving any additional specific information. The fact that artistic talent is not important and that "whatever you do is all right" should be stressed. I have used this procedure with more than five thousand individuals and have faced only four adamant and persistent refusals to draw a person.

If the subject draws an incomplete figure, he is asked to take another sheet and draw a complete one. (The examiner must remember to number each sheet consecutively.) A word of explanation is necessary about what is meant by a "complete figure." A figure that includes the major part of any of the four major areas of the body is acceptably complete. The four areas of the body are the head, the torso, the arms, and the legs. If any *one* of these areas is *completely* omitted, the figure is incomplete. If only a part of an area is omitted, however—for example, the hands or the feet or one of the facial parts—the drawing is acceptably complete.

If the subject draws a cartoon, "stick" figure, stereotype, or abstract representation, he is asked to select an additional sheet and to draw a person; but sterotypes, cartoons, etc. (as the case may be), are not acceptable, and the instructions are repeated until a satisfactory figure drawing results.

The examiner now has in his possession one or more consecutively numbered drawings, at least one of which is an acceptably complete figure. If this figure is a male, the examiner now says: "This is a male figure; now please draw a female." If the first figure is a female, the examiner now says: "You drew a female figure; now please draw a male." The reactions of the subject may vary in ways similar to those previously described, and the examiner's responses are appropriate.

Observations.—This aspect of the technique consists in recording descriptive and interpretive statements about the subject's behavior and drawing.

BEHAVIOR

The behavior of the subject may be described with respect to its orientative, verbal, and motor aspects. He is presented with a somewhat unstructured situation. How does he orient himself? Does he express an acute need for more direction, and, if so, is this need expressed directly and verbally or indirectly through expressive movements and motor activity? Does he venture comfortably and confidently into the task? Does he express doubts about his ability, and, if so, does he express these doubts directly or indirectly, verbally or through motor activity? Is he insecure, anxious, suspicious, arrogant, hostile, negative, tense, relaxed, humorous, self-conscious, cautious, impulsive? The astute clinician will be able to form a fairly illuminating impression of the subject as a result of his preliminary behavior.

ANALYSIS OF THE DRAWING

There are many ways to approach the drawings. After a review of the literature Krim [89] concluded that drawing interpretation divides itself logically into three parts: namely, formal, graphological, and psychoanalytical (content analysis). This is one useful approach to the drawing.

After considerable trial and error I have evolved a technique of analysis based upon the Drawing Analysis Record Form *[93]*. (See Figure 24.) This serves the double purpose of focusing the clinician's attention upon meaningful aspects of the drawing and providing him with uniformly recorded data that facilitate the application of research techniques. There is nothing sacrosanct about this record form, however, or the procedure based upon it. It is expected that each clinician will feel free to proceed in the way that is most comfortable and productive for him.

In the following paragraphs the steps in analysis are described, along with other relevant information and drawings. The drawings are not presented as proof of the interpretive principles described but are included solely for *illustrative* purposes.

FIGURE SEQUENCE

Does the subject draw the male or female figure first? Of 5,000 adult subjects examined, 87 per cent drew their own sex first. Of sixteen overt homosexuals, thirteen drew the opposite sex first. These two facts suggest that it is usual for an unselected group of people to draw their own sex first, and that it is usual for a selected group of homosexuals to draw the opposite sex first. This obviously does not mean that every individual who draws the opposite sex first is a homosexual. The experienced clinician knows how dangerous it is to apply normative generalizations to an individual. If a subject draws the opposite sex first, however, the clinician should be interested in exploring the reason for this atypical procedure. I have found the following explanations for some of the cases cited above in which the first figure drawn was of the opposite sex: sexual inversion, confusion of sex identification, strong attachment to or dependence on parent of opposite sex, strong attachment to or dependence on some other individual of opposite sex. There are probably other explanations as well. Subjects will occasionally verbalize their indecision by asking such questions as: "Which sex shall I draw first?" The clinician should consider the possibility that the subject who raises these questions may be indicating confusion as to his own sexual role. Figures 16A, 16B, and 16C were drawn by overt homosexuals, and Figure 16D by an individual who has had both homosexual and heterosexual experience.

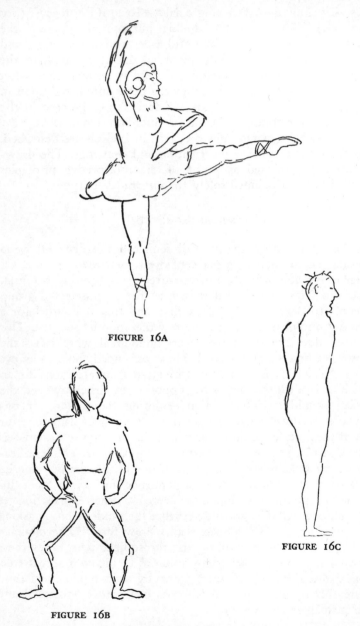

FIGURE 16A

FIGURE 16C

FIGURE 16B

FIGURE 16. Figure Drawings by Overt Homosexuals

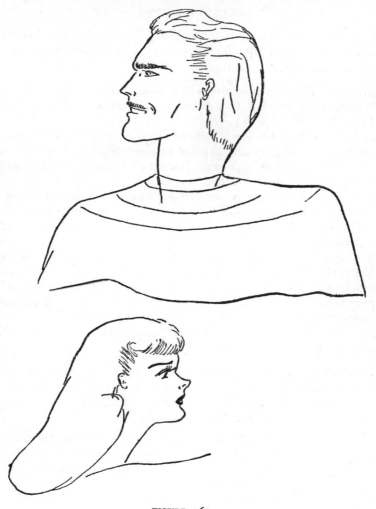

FIGURE 16D

FIGURE 16 (*Cont.*). Figure Drawings by Overt Homosexuals

FIGURE DESCRIPTION

I have found that by simply describing each figure illuminating insights are enticed into consciousness. The following are examples of descriptive statements:

Figure 16A. "This is a muscular female ballet dancer in a toe-dancing position with her left foot pointing and extending horizontally from the body."

Figure 16B. "This looks like a male acrobatic figure in a half-crouching position similar to that assumed by dancers before they receive their partner. He is apparently unclothed except for tights, and the facial features are omitted."

Figure 19A. "This is a very unusual drawing of a large-eyed, long-haired, fancifully clothed, and bearded individual. He is not a contemporary, and his appearance is very immature despite the beard and clothing."

Figure 19B. "This is a drawing of a woman with a stern expression. She is very ornately dressed. Her oval-shaped face is very prominently outlined, and her full mouth has a rather serious expression."

Figure 22A. "This is a very small, dowdy woman with a prominent nose and receding chin. She seems to be self-conscious."

Figure 22B. "This is a grim, tight-mouthed man wearing a high hat, formal attire, and carrying a cane."

It is interesting to note that the person who drew Figures 22A and 22B protested: "I have never been able to draw anything, I just don't know how to draw." Later, while discussing her father, John, she described him as follows:

A very stern man who loved to go out dressed up. He was always meticulous about himself and insisted upon doing the right thing at the right time and criticized other people who do things for the fun of it or because they just want to. Margueritte (Figure 22A) is a young girl who really does not look the way she is pictured to be. But that's the way John makes her feel. John made her feel as though her evening gown were a house dress. She hesitated to accompany him to functions for fear of being criticized.

It is interesting to observe that, in spite of her protestations about lack of drawing skill, the two figures she drew convey with astonishing clarity and economy her feelings about herself and her father.

It is the experience of most clinicians that even untutored and unskilled individuals, including young children, draw figures that convey expressive ideas. The precise way in which this is used by the clinician cannot be specifically formulated. The technique of studying the drawing for a few moments in order to describe the attitudes and feeling tones conveyed by it has proved productive in undefined ways. Perhaps the clinician's mind-set is so structured that the threshold for responding to subliminal cues is lowered. But this is speculation. The fact is that drawings do vary in their expressive aspects, and that recognition and conscious formulation of these differences seem to facilitate further interpretation.

COMPARISON OF FIGURES

Virtually everybody is able to draw two figures that differ from each other in some ways. The particular ways selected (consciously or unconsciously) by a subject are usually informative with respect to psychosexual attitudes. For example, in Figure 17A the male figure is much smaller and less mobile and has shorter arms than the female shown in Figure 17B. That is a descriptive statement of the differences between the two drawings. One possible interpretative statement based upon these objective differences is that the male is a smaller, more passive individual than the female. This interpretation is based upon the following elements: the woman's stance, posture, and arms suggest activity, whereas the male figure's posture, arms, and hands convey the impression that he is not in motion, that he is standing, with his hands in his pockets, watching. From this we may proceed a step further away from the objective drawing to the interpretation that the subject sees the man as inactive (passive), introverted, whereas the female appears to him as active, extroverted. That this is the general feeling conveyed by these drawings can easily be verified in ways similar to the technique used by me. This pair of drawings was presented to five clinicians with a request that they describe each of the figures as succinctly as possible. From the five statements made about the male (all five agreed in the essential characterization), the descriptive words that appeared with most frequency were tabulated. Words implying spectatorship rather than active participation (observer, onlooker, thoughtful, watching) occurred in each of the five de-

FIGURE 17A

FIGURE 17B

FIGURE 17. Drawings of a Male Figure and of a Female Figure

scriptions. Words implying passivity or dependence (less competent, dependent, feels small) occurred in four of the descriptions.

Descriptive words implying activity (aggressive, protective, active) appeared in all of the statements about the woman; and the implication of extroversion (takes care of others, not self-centered, motherly, competent) appeared in all the statements. When the five statements were boiled down into one descriptive passage about each figure, the following descriptions resulted. "Figure 17A is that of a somewhat retiring, sensitive, dependent, thoughtful, idealistic, introverted, gentle individual." "Figure 17B is that of a competent, energetic, active, protective, generous, firm person who is accustomed to taking charge." These two statements, with sexual identification omitted, were presented to five other clinicians with the request that they match each statement with the drawing to which it seemed to apply. In every case the former statement was matched with the male figure and the latter with the female.

There are other factors in each drawing to support these characterizations. Hands and arms are the parts of the human body that "do things," establish contact (shake hands), punish, or defend. In the male drawing the arms are relatively short (limited contact possibilities), pressed close to the body, and the hands are placed in the pockets. In this position there is no suggestion of readiness for activity, attack, manipulation, aggression, or other forms of contact.

The woman's arms are rather long, bent away from the body, with hands outlined. They are in a position from which it is quite easy to establish contact with people or objects. The kinesthesia expressed in the position of the arms suggests activity, whereas arms resting along the sides of the body with hands in pockets imply a lack of muscular tension, ergo passivity. The hair in the female drawing is sketched in single, firm strokes and gives the over-all impression of energy. What kind of woman wears her hair in this way? Observe that the man's hair is not drawn from the center of the head away from the body (as is the woman's), but is drawn from the head *toward* the body for the most part. In my experience with figure drawings stroking toward the body is suggestive of introversive tendencies, whereas stroking away from the body is often associated with extroversive tendencies.

Observe the difference in size. What is the usual association with respect to relative size? Is not the adult bigger and more competent than the child? Observe the differences in detail. The figure given the most care and detail is usually the one in which there is a larger investment of libidinal energy. In these drawings the male figure has two rows of buttons, a carefully knotted tie, clearly sketched eyebrows and features. The face is very carefully outlined. The interpretation may be made that the subject is identifying with the male figure, that his attention is directed toward himself (introverted), and that the female figure incorporates his apperception of women, which may be assumed to be derived from his relationship with his mother or mother surrogate.

The fact that the woman as well as the man is somewhat carefully detailed, with belt and neckline outlined, suggests that the subject who drew these figures is a somewhat compulsive individual with some regard for detail and order. The way in which the outline of the male figure is traced and retraced—the jacket is drawn and then redrawn to correct proportion—reinforces the interpretation of compulsiveness and orderliness. Thus by comparing the man-woman drawings the following interpretative statements may be made about the male subject who drew them: "*S* is an introverted, thoughtful, compulsive, sensitive, passive individual; a spectator rather than a man of action; has a need for nurturance and support and expects to receive these from a maternal figure."

SIZE

The relationship between the size of the drawing and the available space may parallel the dynamic relationship between the subject and his environment or between the subject and parent figures. If the drawing is a projection of self-concept, then the size is suggestive of the way the subject is responding to the environmental press. If the self-concept figure is small, the hypothesis may be formulated that the subject feels small (inadequate) and that he is responding to the demands of the environment with feelings of inferiority. If the figure is large, then the subject is responding to environmental press with feelings of expansion and aggression. These interpretations may be made only after it is established that the drawings are projections of self-concept.

A word is in order about the meanings of "large" and "small." The average drawing of a full figure is approximately seven inches long, or two thirds of the available space. More important than absolute size is the impression conveyed by the relationship between the figure and the surrounding space. If the *impression* of smallness is conveyed in a self-concept drawing, then the interpretation may be made that the subject feels small (inferior) or lost (rejected).

If it has been determined that the drawings are not self-con-

FIGURE 18A   FIGURE 18B

FIGURE 18. Aggressive and Punitive Male and Female Figures

cept figures, two other possibilities must be considered: namely, the drawing is a projection of ideal self-image (wishful image) or is a projection of parent image. In the latter case a large drawing indicates that the parent is strong, capable, dependable, or is threatening, aggressive, punitive. Which of these interpretations is appropriate usually becomes obvious in the context. For example, in Figure 17B, previously described, the mother figure, which is large, implies strength, competence, and dependability. On the other hand the figures in Figures 18A and 18B, which are equally large, may be interpreted as being threatening, aggressive, and punitive.

If the drawings are interpreted as being projections of ideal self-image, then a large drawing may be interpreted to mean that the subject is reacting to feelings of inadequacy with compensatory fantasying. Figures 20A, 20B, and 20C are the male drawings of three sixteen-year-old boys, all of whom are seventy-four inches tall. Figure 20A is the drawing of a weak, ineffectual individual who "talks big"—that is, who compensates for inferiority feelings with fantasy. Figure 20B is the drawing of an adolescent who feels inadequate and who responds to his feelings by withdrawal and inferiority. He frequently becomes "ill," fails in school, and is very dependent and docile. Figure 20C is the draw-

FIGURE 19A

FIGURE 19. Drawings of Immature Male Figure and Ornately Dressed Female Figure

ing of an adolescent who feels competent and independent and does not resort to either fantasy or inferiority as a main mechanism for adjustment.

LOCATION

There are five general placement possibilities. The drawing may be placed in the upper half, the lower half, the left side, the right side, or the center of the sheet.

Children whose drawings are placed in the upper half of the

FIGURE 19B
FIGURE 19 (*Cont.*). Drawings of Immature Male Figure and Ornately
Dressed Female Figure

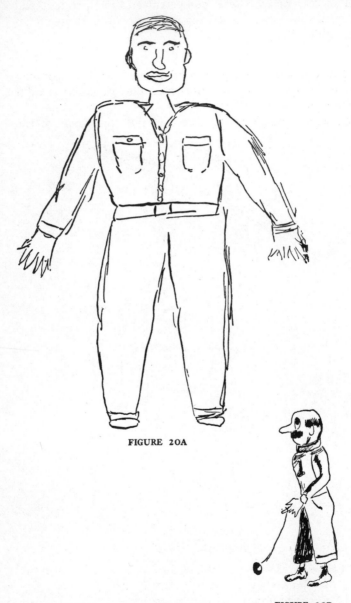

FIGURE 20A

FIGURE 20B

FIGURE 20. Figure Drawings of Adolescent Boys

FIGURE 20C

FIGURE 20 (*Cont.*). Figure Drawings of Adolescent Boys

sheet usually have rather high standards of achievement, for the attainment of which they constantly strive. Adults whose figures are placed in the upper half of the page frequently are those who feel unsure of themselves ("up in the air"). Those whose drawings are on the left side of the page are frequently self-conscious or introverted. Those whose drawings are placed at the bottom of the page seem to be more stable, firmly rooted, calm. Occasionally depressed or defeated individuals will do likewise. Those whose figures are carefully centered are usually self-directed, adaptive, and self-centered. In my experience, drawings rarely occur on the right side of the page. In the few instances where this has been observed, varying interpretations have been made. The only common factor seemed to be in the direction of negativism or rebelliousness.

What has been said of other dimensions of analysis may be said of location. No interpretation should be made out of context or without fitting it into the pattern delineated by the total configuration of interpretive statements.

MOVEMENT

Almost all figure drawings suggest some kind of kinesthetic tension, ranging from rigidity to extreme mobility. A drawing that is suggestive of much activity is frequently produced by those individuals who have a strong impulse toward motor activity. The restless individual, the man of action, the hypermanic, produce drawings that contain considerable movement. Figures that convey the impression of extreme rigidity are frequently produced by individuals with serious and deep-seated conflicts over which a rigid and usually brittle control is maintained. Occasionally the drawing will be that of a seated or reclining individual, in which case it is frequently indicative of low energy level, lack of drive, or emotional exhaustion. If a drawing is a mechanical kind of figure completely lacking in kinesthetic implications, the analyst should be alert for other signs of psychosis. Figures 21A and 21B are mechanical and lifeless and were produced by a schizophrenic.

DISTORTIONS AND OMISSIONS

A distortion or omission of any part of the figure suggests that conflicts may be related to the part so treated. For example, voyeurists frequently omit the eyes or close them. (See Figure 18B.) Individuals with sexual conflicts will omit or distort the areas associated with sexual parts. Infantile individuals with oral needs usually draw enlarged breasts. In a study of World War II leg amputees I found that the lower parts of the body were frequently omitted. (See Figure 23.) Remarks, erasures, shading, and reinforcement are all in the same direction as distortions and omissions and should be explored for possible relationships to conflict areas.

Head Region.—This is usually drawn first. Most individuals' concept of self is focused in the head and face. If the head is markedly enlarged, the subject may either be very aggressive,

FIGURE 21A   FIGURE 21B

FIGURE 21. Figure Drawings of Schizophrenics

have intellectual aspirations, or have head pains or other somatic symptoms. If the head and face are dimmed out, the subject may be extremely self-conscious and shy. If the head is drawn last, the possibility of severe disturbance in interpersonal relationships should be explored. If the head is very clearly drawn in contrast with a vaguely sketched or rejected body, the individual may habitually resort to fantasy as a compensatory device or may have feelings of inferiority or shame about his body parts and function.

The hair is given a great deal of attention and care by narcissistic or homosexual individuals. Hair on the face (beard or mustache) is usually associated with a striving for virility by those who have feelings of sexual inadequacy or doubts about masculinity. The mouth may be portrayed by a straight line, a curved line, an oval, and sometimes with teeth. If teeth are included, the subject may be orally aggressive and sadistic; other characteristics associated with this stage of development should be looked for. If the mouth is indicated by a single line, the individual may be verbally aggressive. If the mouth is oval or full and open, the subject may be an oral erotic, dependent individual. If the lips on the male are full and sensuous, the subject may be effeminate or homosexual.

If the eyes are very large and if those of the male figure have lashes, the subject is almost surely a homosexual. If the eyes are large in outline but the pupils are omitted or absent, the subject is expressing guilt in relation to voyeuristic tendencies. If the eyes are large and have the quality of staring, the clinician should investigate the possibility of paranoid trends.

The nose may portray a social stereotype or may be interpreted as a phallic symbol. If the nose is hooked or broad and flared, the subject is expressing rejection and contempt. If the drawing is a projection of self-concept, then these feelings are directed toward the self. If the drawing is a projection of non-self-concept, then these feelings are directed toward others. If the nose is especially large, it is usually associated with feelings of sexual impotency. Male involutional melancholics usually draw extremely large noses. Adolescents who are aggressively attempting to establish their male role almost invariably draw large noses.

The chin is a social stereotype for strength and determination. If a self-concept drawing has an enlarged chin, it may be an expression of strong drive, aggressive tendencies, or compensatory feelings for weakness and indecisiveness. If the chin is enlarged in a non-self-concept drawing, the subject is expressing feelings of inadequacy in the face of determined, aggressive, strong individuals.

The ear is rarely detailed. If it is enlarged or emphasized, the clinician should explore the possibility of organic damage in the auditory area, or auditory hallucinations in a paranoid individual, or a hearing disability.

The neck separates the head from the body and may be regarded as the link between intellectual control and id impulses. A long neck may suggest that the subject is having difficulty in controlling and directing instinctual drives. A long neck may also indicate somatic symptoms in this area. Individuals who have difficulty in swallowing, globus hystericus, or psychogenic digestive disturbances may draw figures with extremely long necks. Schizoid or schizophrenic individuals frequently draw figures with an exaggerated neck. (See Figures 21A and 21B.) If there is marked difference in the male and female neck, with the female being considerably longer, the subject may be an effeminate, dependent, orally passive individual.

Arms and Hands.—The arms and hands are the contact and manipulatory organs of the body. If the hands are hidden, the subject is expressing contact difficulties or feelings of guilt for manipulatory activities (masturbation). If the hands are shown but are exaggerated in size, this may be interpreted as compensatory behavior for feelings of manipulatory insufficiency, contact difficulties, or inadequacy. If the hands have considerable shading, then the subject may be expressing anxiety with respect to manipulation or contact activities. If the arms are pressed close to the body, the subject may be expressing passive or defensive feelings. If the arms are extended away from the body, the subject may be expressing externally directed aggressive needs. If fingers, fingernails, and joints are carefully sketched, the subject is either compulsive or is expressing difficulties with relation to body concept (as in early schizophrenia). Closed fists suggest repressed aggression.

Other Parts of the Body.—If the legs and feet are drawn first and given considerably more attention than the rest of the body, the subject may be expressing discouragement or depression. If the hip and buttocks of the male figure are rounded and larger than they should be or given an unusual amount of attention, the subject may have strong homosexual trends. If the trunk is rounded or wasp-waisted, a similar interpretation may be made. If the elbow joints and other articulatory regions are delineated, the subject is either a compulsive individual, in which case this trait will be manifested in many other ways, or he is a dependent, uncertain individual who needs familiar perceptual cues for reassurance. If internal anatomy is drawn, the subject is almost surely schizophrenic or manic. If the body is vaguely or bizarrely drawn (Figures 21A and 21B), the subject may be schizophrenic. The treatment of the feminine figure should be carefully observed. Is the drawing a representation of a child, a

FIGURE 22A

FIGURE 22B

FIGURE 22. Figure Drawings Showing Self-consciousness and a Grim,
Tight-mouthed Male

dream girl (Petty model), a maternal figure? What parts of the
female body are emphasized? If the breasts are extremely enlarged and carefully drawn, the subject may be expressing strong
oral dependent needs. If the arms and hands are long and prominent, the individual may be expressing the need for a protective
mother figure. If femininity in the female figure is indicated
through the use of superficial or symbolic details, the subject
may be expressing severely repressed œdipal feelings. If the shoulders and other masculine indicators in the male figure are exaggerated, the subject may be expressing his own insecurity with
respect to masculinity.

Clothing.—Most drawings are clothed. If the figures are nude and the sexual parts prominently displayed, the subject may be expressing rebellion against society (parent figures) or may be consciously aware of sexual conflicts. Individuals in whom there is a large voyeuristic element may draw glorified nude figures. If the self-concept figure is nude and given a great deal of attention, the subject may be expressing body-narcissism. On the other hand, if the self-concept drawing is carefully clothed, the individual may be expressing clothing- or social-narcissism. Both forms of narcissism are found in infantile, egocentric individuals.

Buttons are usually indicators of a dependent, infantile, inadequate personality. If the buttons are drawn along the mid-line, the subject may have somatic preoccupations. If buttons are drawn on cuffs and other equally inconspicuous areas, the subject is probably an obsessive-compulsive individual. The latter will also draw shoelaces, wrinkles, etc.

Pockets, when placed on the breast, are indicators of oral and affectional deprivation and are usually found in the drawings of infantile, dependent individuals. A tie is frequently interpreted as a phallic symbol. If a great deal of care and attention are lavished upon the tie and if the figure is somewhat effeminate, the subject may be a homosexual. A small tie may suggest repressed feelings of organ inferiority. Earrings are frequently drawn by subjects who have sex preoccupations of an exhibitionistic nature. Cigarettes, pipes, and canes are usually interpreted as symbols of striving for virility.

GRAPHOLOGY

The stroking may be described with respect to pressure, direction, continuity, angularity, rhythm. The pressure of the stroke is usually related to the level of energy. Thus an individual with a great deal of drive and ambition will usually draw firm lines. The individual whose energy level is low because of physical or psychic reasons will draw rather light lines. The cyclothymic, unstable, or impulsive individual will show fluctuating pressures.

The direction of the stroke may be vertical or horizontal, determined or undetermined. A marked preference for horizontal movements is frequently associated with weakness, femininity, fantasy living. A marked preference for vertical stroking is often associated with determination, hyperactivity, and assertive masculinity. If the direction of the stroke is determined and unhesitating, the individual may be a secure person with perseverance and persistence in working toward goals. Strokes that are indeterminate or vacillating in direction are frequently associated with a lack of the foregoing qualities. Thus vague, insecure individuals who lack opinions and points of view will draw figures in which the stroking has no determined direction. Uninterrupted straight lines are frequently the product of quick, decisive individuals. Interrupted curvilinear lines are often associated with slowness and indecisiveness. Very short sketchy strokes are often associated with anxiety and uncertainty. If the stroking is performed in a free and rhythmic way, the subject may be an unconstricted, responsive individual. If the stroking is constricted, the individual may be a tense, withdrawn, coarcted person. If the outline of the figure is sharp and clear with an unbroken reinforced line, the individual may be expressing his isolation and a need to protect himself from external pressures. Shading is usually an anxiety indicator. If the shading is found in sexual areas, the anxiety may be in relation to sexual function.

Strokes drawn from the page toward the subject may suggest self-involvement, introversion, or anxiety. Strokes drawn from the subject toward the upper part of the sheet may suggest aggression or extroversion. Strokes drawn from right to left are frequently associated with introversion or isolation. When the direction is from left to right, the figure-drawing analyst may look for tendencies toward extroversion, social stimulation, need for support.

At the risk of repetition, the clinician is again cautioned against using any one area of interpretation as reliably diagnostic unless supported by the total patterning of the drawing analysis.

Miscellaneous.—If the subject draws "stick" figures or abstract representations, they may be interpreted as indicative of evasion. This is frequently characteristic of insecure, self-doubting individuals. If the figures are clowns, cartoons, or silly-looking, the subject is expressing his contempt and hostility for people. This is frequently found in adolescents who feel rejected or inadequate. Witches or similar characters are drawn by individuals who are hostile and express their feelings extrapunitively.

Frequently ancillary material such as lines to represent the ground or a fence to lean on are included. These may be interpreted to express the need for support or succorance. Compulsive individuals are very easily recognized by their drawings. They are unable to leave them alone, and they go over and over an area, adding more and more detail. The hysteric, impulsive, unstable individual presents drawings that reveal these qualities in their lack of preciseness and the lack of uniformity of performance.

VARIATIONS OF THE BASIC PROCEDURE

There are many modifications of the basic figure-drawing test. The most extensive and structured is that described by Machover [102]. The reader is referred to this book for a complete discussion of that technique. There are several as yet unpublished techniques that have been found to be productive.

The Rosenberg Draw-a-Person Technique [136]. In this experimental modification of the "Draw-a-Person" Test the subject is given complete freedom to change his completed drawings in any way that he wishes. By using a carbon copy, one may retain the unchanged or original drawings for comparison with the changed copy.

Procedure.—It is felt that the actual wording of the directions is crucial in obtaining optimal results in this technique. At present research is being done to determine the most effective set of directions.

1. The subject uses a stapled set of two sheets with a carbon between them to do his drawing on. Standard directions for the "Draw-a-Person" Test are given, and a modified inquiry is conducted following the Machover technique, with both man and woman drawings. ("What is this person like?" etc.)

2. The examiner then tears off the top sheet of each set of drawings and retains the carbon copy for comparison with the changed copy. He gives the top sheet to the subject and instructs him: "Now you may have complete freedom to change, mark, or mess up, erase, cross out, or do anything you wish with the drawing you made. Feel as free as you like to change the drawing any way you wish. Now go to work on your drawing and make it as different as you would like." Changes are requested on both the male and female drawings in the same way. In some cases the carbon copy is quite lightly reproduced, but observation of the subject during the test will make clear what changes were made. Finally a post-inquiry is conducted asking about the changes made.

Value of This Modification.—In view of the fact that only preliminary work has been done with this technique, I can suggest possible clinical values only.

1. *Index of hostility.* The aggressive, hostile individual may project his feelings against the human figures he has drawn. The degree and type of change may represent hostility against the self or parent figures. This may be similar to the play-therapy techniques in which children may mutilate dolls representing mother or father figures.

2. *Rigidity-plasticity factors.* The loose, labile individual will be willing to change his original drawing, while the rigid person will be unable or unwilling to make any changes.

3. *Dynamic elements* (complexes, etc.). Sexual disturbances, serious concern over different parts of the body, reflections of core conflicts.

4. *Diagnosis of serious maladjustment.* The nature and degree of the changes made may provide a basis of differential diagnosis between moderate and severe emotional disturbances.

Illustrations of the Method.—1. D, aged 29, was hospitalized because of complaints of depersonalization and loss of affect. His woman drawing was that of a voluptuous nude figure, which he promptly changed into a "devil" when asked to make any changes he wished to. He added a devil's horns, cleft feet, tail, hair on the body, and sharply pointed teeth, and when asked in the inquiry about her, called her a "nymph." Further inquiry revealed that he meant "devil." His male figure, a dressed, well-integrated drawing, was converted into a cowboy, with high heels, and boxing gloves on his hands. Possible interpretations: great hostility against women; association of sex with moral sin; concern over masturbation.

2. C, aged 29, a high-school graduate, was receiving treatment at a mental-hygiene clinic because of depression, "mental blanks," and asocial feelings. He was diagnosed as a schizophrenic in remission with some regressive elements still present. His male figure was a somewhat crude drawing and was described as "a businessman, dressed up, clean-cut, walking along . . . a good talker . . . keeps his sex life under control." When asked to change the figure, he converted the businessman into a "devil" with short cropped hair, walking along with his penis exposed, urinating as he walked. In the post-inquiry, "He is walking along

FIGURE 23. Figure Drawings by a Below-the-knee Amputee Veteran

peeing . . . shrewd, that's why he's a devil . . . when no one is around he does things he wants to." The woman drawing was rather primitive, and in the conversion she was changed into "a donkey" and the sexual parts were heavily indicated (vagina, breasts, horns on head). These changes provide vivid indicators of the primitive and probably regressive impulses of the patient, his sexual preoccupation.

The Draw and Tell a Story Technique.[1] If the subject is a male, he is asked to draw two men and a woman on a single sheet of paper. If the subject is a female, she is asked to draw two women and a man on a single sheet of paper. The subject is then asked to give each figure a first name and to make up a story involving all three figures. It has been found useful to set a time limit of two or three minutes in order to apply pressure to the subject to tell a story with a minimum of ego direction. The time limit is not actually adhered to; its sole purpose is to apply pressure to the subject.

This technique sets up a triangular situation, and the story that is told will frequently be illuminating with respect to the interpersonal attitudes of the subject, who will impose his idiosyncratic interpretation of the situation. Thus in one case the triangle will recall a sibling theme, while in another œdipal dynamics may be revealed. I have found that young children tend to destroy one of the two equivalently sexed figures. In a recent

---

[1] Sidney Levy: "The Draw and Tell a Story Technique." Unpublished thesis, New York University, 1947.

DRAWING-ANALYSIS RECORD BLANK

Subject's Name........... Sex... Age... Education...... Date....

1. *Directions for Administering*

2. *Observations*
   a) **Test Behavior:**

   b) *Sequence:*

3. *Drawing Analysis*

FIGURE 24. Drawing Analysis Record Blank

Figuré 1

Whole

1) Descriptive statement, including age, sex, etc.:

2) Size: 1 2 3 4 5 6 7 8 9 10 11 12 13 14 15 16 17 18 19 20 21 22

3) Location:

4) Aspect: Full Face—— Left Profile—— Right Profile——
                Rear View——

5) Movement: Active—— Mild—— Suggested—— Rigid——
                Absent—— Extensor—— Flexor——

Details

6) List parts omitted:

7) List parts distorted or exaggerated:

8) List articles of clothing included:

9) List ancillary parts external to the figure:

4. *Graphic Analysis*

10) Pressure: High—— Medium—— Soft——
11) Continuity: Unbroken—— Broken——
12) Rhythm: Broad—— Narrow——
13) Direction: Varied—— Up—— Down—— Right—— Left——
14) Motor movement: Restricted—— Free——
15) Amount of detail:
16) Preciseness of form:
17) Balance:
18) Shading

MISCELLANEOUS:

FIGURE 24 (*Cont.*). Drawing Analysis Record Blank

study of World War II amputees,[2] a recurrent theme revealed sexual insecurity (castration anxiety?). The female figure was frequently described as deserting her former husband or lover and going off with "the other man." In schizophrenics' stories each of the figures goes his own way or one or more of the figures is omitted from the story. (See Figure 23.)

CONCLUSION

Figure-drawing analysis is a useful technique for clinical and research purposes. Although it can be used scientifically, the technique itself has not been scientifically validated. If it is used with the same caution, artistry, and skill that are applied to other clinical instruments, it may frequently prove to be a fruitful and economical source of insights about the personality of the subject. Effective utilization of this technique is dependent upon a thorough understanding of personality dynamics and extensive familiarity with the drawings of large numbers of individuals about whom there is available fairly complete psychological information.

REFERENCES

1. ABEL, T. M.: "Free Design of Limited Scope as a Personality Index," *Character and Personality*, Vol. 7 (1938), pp. 50–62.
2. ALLEN, GRANT: *The Color Sense: Its Origin and Development.* London: Kegan Paul, Trench, Trubner & Co.; 1892.
3. ALLPORT, G. W., and ODBERT, H. S.: "Trait Names: a Psycholexical Study," *Psychological Monographs*, Vol. 47 (1936), No. 211, p. 171.
4. ALLPORT, G. W., and VERNON, P. E.: *Studies in Expressive Movement.* New York: Macmillan Co.; 1933.
5. ANASTASI, A., and FOLEY, J. P.: "A Survey of the Literature on Artistic Behavior in the Abnormal: III. Spontaneous Productions," *Psychological Monographs*, Vol. 52 (1941), No. 237.
6. ———: "An Analysis of Spontaneous Drawings by Children in Different Cultures," *Journal of Applied Psychology*, Vol. 20 (1936), pp. 689–726.

---

[2] Lawrence E. Abt and Sidney Levy: "A Psychological Study of World War II Amputees." Unpublished monograph. New York University, 1947.

7. ——: "A Study of Animal Drawings by Indian Children of the North Pacific Coast," *Journal of Social Psychology*, Vol. 9 (1938), pp. 363–74.
8. APPEL, K. E.: "Drawings by Children as Aids to Personality Studies," *American Journal of Orthopsychiatry*, Vol. 1, (1931), pp. 129–44.
9. ASCH, S. E.: "Forming Impressions of Personality," *Journal of Abnormal and Social Psychology*, Vol. 41 (1946), pp. 258–90.
10. AYER, F. C.: *The Psychology of Drawing*. Baltimore: Warwick & York; 1916.
11. BALLARD, F. B.: "What Children Like to Draw," *Journal of Experimental Pediatrics*, Vol. 2, (1913), pp. 127–9.
12. BARNES, E.: "A Study of Children's Drawings," *Pedagogical Seminary*, Vol. 2 (1893), pp. 451–63.
13. BATAILLE, G.: "L'Art primitif," *Documents*, Vol. 7 (1930), pp. 389–97.
14. BAYNES, H. G.: *Mythology of the Soul: A Research into the Unconscious from Schizophrenic Dreams and Drawings*. London: Balliere, Tindall & Cox; 1939.
15. BELO, J.: "Balinese Children's Drawings," *Djawa*, 5 and 6. 1937.
16. BENDER, L.: "Gestalt Principles in the Sidewalk Drawings and Games of Children," *Journal of Genetic Psychology*, Vol. 41 (1932), pp. 192–210.
17. ——, and SCHILDER, P.: "Form as a Principle in the Play of Children," *Journal of Genetic Psychology*, Vol. 49 (1936), pp. 254–61.
18. BERGER, E.: "Der Sandersche Phantasietest im Rahmen der Psychologischen Eignungsuntersuchung Jugendlicher," *Archiv für die gesamte Psychologie*, Vol. 103 (1939), pp. 499–543.
19. BERRIEN, F. K.: "A Study of the Drawings of Abnormal Children," *Journal of Educational Psychology*, Vol. 26 (1935), pp. 143–50.
20. BEST, MANGARD ADOLF: *Method for Creative Design*. New York: Alfred Knopf; 1927.
21. BIBER, BARBARA: *From Lines to Drawings;* New York: 69 Bank Street; 1930.
22. ——: *Children's Drawings: From Lines to Pictures*. New York: Bureau of Educational Experiments; 1934.
23. BILLINGS, M. L.: "A Report of a Case of Inverted Writing and Drawing," *Child Development*, Vol. 6 (1935), pp. 161–3.

24. BRILL, M.: "Study of Instability Using the Goodenough Drawing Scale," *Journal of Abnormal and Social Psychology*, Vol. 32 (1937), pp. 288–307.

25. BROOM, M. E., THOMPSON, B., and BOUTON, M. T.: "Sex Differences in Handwriting," *Journal of Applied Psychology*, Vol. 13 (1929), pp. 159–66.

26. BROWN, D. D.: *Notes on Children's Drawings*. Berkeley: University of California Publications; 1897.

27. BULLOUGH, E.: "Recent Work in Experimental Aesthetics," *British Journal of Educational Psychology*, Vol. 12 (1934), pp. 76–99.

28. BURK, F.: "The Genetic Versus the Logical Order in Drawing," *Pedagogical Seminary* Vol. 9 (1902), pp. 296–323.

29. CAILLE, RUTH KENNEDY: "Resistant Behavior of Preschool Children," *Child Development Monographs, No. 11*. New York: Teachers College, Columbia University; 1933.

30. CALKINS, M. W.: "The Self in Scientific Psychology," *American Journal of Psychology*, Vol. 26 (1915), pp. 496–524.

31. ——: "The Self in Scientific Psychology," *Psychological Bulletin*, Vol. 13 (1916), pp. 20–7.

32. CAMERON, N.: "Individual and Social Factors in the Development of Graphic Symbolizations, *Journal of Psychology*, Vol. 5 (1938), pp. 165–84.

33. CANE, F.: "The Gifted Child in Art," *Journal of Educational Sociology*, Vo' 10 (1936), pp. 67–73.

34. CANTRIL, H., and RAND, H. A.: "An Additional Study of the Determination of Personal Interests by Psychological and Graphological Methods," *Character and Personality*, Vol. 35 (1934), pp. 72–80.

35. CATTELL, R. B.: *Description and Measurement of Personality*. Yonkers: World Book Co.; 1946.

36. CHILD, H. G.: "Measurement of the Drawing Ability of 2177 Children in Indiana City School Systems by a Supplemental Thorndike Scale," *Journal of Educational Psychology*, Vol. 6 (1915), pp. 391–408.

37. COCKRELL, D. L.: "Design in the Paintings of Young Children," *School Arts Magazine*, Vol. 30. (1930), pp. 112–19.

38. COHEN, J.: "The Use of Objective Criteria in the Measurement of Drawing Ability," *Pedagogical Seminary*, Vol. 27 (1920), pp. 137–51.

39. COLE, N. R.: *The Arts in the Classroom*. New York: John Day Co.; 1940.

40. DANZ, LOUIS: *It Is Still the Morning.* New York: William Morrow & Co.; 1943.

41. DILLON, M. S.: "Attitudes of Children Toward Their Own Bodies and Those of Other Children," *Child Development,* Vol. 5 (1934), pp. 165–76.

42. DIXON, C. MADELEINE: *High, Wide, and Deep.* New York: John Day Co.; 1943.

43. DORCUS, R. M.: "The Experimental Study of Forms of Expression," *Character and Personality,* Vol. 2 (1933), No. 2, pp. 168–76.

44. DOWNEY, J. E.: *Graphology and the Psychology of Handwriting.* Baltimore: Warwick & York; 1919.

45. DREVER, J.: "The Analytical Study of the Mechanism of Writing," *Proceedings of the Royal Society,* Vol. 345 (1913), pp. 230–400.

46. DUMMER, ETHEL S.: *Why I Think So: the Autobiography of an Hypothesis.* Chicago: Clarke-McElroy Publishing Co.; 1937.

47. ENG, HILDA: *The Psychology of Children's Drawings: From the First Stroke to the Color Drawing.* London: Kegan Paul, Trench, Trubner & Co.; 1931.

48. ESTES, S. G.: "Judging Personality from Expressive Behavior," *Journal of Abnormal and Social Psychology,* Vol. 33 (1938), pp. 217–36.

49. EAGLESON, O. W.: "The Success of Sixty Subjects in Attempting to Recognize Their Handwriting," *Journal of Applied Psychology.;* Vol. 21 (1937), pp. 546–9.

50. FINDLEY, W. G.: "Factor Analysis of a Short-Item Drawing Test," *Psychological Bulletin,* Vol. 33 (1936), p. 605.

51. FLORINA, A.: "Research into the Drawings of Preschool Children," *New Era,* Vol. 9 (1928), pp. 37–8.

52. FRANK, L. K.: "Projective Methods for the Study of Personality," *Journal of Psychology* (1939), pp. 389–413.

53. FREEMAN, F. N.: "An Experimental Analysis of the Writing Movement," *Psychological Monographs,* Vol. 17 (1914), p. 4.

54. GALLAGHER, M.: "Children's Spontaneous Drawings," *Northwestern Monthly,* Vol. 8 (1889), p. 130–4.

55. GERALD, H. J. P.: "Inverted Positions in Children's Drawings. Report of two cases," *Journal of Nervous and Mental Diseases,* Vol. 68 (1928), pp. 449–55.

56. GESELL, A. L.: "Accuracy in Handwriting as Related to School Intelligence and Sex," *American Journal of Psychology,* Vol. 17 (1906), pp. 394–405.

57. ——, et al.: *The First Five Years of Life: A Guide to the Study of the Preschool Child.* New York: Harper & Bros.; 1940.

58. ——: *Infant and Child in the Culture of Today: Guidance and Development in Home and Nursery School.* New York: Harper & Bros.: 1943.

59. GOODENOUGH, FLORENCE L.: *Developmental Psychology.* New York: D. Appleton & Co.; 1934.

60. ——: *Measurement of Intelligence by Drawing.* Yonkers: World Book Co.: 1926.

61. ——: "Studies in the Psychology of Children's Drawings," *Psychological Bulletin,* Vol. 25 (1928), pp. 272–9.

62. ——: "Children's Drawings," in *Handbook of Child Psychology.* C. Murchison (ed.) Worcester: Clark University Press; 1931.

63. GRIDLEY, P. F.: "Graphic Representation of a Man by Four-Year-Old Children in Nine Prescribed Drawing Situations," *Genetic Psychology Monographs,* Vol. 20 (1938), pp. 183–350.

64. GRIFFITHS, RUTH: *A Study of Imagination in Early Childhood.* London: Kegan Paul, Trench, Trubner & Co.; 1935.

65. GRIPPEN, V. B.: "A Study of Creative Artistic Imagination in Children by the Constant Contact Procedure," *Psychological Monographs* (1933), Vol. 45 (1933), No. 1, pp. 63–81.

66. GUILFORD, J. P. and LACEY, J. I. (eds.): *Printed Classification Tests.* Washington: U. S. Government Printing Office; 1947.

67. HALLOWELL, A. I.: "The Child, The Savage, and Human Experience," *Proceedings of the 6th Institute for Exceptional Children, Child Research Clinic* (1939), pp. 8–34.

68. HARMS, ERNST: "Child Art as An Aid in the Diagnosis of Juvenile Neuroses," *American Journal of Orthopsychiatry,* Vol. 11 (1941), No. 2, pp. 191–209.

69. HATTWICK, LA BERTA A.: "Sex Differences in Behaviour of Preschool Children," *Child Development,* Vol. 8 (1937).

70. HERRICK, M. A.: "Children's Drawings," *Pedagogical Seminary,* Vol. 3 (1893), pp. 338–9.

71. HICKS, M. D.: "Art in Early Education," *Kindergarten Magazine,* Vol. 6 (1894), pp. 590–605.

72. HILDRETH, G.: "The Simplification Tendency in Reproducing Design," *Journal of Genetic Psychology,* Vol. 64 (1944).

73. HINRICHS, W. E.: "The Goodenough Drawing Test in Relation to Delinquency and Problem Behavior," *Archives of Psychology,* Vol. 175 (1935), pp. 1–82.

74. HOMBERGER, ERIK: "Configuration in Play," *Psychoanalytic Quarterly,* Vol. 6 (1937), pp. 139–214.

75. HULL, C. L., and MONTGOMERY, R. P.: "Experimental Investigation of Certain Alleged Relations between Character and Handwriting," *Psychological Review*, Vol. 26 (1919), pp. 63–74.

76. HUNT, J. McV. (ed.): *Personality and the Behavior Disorders*. Vol. I, Chap. VI, by Robert W. White. New York: Ronald Press Co.; 1944.

77. HURLOCK, E. B.: "The Spontaneous Drawings of Adolescents," *Journal of General Psychology*. Vol. 63 (1943).

78. ——, and THOMSON, J. L.: "Children's Drawings: an Experimental Study of Perception," *Child Development*, Vol. 5 (1934), pp. 127–33.

79. HUTT, M. L. in Foreword, *Journal of Projective Techniques*, Rorschach Institute, Vol. 11 (1947), No. 10.

80. JACOBS, MICHEL: *The Art of Color*. New York: Doubleday, Doran & Co.; 1931.

81. JACOBY, H. J.: "The Handwriting of Depressed Children," *New Era*, January 1944.

82. KATO, M. A. "Genetic Study of Children's Drawings of a Man," *Journal of Experimental Psychology*, Vol. 3 (1936), pp. 175–85.

83. KATZ, S. E.: "The Color Preference of Children," *Journal of Applied Psychology*, Vol. 65 (1922), pp. 225–66.

84. ——: "Color Preference in the Insane," *Journal of Abnormal and Social Psychology*, Vol. 26 (1931), pp. 203–11.

85. KERR, M.: "Children's Drawings of Houses," *British Journal of Psychology*, (Med. Sect. 16), 1936, pp. 206–18.

86. KLOPFER, BRUNO: "Personality Differences between Boys and Girls in Early Childhood: Report before the American Psychological Association," *Psychological Bulletin*, Vol. 36 (1939), p. 538.

87. ——: "Rorschach Reactions in Early Childhood," *Rorschach Research Exchange*, Vol. 5 (1940), pp. 1–23.

88. KNAUBER, A. J.: "Art Ability in Children," *Child Development*, Vol. 2 (1931), No. 1, pp. 66–71.

89. KRIM, MURRAY: "Diagnostic Personality Testing with Figure Drawings," Unpublished thesis, New York University, 1947.

90. KROTSCH, W.: "Rhythmus und Form in der freien Kinderziehung. Reported by Viktor Lowenfeld," Leipzig: 1917. In *The Nature of Creative Activity*. New York: Harcourt, Brace & Co.; 1939.

91. LAND, A. H.: "Graphology: a Psychological Analysis," University of Buffalo Studies, Vol. 3 (1924), pp. 81–114.

92. LECKY, P.: *Self-Consistency: a Theory of Personality.* New York: Island Press; 1945.

93. LEVY, SIDNEY: *Drawing Analysis Record Form.* Copyright, 1948.

94. LEWIS, N. D. C.: "Graphic Art Productions in Schizophrenia," *Proceedings of the Association for Research in Nervous and Mental Diseases,* Vol. 5 (1928), pp. 344–68.

95. LISS, E.: "The Graphic Arts," *American Journal of Orthopsychiatry,* Vol. 8 (1938), pp. 95–9.

96. LONG, W. F., and TIFFIN, J.: "A Note on the Use of Graphology by Industry," *Journal of Applied Psychology,* Vol. 25 (1941), pp. 469–71.

97. LORAND, SANDOR (ed.): *Psychoanalysis Today.* New York: International Universities Press; 1944.

98. LOWENFELD, MARGARET: *Play in Childhood.* London: Gollancz; 1935.

99. LUKENS, H.: "A Study of Children's Drawings in the Early Years," *Pedagogical Seminary,* Vol. 4 (1896), pp. 79–110.

100. LUNDHOLM, H.: "The Affective Tone of Lines: Experimental Researches," *Psychological Review,* Vol. 28 (1921), pp. 43–60.

101. MACHOVER, KAREN: "A Case of Frontal Lobe Injury Following Attempted Suicide. (Drawings, Rorschach)," *Rorschach Research Exchange and Journal of Projective Techniques,* Vol. 11 (1947), p. 1.

102. ——, *Personality Projection in the Drawing of the Human Figure.* Springfield: C. C. Thomas; 1948.

103. MAITLAND, L.: "What Children Draw to Please Themselves," *Inland Educator,* Vol. 1 (1895), p. 87.

104. ——, and C. RICCI: "The Art of Little Children," *Pedagogical Seminary,* Vol. 4 (1895), pp. 302–7.

105. MANUEL, H.: "Talent in Drawing: an Experimental Study of the Use of Tests to Discover Special Ability," *School and Home Educational Monographs,* Vol. 3 (1919).

106. ——, and HUGHES, L. S.: "The Intelligence and Drawing Ability of Young Mexican Children," *Journal of Applied Psychology,* Vol. 16 (1932), pp. 382–7.

107. MATHIAS, MARGARET C.: "Encouraging the Art Expression of Young Children," *Childhood Education,* Vol. 15 (1939), No. 7, p. 293.

108. McALLISTER, C. N.: "Researches on Movements Used in Handwriting," *Yale Psychological Laboratory Studies*, Vol. 8 (1900), pp. 21–63.

109. McDermott, L.: "Favorite Drawings of Indian Children," *Northwestern Monthly*, Vol. 8 (1897), pp. 134–7.

110. McElwee, E. W.: "The Reliability of the Goodenough Intelligence Test Used with Subnormal Children Fourteen Years of Age," *Journal of Applied Psychology*, Vol. 18 (1934), pp. 599–603.

111. McIntosh, J.: "An Inquiry into the Use of Children's Drawings as a Means of Psychoanalysis," *British Journal of Educational Psychology*, Vol. 9 (1939), pp. 102–3.

112. Melcher, W.: "Dual Personality in Handwriting," *Journal of Criminal Law and Criminology*, Vol. 11 (1920), pp. 209–16.

113. Miller, J.: "Intelligence Testing by Drawings," *Journal of Educational Psychology*, Vol. 29 (1938), pp. 390–4.

114. Mira, E.: "Myokinetic Psychodiagnosis: a New Technique for Exploring the Conative Trends of Personality," *Proceedings of the Royal Society of Medicine*, Vol. 33 (1940), pp. 9–30.

115. Morgenstern, S.: "Le Symbolisme et la valuer psychoanalytique des dessins infantiles," *Revue française Psychoanalytique*, Vol. 11, pp. 39–48.

116. Murray, H. A., et al: *Explorations in Personality*. New York: Oxford University Press; 1938.

117. Newall, S. M.: "Sex Differences in 'Handwriting," *Journal of Applied Psychology*, Vol. 10 (1926), pp. 151–61.

118. Oakley, C. A.: "The Interpretation of Children's Drawings," *British Journal of Psychology*, Vol. 21 (1930), pp. 256–70.

119. ———: "Drawings of a Man by Adolescents," *British Journal of Psychology*. Vol. 31 (1940), pp. 37–60.

120. Oberlin, D. S.: "Children Who Draw," *Delaware State Medical Journal*, Vol. 10 (1938).

121. Oldham, H. W.: "Child Expression in Form and Color. London: John Lane; 1940.

122. Omwake, K. T.: "The Value of Photographs and Handwriting in Estimating Intelligence," *Public Personnel Studies*, Vol. 3 (1925), pp. 2–15.

123. O'Shea, M. V.: "Children's Expression Through Drawing," *Proceedings of the National Education Association*, 1894, pp. 1015.

124. ———: "Some Aspects of Drawing," *Educational Review*, Vol. 14 (1897), pp. 263–84.

125. PASET, G.: "Some Drawings of Men and Women Made by Children of Certain Non-European Races," *Journal of the Anthropological Institute*, Vol. 62 (1932), pp. 127–44.

126. PFISTER, H. O.: "Farbe und Bewegung in der Zeichnung Geisterkranker," *Schweizer Archiv für Neurologie und Psychiatrie*, Vol. 34 (1934), pp. 325–65.

127. PINTNER, R.: "Aesthetic Appreciation of Pictures by Children," *Pedagogical Seminary*, Vol. 25 (1918), pp. 216–18.

128. ——, and TOOPS, H. A.: "A Drawing Completion Test," *Journal of Applied Psychology*, Vol. 2 (1918), pp. 164–75.

129. POFFENBERGER, A. T., and BARROW, B. E.: "The Feeling Value of Lines," *Journal of Applied Psychology*, Vol. 8 (1924), pp. 187–205.

130. POWERS, E.: "Graphic Factors in Relation to Personality: an Experimental Study." (Unpublished thesis) Dartmouth College Library, 1930.

131. PRINCE, M.: *Clinical and Experimental Studies in Personality.* Cambridge, Mass.: Sci-Art Publishers; 1929.

132. PRINZHORN, H.: *Bildnerei der Geisteskranken.* Berlin: Springer; 1923.

133. READ, H.: *Education through Art.* London: Faber & Faber; 1944.

134. *Review of Educational Research*, Vol. 14, No. 1, Chap. VI. Washington: National Education Association; 1944.

135. REITMAN, F.: "Facial Expression in Schizophrenic Drawings," *Journal of Mental Science*, Vol. 85 (1939), pp. 264–72.

136. ROSENBERG, LOUIS: "Modifications of 'Draw-a-Person' Test." Unpublished thesis, New York University, 1948.

137. SACHS, H.: *The Creative Unconscious.* Cambridge, Mass.: Sci-Art Publishers; 1942.

138. SAUDEK, R.: *Experiments with Handwriting.* New York: William Morrow & Co.; 1928.

139. SEARS, R. R.: "Experimental Studies of Projection: 1. Attribution of Traits," *Journal of Social Psychology*, Vol. 7 (1936), pp. 151–63.

140. SCHILDER, P.: *The Image and Appearance of the Human Body.* Psychic Monographs. No. 4. London: Kegan Paul, Trench, Trubner & Co.; 1935.

141. SCHUBE, K., and COWELL, J.: "Art of Psychotic Persons," *Archives of Neurology and Psychiatry*, Vol. 41 (1939), pp. 709–20.

142. SCHUBERT, A.: "Drawings of Orotchen Children and Young People," *Journal of Genetic Psychology*, Vol. 37 (1930), pp. 232–44.

143. SPOERL, D. T.: "Personality and Drawing in Retarded Children," *Character and Personality*, Vol. 8 (1940), pp. 227–39.

144. *The Visual Arts in General Education: Report of Committee on Function of Art in General Education, Progressive Education Association Commission on the Secondary School Curriculum.* New York: D. Appleton-Century Co.; 1940.

145. THORNDIKE, E. L.: "The Measurement of Achievement in Drawing," *Teachers College Record*, Vol. 14 (1913), 30–6.

146. TRAUBE, T.: "La valeur diagnostique des dessins des enfants difficiles," *Archives de psychologie*, Vol. 26 (1937), pp. 285–309.

147. WACHNER, T. S.: "Interpretation of Spontaneous Drawings and Paintings," *Genetic Psychology Monographs*, 1946, pp. 3–70.

148. WOLFF, W.: "Projective Methods for Personality Analysis of Expressive Behavior in Preschool Children," *Character and Personality*, Vol. 4 (1942), pp. 309–30.

149. ——: *The Expression of Personality.* New York; Harper & Bros.; 1943.

150. ——: *The Personality of the Preschool Child.* New York: Grune & Stratton; 1946.

151. YEPSEN, L. N.: "The Reliability of the Goodenough Drawing Test with Feeble-Minded Subjects," *Journal of Educational Psychology*, Vol. 20 (1929), pp. 448–51.

▼

ORGANIZED around the clinical application of the Szondi Test in the measurement of the effects of electric-shock therapy, Mrs. Susan K. Deri's chapter which follows represents one of the few authoritative statements in American psychological literature about the use of the test. In recent years, as the Szondi Test has grown in use in this country, there has been an increased concern expressed for understanding the theory on which the method rests. We are of the opinion that not many American psychologists are likely to find themselves in sympathy with the theory, and Mrs. Deri has found no need to state it even briefly here.

In seeking to present this projective test through its application in a specific clinical psychological inquiry, she has managed to convey to a remarkable degree the type of information provided and the nature of the inferences that may be drawn by the clinician who proposes to use this method.

▼

The Szondi Test

ITS APPLICATION IN A RESEARCH STUDY OF
DEPRESSIVE PATIENTS BEFORE AND AFTER
ELECTRIC-SHOCK TREATMENT

Susan K. Deri

INTRODUCTION

WITHIN recent years there has been a growing interest among clinicians in the possibilities afforded diagnostic workers by the addition of the Szondi Test to a battery of other instruments of evaluation. Recently I brought out the first full statement in English of the underlying principles of the test and the factors that must be taken into account in clinical practice with it [4]. The English translation of Szondi's basic book [11] is well under way, and when it is available it will present in full the underlying conceptions that have been employed in the development of the test.

It has been decided to offer a specific piece of work in which the Szondi Test was used as the most suitable brief approach to understanding its applications and uses in clinical work. The results of this one study, paradoxical as it may seem, furnish more convincing answers to a few general questions about the test— mainly regarding its validity and reliability—than would any detailed description of the theory underlying this projective method and the practice of interpretation. One may make this assertion with some conviction, for this is the first systematic study to be carried out in this country, it utilizes widely employed statistical methods for the treatment of the data, such as the significances of differences and the establishment of reliability by test-retest methods, and it is a good example of how the Szondi Test may be used in clinical psychological research.

In Szondi's book *[11]* many quantitative data are presented and constitute the basis on which the scheme of test interpretation ultimately rests. Owing to the different conceptions of psychology and of appropriate methods of data treatment that exist in Europe, however, questions of validity and reliability of this projective technique are not readily answered on the basis of quantitative data provided by Szondi. In point of fact, one may state that Szondi Test results do not usually lend themselves to ordinary methods of treatment, owing chiefly to reasons inherent in the basic assumptions on which the test is based. It is possible, however, to collect such data, even though, as in the present instance, one has to be prepared to sacrifice many of the clinically more important aspects of interpretation.

The present study illustrates how the Szondi Test may be used as a research tool in studying the typical changes that occur in one specific group of subjects who underwent electric-shock treatment during the period between test and retest, and in comparing the reactions of this group with those of control groups who did not undergo shock treatment. If the results of this study show significant differences, and if the trends are consistent with theoretical expectations, then the basic question regarding the test's validity and the assumptions involved in its interpretation may be partially answered.

A BRIEF DESCRIPTION OF THE TEST

Before presenting and discussing the data of the present study, I offer a brief general description of the Szondi Test. For a somewhat more detailed discussion of the underlying psychological assumptions and the principles of interpretation, the reader is referred to the paper read by me at the twenty-fifth annual meeting of the American Orthopsychiatric Association [5].

The test material consists of six sets of pictures, each set containing eight photographs of various types of mental patient. Pictures of eight different types of patient are to be found in each set. These are: a homosexual, a sadist, an epileptic, a hysteric, a catatonic schizophrenic, a paranoid schizophrenic, a manic-depressive depressive, and a manic-depressive manic. Thus each disease category is represented by six photographs. The eight types of mental disorder will be referred to from now on as the eight "factors." The subject is presented with the single series consecutively, with instructions to choose the two pictures from each set that he likes most and the two he dislikes most. Thus, finally, twelve pictures are chosen as liked and twelve as disliked. These twenty-four choices are recorded graphically in the form of a test profile.

Figure 25 shows a sample profile. The eight vertical columns correspond to the eight factors; the heavy horizontal dividing line separates the "like" choices (these will be referred to as "plus" choices) from the "dislike" choices (to be referred to as "minus" choices). Each choice is represented by the shading of the appropriate square. The eight small initials, "h," "s," "e," "hy," "k," "p," "d," and "m," stand for the names of the eight mental disorders listed above. The eight factors are grouped into four so-called "vectors," which are marked on the scoring sheet with the capital initials "S" for sexual vector, "P" for paroxysmal vector, "Sch" for schizophrenic vector, and "C" for circular vector. Psychological interpretation of the factors relevant to our present study will be given later.

The stimulus material has been selected on the basis of Szondi's theory, which he calls "genotropism." For a detailed presentation of this theory see Szondi's books, *Schicksals Analyse* [12] and *Experimentelle Triebdiagnostik* [11]. As the word "genotropism" indicates, the theory implies that genes—more precisely, the latent recessive genes—exercise some sort of power of attraction, or, in Szondi's words, the psychological function of the latent recessive genes consists in directing our instinctive (spontaneous) choice reactions. One manifestation of this "directing" is supposedly that our libido is attracted by, or directed toward, individuals who to some extent have a gene stock that is similar

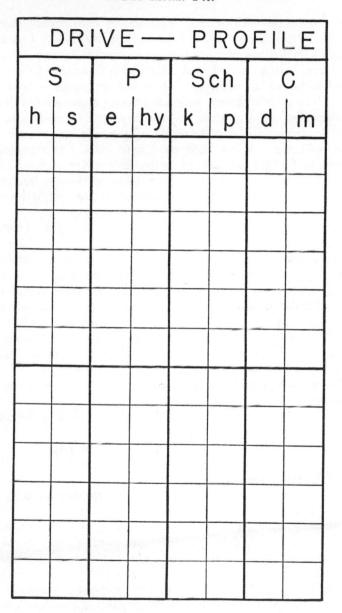

FIGURE 25. Sample Szondi Test Profile

to our own. Szondi's original intention in constructing his test was to demonstrate his hypothesis experimentally. The eight types of mental disorder were selected on the basis of his belief that these eight mental and emotional disorders follow the Mendelian laws of inheritance. This last statement is according to Szondi's genetic theory, which is actually a much more flexible and inclusive concept than may be apparent to readers of this highly condensed presentation. Since, however, my interest and work with this test are concerned with its use as a projective technique for the purpose of personality investigation, I shall not try to prove or disprove Szondi's gene theory, but rather attempt to present a purely psychological set of assumptions as a theoretical frame of reference.

The eight factors of the test have to be thought of as corresponding to eight different need-systems. The assumption that manifest mental and emotional diseases are extreme manifestations of certain emotional needs or drives operating to some extent in everybody accounts for the fact that the test can be used with the so-called "normal" population as well as with cases of psychopathology. The eight kinds of emotional needs represented in the test by their extreme pathological representatives are assumed to be the eight basic divisions of emotional life in regard to which we have to evaluate any personality.

The most general description of these eight needs is the following:

1. The "h" factor represents the need for tender, "feminine" love.

2. The "s" factor represents the need for physical activity and aggression, the need for "masculinity." The "h" and "s" factors together form the "sexual vector."

3. The "e" factor indicates the way the person is dealing with his crude, aggressive emotions.

4. The "hy" factor represents the person's need to exhibit his emotions. Together the "e" and "hy" factors form the "paroxysmal vector," which indicates the degree and kind of emotional control.

5. The "k" factor represents the narcissistic ego-needs.

6. The "p" factor indicates the expansive tendencies of the ego. The "k" and "p" factors together form the "schizophrenic vector," or, as we may call it, the "ego vector."

7. The "d" factor indicates the need for acquiring and mastering objects.

8. The "m" factor indicates the need for clinging to objects for the sake of enjoyment. Together the "d" and "m" factors form the "circular vector," the vector that indicates the way the person relates to the objects of the environment.

The function of the test is to indicate the degree or state of tension, and the individual's conscious or unconscious attitude to this tension, in each of the eight need-systems described above. The pictures of one factor assume valence character if the corresponding need-system is in a state of tension. In this case the subject *chooses* pictures from the factor that corresponds to his own need-tension. The *absolute* number of choices within one factor has to be interpreted according to this principle. On the other hand, no choice or a maximum of two choices (only if the two choices are distributed as one "plus" and one "minus") within one factor indicates that the corresponding need-system is *not* in a state of tension. Theoretically this may be due either to an original weakness of the particular drive or to the subject's having released the tension. Emotional tension can be released by "living out" the particular drive through adequate activity.

The direction of the choices—whether certain pictures are chosen as liked or as disliked—depends, besides the existence of a need-tension, upon the person's acceptance or nonacceptance of this particular drive. If the person identifies himself with the psychological tendency expressed by the pictures of a certain category, the corresponding reaction in that facotor will be "plus." In the event of a counter-identification, the reaction will be "minus." The implicit assumptions in all these statements are evidently (a) that essential emotional characteristics are expressed through the photographs used in the test, and (b) that in the subject's taking the test there is an unconscious recognition of and responding to these essential psychological qualities.

The fact that the test "works"—in other words, that we can give meaningful interpretations on the basis of the choice-reactions —proves the validity of the above assumptions. The results of the following study will serve as a concrete example, which in itself can serve to validate the underlying hypothesis.

Since a detailed description of the meaning of each factor and of the correlation between the factors is beyond the scope of this paper, I shall limit myself to a brief presentation of the psychological interpretation of the two factors that turned out to be the most important from the point of view of my study of the psychological effects of the electro-shock treatments on depressive patients.

GENERAL HYPOTHESIS UNDERLYING THE EXPERIMENTAL STUDY

First, something has to be said about the "clinical hunch" preceding this research which led to the selection of the experimental procedure. The hypothesis was that the artificial seizures serve to release the depressed patient's accumulated introverted aggression. The hunch was based partly on clinical observations, partly on Freud's theory in regard to the unconscious psychodynamics involved in the psychotic depression [6]. Depressive patients' most apparent symptoms are their constant self-accusations and guilt-feelings. Freud relates these symptoms to aggressive feelings against an object that originally had strong ambivalent libido cathexis. The person, not being able to endure this acute ambivalence, introjects the object into his own ego. This introjection serves the original ambivalent cathexis by "killing" (eliminating) and securing the object at the same time. The aggression, originally directed against the outside object, is now directed against the introjected object; that is, against the individual's own ego. In this way depressive patients' self-accusations acquire the meaning of aggression against the ambivalently cathected love-object. The whole mechanism is a kind of defense-reaction whose function is to prevent open aggression against an outside person.

The hypothesis was that the artificial seizures serve to discharge the patient's introjected aggression without having it directed against any outside object and therefore without the danger of ensuing punishment from the superego. In this way the ego is freed from the paralyzing effect of inhibited aggression. That the inhibition of aggression against a highly cathected object will tend to spread over the whole personality, in the sense of inhibiting free behavior in general, was a further elaboration of the original hypothesis. The more desirable an action seems to a depressed patient, the stronger will he experience the effect of restraining forces that keep him from acting freely in the desired direction. A general motor inefficiency was assumed on the basis of the same principle.

The selection of the experiments and tests administered to the patients before and after shock treatment was determined according to the above-mentioned theoretical considerations. Various experiments were included to measure motor speed and efficiency. Satiation time was measured in connection with an unpleasant and meaningless task. Five of the TAT pictures were used in order to follow up changes in the content and the more formal qualities of the stories. Finally the Szondi Test was chosen because of its effectiveness in indicating inhibited aggression as well as release of this inhibition. The decision time needed for choosing likes and dislikes was measured. In this paper only the results of the Szondi Test will be discussed.

According to the hypothesis established for this research, the most significant changes after shock treatment were expected in the "s" factor. This factor has to be interpreted as corresponding to the psychological dimension, active-passive. Theoretical considerations, as well as experience with the Szondi Test, showed that the degree of motor activity is closely linked with the amount of open or repressed aggression in general. The relationship between aggression and general motor drive has also been suggested by Schilder and Bender [8] and by Caille [3].

In interpreting the test profiles we find that a "plus s" (pictures of sadists chosen as liked) indicates a generally high degree of physical activity as well as a tendency for uninhibited aggressive manifestations. Whether the interpretation should follow more the line of aggression or merely that of activity, which can in some instances mean socially valuable activity, depends upon the rest of the profile. Similarly to all other projective techniques, the exact meaning of one factor cannot be determined without considering the whole configurational pattern of all the factors. There is some basic interpretation, however, for "plus s" which holds under any circumstances, and that is the tendency to manipulate real objects of the environment, a certain extrovert object-mindedness, or using Goldstein's concept, a rather concrete behavior.

On the other hand, "minus s" indicates a low level of physical activity as well as the tendency to inhibit open aggressive manifestations. In terms of the most general interpretation, it means the tendency to prefer manipulation of concepts and ideas to the manipulation of real objects. To follow the parallel with the interpretation of "plus s," "minus s" means a certain tendency toward introversion or what Goldstein calls "abstract behavior."

"Open s" reaction (no choice, or a maximum of two choices if the two are distributed as one "plus" and one "minus") means, in accordance with the general theory already presented, lack of tension in this area, which may be due to actual release of the tension through adequate activity. Individuals who live out their aggressive needs through some kind of constant activity give "open s." Again depending on the rest of the factors, this steady discharge of activity might take a socially positive form as well as a negative one.

In accordance with the hypothesis concerning the function of convulsions, the Szondi Test was expected to show that electric-shock treatments serve to release inhibited aggression. The "s" factor was expected to show a strong negative tendency before shock, and a change toward the plus direction after shock treatment was finished. Change toward "plus" includes the change of becoming simply less negative or closer to "open" reaction.

The other factor that has to be discussed before presenting the results is the "k" factor (reaction to photographs of catatonic schizophrenics). Since the changes in this factor were not part of the original theoretical expectations, this necessitated the reformulation of the initial hypothesis about the psychological function of the seizures.

The "k" factor corresponds to the organizing power of the ego. The function of this organizing power is to establish certain structures by keeping up the boundaries that separate the person from the environment, as well as the boundaries between the inner-personal regions. In other words, this factor can be characterized as determining the degree of fluidity or rigidity of the ego. It is relatively easy to understand why reactions to pictures of catatonics can be used as some sort of measuring stick for this particular quality of the ego, since catatonic schizophrenia is known to imply a pathologically high degree of rigidity of the ego.

This organizing tendency of the "k" factor is assumed to counteract emotional drives originating from the id and wanting to enter the ego. For the organizing tendency of the "k" factor, there are two ways to deal with such emotional drives. Either serves the purpose of trying to save the narcissistic integrity of the ego by diverting the original object-libido toward a narcissistic goal. The purpose of the "k" factor is to keep the ego relatively tension-free. One way to reach this goal is to neutralize the id-drives through sublimation or conscious intellectualization. The dynamic character of the drives is thus taken away so that they can be incorporated into the ego without danger of disrupting its organization. The "plus k" reaction indicates that the person is able to use this more constructive type of defense mechanism. For instance, "plus k" is characteristic of individuals who neutralize their id-drives through intellectual channels such as sublimation in a profession. This does not mean, however, that in certain configurations "plus k" cannot result in pathological symptoms, especially in connection with highly narcissistic disturbances.

The other method by means of which the "k" factor can rid the ego of the disturbing tension that results from the id-drives is by repressing them. The goal, to deprive the emotional needs of their dynamic character and to keep up the undisturbed organization of the ego, is reached again, although probably only temporarily and superficially. "Minus k" is the sign on the profile for this kind of defense mechanism; it can be called organization through repression. In psychopathology "minus k" prevails in hysteria and compulsion neurosis; this does not mean, however, that in some instances the repression, as indicated by the "minus k," does not have socially desirable effects.

From a theoretical point of view, one of the most interesting findings on the Szondi Test was that the close relationship between sublimation and repression was made evident as being both functions of the same "organizing tendency" of the "k" factor. Theoretically, the similarity between these two mechanisms had been pointed out by various psychoanalysts previously. The Szondi Test, however, is probably unique in being able to show this relationship in such a tangible, empirical way.

DESCRIPTION OF THE EXPERIMENT

1. The experimental subjects were nineteen patients from the psychopathic hospital of the State University of Iowa. Between the two testing sessions all underwent electric-shock treatment.

The number of treatments for one patient ranged from 5 to 20, with a mean of 9.6. The time interval between test and retest ranged from 16 days to 40 days, with a mean of 27 days. The chronological age of the patients ranged from 19 to 56, the average being 37 years. There was no patient whose I.Q. on the Wechsler-Bellevue Test fell below the range of average intelligence. In educational level, expressed in number of years, the range was from 8 to 14 years of school education, with a mean of 11.5 years.

In selecting the subjects we took their clinical symptoms into consideration rather than the official final diagnosis, the criterion being that the main symptoms should include depressive mood and guilt-feeling. These seem to be the common features in cases that benefit from shock treatment. (See Kennedy's comprehensive critical review [7].) This method of selecting the subjects was preferred because it is a well-known fact that the nosological classification of mental patients is at present far from universal. Such questions as that of diagnosing a patient as manic-depressive with schizoid features or schizophrenic with manic-depressive features are many times decided in a rather arbitrary way, and the decision may, of course, vary from one hospital to another.

From the point of view of our initial hypothesis, the presence of depressed mood, guilt-feelings, and self-accusation were essential. Of the nineteen experimental subjects, seventeen exhibited the above symptoms. One of the two patients who did not display these symptoms was a manic-depressive girl in manic state who had had a depressive period a year earlier, at which time she attempted suicide. The other was a woman who at the beginning of her hospital stay showed depressive features, but who developed a clear-cut paranoia while she was in the hospital. The elimination of the results of these two subjects from the computation of data would have made the differences obtained as a result of the shock treatment even more definite. The distribution of the official hospital diagnoses was as follows:

	No. of Cases
Involutional melancholia	7
Involutional psychosis, paranoid type with depressive symptoms	1

	No. of Cases	
Manic-depressive, depression	5	
Manic-depressive, manic	1	
Reactive depression	1	
Schizophrenia, unclassified; *post partum* depression	1	
Schizophrenia, unclassified; perplexed depression	1	
Schizophrenia, hebephrenica	1	(guilt-feelings, attempted suicide)
Schizophrenia, paranoid type	1	(described above)

2. The hospital control group consisted of ten patients in the same hospital who did not undergo shock treatment, at least before the second testing. The selection of this group presented considerable difficulties, since exact matching of the diagnoses was not feasible. Patients with clear-cut depressive symptoms were started on shock treatment a few days after having entered the hospital unless there was some special contraindication to this treatment. Still, our reason for including this group, besides our desire to use a normal control group, was to counteract a possible criticism that any change between test results before and after shock treatment in the experimental group might be due to the greater instability of mental patients as compared with normal subjects. The distribution of the official diagnoses for the hospital control group is given below:

	No. of Cases
Involutional melancholia	2
Undiagnosed (later this patient was started on shock treatment because of her depressive symptoms)	1
Schizophrenia, paranoid type, or manic-depressive depressive with paranoid traits	2
Paranoid condition (symptoms of	

No. of Cases

anxiety and guilt-feelings)	1
Schizophrenia, hebephrenic type (fatigue and loss of interest)	1
Psychotic episode in psychopathic personality	1
Behavior disorder	2

The hospital control group and the experimental group were matched in regard to the time interval between test and retest, range of chronological age, range of I.Q., and educational level.

3. A normal control group consisting of ten hospital employees was used. The time between test and retest was matched with the two previous groups. The chronological ages of this group ranged from 22 to 45 years, the educational level ranged from 12 to 16 years of schooling, with a mean of 13.2 years.

PRESENTATION OF RESULTS

The first step in analyzing the Szondi Test results was to determine the amount of change that occurred from test to retest for the three groups. When we talk about changes occurring in the single factors, we can refer either to changes from a purely quantitative point of view or to changes in direction. By "direction" is meant the four possible modes of reaction in each factor, as follows:

1. "Plus": if all choices, or if the majority of choices, fall into the category "liked" (with the exception of the proportion 3 to 2).

2. "Minus": if all choices, or if the majority of choices, fall into the category "disliked" (with the exception of the proportion 2 to 3).

3. "Ambivalent": if there is an equal number of choices in the "like" and "dislike" category, or if there are 2 likes and 3 dislikes or 3 likes and 2 dislikes.

4. "Open": if there are no choices, or there is a maximum of one as "liked" and one as "disliked."

Any change that involves changing the direction of the factor is more important in qualitative clinical interpretation than a change that merely involves the increase or decrease of the number of choices within the same direction, even though the actual number of choices that have changed may be the same in the two instances. Rapid changes in direction from one testing to the other, especially if it is a so-called complete reversal from "plus" to "minus" or from "minus" to "plus," are the most significant indications for serious emotional or mental disturbance, the maximum number of such changes being reached in manifest schizophrenia.

TABLE 9

Percentage of Subjects Showing No Change in Direction from Test 1 to Test 2

EXPERIMENTAL GROUP N=19		HOSPITAL CONTROL GROUP N=10		NORMAL CONTROL GROUP N=10	
"p" factor	78.9%	"h," "s," "d" factors	70%	"m" factor	90%
"h" and "hy" factors	68.4%	"m" factor	60%	"d," "hy," "s," "k" factors	80%
"k" factor	63.1%	"e," "k," "p" factors	50%	"h" factor	60%
"d," "m," "e" factors	47.4%	"hy" factor	30%	"p," "c" factors	40%
"s" factor	15.0%				
Mean	54 %	Mean	56%	Mean	69%

Legend: h=homosexual e=epileptic k=catatonic d=depressive
         s=sadist   hy=hysteric   p=paranoid m=manic

Comparison of the three groups shows that both the mean and the maximum percentages of "no change" are highest in the normal control group, which means that the normal subjects were more consistent in their reactions to the pictures than were the other two groups. This finding is in accordance with our theory about the psychological meaning of the changes in direction.

The percentages for the experimental group show that the "s" factor is the least stable so far as this group is concerned. In only 15 per cent of the cases does "s" stay within the same direction after shock treatment as before. On the other hand, the "s" factor shows rather high stability in the two control groups. It is the most stable factor in the hospital control group and one of the two most stable factors in the normal control group.

Our original hypothesis that the shock treatment brings about changes in the area of aggression seems to be supported by the above data.

As has been said, complete reversals of direction (from "plus" to "minus" or reverse) have the greatest pathodiagnostic significance. Therefore we were interested in the percentages of such complete reversals for the three groups.

TABLE 10

Frequency of Reversal of Direction

EXPERIMENTAL GROUP N=19		HOSPITAL CONTROL GROUP N=10		NORMAL CONTROL GROUP N=10	
"s" factor	36.8%	"k" factor	30%	·"h," "s," "e," "hy,"	
"k," "h," "hy"		"s," "e," "d"		"k," "p," "d,"	
factors	10.5%	factors	10%	"m" factors	0%
"e," "p," "d,"		"hy," "p," "h"			
"m" factors	5.2%	factors	0%		
		"m" factor	0%		
Mean	11.3%	Mean	7.5%	Mean	0%

The data of Table 10 confirm the results obtained on the previous one. The entire absence of changes involving reversal of direction within the normal group again indicates the significantly higher stability of the reactions of this group as compared with the two hospital groups; it does not mean, however, that the so-called "normal" subjects actually never show reversals of direction in any factor. The 0 per cent of such changes in our ten clinically healthy subjects must have been due either to chance or to the function of some sort of unknown selective factor operating in a group of hospital employees (mainly nurses and attendants). Either way, it still warrants the interpretation that subjects without clinical symptoms are much more stable in their reactions than patients of a psychopathic hospital.

The previous finding that the "s" factor is the least stable in the experimental group is also confirmed. It is the factor that shows the highest percentage of reversals (36.8 per cent) in the experimental group, while the hospital group not undergoing shock treatment showed only 10 per cent of reversals in the "s" factor. This is a further corroboration of the assumption that the changes in the "s" factor in the experimental group are to a high degree a function of the electric-shock treatment.

The second type of analysis of the Szondi Test results is to determine the number of changes, disregarding whether they result in changes of direction or not. In order to illustrate these changes in the most apparent way, the algebraic sum of the choices in each factor was computed and their means represented graphically in Figure 26.

Taking the algebraic sum of the choices for each factor and then averaging the results thus obtained is a crude way of dealing with the data and should never be used except for the purpose of statistical group analysis. In the present case it was permissible because our main interest was to determine the major trends of the changes in three groups of subjects. The purpose of using the Szondi Test in this study was rather to prove or disprove our prediction in regard to the greatest changes occurring in the "s" factor after shock treatment than to use the test results for thorough qualitative analysis.

After having obtained the profiles of the means of the algebraic sums of choices for each group, we tested the changes from test 1 to test 2 for statistical significance with the test. The obtained values corresponded to the .05 per cent level of significance concerning the change in the "s" factor in the experimental group, and the .01 per cent level of significance for the change in the "k" factor in the experimental group. None of the other factors in either of the three groups showed statistically significant changes.

In the experimental group the values for the "s" factor are minus 1.4 before shock and minus .1 after shock. This change bears out the hypothesis that after shock treatment the patients are repressing aggression less and that they become "free" in physical activity.

The change in the "k" factor showed the opposite direction, the mean before shock being minus .9 and after shock minus 2.0. The fact that the absolute value of the factor increased has to be interpreted as indicating the strengthening of the organizational

Szondi Test

Profile of the Means of Algebraic Sum for each Single Factor

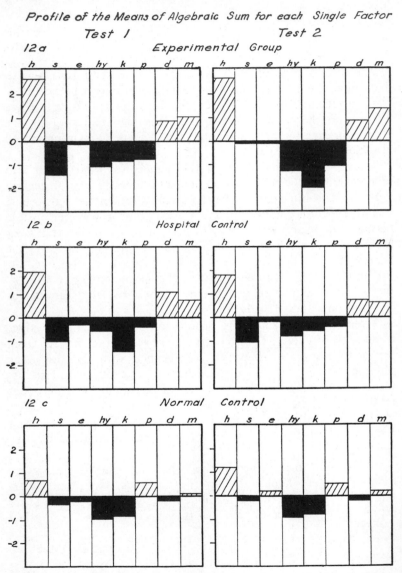

FIGURE 26. Profile of the Means of Algebraic Sum for Each Single Factor

power of the ego. That this increase occurred in the negative direction shows that this is obtained by means of reinforcing the mechanism of repression.

Neither control group showed changes as large as those for the "s" and the "k" factors in the experimental group. The relatively largest change within the hospital control group occurred in the "k" factor. This change was in the opposite direction, however, to that of "k" in the experimental group. According to the Szondi Test theory, the decrease in minus "k" means a weakening of the repressive forces in the ego. This interpretation would be in line with the fact that the hospital control group was partly under psychotherapy, partly under drug treatments, such as sodium amytal, since either of these treatments aims at relieving inhibitions.

The normal control group showed no change at all or very little in any of the eight factors. The expected relative stability of the choices of clinically healthy individuals, as opposed to the instability of choices of the various pathological groups, has been mentioned previously. It should be added, however, that a maximum degree of constancy in all the eight factors—in other words, a reliability coefficient of 1.0 or very close to 1.0—is not expected from the average clinically healthy population. As a matter of fact, the highest "reliability" of choices at various testings has been found in compulsive neurotics or compulsive characters. The stability of choices in our normal control group is almost suggestive of some common compulsive traits in this group which may have been a selective factor in individuals choosing this kind of occupation. This is probably just one of the many instances when psychologists find themselves more at a loss in finding a truly "average" normal population than in satisfying the criteria for the definitions of various pathological groupings. For this reason the contrasting of well-defined clinical groups may be a psychologically sounder procedure, especially in using projective techniques, than the comparison of pathological and "normal" groups.

Finally, something should be mentioned about the initial differences between the two hospital groups and the normal control group. Greatest initial differences were found in the "h," "s," "p," "d," and "m" factors. The "h" factor shows less positive tendency for the normal group than do the hospital groups. The "p" factor is positive in the normal and negative in the other two groups of patients. On the other hand, "d" is positive in the experimental and the hospital control groups as versus slightly negative in the normals. The "m" is less positive in the normals than in the two other groups. The "s" is more negative in the hospital patients, especially in the experimental group.

With the exception of the "s" factor, neither of these factors in the experimental group, originally diverging from the test pattern of the normal group, came closer to the "normal" pattern after shock treatment. The only change in the experimental group, where the mean value of the normal group has been practically reached after shock treatment, occurred in the "s" factor. The other factor that showed statistically significant change after shock was the "k." The mean value of the "k" factor, however, was practically identical with the normal group before shock and changed in a direction away from the normal pattern after shock. The interpretation of these two (at first impression) somewhat contradictory changes will be given in the discussion of results.

Since the clinical interpretation of all the other initial differences that did not change significantly from first to second testing would require a thorough knowledge of the meaning of all the eight factors, it is thus beyond the scope of this paper. All that can be said here is that the constellation of factors in the normal group indicates better possibilities for sublimation than the test pattern at either the first or second testing of the two hospital groups.

DISCUSSION AND CONCLUSION

The Szondi Test results of this piece of research can be discussed from the point of view of the test as a research instrument and in regard to what they contribute to a theory about the psychological effects of electro-shock treatment.

The results have shown that the retest constancy of the test with respect to the normal group is high. Significant changes after shock in the experimental group took place only in two factors, the "s" and the "k." One of these two changes, that in the "s," was in accordance with our original prediction; the change in the "k" was not predicted, but could be well integrated in our final hypothesis since practically all the results obtained through the other tests and experiments used in this study, but not reported in this chapter, confirm the interpretation of the increase in "minus k" after shock.

These were the results referred to at the beginning of the chapter as furnishing more convincing evidence in regard to the validity of the assumptions underlying the test than would a detailed description of the theory and principles of interpretation. By that it is meant that the results of this one study help to validate the assumption that these photographs of mental patients do convey some essential psychological characteristics to which individuals react in the testing situation in a psychologically valid way. If this had not been the case, we could not have obtained meaningful results, differentiating according to our predictions among the three various groups of subjects used in the study.

To recapitulate the differential reactions of the three groups, they were the following:

1. The difference between the normal group as against the two groups of patients in regard to the constancy of the reactions has been shown by three different methods of analysis of the results.

(a) By the percentage of subjects showing no change in "direction" from test 1 to test 2.

(b) By the frequency of "reversals of direction."

(c) By comparing the profiles of the means of the algebraic sums of choices for the three groups.

In all these comparisons the group of normal subjects stood out with its relative constancy of the reactions in each factor.

2. The comparison of the profiles of means of algebraic sums of the choices has also shown the initial similarity of the reaction patterns of the two hospital groups as against the reaction pattern of the normal group.

The specific changes occurring in the experimental group after shock proved more than just the general fact that the choices are not due to chance, and that groups of subjects varying in their degree of emotional stability react to it differently. These changes asserted the validity of the more specific theory in regard to the principles involved in reacting to the pictures in the testing situation as stated above in connection with the general description of the test. On the basis of this theory the greatest qualitative changes occurring in the "s" factor after shock were predicted. Actually the "s" factor turned out to be the most changing one so far as changes in direction are concerned. The theoretical reasons for having expected the changes in the "s" factor have been described previously. The interpretation of the only other factor, the "k," which changed significantly after shock, helps to round out our initial hypotheses in regard to the psychological effects of electric shock.

On the basis of the results of this research the following theory has been developed.

The basic idea of the theory follows the psychoanalytic assumption that the state of pathological depression results from the inhibition of aggressive tendencies originally directed against an ambivalently cathected object. The inhibition serves as a defense mechanism, but owing to the strength of the undesirable id-wishes it has to affect practically the total behavior in order to assure successful inhibition of open aggression. This psychological state corresponded to the pre-shock test results. The strength of the "minus s" reaction before shock has to be interpreted according to this theory, and the general motor inefficiency (results of "tower building"), lack of own initiative (satiation experiment and decision time), and lack of power of structurization (TAT stories) are all in line with this interpretation.

From the first to the second testing the experimental group (but neither of the two control groups) showed statistically significant changes in connection with all the tests, indicating better motor efficiency, decrease in satiation time, decrease in decision time, and better structurization of the personality.

The results of the Szondi Test after shock showed that the "s" and "k" factors changed in opposite directions. Factor "s" changed toward the mean value of the normal group, indicating less inhibition of aggression and more uninhibited physical activity, while the shift in the "k" factor was away from the mean value of the normal group, indicating the strengthening of repression in the ego.

These seemingly contradictory results can be interpreted as follows: The inhibition indicated by the originally strong "minus s" served as one kind of defense mechanism against open aggressive manifestations—namely, defense through becoming inactive. The constellation in "s" and "k" after shock indicates a change in the type of defense mechanism used against aggression. Instead of securing nonaggressive behavior through inactivity, the strong "minus k" indicates the strengthening of a more underlying repression operating in the ego. If this underlying repression is strong enough to exclude successfully any thought or feeling connected with the basic conflict of aggressive tendencies, then the person no longer needs to be inactive in his behavior. Accordingly, the stronger repression of the basic conflict (increase in "minus k") means a change toward normality in regard to the organizational power of the person, although this apparently better organized and more efficient behavior is based on more "efficient" repression.

In the light of this theory one has to conceive of the electric shock as representing a danger situation for the patient, giving rise to feelings of intense anxiety, which in turn mobilizes the use of stronger repression in order to restore the unity of the ego. On the other hand, psychotic depression can be looked upon as the result of unsuccessful repression when wishes and intentions disapproved by the superego cannot be completely isolated from the rest of the personality, a process that accounts for the development of subsidiary reaction formations and defense mechanisms. The depressive patients' repetitive self-accusations and general retardation symptoms are manifestations of such subsidiary mechanisms which can be given up, once the basic repression is re-established. We know that a certain amount of ability to repress is required by any well-functioning individual. Since, however, the needs that endanger the smooth functioning of the ego are much stronger and more antisocial in their original character in the depressive patient than in a healthy personality, the absolute strength of repression has to be proportionally stronger in the depressive if the same degree of organizational unity of the ego should be reached as in individuals without extremely strong basic conflicts.

In the Szondi Test results this state of affairs is indicated by the correlation of the "k" and "s" factors in the experimental group, and the comparison with the constellation of the same two factors in the normal control group. (See Figure 26.) At first testing, where the value of the "minus k" is equal for the two groups, the rest of the Szondi factors, as well as the results of the other experiments and their open behavior, showed much greater discrepancy in the sense that members of the experimental group were apparently more disturbed in every manifestation of their personality. At second testing, where the "minus k" became significantly stronger in the experimental group, the discrepancy in the rest of the test results, as well as in their manifest behavior, disappeared. The experimental group apparently needed stronger repressive forces in order to function efficiently, at least on the surface.

The conclusions of this study are in partial accord with the views of several authors, particularly with those of Abse [1, 2]. Abse contends that the effect of shock treatment consists in strengthening the resources at the disposal of the ego in order to make repression of disturbing id-contents successful. To quote him: "In this way we can regulate the conflict to a less dominating position, even make it submerge in the deepest strata of the mind."

The final hypothesis arrived at, mainly on the basis of the Szondi Test results, also finds support in observational studies; see Schilder [9], Shapiro [10], Weigert [13], all stressing the fact that patients after shock treatment insist that they do not remember their original complaints and that any mention of their previous complaints is distasteful to them, and in cured patients' own descriptions of the psychological change they have experienced after shock.

REFERENCES

1. ABSE, D. W.: "Rationale of Convulsive Therapy," *British Journal of Medical Psychology*, Vol. 19 (1942), pp. 262–70.
2. ———: "Psychology of Convulsion Therapy," *Journal of Mental Science*, January 1940.
3. CAILLE, R. K.: "Resistant Behavior of Preschool Children," *Child Development Monographs*, Vol. 11 (1938), p. 142.
4. DERI, S. K.: *Introduction to the Szondi Test: Theory and Practice.* New York: Grune & Stratton; 1949.
5. ———: "The Szondi Test," *American Journal of Orthopsychiatry*, Vol. 3 (1949), pp. 447–54.
6. FREUD, S.: "Trauer und Melancholie," *Internationaler Psychoanaltischer Verlag*, 1931.
7. KENNEDY, A.: "A Critical Review of the Treatment of Mental Disorders," *Psychiatry*, January 1940.
8. SCHILDER, P., and BENDER, L.: "Aggressiveness in Children, II,"

Genetic Psychology Monographs, Vol. 18 (1936), pp. 410–525.

9. SCHILDER, P.: "Psychology of Metrazol Treatment in Schizophrenia," *Journal of Nervous and Mental Diseases*, Vol. 89 (1939), pp. 133–44.

10. SHAPIRO, H. D., and FREEMAN, W.: "Shock Therapy in the Neuroses," *Medical Annals of District of Columbia*, Vol. 8 (1939), p. 65.

11. SZONDI, L.: *Experimentelle Triebdiagnostik*. Bern: Verlag Hans Huber.

12. ———: *Schicksal Analyse*. Basel: Benno Schwabe & Co.

13. WEIGERT, V. E.: "Psychoanalytic Notes on Sleep and Convulsion Treatment in Functional Psychoses," *Psychiatry*, Vol. 3 (1940), pp. 189–209.

▼

THE following paper on the Bender Visual Motor Gestalt Test has been written by Adolf G. Woltmann, long-time practitioner of the procedure, and prepared by him under the supervision and sponsorship of Dr. Lauretta Bender. For some clinicians the Bender Gestalt Test, as it is popularly known, has been a very useful diagnostic instrument, and it is likely that other clinicians may now decide to add this projective procedure to their assessment and diagnostic batteries.

In the Bender Gestalt Test one can detect the strong contributions that Gestalt psychology has made to the entire field of projective psychology, a situation that is reflected in this method not alone in the choice of Gestalt figures but also in the interpretative significance of an individual's projective productions.

▼

The Bender Visual-Motor Gestalt Test

Adolf G. Woltmann [1]

BACKGROUND

THIS test, which consists of nine geometrical figures that are copied by the person to be tested, was first published by Dr. Lauretta Bender in 1938 as Research Monograph No. 3 of the American Orthopsychiatric Association and appeared under the title "A Visual-Motor Gestalt Test and Its Clinical Use" [3]. The Gestalt Test at first was not very well known because the test cards that contain the figures to be copied were reproduced in the book and were not available separately. Early users of the test frequently had to make their own test cards. The demands of the war upon psychology for quicker and more effective methods for differential diagnosis gave new applications to the test. It was widely used in various installations of the armed forces, where its simplicity and quickness of administration and its rapid evaluation for clinical patterns were a time-saving device toward

---

[1] I am indebted to Dr. Lauretta Bender for a multitude of suggestions concerning the writing of this chapter.

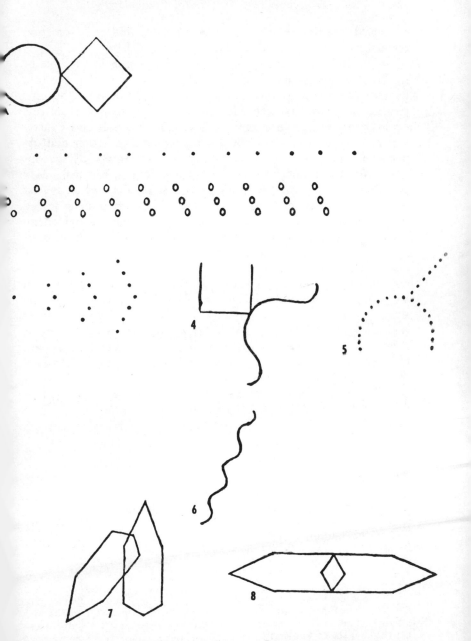

FIGURE 27. Bender Visual-Motor Gestalt Test Figures

clinical disposition. Since 1946 the test cards and an instruction manual have been available to the profession [4].[2]

At this point it is necessary to say a few words about some of the fundamental concepts of Gestalt psychology so that the test, its underlying assumptions, and its clinical application will become clearer. Scientific research has not always progressed from one problem to another in a straight line. Controversies and contradictions, more often than not, have stimulated thinking and experimentation. Gestalt psychology is the outgrowth of the opposition that a number of German psychologists, primarily Max Wertheimer, Wolfgang Koehler, and Kurt Koffka, voiced against the traditional association psychology. These men investigated phenomena for which a mechanistic point of view provided no adequate explanation. Research in perception and organization of stimuli led to the formulation of so-called Gestalt principles, or laws of perception, on the basis of proximity, similarity, direction, and inclusiveness of a given stimulus. We do not see parts which we group together and build up as an image, but we perceive the whole or total quality of a stimulus. A triangle of which one corner is missing or a circle that has a part of its periphery missing is nevertheless seen as a triangle or a circle, respectively. Gaps seem to close; figures have background and spatial positions in regard to above and below.

When we see an object, we see more than just the parts that form the whole. We perceive the total configuration, which is more than the sum of the parts. Within the total configuration there are elements of greater and lesser importance. The perception of a Gestalt changes to the degree in which these important or unimportant elements are changed. We can think of a landscape that shows little detail in the foreground, but of which the background may contain important buildings or a mountain. Our eyes immediately are attracted to the background. A change in shading of color or the inclusion of more worked-out detail in the foreground may make us overlook the formerly important background because our eyes become focused on the

---

[2] The test cards were copyrighted in 1946 by Dr. Lauretta Bender and the American Orthopsychiatric Association. The descriptions, remarks, and interpretations in this chapter, unless otherwise stated, pertain only to the copyrighted set of test cards.

foreground. The picture is essentially the same, but our mode of perception has changed. The changed mode of perception is conditioned by inner psychological determinants, which may be the result of motor development and maturation, neural defects, a multitude of emotional factors, such as stress, anxiety, or insecurity, and physiological states, such as exhaustion. Various social factors likewise play an important part in this process of perception. Traditional Gestalt psychology has been hesitant to consider the emotional components inherent in perceptual processes. Schilder [19] has pointed out that physiological-motor activities are involved, which lead to contact with reality. Contact with reality and reality-testing are intimately bound up with emotions or the person's own idiosyncratic reaction to the world around him. Physiological-motor functions are also dependent upon processes that, according to Schilder, lead to the concept of the body-image. The shift from horizontal to vertical patterns in young children is a maturational component of the change from sitting and crawling to the straight standing posture. Perception of visual stimuli may therefore be regarded as a dynamic process in which selection, organization, differentiation into foreground and background, and action or motility take place in an interchangeable pattern. According to Schilder [20], "organization gets its final meaning only in relation to concrete situations of life which adapt the patterns to the actions and experimentations of individuals."

Psychoanalysis has taught us that life is a continuous struggle between constructive drives and destructive or negative impulses. These entities do not inhabit some specific phases of our affective qualities, but are part of our total personality, which includes processes of and reactions to perceptual experiences. The constructive forces in our perceptual organizations are referred to by Bender as "the factor of becoming," meaning the tendency to sift, to select, to organize, and to react to a stimulus as a whole. The factor of becoming integrates configurations not only in space but also in time. We not only perceive Gestalten but we also have an innate tendency to complete Gestalten. This process leads to reorganizations that are biologically determined by the sensory motor pattern of action. Variations are produced by differences in maturation or growth levels and also by organic or functional pathological states [6]. Negative forces tend to destroy or to interfere with such total dynamic processes. It is this deviation from good perceptual organization that has given us knowledge and understanding of psychopathological states and has helped us to refine some of our diagnostic techniques.

Bender *[3]* enumerates the following factors that determine the Gestalt:

(1) The stimulating pattern in the physical world, which must obey certain laws of Gestalt. (2) The motility of the visual field, which determines spatial relationships. (3) The temporal factor determined by the motility and sequential relationships, which tend to become more intricately integrated into the spatial relationships with maturation processes and are determined therefore by the temporal factor of the life span of the individual. (4) The motor reaction pattern of the individual, his attitude toward and actual participation in the individually created experience. (5) The immediate tendency for each of these factors to be nonseparable from the others.

The factors that play an important part in the process of integration are defined by Bender *[3]* as follows:

(1) The biological character of the visual field or the principles of perception based upon spatial relationships. (2) Temporal relationships based upon the span of the preceding experiences of the individual and therefore upon the length of the maturation process. (3) Motility factors which are closely related in the impulses and attitudes toward the problem itself.

It should be clear from these brief remarks that seeing and reproducing geometrical designs is not merely a simple task of learning, but that numerous factors are involved in such a process. It remains Bender's merit to have investigated this complex problem. By doing so she has shown that the physical laws of Gestalt psychology are applicable to the investigation of personality problems and deviations.

THE BENDER GESTALT TEST

The material of this visual-motor Gestalt test consists of nine geometrical figures which were part of Wertheimer's classical "Studies in the Theory of Gestalt Psychology" *[27]*. (See Figure 27.)

Figure A consists of a circle and a square; the linear figure touches the circle in such a way that it is perceived as a diamond. This design was chosen as an introductory figure because "it soon became evident that it was readily experienced as closed figures on a background." According to Wertheimer, "this configuration is recognized as two contingent figures because each represents a 'gute Gestalt.' . . . This principle overrules the principle that parts which are close together are usually seen together. In this instance the contiguous parts of the circle and square are closer to each other than the two sides of the square."

According to Wertheimer:

Figure 1 should be so perceived that the dots appear as a series of pairs determined by the shortest distance, or with "remnants" left over at each end. Such a pairing would be more readily perceived if the differences in the distances were greater. This is an example of a Gestalt formed on the principle of the proximity of parts.

Figure 2 is perceived usually as a series of short, slanting lines consisting of three units (of loops) so arranged that the lines slant from the left above to right below. It is also determined by the principle of proximity of parts.

This is also true of *Figure 3*, formed by dots arranged in such a way that one, three, five, and seven dots form a design in which the middle dot of all these parts lies on the same level and the added dots are arranged in relation to this mid-line like the two sides of a diamond, converging toward the first single dot.

Figure 4 is ordinarily perceived as two units determined by the principle of continuity of geometrical or internal organization, the open square with the bell-shaped form at the lower right-hand corner.

The same principle holds true for the introductory *Figure A* and also for *Figure 5*, which is seen as an incomplete circle with an upright slanting stroke made in dotted lines.

Figure 6 is seen as two sinusoidal (wavy) lines with different wave lengths, crossing each other at a slant.

Figures 7 and *8* are two configurations made up of the same units, but they are rarely perceived as such because in *Figure 8* the principle of continuity of geometric form prevails, which in this instance is the straight line at the top and the bottom of the figure.

This test is so easily administered that specific test instructions are almost unnecessary, but they have been offered nevertheless. In this connection it is noted that Bender did not include instructions for administration in her 1938 monograph. This omission has been corrected in the 1946 *Instructions for the Use of the Visual-Motor Gestalt Test,* where she points out that this is a clinical test that should not be so rigidly formalized as to destroy its function, which is to determine the individual's capacity to experience visual-motor Gestalten in a spatial and temporal relationship. Deviate behavior in the course of the test should be observed and noted. It never represents a test failure. Notes may be made on the test paper of anything unusual in the way the test is organized or in the manner and behavior of the individual being tested, and his reaction to the test situation.

TEST ADMINISTRATION

The testee is put into a comfortable sitting position similar to that assumed for the purpose of writing. The examiner places a white, unlined sheet of paper, 8½ by 11 inches in front of the subject so that the shorter sides of the paper form the top and the bottom of this rectangle. Several sharpened pencils of medium softness, preferably not harder than the ordinary No. 2, are put next to the paper. The examiner may hold the test cards in his hands or he may place them on the desk, face down, with Card A on the top and Card 8 at the bottom. There is no objection to the presence of erasers, but mechanical aids such as rulers or coins should not be within reach of the testee.

The subject is told reassuringly: "I have here some cards with very simple designs on them. I want you to copy these designs. Draw what you see!" With that, Card A is laid next to the top part of the sheet of paper. This brief introduction is sufficient in most cases. After the Gestalt on Card A has been copied, Card 1 is placed on top of it, then Card 2, and so on until all the figures have been drawn. Each Gestalt figure remains in full sight of the subject until he has finished his drawing. Should the subject have difficulty in properly seeing the design, he may be permitted to bring the cards closer to his eyes. Turning the cards around, however, should not be condoned. If this happens, the examiner may reach over silently and restore the card to its original position. Should the subject insist upon turning the card, or perhaps upon moving the paper to an angle of ninety degrees, nothing further should be said about it, but a note of such deviation should be made. There is an exception to this. It may happen that a subject has more or less covered the sheet with the drawings by the time that he is confronted with Gestalt 8, an elongated figure. In such a case it is permissible to let the subject turn the paper to an angle of ninety degrees in order to have sufficient space at the new bottom of the sheet to execute this figure.

A subject may ask: "Where do you want me to start? Up here at the top, or in the middle of the sheet, or where?" Such a person is told that it does not matter where the first figure is placed so long as all the nine designs appear on the same sheet. The use of several sheets of paper seldom occurs, as is pointed out elsewhere in this chapter.

Aside from presenting the cards in their proper order, the examiner remains passive and silent. It may be necessary to tell the subject that the exact number of dots or loops is not important, and that he is expected to draw what he sees. Such a remark may be made with the presentation of Card 1 if the subject begins to count the dots on this figure. This remark, however, should not be repeated, because the number of dots on Card 3 is important. Another reason for refraining from insisting on the general Gestalt and not so much on correct detail lies in the fact that severely compulsive persons will persist in counting and thereby reveal some of their major difficulties.

The process of perceiving configurations takes place in time as well as in space. An evaluation of the Gestalt test therefore should not only pay attention to the finished copies of these figures (space factor), but also consider the motor process of copying (time factor). The examiner may not interfere while these figures are copied by the subject. He should watch, however, and if necessary make notes on a separate sheet of paper. The manner in which the Gestalten are copied may reveal important clues that are undiscernible in the finished test record.

Normally the nine geometrical figures are drawn as follows:[3]

Figure A. First the circle and then the diamond.

Figure 1. The dots begin at the left and are continued toward the right.

---

[3] Card and *Figure* are synonymous.

Figure 2. The loops begin at the left and are drawn as sets of three slanting loop units.

Figure 3. The single dot at the left is drawn first. Three, five, and seven dots are added from left to right.

Figure 4. First the open square and then the bell-shaped curve.

Figure 5. First the semicircle of dots, to which is added the slanting straight line of dots. It is fairly common practice to draw first the line and then the semicircle.

Figure 6. Horizontal wavy line first, vertical slanting wavy line second.

Figure 7. Vertical figure first, slanting intersecting figure second. The reversal is fairly common.

Figure 8. Elongated figure first, diamond in center second.

These brief instructions are added for the benefit of the examiner only. The subject should be unaware of the correct way of copying the figures, so that his deviations reveal diagnostic clues.

The test record that follows this set of directions does not require further comments. There are, however, many different ways in which these figures can be drawn. Figure 28 is offered as a helpful suggestion to the examiner for keeping track of deviations that may occur in the process of drawing. Numbers and arrows were found to be the easiest means of marking deviations. If in *Figure A* the diamond is drawn first and the circle second, the numbers 1 and 2 will indicate this (Figure 28, ①). If there has been a clockwise or counterclockwise rotation, a small arrow will be helpful (Figure 28, ②). Should the subject turn the card, mark the figure "C.R." (card rotation). A turning of the paper is indicated by "P.R." (paper rotation). An arrow next to these initials will give the directions of the rotations (Figure 28, ③).

Arrows will indicate change of directions on *Figures 1* and *2* (Figure 28, ④ and ⑤). Rotations are marked the same as on *Figure A*. This applies to rotations that may appear on the following figures.

A most frequently observed deviation on *Figure 3* consists of drawing the four dots that form the center backbone of this configuration, to which are added the dots above and below. A straight arrow will indicate this mode of drawing (Figure 28, ⑥).

Arrows and numbers describe deviations in drawing *Figures 4, 5,* and *6* (Figure 28, ⑦, ⑧, and ⑨). *Figure 7* seldom needs explanatory markings, but it happens that the diamond in *Figure 8*

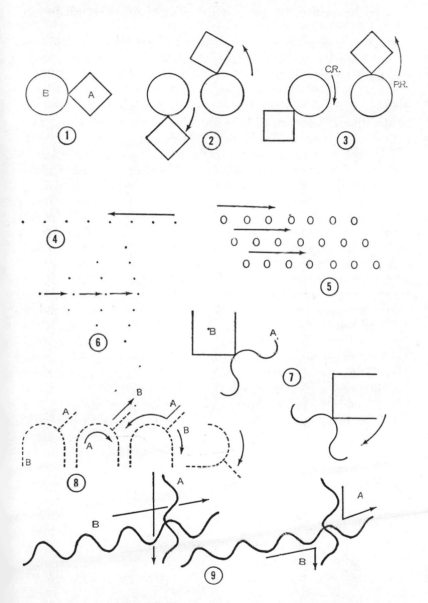

FIGURE 28. Method for Indicating Distortions in Bender Visual-Motor Gestalt Test Reproduced Figures

may be drawn first. In that case the same numbers are used as in *Figure A*.

Bender's monograph *[3]* contains many enlightening examples of psychopathological deviations. Many of her examples are obvious and lend themselves readily to clinically valid interpretations. The psychologist who uses this test in his everyday work will not always find such marked deviations. It is for this reason that the observation of the act of copying is of great importance. The following example will make this point clearer:

I recently had to examine an eighteen-year-old college student who had difficulties in reading. A check with a remedial reading test revealed that this girl did not suffer from any known reading disability. She scored in the 99 percentile on vocabulary, paragraph reading and meaning, and speed of reading. Her chief complaint was an inability to retain what she had read.

She copied the Bender Gestalt figures in a most correct and perfunctory manner. An important clue to her difficulties was found while observing the way in which she drew *Figure 3*. She started out by drawing the four middle dots, making sure that they were equally spaced. Then she added two dots, one above and one below, to the mid-line dots two, three, and four. Then she added two more dots to the mid-line dots three and four and finally finished by adding one dot above and below mid-line dot four. This careful construction revealed lack of spontaneity and imagination, a desperate clinging to geometrical or rational space-time relationships, and an obsessive-compulsive trend. The referring psychiatrist later on confirmed the correctness of this observation and stated that this girl had been under psychiatric treatment for some time because of suffering from a severe obsessive-compulsive neurosis. The so-called reading disability was primarily due to severe rigidity and blocking in her personality. Without the close observation of her test performance this clue would not have come to light, because her finished performance did not reveal any of her real difficulties.

It has been indicated that this test should not be given and evaluated as a single entity, but that it should form part of a test battery. At which point within a test battery should the Bender Gestalt Test be administered? One cannot set up a hard and final rule because test selection will depend upon the needs and objectives in each case. I have found it most helpful to administer the Bender Gestalt Test after the Rorschach Test has been given. Owing to its inherent simplicity, the Bender Gestalt Test offers a sort of a breathing spell, gives the subject an active role in the test situation after the passivity of forming concepts to ink blots, and also prepares the way for the drawings of human figures. Yet it may be necessary to give the test as the first task in a test battery if the subject is tense or worried and if he feels that he cannot do justice to the other tasks imposed upon him. His ability to copy simple figures may serve as a reassurance for the rest of the testing session. Each psychologist, according to his own discretion and awareness of the special needs of the subject in each case, should use this test at the proper time in a battery of tests. The clinician must determine the proper moment for himself. For reasons expressed elsewhere in this contribution, the Bender Gestalt Test should be given *before* the drawings of human figures and not after them.

Usually one encounters very few difficulties with the copying of the single figures, but the placement of the figures on the same sheet constitutes in itself a very interesting and often a very revealing Gestalt pattern. Some persons start at the top of the sheet and place the next figure directly under the preceding one. Their final production may look very neat and orderly, but very often there is a tense, constricted, and perhaps a compulsive or inhibited quality in the organization of the figures. This becomes more apparent when all the figures occupy less than one half of the sheet. The numbering of each design usually is a neurotic manifestation. Fencing off each figure from the next by pencil lines must be regarded, according to our present empirical knowledge of this test, as a sign of a severe neurosis or perhaps even as a prepsychotic danger signal. Another person may start at the middle of the sheet, work down, and then utilize the empty top part of the sheet for whatever figures remain to be drawn. Ordinarily such a practice may not have significant clinical-diagnostic values other than perhaps an indication of poor planning ability and a lowered threshold for anticipation. An overlapping of figures is not infrequent. The wavy lines of *Figure 6* may extend into some of the other figures. *Figures 7* and *8* may reach into *Figures A, 1, 2,* or any one of the others. When that happens, figures lose their individuality and the result is some sort of sloppy, disorganized pattern. The impression of something being messy or unclear in the personality that is being evaluated is usually confirmed by other test data.

Bender's omission of test instructions in her 1938 monograph has led to a variety of administrative procedures. Those of us who worked very closely with Bender have more or less followed her manner of approach.

Wherever possible it is desirable to have all nine figures on the same sheet of paper. Bender has pointed out that the organization of all these figures on the same sheet of paper is in itself a Gestalt function. Hutt [13, 14], who was introduced to the Gestalt test by me, attempted to work out suitable instructions for administration, which cover several mimeographed sheets. Such overrefinement of instruction is unnecessary for this simple test. In his *Tentative Guide* he advocated that the subject may use as many sheets of paper as he desires. Such a procedure overlooks and neglects the diagnostically important fact that the final organization or distribution of the nine figures on the same sheet constitutes an added Gestalt function in the sense that the handling of such a task reveals whether a person is greatly inhibited, obsessive, careless, meticulous, disturbed, or perhaps disoriented. Bender herself has not stressed too strongly the one or the other mode of administration, but she leans toward the use of one sheet. It is true that when the subject is told beforehand that the figures should all be drawn on the same sheet of paper, an element of frustration or perhaps inhibition is added to the task. The final completion of the test therefore not only tells us how a given subject functions in his visual-motor sphere, but also reveals his handling of, or reaction to, limitations which, in a wider sense, are almost always experienced as frustrations.

The cases where several sheets of paper are necessary for the completion of this test are rare. In less than one per cent of all instances where this test was given has it been necessary to supply additional sheets. Such deviations in themselves are of important diagnostic value, especially in severely disturbed persons, where the test may become a vehicle through which idiosyncratic preoccupations may be expressed. The case of a ten-year-old schizophrenic boy may be cited as an example. This child needed three sheets to complete the drawings. Instead of copying *Figure A*, he put three horizontal pencil lines on the first sheet. Then he drew *Figure A* in the center and fenced it off to the right and left with broken pencil strokes. He then divided the circle of this figure into eight parts and labeled the segments alternately A and B. He called his final production a "compass," and elaborated upon the relative position of each segment. Several figures were joined together with pencil lines, thus destroying the original Gestalt and creating something new which served his ideologies. There was an utter disregard for the reality element of the test. The tendency to place most of his figures in the center of the paper has a certain similarity to the clinging to the mid-line in the Rorschach Test.

The diagnosis of personality factors and of possible deviations should not be based solely upon the findings of this test. Bender points out in her *Instructions* that this test should be used in connection with regular batteries of exploratory methods. Billingslea [8] also indicates that the observations from this test "should be linked with knowledge gained from other clinical data before a total personality picture is attempted."

This Gestalt test has additional advantages when given in a battery of tests. It is so simple that most subjects readily copy the figures without much questioning. When the subject is asked to draw a human figure, he may balk and state: "That I can't do. I don't know how to draw. I am the world's poorest artist." Or he may give similar reasons to demonstrate his inability to draw a person. In such cases one may point to the Gestalt drawings of this person and say reassuringly: "See how nicely you drew on this test! You have already shown that you can draw." Only a very disturbed individual will try to offer other arguments after such an object lesson which proves his own graphic ability beyond any question.

Another advantage of the test lies in the fact that it is not timed and that it can be administered with equal validity to the young child as well as to the senile adult.

INTERPRETATION OF BENDER GESTALT TEST DATA

Before an investigation into the clinical application of this test is undertaken, one must first search out the genetic development of the visual-motor function in the human being. We are not born with a ready-made apparatus through which we perceive, interpret, integrate, and organize stimuli. We have to learn, or, better, we must master these processes through successive stages of maturation. The small child does not experience perception as the adult does. Goodenough *[11]*, in her drawing scale and bibliographic annotations, points out that the first graphic attempts of small children are pure motor play. Bender states that the scribbles of the very young child "are done for the pleasure of the motor expression, the scribbled pictures being a by-product and having no meaning. They are performed by large arm movements in a dextrad, clockwise whirl, or pendulum waves if the child uses its right hand, and in sinistrad, counterclockwise whirls if the left hand is used" *[3]*. Krautter *[15]* and Bender and Woltmann *[7]* have described the maturational motor factors that lead to object representation with plastic material.

An investigation into the maturation cycle of graphic representation shows that in the beginning motor energy of the arm forms the springboard for action. The small child has no intention of representing or copying specific forms. Undistinguishable zigzag lines, dots, and dashes become curved and round. This is partially the result of anatomical limitations because the arm is fixed at the shoulder. A free swinging of the arm results in curved, round, and circular movements. Another reason for the formation of and preference for the round figure lies in the anatomical construction of our visual apparatus, which is a sphere.

Through various motor experiences, either by the child himself or observed by him in others, he learns to draw a loop. The enclosed loop is the basis for all perceived form. Once this form has been consciously mastered, it leads to repetitions, groupings, and various types of experimentations.

These early graphic attempts constitute a very important developmental phase for the growing child. They mark the beginning of motor-energy discipline and the transition from wild scribbling to motor co-ordination and organization. The child becomes conscious of the fact that motor impulses result in permanent visible records that can be seen, admired, or criticized by others. This adds a note of social recognition and participation. The impulses also enable the small child to express himself in a medium other than language by attaching meanings and ideologies to these "non-object representations." A three-year-eight-month-old girl drew a number of closed and open loops and explained that the open loops were houses with open doors. The closed loops to her were houses at nighttime after the children had gone to bed and the front door had been closed.

Wertheimer's Gestalt principles do not apply to these early graphic maturation phases. Direction is more important to the small child than distance, size, proximity, and continuity. The small child grasps the meaning of "masses," "series," or "bunches of things," but is not impressed by absolute numbers or sizes.

Maturation in the Normal Child.—Rapid differentiation of form, maturing of the motor apparatus, and the capacity for object representation take place between the fourth and seventh year. By this time the child begins to go to school, is taught formalized social concepts, learns to inhibit his own motor impulses, is instructed to copy forms with definite meanings, such as the letters of the alphabet, and at the same time is introduced to reading, which is the complicated function of not only recognizing each letter but also combining the form with phonetics. It is at this stage of maturational development that Wertheimer's Gestalt principles acquire validity. Social-emotional development and the search for cognitive growth likewise play a very important part in this development. The child, according to Bender [3] actually experiments with the different phenomena, getting satisfaction with each new experience which is complete enough for that stage of maturation of the developing organism from preceding experience levels. There is, moreover, a continuous reaching out for new experiments in which the child freely gives himself so that his activities become an active part of the knowledge obtained. This becomes a continually expanding "Gestaltung," which is continually reshaping itself in the experience of the growing child.

On the basis of these findings, Bender attempted to standardize her material as a performance test for children. Related studies with the Gestalt figures had convinced her that the "visual-motor Gestalt function is a fundamental function associated with language ability and closely associated with various functions of intelligence, such as visual perception, manual motor ability, memory, temporal and spatial concepts, and organization or representation." She found no valid criteria in young children below the age of four. Up to that age the small child usually produces scribbles. It is true that the Goodenough drawing test of a man starts with a basic mental age of three years, but really good attempts to draw a man seldom occur below the four-year

AGE	A	1	2	3	4	5	6	7	8
				F I G U R E					
Adult	100%	25%	100%	100%	100%	100%	100%	100%	100%
11 yrs.	95%	95%	65%	60%	95%	90%	70%	75%	90%
10 yrs.	90%	90%	60%	60%	80%	80%	60%	60%	90%
9 yrs.	80%	75%	60%	70%	80%	70%	80%	65%	70%
8 yrs.	75%	75%	75%	60%	80%	65%	70%	65%	65%
7 yrs.	75%	75%	70%	60%	75%	65%	60%	65%	60%
6 yrs.	75%	75%	60%	80%	75%	60%	60%	60%	75%
5 yrs.	85	85	60	80	70	60	60	60	75
4 yrs.	90%	85%	75%	80%	70%	60%	65%	60%	60%
3 yrs.	— — — — — Scribbling — — — — — — — —								

FIGURE 29. Summary of Genetic Changes in Capacity to Reproduce Gestalt Figures

level. Bender's standardization of Gestalt maturation and function covers the ages of four to eleven, which is the age when language function, including reading and writing, is developing. The results of attempted standardization are shown in a chart that is reproduced in the original monograph [3] as well as in the instruction manual [4]. (See Figure 29.) Since this is a performance type of developmental visual-motor factor, complete mastery is usually achieved with the beginning of adolescence. Bender therefore points out that this scale is not valid for normal individuals whose mental age is above the eleven-year level. This is in agreement with the Goodenough drawing scale, which likewise ceases to operate as an indicator of intelligence above this level.

The concept of mental age is still widely used as a psychological measuring device for defining different degrees or levels of intelligence. It has practical value when applied to children, but it becomes meaningless when applied to adult intelligence. The interested reader is referred to Wechsler's chapters on "The Concept of Mental Age and Intelligence Quotient" *[24]* and on "Abandoning the Mental Age" *[25]* for a more thorough discussion. To say that the configurations of an adult schizophrenic patient show deterioration of functional Gestalt concepts and relationships and the emergence of primitive Gestalt factors is more meaningful than to state that his Gestalt drawings show a mental age of, shall we say, seven years. In such a patient, personality integration is distorted in such a complicated manner that the assignment of mental age levels on the basis of similarities to performance achievements in growing and developing children does not settle the issue.

Bender's findings, as stated in her chart, may be used as points of comparision when applied to adults who suffer from Gestalt-distorting mental diseases. Gestalt maturation, as shown in this chart, is not an even process. More four-year-old children can draw *Figure A* than *Figures 5, 7,* and *8.* Mastery in these last-mentioned figures is not fully achieved until the child is ten years old. The percentages given in this chart refer to the number of children in each age group who were able to draw the figures. The percentages of children who were able to draw these figures are based on the results of 800 children who were used for the standardization.

A few explanations are necessary at this point. It will be noticed that only 25 per cent of the adults seem to be able to copy *Figure 1* correctly. The deciding factor here is the pairings of dots, a process grasped by only one fourth of the adult population. Successes are rated not so much on the basis of correct graphic representation as upon recognition of the Gestalt principles involved. For instance, 90 per cent of children on the four-year level do not draw *Figure A* as a circle and a diamond, but rather as two circles whose peripheries meet. Some 60 per cent of children in the same age group can copy *Figure 8*, not as an elongation with a diamond in the middle, but as a circle within a circle. The chart shows that different figures are mastered at different ages in the following distribution:

6 years: *Figure A, Figure 1, Figure 4, Figure 5;*
7 years: *Figure 8;*
8 years: *Figure 6;*
10 years: *Figure 2, Figure 7;*
11 years: *Figure 3.*

The tracing of the genetic development of visual-motor patterns applies, of course, to the development of the so-called normal child.

Mental Deficiency.—There are adults whose motor reaction patterns appear to be mature but whose intellectual level is very low. Bender therefore investigated the visual-motor Gestalt functions in low-grade mental defectives quite early in her experimental studies. A detailed analysis of these motor forms drawn by adult mental defectives revealed that the first evidence of expressing forms appeared on a mental level of two years, where little units of loops or whirls are perseverated in the horizontal plane. Bender feels that this is primarily a motor expression and as such has little to do with reproduction of form. The tendency toward Gestalt formation appears on the three-year level in the shape of rectangular forms either near or inside of each other. The close dependency of the visual-motor functions on maturation seems to apply to low-grade mental defectives in the same way as it applies to the growing child. Some of the Gestalt principles are functions of the more highly elaborated perceptual motor capacities and appear only at the higher intellectual levels. Therefore in the low-grade mental defectives with mental ages up to the three-year level one gets a kind of scribbling similar to that observed in the small child. "Above three years there is the tendency to accentuate the horizontal base line, to control perseveration, and to produce wavy lines instead of broken ones for the representation of straight lines, and some efforts to cross lines. At the five-year level there is a tendency to reduce the primitive loops to points (but this tendency is reversible even at the superior adult level) and there is a tendency to make straighter lines and better recognized Gestalten" *[3]*.

Approximately 2 per cent of the population fall within the above described defective range of intelligence. The majority of people with such low and inadequate intelligence are institutionalized and seldom come to the attention of the medical and psychological professions outside of these special protective environments. However, roughly 22 per cent has intellectual deficiencies ranging from dull-normal to borderline intelligence. Bender, on the basis of years of clinical experience, regards mental deficiency as a condition that is neither an entity in itself nor an isolated deficiency in endowment, but rather a symptom that may be associated with many different conditions. The Gestalt test was found to be of special value when administered to this comparatively large group of people with below average intelligence because, owing to its structure and simplicity, it has helped to clarify doubtful diagnostic clues and has aided in the clinical understanding of subnormal personality constellations.

After surveying the Gestalt drawings of children and adults whose intelligence was below the average norm, Bender arrived at the following conclusions:

The study of the visual-motor Gestalt function shows that the problem of mental deficiency is not a simple one. If we were to assume a slow-up or simplification of the maturation process in a unified way, we would expect less differentiation, a more unified system, a stronger and simpler Gestalt, such as we find in the younger normal child. This does occur in some individuals, especially among the higher-grade defectives. Such individuals usually seem to represent the hereditary constitutional defective. Even in these cases we do not find a simple retardation in all the principles of the integrated visual-motor Gestalt function. Motor control is usually better than in the normal children of the younger age. Small, energy-conserving figures are the rule. The primitive loop is freely used with less motor play or experimentation. The patterns are more rigid. In the majority of the responses of all the mental defectives investigated, other features are also seen. It must be realized that many individuals who function as mental defectives do so not because of hereditary retardation in maturation, but because they are constitutional deviates of some other sort, or because of some subsequent brain pathology. It is therefore possible to get every sort of deviation in the personality reaction and in the Gestalt function. Detailed analysis leads to the conclusion that many individuals who are functioning as mental defectives show evidence in their Gestalt drawings of more or less aphasic disturbances, which are characterized by the use of a perseverated primitive symbolic unit, while others show the dissociative phenomena characteristic of schizophrenia; still others show disturbances in impulses with a poverty of responses or hyperkinetic features; and, finally, others show perceptive difficulties, confusional features, with disorientation of whole figures or parts of figures on the background [3].

The importance of Bender's conclusions lies in the fact that this Gestalt test not only allows for a sorting out of various clues which supplement other diagnostic findings but also makes possible a better differentiation and understanding of what really might be involved in a condition that outwardly resembles mentally deficient behavior.

Organic Brain Disease.—"This is the place where the dead are glad to help the living" is written over the portals of a famous European anatomical institute. Medical science has learned from the diseased, the abnormal, and the deviates. We cannot always be sure what is a normal process or a normal functioning until we meet with an obvious deviation in which certain functions are impaired. The absence of certain reflexes, paralysis of parts of the body, motor disturbances, and many other symptoms allow us to understand which part or parts of the functioning body are involved. It was therefore natural for Bender to investigate whether organic brain disease, which tends to disorganize cerebral functions, will reduce the sensory experiences to independent disconnected sensations or to simpler levels of integration of whole figures. She studied eight cases of organic brain disease in which sensory aphasia was a conspicuous symptom. Case 1 was a sixty-five-year-old man who suffered from senile arteriosclerosis, slight hemiparesis, increased right tendon reflexes, and a slight homonymous hemianopia. It was felt that this patient had a probable hemorrhage in the left temporoparietal lobe. He displayed severe disturbances in the more highly integrated functions of speech, thought processes, and sociopersonal habits. When he was asked to copy the Gestalt figures, he drew various kinds of loops, thus demonstrating a disintegration of the more intricate, internal, detailed organization of the Gestalten, with a perseveration of the fundamental Gestalt principle, the loop. He had lost the higher integrative capacities, but was able to express himself on a lower maturational level by producing loops which represent the Gestalt on its indifferent background. Case 2 describes a forty-three-year-old man who suddenly developed a right facial paresis and an aphasia ten days after having been admitted to the hospital for heart trouble. Upon admission this patient had not displayed mental or neurological disturbances. Bender followed the recovery of this patient in day-by-day presentations of the Gestalt cards from the fifth day after the cerebral embolism until the twelfth day, when the patient was taken home by relatives.

These day-by-day productions showed the following tendencies in visual-motor responses: (1) perseveration of the larger principles of Gestalt; (2) emergence of primitive response; (3) utilization of the compact, enclosed, energy-saving unit symbols to show relationships; (4) perseverative tendencies that led to confusion and blocking; (5) recovery accompanied by progressive integrative maturation, with sudden episodes of insight.

A description of the six other cases is omitted here. The reproduction of the Gestalt figures of all these eight cases, to be found in Bender's monograph [3], proves beyond doubt that organic brain disease does interfere with the visual-motor Gestalt functions. A knowledge of how visual-motor patterns disintegrate in the process of organic brain disease undoubtedly helps the brain surgeon, the neurologist, the psychiatrist, and the clinical psychologist to interpret more correctly the at times bizarre and euphoric manifestations of brain-injured persons. Although the brain-injured person tends to show in his motor behavior a regression toward more primitive levels, his graphic reproductions of Gestalt figures differ markedly from those of mentally deficient persons. The mentally deficient person has fixed upper limits that do not permit growth and further integration. The brain-injured person, provided he is not mentally deficient, experiences changes that manifest themselves as regressions toward more primitive modes of integration. The regression is conditioned by the basic biological matrix, by the previously reached and maintained level of integration, the locus and extent of the lesion, and the emotional involvement of the individual as a whole. Since all of these factors and their relative strength relate to each other in dynamic relationships, perception is never a static process, but differs from case to case. Very often there are day-by-day changes in the same brain-injured person. "These studies of disturbances in perceptual motor Gestalten in organic brain disease indicate that the Gestalt principles are never fixed but are the integrative responses of the personality as a whole in any given situation; in disintegrating cerebral lesions they tend to revert to more primitive levels and, as the brain recovers from the insult, they tend to follow the laws of developmental maturation in returning to the higher integrative responses" [3].

Alcoholic and Traumatic Psychoses.—Disturbances in visual-motor Gestalten were studied by Bender in patients who suffered from alcoholic and traumatic psychoses. She found that the acute stages of these psychoses were marked by confusion and clouding of consciousness, resulting in difficulties in the synthesis of perceptual activities. In most cases the patients were able to perceive the configurations as a whole, but there also appeared tendencies toward reverting to more primitive forms. Acute confusional states or amentia, which are described by Schilder as manifestations in which "perplexity is the correlate of an inadequate comprehension of the environment, with the additional symptom of dissatisfaction with the inadequacy" [20], do show up in the Gestalt test. "The disturbance in acute confusional states resolves itself into a disturbance in the integration of the parts of the figure to the whole, and of the whole to its background or situation. The primitive reversions are secondary to this primary difficulty. When micrographia occurs, it is associated with the poverty of impulses observed in cases showing lethargy or dullness" [3].

Schizophrenia.— Bender's first attempts to study deviations of visual-motor Gestalt patterns were carried out on schizophrenic patients. This is not surprising, because the major psychoses with their bizarre distortions and disintegrations of normal modes of behavior have been used in many instances as focal points of research. Aside from the fact that such studies have led to a better understanding of the disease processes themselves, they have also contributed greatly to our knowledge of so-called normal or undisturbed human dynamics. Diagnostic criteria for schizophrenia, of course, were already known, thanks to the labors of Kraepelin, Bleuler, and Adolf Meyer; but a refinement of differential diagnosis was still wanting. Little was known about childhood schizophrenia, and as late as 1938 Bender could write that "schizophrenia in children is rare, so rare that usually psychiatrists do not agree in the diagnosis" [3]. Concentrated and intense research since then has led to a quicker recognition of schizophrenic disease entities in children and has prepared the way for more hopeful methods of treatment. Investigations by Bradley, Despert, Kanner, Schumacher, and others have given us salient facts but have failed to unify diagnostic and prognostic procedures. Bender's approach and the fruit of her labors, based upon many years of daily contact and study of the schizophrenic child, are documented in her 1947 publication on "Childhood Schizophrenia" [5] in which she defines this disease as revealing

> pathology in behavior at every level and in every level of integration or patterning within the functioning of the central nervous system, be it vegetative, motor, perceptual, intellectual, emotional, or social.
>
> This behavior pathology disturbs the pattern of every functioning field in a characteristic way. The pathology cannot, therefore, be thought of as focal in the architecture of the central nervous system, but rather as striking at the substratum of integrative functioning or biologically patterned behavior.

Studies of the visual-motor Gestalt functioning in the schizophrenic child were part of this whole or configurational approach to a baffling problem. After briefly restating the genetic development of visually perceived form which begins with a "whole arm circular scribble" and which, with the beginning controlled vortical movements, leads to the formation of the circle, of the square, of the triangle, and finally of the diamond, Bender summarizes the visual-motor Gestalt functions in schizophrenic children as follows:

The schizophrenic child copying these figures shows many of the same problems that are shown in his motility. There is a tendency to use old primitive responses interlocked with the more mature capacities that are expected from the maturational level of the child. There is therefore an excessive use of vortical movement even with good diamond form. A series of figures on a horizontal plane may be pulled around into a vertical figure. The boundaries of circles are uncertain and may be gone over several times. The centers of circles are uncertain; there are no points, but many little circles, and for the same reason angular and crossed forms are fragmented. Action cannot be readily controlled and figures are elaborated, enlarged, repeated. The total product makes a pattern itself with a great deal of fluidity to it, based upon vortical movement. The perceptual patterns lose their boundaries and therefore their relationship to the background. One may speak also of a motor compliance and cohesiveness between the boundaries of two objects. There is also an effort to explore and to fixate depth or third and fourth dimensions. In this well-patterned fluid matrix are areas in which the pattern is broken; a part of a figure is separated from the whole and made to rotate faster; a group of small circles is separated from the whole mass. It is as though in a circular stream of rippling water a pebble were thrown, causing a new wave movement. One's best understanding is to think in terms of a disturbance in the time factor in patterned behavior characteristic for each field of behavior, such a time factor being of biological origin and related to this disease process alone. Other forms of behavior, such as regressive, projective and introjective, elaborative, inhibitive, distractive and concretistic, are efforts on the part of the personality to orient itself to this pathology and, if possible, control it.

Bender's studies of schizophrenic children confirmed her previously made observations with schizophrenic adults [3], in which she stated that we can understand the visual-motor patterns of this group of mental patients "if we realize that all form arises from motion, which is vortical, and that the schizophrenic disturbance in function is such a fundamental one that there tends to be disturbance in this motion which distorts the form of the units and the relationship of the Gestalt configuration" [3]. Gestalt drawings of typical schizophrenic patients are easily recognized by the bizarreness of the configurations produced, the frequent splitting in figures, an unusual cohesion between all the figures, and an increase in movement in the figures. Attempts to use these figures as matrices for delusional ideations by ornamenting them with connecting lines, destroying the original Gestalt, and creating new figures are usually noticeable. In such instances the Gestalt test really becomes a projective technique by allowing the person to be tested to project his own ideations into the test performance.

Manic-depressive Psychoses.—In the manic-depressive psychoses the organization of the personality is more intact than in schizophrenia. The disturbances in psychic functions are less profound. Gestalt figures may be embellished with ornaments, but there is less tendency to destroy the figures.

Malingering and Ganser Syndrome as Checks on the Validity of the Bender Test.—Interesting observations are found in Bender's chapter on the Gestalt functioning in malingering and the Ganser syndrome. Physicians, medical students, and nurses who were not acquainted with the principles of the work on Gestalt function were asked to copy the Gestalt figures as if they themselves were mental defectives and therefore could not draw correctly what they saw. It was found that in all these experimental cases the basic Gestalt principles had not been violated. Basically these volunteers copied all of the Gestalt principles correctly. This bears out Schilder's contention "that it is a human necessity to respond truthfully to the perception of a situation; the world of reality has to be respected" [20]. This finding of Bender's is of very great importance because, although not specifically mentioned as such, this experiment really is a test of validity. Various types of deviations may occur, but real destruction of the Gestalt forms and their conversion into new configurations occurs in psychotic individuals only. In other words, a nonpsychotic person cannot react to reality in an unreal way. He cannot deny or destroy the basic principles that enable him to function as an individual who is in contact with reality. In this way the cards and the stimuli they respect are valid and nondestructive in their reality-testing functions. Bender found that in cases where persons are specifically asked to violate the forms, not only an inhibition of impulses takes place but also a diminishing of reality perception is absent.

The practical implications of these findings become of value when one deals with a person who tries to simulate a psychotic condition in order to escape unpleasant consequences of his acts. Such attempts may be ordinary malingering of the kind found in army installations where soldiers tried to get off shipping lists or desired to be separated from the service. A more serious form of simulation is found in the Ganser syndrome. This is a mental disorder occurring most frequently in prisoners under detention awaiting trial, and should not be confused with a true prison psychosis, which usually occurs after the prisoner has been sentenced. The hysteric element in this condition does not exclude underlying psychotic trends. The administration of the Gestalt test has proved itself very valuable in determining whether or not the Gestalten have been destroyed, as one expects in a psychotic performance, or whether no violence has been done to the reality element of the test with a resulting inhibition of impulses.

Psychoneurosis.—It was stated earlier in this chapter that the Gestalt test should be included in a battery of tests instead of being used as a single measure. Organic conditions and psychotic disturbances usually produce a telltale pattern with obvious deviations in the copying of the Gestalt figures. Yet it happens very often that a clearly established diagnosis of psychoneurosis from the test battery is accompanied by very normal copies of the Gestalt figures. This does not render the Gestalt test invalid, because personality disturbances in the neurotic personality seldom invade the visual-motor sphere.

Bender's position is that we do not expect to find disturbances in perception or in the visual-motor Gestalt function in the psychoneuroses. In these conditions we find disturbances in the normal emotional development through the infantile stages. The child who is thwarted or overindulged in his demands for satisfactions arising from his relationship to his mother or father or his own bodily needs will tend to show a persistent demand for the same type of satisfaction. Since the reasons for the thwarting or overindulgence occur in the infantile stage, when consciousness is not fully developed, it usually happens that the individual throughout his life may be unconscious of this reason—unless it can be brought into consciousness by a special method such as psychoanalysis. The unacceptable demand for satisfaction is usually presented by some other activity which stands as a symbol for the real desires and drives of the personality. Since the stage of dawning consciousness is also the stage of maturation of the perceptual motor Gestalten, it would not be surprising to find that some such Gestalten might become the symbol of the individual's unsatisfied infantile drives. In other words, they might represent the individual preoccupations, obsessions, and compulsions.

Obvious distortions may be absent from the psychoneurotic Gestalt record, but an evaluation of the test performance, referred to briefly above, usually will produce clues that tell how a person approaches and organizes a given task. Some people may ask many specific directions and may look to the examiner for help and guidance. The nine figures may be spread out or be bunched closely together. Some persons erase a great deal and try to copy the test forms as correctly as possible. Others may show the opposite type of behavior by quickly drawing approximations. Whereas one person may be too critical, dependent, and perfectionistic, another personality will stand out by his lack of insight, absence of critical evaluation, and a slightly manic tendency to comply without conforming. It is true that these and innumerable other forms of test behavior are found in every type of normal and abnormal personality patterns. At the present state of our knowledge one cannot differentiate, on the basis of this test alone, between an anxiety neurosis, a mixed neurosis, and an anxiety hysteria, to mention only a few of the better-known neurotic deviations. The clues mentioned above and many others, taken primarily from an observation of the test performance and sometimes also from the final arrangements of the figures on paper, will serve as helpful additions in describing functional aspects of a personality. It is not necessary to attach diagnostic labels to these observations. A good description of what actually took place during the copying of these figures will be sufficient and enlightening.

Billingslea [8] in his study of the Bender Gestalt Test also found psychoneurotics do not seem to produce specific deviations in their visual-motor functions, and he states that "the general conclusion from this sampling must support Bender that a clear syndrome for distinguishing the psychoneurotic test record cannot be established." The full meaning of this statement must be understood in terms of the objectives that Billingslea investigated. Since copyrighted test cards were not available at that time, Billingslea used a slightly modified set of Gestalt figures which had originated at the Adjutant General's Army School. The Gestalt test was administered to an experimental group of one hundred psychoneurotic adult male patients, all soldiers in an army hospital, and to a group of fifty adult male soldiers judged to fall within the normal range. None of the experimental subjects had major organic injuries or defects, although fifty did have records of injuries sustained either in combat or in accidents at some time during their army careers. According to Billingslea, the judgments for the experimental group were made by four psychiatrists and himself. Data were collected from personal interviews, medical and life histories, and a battery of tests, which included the Wechsler-Bellevue Intelligence Scale, the Rorschach Test, the Minnesota Multiphasic Personality Inventory, and the Kuder Preference Record. The experimental and the normal group "were of comparable age, intelligence, civilian and army occupational experience, army combat experience, and home town population." All subjects were fully ambulatory.

The purpose of this study was to do the following:

1. To develop an objective scoring method for the Bender Gestalt Test.

2. To objectify, by means of operational definitions as far as practicable, the perceptually meaningful factors of the test.

3. To give some measure of the test's reliability and validity by (a) comparing the test results of individuals judged emotionally neurotic with those judged emotionally normal; and (b) comparing the test results of individuals judged to have different types of neurotic emotional adjustment patterns.

The evaluation of the test results led to the establishment of sixty-three indices, including measurement of length of lines, angles, areas, irregularities in shape and rotations of a whole figure or parts of a figure relative to each other to give quantifying coefficients to twenty-five test factors. Billingslea defines a factor as a "rather clearly detectable test behavior in one or more of the figures" *[8]* such as angulation, closure, fragmentation, overlapping, and so on. "Indices, on the other hand, involve the measurement on only one figure." Billingslea constructed a special measurement scale for the investigations of the various indices.

The greater part of Billingslea's fine and scholarly paper deals with scoring methods and the establishment of reliability and validity. His data on these must be omitted here, but his publication should be consulted for more comprehensive information.

Aside from the statistical comparison of the various test factors, the test results also were compared "with the test factor syndrome set forth by Hutt [14] as distinctive of the psychoneurotic record." From the results the following conclusions were reached:

1. The instrument in the hands of a trained clinician is excellent for establishing rapport and observing the client's behavior in a standard situation.

2. Though three factors show a degree of interfigure reliability, test factors with indices from several of the figures tend to be unreliable and to lack validity. The exception is the factor of size differences.

3. Hutt's syndrome for the psychoneurotic record is not, in general, supported.

Experiments with Optic Imagery.—Bender investigated optic imagery and movement as the means of organizing representation. She selected four subjects for this experiment after having found that not all persons seem to be suitable for such a type of study because "they do not seem to experience optic images, at least not adequately enough to describe them" [3]. The subjects had to study each card for about one minute, close their eyes, try to imagine the object, describe it, hold the memory image as long as possible, and tell what happened to it until the optic field was again at rest. Afterwards they were asked to draw a picture of the different images they experienced. It should be noted here that the Gestalt figures as such were not changed, but that movement in the optic field and, to borrow a term from Schilder, the constructive energies of the psyche remodeled and reshaped these stationary objects into moving and changing concepts. The final results allowed Bender to reach interesting conclusions about individual differences in stimulus perception and integration and about processes through which a stimulus is incorporated into the personality structure and related to cognition, affect, and idiosyncratic concepts. Intense study and research are needed in this field before more conclusive facts can be stated about the underlying dynamics involved in such processes and about how they relate to other aspects of personality organization.

Psychosomatic Symptoms.—The application of the Bender Gestalt Test has been most fruitful in investigating organic and psychotic deviations. Unfortunately, the Gestalt Test has not been applied sufficiently toward a study of psychosomatic disorders. There are some studies on the way, but findings are not available.

It is true, as Billingslea states, that the test has not amassed an impressive bibliography. Yet some studies are on record in which the Bender Gestalt Test assumed prominence as a valid clinical tool. Orenstein and Schilder [17] made patients draw these figures before and after insulin-shock treatment. They found that there were fewer destructions of the Gestalt principles in the post-shock stage. Stainbrook and Lowenbach [22] administered this test during periods of postconvulsive reintegration. Drawings were repeated at various intervals after the convulsion. They noted that early attempts of Gestalt figure drawings resulted in primitive loops, and that there was a progressive improvement in drawing in line with recovery from the convulsive attack.

The Bender Gestalt Test was employed in a battery of tests for a study on hypnotic ablation [21], carried out at the Mason General Hospital. Fabian [9] used the Bender Visual-Motor Gestalt Test in his study of vertical rotations in visual-motor performance and its relationship to reading reversals. Five hundred and eighty-six so-called normal schoolchildren and 106 boys from the Children's Observation Ward of the Psychiatric Division of Bellevue Hospital were tested. Fabian found that "the tendency to rotate horizontally directed configuration to the vertical position is found in the normal child of preschool and beginning school age. It is a developmental phenomenon which is gradually corrected as the child matures, but does not disappear until he is seven or eight years of age. When configurational horizontality is accentuated, 'verticalization' becomes more compelling for the child." The persistence of the "verticalization," according to Fabian, should be checked through the use of visual-motor tests because such persistency may indicate either mental deficiency or some organic brain disease where it is a regressive feature. "In the general school population, however, the abnormal conditions are relatively infrequent and, if present, they can be readily ascertained. Much more common are infantile patterns of behavior due to emotional difficulties or environmental handicaps which inhibit the learning process and which betray themselves by primitive visual-motor tendencies such as 'verticalization.' "

Harrower [12], describing a neurotic depression in a child, included the Bender Gestalt Test in her battery of tests.

Israel Wechsler has included the Bender Gestalt Test in his sixth edition of *A Textbook of Clinical Neurology* [26], where he writes: "The clinical use of this test depends upon the fact that visual-motor organization is a maturation process which may be arrested, regress after maturity is reached, and be variously affected by neuropsychiatric disorders."

Recently the Bender Gestalt Test, together with the abbreviated Thematic Apperception Test and the Group Rorschach Test, were administered by Wayne et al. [23] to inmates of a military disciplinary barrack in an effort to determine homosexual tendencies in the men. Overt homosexuals were matched with a control group of nonhomosexuals picked at random. The authors found that the Bender Gestalt Test revealed sexual conflicts, but the exact nature of these conflicts could not be determined. The mere fact that the Bender Gestalt Test shows up sexual conflicts attests to its sensitivity when applied to personality problems. A more conclusive correlation between the Bender Gestalt Test findings and homosexual conflicts will result when the psychological nature of homosexuality is better known and understood.

A novel departure from the application of visually perceived Gestalten is Barkley's [1] introduction of the Hapto-Kinesthetic Gestalt Test for the investigation of brain injuries. He uses plastic cards which contain exact reproductions of Bender's Gestalt figures which are raised in relief one sixteenth of an inch in height. A subject has to feel the designs and draw what he has felt. After the hapto-kinesthetic test has been completed, the regular Bender Gestalt Test is administered under standard conditions. Barkley writes:

Only a minor pilot study has been run to date, but there appear to be marked and significant difference between the performances of the brain damaged and of normal subjects. It has also been found that many subjects suffering from organic brain pathology who give a good reproduction of the visual stimuli exhibit marked distortion on the reproductions of the hapto-kinesthetic perceptions.

CONCLUSIONS

The Bender Gestalt Test has been used as a maturational test in visual Gestalt function in children and to explore retardation, loss of function, and organic brain defects in children and adults. Personality deviations that show regressive phenomena have been studied successfully with its help. Conclusive diagnostic data are incomplete for psychoneurosis, psychosomatic conditions, and hapto-kinesthetic modes of perception.

The Bender Gestalt Test is a projective technique as well as a simple, easily administered, nonsocial, neutral, apparently innocuous test. Among the projective techniques, it is "the pause that refreshes."

REFERENCES

1. BARKLEY, BILL J.: "A Note on the Development of the Western Reserve Hapto-Kinesthetic Gestalt Test," *Journal of Clinical Psychology*, Vol. 5 (1949).
2. BELL, JOHN ELDERKIN: *Projective Techniques*. New York: Longmans, Green & Co.; 1948.
3. BENDER, LAURETTA: "A Visual-Motor Gestalt Test and Its Clinical Use," *Research Monograph No. 3*, American Orthopsychiatric Association, 1938.
4. ———: *Instructions for the Use of the Visual-Motor Gestalt Test*, American Orthopsychiatric Association, 1946.
5. ———: "Childhood Schizophrenia," *American Journal of Orthopsychiatry*, Vol. 17 (1947).
6. ———: "Psychological Principles of the Visual-Motor Gestalt Test," *Transactions of the New York Academy of Sciences*, March 1949.
7. ———, and WOLTMANN, ADOLF G.: "The Use of Plastic Material as a Psychiatric Approach to Emotional Problems in Children," *American Journal of Orthopsychiatry*, Vol. 7 (1937).
8. BILLINGSLEA, FRED Y.: "The Bender Gestalt: an Objective Scoring Method and Validating Data," *J. Clin. Psychol.*, Vol. 4 (1948).
9. FABIAN, A. A.: "Vertical Rotation in Visual-Motor Performance: Its Relationship to Reading Reversals," *Journal of Educational Psychology*, 1945.
10. FRANK, LAWRENCE K.: "Projective Methods for the Study of Personality," *Journal of Psychology*, Vol. 8 (1939).

11. GOODENOUGH, FLORENCE L.: *Measurement of Intelligence by Drawing.* Yonkers: World Book Co.; 1926.

12. HARROWER, MOLLY R.: "Neurotic Depression in a Child," in Arthur Burton and Robert H. Harris (eds.): *Case Histories in Clinical and Abnormal Psychology.* New York: Harper & Brothers, 1947.

13. HUTT, MAX L.: "The Use of Projective Methods of Personality Measurement in Army Medical Installations," *J. Clin. Psychol.,* Vol. I (1945).

14. ———: *A Tentative Guide for the Administration and Interpretation of the Bender Gestalt Test.* U. S. Army: Adjutant General's School; 1945. (Restricted.)

15. KRAUTTER, OTTO: "Die Entwicklung des plastischen Gestaltens beim vorschulpflichtigen Kinde," *Beiheft 50 zur Z. angew. Psychol.,* 1930.

16. NOYES, ARTHUR P.: *Modern Clinical Psychiatry.* (2nd ed.) Philadelphia: W. B. Saunders Co.; 1939.

17. ORENSTEIN, L. I., and SCHILDER, PAUL: "Psychological Considerations of Insulin Treatment in Schizophrenia," *Journal of Nervous and Mental Diseases,* Vol. 88 (1938).

18. SARGENT, HELEN: "Projective Methods," in L. A. Pennington and I. A. Berg (eds.): *An Introduction to Clinical Psychology.* New York: Ronald Press Co.; 1948.

19. SCHILDER, PAUL: *Mind: Perception and Thought in Their Constructive Aspect.* New York: Columbia University Press; 1942.

20. ———, and BENDER, L.: "A Visual-Motor Gestalt Test and Its Clinical Use," *Research Monograph No. 3,* Amer. Orthopsychiat. Ass., 1938.

21. SPIEGEL, H., SHOR, J., and FISHMAN, S.: "A Hypnotic Ablation Technique for the Study of Personality Development," *Psychosomatic Medicine,* Vol. 7 (1945).

22. STAINBROOK, E. J., and LOWENBACH, H.: "Writing and Drawing of Psychotic Individuals after Electrically Induced Convulsions," *J. Nerv. Ment. Dis.,* Vol. 99 (1944).

23. WAYNE, D. M., ADAMS, M., and ROWE, L. A.: "A Study of Military Prisoners at a Disciplinary Barracks Suspected of Homosexual Activities," *Military Surgeon,* Vol. 101 (1947).

24. WECHSLER, DAVID: *The Measurement of Adult Intelligence.* (3rd ed.) Baltimore: Williams & Wilkins; 1944.

25. ———: *Wechsler Intelligence Scale for Children.* New York: Psychological Corporation; 1949.

26. WECHSLER, I.: *A Textbook of Clinical Neurology.* (6th ed.) Philadelphia: W. B. Saunders Co.; 1947.

27. WERTHEIMER, MAX: "Untersuchungen zur Lehre von der Gestalt," *Psychologische Forschung,* Vol. 4 (1923).

▼

In "The Sentence Completion Test" Dr. Joseph M. Sacks and Dr. Sidney Levy offer a useful survey of the rapidly increasing literature on the incomplete sentences method. In addition they have made available a new sentence completion test that clinical psychologists may find more acceptable than certain earlier versions on which it is based. Although of potentially wide application, this technique has not as yet been fully explored; and it is our belief that the present contribution will serve to awaken new interest in the possibilities of the method.

The problem of interpretation of sentence completion materials has been a bothersome one, and we feel that the authors have made a contribution in this direction by stressing some interpretative principles that may sharpen our skills in using this projective method.

▼

The Sentence Completion Test*

Joseph M. Sacks and Sidney Levy

INTRODUCTION

A SENTENCE completion test consists of a number of incomplete sentences presented to the subject for completions; for example, "I get angry when . . ." Usually there are no instructions except "Complete these sentences as rapidly as you can. Don't stop to think about it, but say the very first thing that occurs to you." The test is usually *not* a standardized test and is rarely treated quantitatively. It may be administered to a group or as an individual test. It requires a minimum of supervision and this fact may be an important consideration in many clinical situations.

Usually sentences are selected which explore significant areas of an individual's adjustment, or in special situations tests may be used for the purpose of investigating some specific cluster of attitudes. An example of the former, which is presented later in this chapter, consists of questions designed to elicit feelings and attitudes in various basic areas of interpersonal relationships. An

---

* Published with permission of the Chief Medical Director, Department of Medicine and Surgery, Veterans' Administration, who assumes no responsibility for the opinions expressed or the conclusions drawn by the authors.

example of the latter is an attitude scale administered to a physically handicapped group for the purpose of determining the attitudes of the group toward the specific handicap.

Some clinicians have rejected the claim that sentence completion is a projective technique. The possibilities for imposing one's idiosyncratic meaning into an almost completed sentence are distinctly more limited than the possibilities inherent in an amorphous portion of an ink plot. Still the projective qualities that are inherent in the sentence completion technique are considerable. To convince himself of the plasticity of the sentence completion technique, the reader may wish to duplicate the following simple experiment.

An incomplete sentence was presented to ten unsophisticated subjects, all clerical workers: "The way my father treated my mother made me feel . . ." Each was asked to read the sentence and to complete it as rapidly as possible without thinking about it. The following ten responses were received, and the response times varied from four to thirty-five seconds.

The way my father treated my mother made me feel . . .

1. very happy.
2. rather indifferent.
3. like killing him.
4. like forming an example after him.
5. good.
6. rebellious.
7. all right.
8. very happy.
9. horrid.
10. he was a sucker.

Only two of the above responses are identical: namely, 1 and 8. The others are unique in this series. These responses to a single incomplete sentence can be evaluated from the point of view of formal characteristics or with respect to content. Some of the formal characteristics include the reaction time, number of words, precision of expression, quality, modifiers, simplicity, obsessiveness, verbosity, and so on. The content may be analyzed from the point of view of the emotional quality, intensity, passivity, symbolism, and so on. For the sake of illustration, let us compare some of the responses listed above.

First let us notice that five of the responses have a positive orientation and that five are negative. The difference in the attitude and affect of the subject who said "very happy," as compared with the one who said "like killing him," is striking. But even among the five negative responses there is considerable variation. Let us examine them.

2. rather indifferent.
3. like killing him.
6. rebellious.
9. horrid.
10. he was a sucker.

The subject who said that he felt "like killing him" expressed a forceful, spontaneous, relatively uninhibited emotion. The feeling was recognized, accepted, and expressed without serious modification, distortion, or apology. It is similar to a pure C response on the Rorschach Test. The individual who said he felt "rather indifferent" is also expressing a negative feeling. But it is a feeling lacking in spontaneity. The mechanism for evading the expression of emotion is akin to a retreat into superiority. The subject implies that his parents' relationship did not interest him, that it was unimportant, that he is "above that kind of thing" (the subject's own association). Note the use of the word "rather." It does not modify the attitude or the nature of the feeling; it is a verbal way of removing oneself even further from the situation. It has a connotation of posturing, a kind of verbal narcissism. It cannot be said at this point whether the feeling and the mechanism for handling it are specific for the parental figures or are an indication of this subject's adjustment in general. If this kind of response were found consistently throughout a sentence completion test, it could be interpreted as indicating a general pattern, rather than related to a specific psychological field.

How does "rebellious" compare with "like killing him"? This also expresses disapproval of the male parent, but, although spontaneous, it is somewhat more controlled. Both subjects were disturbed. One proposes to destroy the cause of the disturbance, the other simply feels like changing the situation. The latter implies intense feeling, recognition, and acceptance of such feeling, but controls the impulse to action. "Rebellious" may be likened to an Fc response on the Rorschach Test as compared with the pure C of "like killing him."

"Horrid" also expresses negative feelings toward the parental situation. But note the difference in quality between it and "like killing him" or "rebellious." The latter two are in the direction of action; one is expressive of direct action, the other an inhibited tendency toward action. "Horrid" has no connotation of action. It is a passive feeling. It suggests shrinking from rather than action toward. There is an undertone of effeminacy (the subject is a male).

"He was a sucker" is quite different in quality from the previous four negative responses. First it differs with respect to the object of disapproval. The others directed their antagonism toward the father, whereas this subject implies hostility toward the mother as well as scorn for the father. In addition to that, this subject removes himself from the situation. He does not feel like killing, or being rebellious, or horrid, or—anything. He is not involved. He is a spectator, looking on with scorn. The quality of his insulation from the situation is subtly different from the individual who feels "rather indifferent." The former finds it possible to admit and to express an attitude, however hard and cynical. "Rather indifferent" denies any emotional involvement and by its very denial reveals the traumatic nature of the situation.

Thus the five statements, although all are negative, differ from one another with respect to intensity, inhibition, evasiveness, passivity, involvement, and attitude.

The five positive statements differ among themselves, too. Let us compare "very happy," "all right," and "like forming an example after him." The first two describe feelings. These feelings, however, appear to be on different levels of intensity. It is not possible to say whether they are evasions or accurate expressions of feeling. In any case one has a greater energy investment than the other. If this were a pattern in all his responses on a sentence completion test, one would conclude that the subject who said "very happy" was considerably more energetic than the one who said "all right." Of course, other interpretations are possible. The subject who felt "like forming an example after him" expressed a different kind of emotion. There is idolatry, a suggestion that he is not so good as his father, a feeling of meekness, and perhaps a suggestion of dependence.

Thus it is possible to form certain hypotheses about emotions, attitudes, and mechanisms from the response to even a single incomplete sentence. The possibilities inherent in fifty or sixty such sentences are impressive. It is frequently feasible for a skilled and experienced clinician to formulate fairly complete and complex patterns of personality, filling in fine nuances as well as the broad strokes. It is apparent that the experience, insight, and understanding of the clinician are of exceptional importance in working with a projective procedure like the sentence completion test.

Before reviewing research in this field, we may find a digression profitable. Personality is a complicated and dynamic cosmos. There is a tendency, in the enthusiasm of discovery, toward grand and extravagant claims. Those who demand perfection, on the other hand, seem unable to resist the compulsive pessimism of sweeping and absolute denial. There is no single way to encompass all of personality. We are in the very primitive stages of a personalistic science and so we cannot afford the luxury of being too fastidious. We must come to grips with personality in any and every way that proves useful.

In reviewing the literature the reader will note a recurring tendency on the part of investigators toward glib generalizations and facile categorizations. Taxonomy is a late phase in the scientific process. Therefore it would seem advisable to resist the temptation toward formulation of rigid rules. At this stage in the development of the psychology of personality a flexible— that is, a clinical—approach recommends itself.

HISTORICAL BACKGROUND AND REVIEW OF RESEARCH

Since the Sentence Completion Test (SCT) is a variation of the Word-Association method, the two techniques have been compared frequently, generally to the advantage of the SCT. It is claimed that the SCT cuts down the multiplicity of associations evoked by a single word; that it is better able to suggest contexts, feeling tones, qualities of attitude, and specific objects or areas of attention; that it allows greater individual freedom and variability of response; and that it taps a larger area of the subject's behavioral world [51, 54, 38, 60].

In 1897 Ebbinghaus used incomplete sentences to test intelligence, which he defined as the ability to combine or integrate.

One of the pioneer workers with the Sentence Completion method in the field of personality was Tendler [60, page 136], who distinguished between diagnosis of thought reactions and of emotional responsiveness. He offered the following criteria for tests in the field of emotional behavior: the use of devices that will (a) directly evoke emotional response, (b) allow for free response, and (c) avoid discrimination or choice (as in personality inventories). He presented the SCT as a method meeting these criteria under the heading of a "test for emotional insight." Insight is defined as "knowledge of the situations under which particular emotional reactions are made" [60, page 124]. The test items were intended to stimulate admiration, anger, love, happiness, hate, self-abasement, worry, compensatory make-believe, regret, boastfulness, pride, grudge, negativism, pity, shame, fear, interest, disgust, evasion, and desire.

These so-called emotional states were selected on an empirical basis. Tendler believed that the presentation of stimuli in this manner would arouse a particular emotional set and yet allow for free responses. The items used were of this type: (2) I get angry when . . . (3) I feel happy when . . . (4) I love . . . (5) I hate . . . (12) I have a grudge against. . . . In analyzing the responses of 250 college girls Tendler noted: the same stimulus evokes different responses from different individuals; individuals differ in the associative flow of responses; responses indicate fears, aversions, likes, interests, and attachment; they may have positive or negative ego-reference or social reference.

Tendler attempted to validate his test of emotional insight against scores on the Woodworth Personal Data Sheet. The first and fourth quartiles of 190 college women on the Woodworth were chosen as representing, respectively, "favorably organized" and "unfavorably organized" groups, from the emotional standpoint. The Tendler test was then scored as follows: responses given by individuals of the first quartile, or "good" group, were given a value of 1; responses given by members of the fourth quartile, or "poor" group, were given a value of 3. The final value of each response was the average of 1's and 3's it received. Results showed that while the poor and good groups did not differ significantly in intelligence, according to their Otis scores: "both the Woodworth Personal Data Blank and the Tendler Emotional Insight Test show significant differences, the latter being somewhat more discriminative" *[60]*.

Tendler's work is open to much criticism on both theoretical and experimental grounds. His definition of insight is a highly questionable one; for an individual may have knowledge of the particular situations under which certain emotional responses are made, yet lack insight because he is unaware of any relationship between these reactions and his past experience. The premise that the stimuli used in this test are adequate to arouse the wide variety of emotional responses expected is quite naïve. Finally, his method of validation is faulty. He criticized personality inventories as inadequate, yet he used one as a criterion of emotional organization. He loaded his own scores in accordance with the criterion and concluded that his method is more discriminative than the criterion itself! However faulty his assumptions and methods, Tendler does emerge with a sound conclusion when he says: "Clinically this instrument has been found to be of value as a device for eliciting attitudes, trends, and significant clues to be followed up by further questioning" *[60, page 136]*.

Lorge and Thorndike *[39]* applied considerable effort and statistical tabulation to the problem of the value of responses in the SCT as indications of personal traits. A group of thirty adults was given 240 sentences to complete with a single word. The following are examples of the items: (1) Animals are . . . (20) I dislike . . . (80) Women want . . . (121) . . . is pleasant. (160) Rich people can buy . . . Each author made up a list of traits, interests, and attitudes and scored the responses as symptomatic of these. For example, "Animals are dangerous," was scored plus 1 on Thorndike's list under "liking for security." The experiment was performed twice, three months elapsing between sessions. Thirty per cent of the 480 responses were found "significant" and were used. Split-half reliabilities were low, and validity correlations were correspondingly lower. An example of a validity criterion was a person's rating of his liking to play a musical instrument and to listen to music. The authors concluded: "We fear that the verbal replies in association and completion tests are largely unrelated to the real behavior of a person. . . . The person may be largely influenced by special symbolic and verbal habits" *[38, page 99]*. This conclusion is clearly too broad for the amount and type of investigation conducted. The method of restricting completions to a single word limited freedom and variability of response, and the methods of validation and interpretation were personal and arbitrary.

A later inquiry was made by Rohde [49], who advocated use of the SCT as a tool for clinical psychologists and other professional people who deal with youth problems and who need to become intimately acquainted with the needs, inner conflicts, fantasies, sentiments, attitudes, aspirations, and adjustment difficulties of their clients. Direct questioning tends, she maintained, to make the individual self-conscious and puts him on the defensive. Freedom of expression is limited in that the questions usually control the answers; but projective techniques avoid such resistance or control. They reveal latent needs, sentiments, attitudes, and aspirations which the subject would be unwilling or unable to recognize or to express in direct communication.

> The sentence completion device in which the subject is asked to read to himself the forepart of a sentence is essentially a projection technique utilizing free association. In unconstrained response to sentence beginnings, the subject inadvertently reveals his true self, since there is no way in which he can anticipate the significance of his answers for personality study [49, page 175].

Rohde revised Payne's list of questions [44] to be used as a projective technique for studying the personality characteristics of young people. Her criteria in selecting and constructing items were the following: (1) The range of the different stimuli must be broad enough to elicit information concerning all phases of personality. (2) The response must be controlled as little as possible by the stimulus-phrase so that the subject may have freedom of expression. (3) The total time required for the test must not exceed a period convenient for schedule of schools and institutions. In final form the Rohde-Hildreth Completions Blank consists of sixty-four items of the following kind: "My school work . . . I want to know . . . There are times . . . ," etc. It is intended for individuals approximately twelve years of age, and it can be given as either an individual or a group test. The author claims that her test reveals not only the subject's needs, inner states, traits, and press, but also his tastes, sentiments, ideology, ego structure, intellectual status, and emotional maturity.

Attempts at deception, false or cryptic answers of suspicious persons, are not less revealing than those of others who give full, free responses—because such a person always writes what to him seems a good response, thus projecting his personality regardless of his intentions [49, page 173].

The test was validated on 670 high-school pupils. Responses were interpreted according to thirty-nine personality categories based on Murray's concept of personality. Results were quantified in terms of frequency and intensity of needs and press, and were correlated with combined ratings obtained from teachers, administrators, and guidance counselors and from school records. Validity coefficients of .79 for girls and .82 for boys are claimed. Details of the methods of quantifying the above variables are not given. Rohde makes several statements about the range of stimuli, the depth to which this technique can reach, the subject's inability to mask his true personality on it, and the over-all amount of revelation that can be obtained. Some psychologists regard these claims as extravagant. Shor [54] repeated the criticisms of the word-association method noted above, and added the point that lists of stimulus words are not planned for range of content or sequence but are arranged in an arbitrary, random order. In Shor's Self-Idea-Completion Test (SIC) the stimuli are sentence beginnings that are supposed to suggest contexts, feeling tones, qualities of attitude, and specific objects or areas of attention. The fifty items "are arranged in a definite sequence to permit a carry-over or generalization of attitude from immediate to basic human interest" [54, page 280]. The author emphasizes the importance of adapting stimuli to the current situation and cultural background of the groups tested. Items like the following were used: (1) I want to know . . . (4) Army food . . . (6) Back home . . . (10) If my mother . . . Shor suggests that administration be adapted to the dynamics of each case. An actively anxious patient, for example, might release rich material by the oral method, while another patient might be able to express himself better if left alone. No formal scoring system is offered, but Shor recommends investigating areas of rejection, evidences of resistance, and other methods of evasion, noting recurrent themes and atypical associations and evaluating the level of personality projected. The SIC test, he admits, may evoke only superficial rationalizations. "Personality dynamics include more than semispontaneous verbal associations or the responses to ambiguous ink blots, but this test may provide individually crucial data, and it is felt to be a valuable addition to the array of projective methods" [*54, page 282*]. Shor's is a well-considered and truly clinical approach. He does not make a sweeping denial of the value of the sentence completion method, as Lorge and Thorndike did on the basis of inconclusive experimentation, nor does he go so far in his claims for it as Tendler and Rohde did. He evaluates it sympathetically but with regard for its limitations.

Stein [*56*] described a sentence completion test that is now used as part of the battery of tests of the Veterans Administration Mental Hygiene Clinic of the New York Regional Office. This device was originally developed as an aid in the selection of Office of Strategic Services personnel during the war. It was used to provide interviewers with data that could yield brief personality descriptions of the candidates. The test consists of two parts of fifty incomplete sentences each. Items were selected to contribute relevant information concerning at least one of ten areas considered important for personality evaluation: family, past, drives, inner states, goals, cathexes, energy, time perspective, reaction to others, and reaction of others to the subject. While efforts were made to eliminate items tending to provoke stereotyped responses, practice has shown that this attempt was not entirely successful. It is also true that responses to items are not alway pertinent to the area that is supposed to be tapped. In this test, for the first time, two different types of items are used: the more "projective" questions in which the proper name of some person or the third-personal pronoun is employed, and personal questions in which the first person is used. The two types are mixed in random order. In this way the authors of the test attempted to camouflage the aim of the test, to lead subjects to believe that it is a test of speed. At the same time they aimed to take advantage of the possibility that in talking about others individuals are more likely to reveal themselves.

It is emphasized by Stein that the validity of the personality description written by the psychologist on the basis of the responses to this test is highly dependent on his experience, insight, and knowledge of the dynamics of behavior. In analyzing the material, he says, the clinician accepts the following assumptions:

1. When an individual is put under pressure to respond with the the first idea that occurs to him, he usually offers significant material that he does not censor.
2. When faced with the problem of completing or structuring an unstructured situation, an individual's responses will be indicative of the true nature of his own reactions and sentiments.
3. In talking about others, an individual is apt to reveal himself [56].

Suggestions are offered for analysis of responses, taking into consideration the following factors: significance, frequency, and rarity; reaction time to individual sentences and to the test as a whole; erasures, omissions, and the intensity of the language used.

Symonds [58] has reported on studies using this type of test in the Office of Strategic Services assessment program. Comparisons were made between the test responses of candidates and data from Office of Strategic Services records. The latter included an interview covering the candidate's family background, education, work experience, and personality characteristics; observations of the candidate during the assessment period; and the summary and recommendations of the assessment staff. SCT responses of four individuals with high over-all ratings and high emotional-stability ratings were compared with responses of four individuals with low over-all and emotional-stability ratings. This preliminary survey showed no differentiation by the individual SCT items between superior and inferior individuals. Two contrasting groups of twenty-five individuals each were studied: those with high emotional-stability ratings and those with low stability ratings. Their SCT and Office of Strategic Services records were compared with respect to persistence, striving for success, feelings of inferiority, doubt and worry, depression and discouragement following failure, high standards, and emotional stability in stressful situations. There was no observable differentiation of these groups by the SCT. It was tentatively concluded that "the sentence completion test cannot be used to differentiate good and bad adjustment by any direct comparison of items or by psychometric methods. The sentence completion test is descriptive and not evaluative" [58, page 321].

Ten cases were then studied in detail to learn in exactly which areas there would be agreement and disagreement. Examples of divergence between the Office of Strategic Services report (R) and the Sentence Completion Test (SC) were:

1. Passive trends (SC) covered up by compensating reaction formation of dangerous and aggressive occupation and sports (R).
2. Physical symptom rejected in R was welcomed in SC as a possible escape from army duty.
3. Low ambition (R); high but shadowy ambition (SC), etc. *[58, page 326]*.

Included among the conclusions of these studies are the following statements:

> The sentence completion test gives unconscious projections in the third person of basic trends in the form of wishes, hostilities, loves, fears, and impulses. The interpretation of the sentence completions as projections is doubtful, questionable, hypothetical, conjectural, and supposititious, and cannot be the substitute for a complete analysis. According to the projective hypothesis, the sentence completions refer only to fantasies or unconscious impulses, and may or may not have counterparts in behavior and attitudes of real life. . . . Not enough is known about the dynamics of unconscious processes to use them in predicting how they will influence future behavior, but future behavior can be explained in terms of breaking through into reality of unconscious forces which the Sentence Completion Test may help to reveal" *[58, pages 327 ff.]*.

Rotter and Willerman *[51]* claimed fairly high validity for the sentence completion method as an evaluative technique. Their Incomplete Sentence Test (IST) was used as a screening device in Army Air Force convalescent hospitals. It consists of forty items, which are very loosely structured, such as: (1) I like . . . (8) The best . . . (28) Sometimes . . . (37) I . . . Responses were scored according to three categories: conflict or unhealthy responses, positive or healthy responses, and neutral responses. The conflict responses were scored from plus 1 to plus 3, the neutral responses 0, and the positive responses from minus 1 to minus 3. The average intercorrelation for seven scorers of fifty records was .89. The validity of the test was determined by correlating the psychologists' initial evaluation of the severity of each patient's disturbance with the patient's total score on the test. The evaluations were based on case-history information, health and personality inventories, admission diagnoses, a test of mental dysfunctioning, and a psychological interview. Each patient was then classified in one of the following categories: (I) psychologically fit for duty; (II) psychologically unfit for duty; (III) seriously disturbed. A triserial coefficient of .61. (SE.05) was obtained for the three evaluations versus the IST scores. When subjective estimates of degree of disturbance based on general inspection of test responses by two experienced clinical psychologists were correlated with admission diagnoses, biserial coefficients of .41 (SE.07) and .39 (SE.07) were obtained. The authors concluded that "The method shows potentiality as a means for studying attitudes in which freedom of response and reasonably objective scoring can be combined" [51, page 47].

Carter [5] combined a modification of Tendler's Emotional Insight Test with a psychogalvanometer to investigate certain affective processes. Stimuli were presented tachistoscopically, and subjects' responses were oral. The exact words used by the subject were recorded, together with changes in palmar skin conductivity and in reaction time required to complete the sentence orally. A control group consisted of twenty so-called "normal" individuals who reported no maladjustments. One experimental group consisted of twenty individuals who reported fears and worries that, in their opinion, interfered with their academic and social adjustment. A second experimental group consisted of twenty individuals who, after a psychiatric examination, were diagnosed as psychoneurotic. Responses were classified according to six categories: ego-positive, ego-negative, social-positive, social-negative, fear, aversion, and unclassified. Carter found that changes in palmar skin conductivity and reaction time were significantly greater in individuals with problems and in psychoneurotics than in normals.

Apparently what individuals said in response to the twenty stimuli does not differentiate either those with problems or the psychoneurotics from the normals. Individuals making up the three groups did not always reveal in words the specific area of their conflict [5, page 274].

One of the conclusions drawn from the study does not seem to be borne out by the data presented; namely:

A marked change in Delta R in reaction to a stimulus suggesting an emotional response, and especially when accompanied by a prolonged reaction-time, suggests not only a locus of conflict but also the intensity of the conflict [5, *page 275*].

Although it is not stated as a conclusion, it is evident from the results that while the technique could differentiate individuals with problems and psychoneurotics from normals, it could not differentiate between the first two groups.

THE SACKS SENTENCE COMPLETION TEST (SSCT)

A sentence completion test designed to obtain significant clinical material in four representative areas of adjustment was developed by Joseph M. Sacks and other psychologists of the New York Veterans Administration Mental Hygiene Service. The four areas covered by that test are family, sex, interpersonal relationships, and self-concept. It is felt that the items included in these areas present the subject with sufficient opportunities to express his attitudes so that a clinical psychologist may infer his dominant personality trends. Such information is useful in screening patients for therapy, and it offers the therapist significant clues to the content and dynamics of the patient's attitudes and feelings.

The family area includes three sets of attitudes, those toward mother, father, and family unit. Each of these is represented by four sentence completion items that stimulate the subject to express attitudes toward his parents individually and toward his family as a whole. "My mother and I . . ." "If my father would only . . ." and "My family treats me like . . ." are examples of the items designed to elicit these attitudes. It is hoped that even when the subject tends to be cautious and evasive he will reveal significant material in response to at least one of the four items.

The sex area includes attitudes toward women and toward heterosexual relationships. The eight items in this area allow the subject to express himself with regard to women as social individuals, toward marriage, and with respect to sexual relationships themselves. "I think most girls . . ." and "If I had sex relations . . ." are typical items in this area.

The area of interpersonal relationships includes attitudes toward friends and acquaintances, colleagues at work or school, superiors at work or school, and people supervised. The sixteen items in this area afford an opportunity for the subject to express his feelings toward others outside the home and his idea of others' feeling toward him. "When I'm not around, my friends. . ." "When I see the boss coming . . ." "The people who work for me . . ." and "At work I get along best with . . ." are examples of the items in this area.

Self-concept involves fears, guilt feelings, goals, and attitudes toward one's own abilities, past, and future. The attitudes expressed in this area give the psychologist a picture of the subject's concept of himself as he is, as he was, as he hopes to be, and as he thinks he actually will be. Among the twenty-four items in this area are "I wish I could lose the fear of . . . ," "My greatest mistake was . . . ," "I believe I have the ability to . . . ," "When I was a child . . . ," "Some day I . . . " and "What I want most out of life . . ."

CONSTRUCTION OF THE TEST

The complete test consists of sixty items, of which four represent each of the fifteen attitudes enumerated above. The test was constructed in the following manner: Twenty clinical psychologists were asked to submit three sentence completion items, purporting to elicit significant attitudes in each of these categories. To these were added items culled from the literature on sentence completions. In this way 280 items were obtained. They ranged in number from fourteen to twenty-eight items per category. For example, nineteen items were listed for attitude toward mother, twenty-two items for attitude toward father, and so on. The twenty psychologists were then requested to select in each category the four items they considered best suited to elicit significant attitudes in that category. The items chosen most frequently became the final test items.

RELIABILITY AND VALIDITY OF THE TEST

Three psychologists rated the degree of disturbance of one hundred subjects in each of the fifteen categories on the basis of the subjects' sentence completion responses. The psychiatrists who treated these subjects made independent ratings of their degree of disturbance in each of the fifteen categories, based on their clinical impressions of the subjects. Reliability of the psychologists' judgments of degree of disturbance is indicated by agreement of two out of three psychologists on 92 per cent of 1,500 ratings. The psychiatrists had no knowledge of the SSCT responses. When the ratings of the psychologists were correlated with those of the psychiatrists, contingency coefficients of .48 to .57 were found, with standard errors of .02 and .03. These figures indicate that the ratings of the psychologists had a significant, positive relationship with those of the psychiatrists. For fifty subjects psychologists wrote interpretative summaries of the fifteen attitudes, based upon the subjects' responses to the four items included under each attitude. These interpretative summaries were submitted to the psychiatrists, who rated them with respect to their agreement with clinical findings. Some 77 per cent of the statements were rated in close agreement or partial agreement with clinical findings. These results of the SSCT compare favorably with those found in validation studies of such other methods of personality study as the Rorschach Test and the TAT *[23, 40, 52]*.

Experience with the test thus developed has demonstrated the need for minor revisions in the wording of some items to allow greater freedom of response, and for the substitution of new items for those which tended to elicit stereotypes and clichés. These revisions are now in process.

ADMINISTRATION OF THE TEST

The SSCT can be administered individually or to groups, and requires from twenty to forty minutes. The subject is asked to read the following instructions and to ask any questions he may have about them.

Instructions: "Below are sixty partly completed sentences. Read each one and finish it by writing the first thing that comes to your mind. Work as quickly as you can. If you cannot complete an item, circle the number and return to it later."

Subjects frequently ask: "Should I take time to think of a sensible answer?" It is emphasized that responses should consist of the first spontaneous reaction to each stimulus item, and that the subject should not stop to think of a logical completion. Another common question is: "Must I write only one word?" He is told that either a single word or a group of words is acceptable, and that it is the subject's spontaneous *thought* that is desired. Subjects sometimes ask the examiner to look at a response and tell them if it is all right. They should be assured that it is a good response if it represents a spontaneous reaction to the stimulus item. Occasionally an examiner is asked the meaning of words in the sentence beginnings. It is permissible to say, for example, that "seldom" (in item 1) means "hardly ever." But if the subject asks the examiner to explain the meaning of an entire item he should be told to respond in terms of the item's meaning to him.

When the subject is ready to respond to the first item, the beginning time should be noted in the upper right-hand corner of the page. When he turns the paper in, the finishing time should be marked.

'Whenever possible, an inquiry should be conducted. The examiner selects responses that appear to be significant or cryptic and asks the subject to "tell me a little more about this." The value of this procedure is demonstrated by the following incident: One of the responses of a depressed, unproductive patient was: "My most vivid childhood memory *is an accident.*" When he was asked to tell more about this, he related an event that occurred during his fifth year. While playing with another child in the kitchen he upset a pot of hot water, which scalded his playmate and resulted in the latter's death. He was later able to discuss this incident with his therapist.

While the standard method of administration requires that the subject should read the stimulus and respond to it in writing, with some anxious patients it is fruitful to administer the items orally and to record the patient's oral responses. This process provides an opportunity for ventilation. These patients often use the SSCT items as a stimulus to abreact, and they tell you afterward that they "feel much better." The oral method also provides an opportunity to note specific items on which the subject blocks by observing his reaction time, flushing, facial expression, changes in tone or volume of voice, and general behavior.

Interpretation and Scoring.—A Rating Sheet has been devised for the SSCT which brings together, under each attitude, the four stimulus items and the subject's responses to them. For example:

ATTITUDE TOWARD FATHER
Item
   1. I feel that my father seldom *works*.
   16. If my father would only *do better*.
   31. I wish my father *was dead*.
   46. I feel that my father is *no good*.

The italicized words are the subject's responses. These four responses are considered together and an Interpretative Summary is made that crystallizes the clinician's impression of the subject's attitude in this area. In this case the summary stated: "Extreme hostility and contempt with overt death wishes."

A rating is then made of the subject's degree of disturbance in this area, according to the following scale:

   2. Severely disturbed. Appears to require therapeutic aid in handling emotional conflicts in this area.
   1. Mildly disturbed. Has emotional conflicts in this area, but appears able to handle them without therapeutic aid.
   0. No significant disturbance noted in this area.
   X. Unknown. Insufficient evidence.

This method of rating four responses together differs from the procedures used by Tendler, *[60]*, Rotter and Willerman *[51]* and others who have employed the sentence completion technique. The traditional method has been to rate individual responses and to arrive at a final rating of adjustment by addition of the individual ratings. The author of the SSCT feels that it is more desirable simply to point out areas of disturbance and to determine these through a constellation of responses. The validity of the rating is dependent, of course, upon the clinical background and acumen of the examiner as well as upon the material produced by the subject. For those who have little experience with this method, an example of interpretations and ratings is presented.

Following the summaries and ratings of the individual attitudes, an outline is presented for a General Summary of the SSCT findings. This includes the following:

   1. A statement of those areas in which the subject shows the most disturbed attitudes. This may provide significant clues for the therapist.

   2. A description of the interrelationships between attitudes with respect to content. This often illuminates dynamic factors

in a case. For example, subject No. 1 described his mother as "too nervous" and "petty." He thinks that most mothers "have too much of a liking for their children and spoil them." He feels that his family is "all right," but they treat him like a "little boy." He is extremely hostile to women whom he considers "untrustworthy and untruthful." He is cautious about marriage—"It's good if everything is worked out beforehand." He considers his father a good man, but wishes he would "stop being so stubborn." He is somewhat contemptuous of superiors. He does not like persons who are petty. His most vivid childhood memory "is of wrongs done me." He is afraid of himself, and when the odds are against him, he quits. Yet he believes he has the ability to "do anything." His attitude toward the future is superficial and somewhat unrealistically optimistic. Some day he expects "to make a million."

EXAMPLES OF SSCT DATA TO BE CORRELATED WITH
THOSE OBTAINED FROM OTHER PROJECTIVE TECHNIQUES

The degree of structuring of a projective stimulus field usually affects the significance of the response in terms of personality description. Thus the Rorschach ink blots may bring out modes and patterns of reaction which tell us a great deal about the subject's basic personality structure. TAT pictures may elicit material related to the dynamics of the subject's problems. The SSCT may reflect conscious, preconscious, or unconscious thinking and feeling. Consideration of the material obtained from various techniques gives us a more rounded picture of the personality than we can obtain from any one technique.

For example, one patient revealed considerable hostility in his Rorschach responses. The two animals in Card VIII were about to "devour a prey." The top detail of Card X reminded him of a "windpipe to be strangled." His TAT stories were replete with themes of violence, rape, and murder. But in the SSCT he made responses reflecting an exaggerated altruism and idealism: "If people work for me *I will pay them more than anyone.*" "My secret ambition in life *is to reform society so that everyone will be happy.*" We may, then, expect that this subject will adjust to his violently aggressive impulses by means of the mechanism of reaction formation.

In the same way inferences about personality structure can be made on the basis of the SSCT, and these may be collated with conclusions drawn from other techniques.

1. Does the individual respond primarily to impulses from within or to stimuli from the environment? Subject No. 6 is afraid of "being outstanding and rejected." He wishes he could lose the fear of "letting myself go." His fears sometimes force him to "draw into my shell and even throw up." These are the responses of an individual who responds primarily to his inner impulses. In contrast with these are the responses of subject No. 15 who is afraid of "almost nothing. However, loud noises make me shy." He wished he could lose the fear of "jumping when loud noises are made."

2. Are his emotional reactions impulsive or well controlled under stress? Subject No. 6 said: "When the odds are against me, *I try to figure my best chances*" (controlled). Subject No. 25 responded to the same item: "I become frightened" (probably impulsive).

3. Is his thinking predominantly mature, showing adequate consideration for his responsibilities and the interests and needs of others, or is it immature and egocentric? Subject No. 5 expresses the following goals: "I always wanted to *sing*." "I could be perfectly happy if *I do as I please*." Subject No. 43 gave as his secret ambition in life "to conduct an orchestra, travel and live abroad, become successful in our culture and society as having helped improve the world." The latter is clearly the more mature outlook.

4. Is his thinking realistic or autistic and fantastic? Attitudes toward the future and toward his own abilities, goals, fears, and guilt feelings provide answers to this question; for example, ambition to be a movie star; feeling he has the ability to play ball with the Yankees; desire to "create something fantastic" and to "ride to the stars"; "I always wanted to *kill someone*"; "My idea of a perfect woman *is a tigress*"; "I know it is silly, but I am afraid of *you*"; "My fears sometimes force me to *commit suicide*"; "My greatest mistake was *being born*," are examples of unrealistic responses given by various subjects.

Other aspects of the SSCT responses can be used to complement TAT findings with regard to a subject's needs and the environmental pressures to which he is responding. Attitudes toward heterosexual relationships and his own abilities, fears, and goals often illuminate these factors. Subject No. 15 stated: "If I had sex relations, *I'd take precautionary measures before and after the acts*," while the response of subject No. 16 to the same item was: "I'd want them to be the result of a fine relationship." Needs for health, peace of mind, and economic security are frequently expressed. Fear of other persons and of difficult situations are commonly found in the responses.

The SSCT form, together with the Rating Sheet and the outline of the General Summary, are reproduced below.

Sacks Sentence Completion Test (SSCT)

Time Began:——
Time Finished:——

NAME: SEX: AGE: DATE:

INSTRUCTIONS: Below are sixty partly completed sentences. Read each one and finish it by writing the first thing that comes to your mind. Work as quickly as you can. If you cannot complete an item, circle the number and return to it later.

1. I feel that my father seldom
2. When the odds are against me
3. I always wanted to
4. If I were in charge
5. To me the future looks
6. The men over me
7. I know it is silly but I am afraid of
8. I feel that a real friend
9. When I was a child
10. My idea of a perfect woman
11. When I see a man and a woman together
12. Compared with most families, mine
13. At work, I get along best with
14. My mother
15. I would do anything to forget the time I
16. If my father would only
17. I believe that I have the ability to
18. I could be perfectly happy if
19. If people work for me

Sacks Sentence Completion Test (Cont.)

20. I look forward to
21. In school, my teachers
22. Most of my friends don't know that I am afraid of
23. I don't like people who
24. Before the war, I
25. I think most girls
26. My feeling about married life is
27. My family treats me like
28. Those I work with are
29. My mother and I
30. My greatest mistake was
31. I wish my father
32. My greatest weakness is
33. My secret ambition in life
34. The people who work for me
35. Some day I
36. When I see the boss coming
37. I wish I could lose the fear of
38. The people I like best
39. If I were young again
40. I believe most women
41. If I had sex relations
42. Most families I know
43. I like working with people who
44. I think that most mothers
45. When I was younger, I felt guilty about
46. I feel that my father is
47. When luck turns against me
48. In giving orders to others I
49. What I want most out of life
50. When I am older
51. People whom I consider my superiors
52. My fears sometimes force me to
53. When I'm not around, my friends
54. My most vivid childhood memory
55. What I like least about women
56. My sex life
57. When I was a child, my family
58. People who work with me usually
59. I like my mother but
60. The worst thing I ever did

SSCT Rating Sheet

SUBJECT: SEX: DATE: TIME:

AGE:

INSTRUCTIONS: On the basis of your clinical judgment, taking into account such factors as inappropriate responses, sysphoric references, and manifestations of conflict, rate the SSCT responses of the subject in the fifteen categories listed below, according to the following scale:

2—Severely disturbed. Appears to require therapeutic aid in handling emotional conflicts in this area.

1—Mildly disturbed. Has emotional conflicts in this area, but appears able to handle them without therapeutic aid.

0—No significant disturbance noted in this area.

X—Unknown. Insufficient evidence.

NOTE: The SSCT stimulus is typed in lower-case letters, the subject's response in capitals. When the number of an item is circled, it means that the subject did not complete it at first but returned to it later.

I. ATTITUDE TOWARD MOTHER. *Rating:*
   14. My mother
   29. My mother and I
   44. I think that most mothers
   59. I like my mother but
INTERPRETATIVE SUMMARY:

II. ATTITUDE TOWARD FATHER. *Rating:*
    1. I feel that my father seldom
   16. If my father would only
   31. I wish my father
   46. I feel that my father is
INTERPRETATIVE SUMMARY:

III. ATTITUDE TOWARD FAMILY UNIT. *Rating:*
   12. Compared with most families, mine
   27. My family treats me like
   42. Most families I know
   57. When I was a child, my family
INTERPRETATIVE SUMMARY:

SSCT Rating Sheet (Cont.)

IV. ATTITUDE TOWARD WOMEN. *Rating:*
10. My idea of a perfect woman
25. I think most girls
40. I believe most women
55. What I like least about women
INTERPRETATIVE SUMMARY:

V. ATTITUDE TOWARD HETEROSEXUAL RELATIONSHIPS. *Rating:*
11. When I see a man and a woman together
26. My feeling about married life is
41. If I had sex relations
56. My sex life
INTERPRETATIVE SUMMARY:

VI. ATTITUDE TOWARD FRIENDS AND ACQUAINTANCES. *Rating:*
8. I feel that a real friend
23. I don't like people who
38. The people I like best
53. When I'm not around, my friends
INTERPRETATIVE SUMMARY:

VII. ATTITUDE TOWARD SUPERIORS AT WORK OR SCHOOL. *Rating:*
6. The men over me
21. In school, my teachers
36. When I see the boss coming
51. People whom I consider my superiors
INTERPRETATIVE SUMMARY:

VIII. ATTITUDE TOWARD PEOPLE SUPERVISED. *Rating:*
4. If I were in charge
19. If people work for me
34. The people who work for me
48. In giving orders to others, I
INTERPRETATIVE SUMMARY:

SSCT *Rating Sheet* (*Cont.*)

IX. ATTITUDE TOWARD COLLEAGUES AT WORK OR SCHOOL. *Rating:*
13. At work I get along best with
28. Those I work with are
43. I like working with people who
58. People who work with me usually
INTERPRETATIVE SUMMARY:

X. FEARS. *Rating:*
7. I know it is silly but I am afraid of
22. Most of my friends don't know that I am afraid of
37. I wish I could lose the fear of
52. My fears sometimes force me to
INTERPRETATIVE SUMMARY:

XI. GUILT FEELINGS. *Rating:*
15. I would do anything to forget the time I
30. My greatest mistake was
45. When I was younger, I felt guilty about
60. The worst thing I ever did
INTERPRETATIVE SUMMARY:

XII. ATTITUDE TOWARD OWN ABILITIES. *Rating:*
2. When the odds are against me
17. I believe that I have the ability to
32. My greatest weakness is
47. When luck turns against me
INTERPRETATIVE SUMMARY:

XIII. ATTITUDE TOWARD PAST. *Rating:*
9. When I was a child
24. Before the war, I
39. If I were young again
54. My most vivid childhood memory
INTERPRETATIVE SUMMARY:

SSCT Rating Sheet (Concluded)

XIV. ATTITUDE TOWARD FUTURE. *Rating:*

  5. To me the future looks
 20. I look forward to
 35. Some day I
 50. When I am older

INTERPRETATIVE SUMMARY:

XV. GOALS. *Rating:*

  3. I always wanted to
 18. I could be perfectly happy if
 33. My secret ambition in life
 49. What I want most out of life

INTERPRETATIVE SUMMARY:

General Summary

1. Principal areas of conflict and disturbance

2. Interrelationships among the attitudes

3. Personality structure

  A. Extent to which subject responds to inner impulses and to outer stimuli

  B. Emotional adjustment

  C. Maturity

  D. Reality level

  E. Manner in which conflicts are expressed

Scoring and Summarizing Responses.—Examples of the way in which responses are rated for degree of disturbance and typical summaries of responses are given below. In each case the same rating was made by three psychologists who worked independently.

Examples of SSCT Scoring

I. ATTITUDE TOWARD MOTHER

Case No. 2   Rating: 2

Item

14. My mother *is a nagging woman.*
29. My mother and I *are quite different from each other.*
44. Most mothers *are too dependent on their children.*
59. I like my mother, but *I don't like my mother.*

Interpretative Summary: Completely rejects and deprecates mother, whom he considers overdemanding.

Case No. 23   Rating: 1

Item

14. My mother *is thrifty.*
29. My mother and I *are good friends with different opinions.*
44. I think that most mothers *allow their love to ruin their reason.*
59. I like my mother *but there is no but.*

Interpretative Summary: Sees mother's faults but accepts them and tolerates their differences.

Case No. 56   Rating: 0

Item

14. My mother *is a wonderful woman.*
29. My mother and I *are great pals.*
44. I think that most mothers *are swell.*
59. I like my mother but *my father is O.K.*

Interpretative Summary: Expresses only positive feelings toward mother.

II. ATTITUDE TOWARD FATHER

Case No. 52   Rating: 2

Item

1. I feel that my father seldom *works.*
16. If my father would only *do better.*
31. I wish my father *was dead.*
46. I feel that my father is *no good.*

Interpretative Summary: Extreme hostility and contempt with overt death wishes.

Case No. 71   Rating: 1

Item

1. I feel that my father seldom *gets together with me as father and son.*
16. If my father would only *listen to things.*
31. I wish my father (no response)
46. I feel that my father is *swell.*

Interpretative Summary: Admires father but wishes their relationship were closer.

Case No. 14   Rating: 0

Item

1. I feel that my father seldom *lacks humor.*
16. If my father would only *take a vacation.*
31. I wish my father *would stay as he is.*
46. I feel that my father *is a very fine person.*

Interpretative Summary: Expresses complete satisfaction with father's personality.

III.   ATTITUDE TOWARD FAMILY UNIT

Case No. 12   Rating: 2

Item

12. Compared with most families, mine *was not together much.*
27. My family treats me like *an outsider, but don't seem to.*
42. Most families I know *have a misery of some sort.*
57. When I was a child, my family *was all messed up and unsettled.*

Interpretative Summary: Feels rejected by family, which has always lacked solidarity and which has constantly contended with difficulties.

Case No. 10   Rating: 1

Item

12. Compared with most families, mine *is all right.*
27. My family treats me like *a little boy.*
42. Most families I know *are like mine.*
57. When I was a child, my family *treated me good.*

Interpretative Summary: Aware that family does not recognize him as a mature person, but feels no difficulty in identifying with them.

Case No. 16   Rating: 0

Item

12. Compared with most families, mine is *exceedingly fine.*
27. My family treats me like *a close friend.*
42. Most families I know *are fine people.*
57. When I was a child, my family *moved many times.*

Interpretative Summary: Instability of family domicile has had little effect on his favorable feeling toward them.

IV. ATTITUDE TOWARD WOMEN

Case No. 1   Rating: 2

Item

10. My idea of a perfect woman, *no such thing.*
25. I think most girls *are untrustworthy.*
40. I believe most women *are untruthful.*
55. What I like least about women *is that they are the opposite sex.*

Interpretative Summary: Extremely suspicious. Possible homosexual tendency.

Case No. 26   Rating: 1

Item

10. My idea of a perfect woman *is an understanding and beautiful one.*
25. I think most girls *are common.*
40. I believe most women *are good.*
55. What I like least about women *is their make-up.*

Interpretative Summary: High ideals but ambivalent feelings.

Case No. 31   Rating: 0

Item

10. My idea of a perfect woman *is ideal.*
25. I think most girls *are nice.*
40. I believe most women *are attractive.*
55. What I like least about women *is long skirts.*

Interpretative Summary: Only criticism is minor and superficial.

V. ATTITUDE TOWARD HETEROSEXUAL RELATIONSHIPS

Case No. 17   Rating: 2

Item

11. When I see a man and woman together *I just look and walk by.*
26. My feeling about married life is *something I use to think of.*
41. If I had sex relations *I wouldn't care.*
56. My sex life *is nothing to brag about.*

Interpretative Summary: Appears to have given up hope of achieving a good sexual adjustment.

Case No. 25   Rating: 1

Item

11. When I see a man and a woman together *I wonder about how they get along.*
26. My feeling about married life *is that it can be pleasant if both parties meet each other halfway.*
41. If I had sex relations *I'd be more contented.*
56. My sex life *hasn't been too interesting.*

Interpretative Summary: Desires sexual experience but has reservations about his ability to maintain a marital relationship.

Case No. 70   Rating: 0

Item

11. When I see a man and a woman together *I am content.*
26. My feeling about married life *is that it is a wonderful experience.*
41. If I had sex relations *but I do.*
56. My sex life *is happy.*

Interpretative Summary: Indicates satisfaction in this area.

VI. ATTITUDE TOWARD FRIENDS AND ACQUAINTANCES

Case No. 83   Rating: 2

Item

8. I feel that a real friend *tries to help you out.*
23. I don't like people who *stare at me.*
38. The people I like best *are few.*
53. When I'm not around, my friends, *I don't believe too much in friends.*

Interpretative Summary: Suspicious and apparently seclusive.

Case No. 22　　Rating: 1

Item

8. I feel that a real friend *is one who is sincere.*
23. I don't like people who *are false.*
38. The people I like best *are those who like me.*
53. When I'm not around, my friends *sometimes talk about me.*

Interpretative Summary: Seems to wait for approval of others before committing himself emotionally.

Case No. 76　　Rating: 0

Item

8. I feel that a real friend *would help me.*
23. I don't like people who *are loud.*
38. The people I like best *are close to me.*
53. When I'm not around, my friends *look for me.*

Interpretative Summary: Expresses mutual good feeling between friends and self.

VII.　ATTITUDE TOWARD SUPERIORS AT WORK OR SCHOOL

Case No. 48　　Rating: 2

Item

6. The men over me *are sometimes unfair.*
21. In school, my teachers *are too bossy.*
36. When I see the boss coming *I duck.*
51. People whom I consider my superiors *I fear.*

Interpretative Summary: Resents and fears authority.

Case No. 45　　Rating: 1

Item

6. The men over me *are okay.*
21. In school, my teachers *were mostly okay.*
36. When I see the boss coming *I get a bit tense.*
51. People whom I consider my superiors *I treat as such.*

Interpretative Summary: Mild difficulty in accepting authority.

Case No. 98　　Rating: 0

6. The men over me *like me.*
21. In school, my teachers *were very nice.*
36. When I see the boss coming *I continue as usual.*
51. People whom I consider my superiors *are my parents.*

Interpretative Summary: Expresses no conflict with authority-figures. Feels accepted by them.

VIII. ATTITUDE TOWARD PEOPLE SUPERVISED

Case. No. 55   Rating: 2

Item

4. If I were in charge *I'd be stricter.*
19. If people work for me *I'd be a poor boss.*
34. The people who work for me *will be sorry.*
48. In giving orders to others, I (no response)

Interpretative Summary: Feels he would be unable to control his hostility in supervising others.

Case No. 22   Rating: 1

Item

4. If I were in charge *I'd see that the best were done.*
19. If people work for me *I would treat them well.*
34. The people who work for me *are satisfied.*
48. In giving orders to others, I *am sometimes uneasy.*

Interpretative Summary: Feels capable of doing good supervisory job but has some misgivings about assuming an authoritarian position.

Case No. 79   Rating: 0

Item

4. If I were in charge *I would do my best.*
19. If people work for me *I would be nice to them.*
34. The people who work for me *think I am all right.*
48. In giving orders to others, I *am okay.*

Interpretative Summary: Feels comfortable and well accepted by subordinates.

IX. ATTITUDE TOWARD COLLEAGUES AT WORK OR SCHOOL

Case No. 9   Rating: 2

Item

13. At work I get along best with *nobody.*
28. Those I work with are *bad.*
43. I like working with people who *are friendly.*
58. People who work with me usually *dislike me.*

Interpretative Summary: Feels rejected by colleagues and condemns them.

Case No. 39   Rating: (1)

Item

13. At work I get along best with *my co-workers.*
28. Those I work with are *very helpful.*
43. I like working with people who *are happy.*
58. People who work with me usually *think me rather incompetent.*

Interpretative Summary: Has some difficulty with his work and depends on his colleagues for help. Has confidence in them.

Case No. 2   Rating: 0

Item

13. At work I get along best with *most everyone.*
28. Those I work with are *mostly pleasant people.*
43. I like working with people who *are pleasant.*
58. People who work with me usually *like me.*

Interpretative Summary: Expresses mutual good feeling.

X. FEARS

Case No. 40   Rating: 2

Item

7. I know it is silly but I am afraid of *sleep.*
22. Most of my friends don't know that I am afraid of *height.*
37. I wish I could lose the fear of *sleep.*
52. My fears sometimes force me to *worry and I wonder what I can do to overcome them.*

Interpretative Summary: Disturbed by apparent fears of losing identity or consciousness, and possibly control of his impulses.

Case No. 68   Rating: 1

Item

7. I know it is silly but I am afraid of *some people.*
22. Most of my friends don't know that I am afraid of *(no response)*
37. I wish I could lose the fear of *talking to a group.*
52. My fears sometimes force me to *retreat.*

Interpretative Summary: Fear of self-assertion, which is fairly common and not pervasive.

Case No. 84   Rating: 0

Item

7. I know it is silly but I am afraid of *nothing*.
22. Most of my friends don't know that I am afraid of *no one*.
37. I wish I could lose the fear of *can't think of any*.
52. My fears sometimes force me to *(don't have any.)*

Interpretative Summary: Expresses lack of overt fear.

XI. GUILT FEELINGS

Case No. 74   Rating: 2

Item

15. I would do anything to forget the time I *did certain uncouth things*.
30. My greatest mistake was *retreat and surrender*.
45. When I was younger, I felt guilty about *masturbation*.
60. The worst thing I ever did *was to lose faith in God*.

Interpretative Summary: Concerned with spiritual failings and physical desires.

Case No. 13   Rating: 1

Item

15. I would do anything to forget the time I *had troubles as a kid*.
30. My greatest mistake was *running away from troubles*.
45. When I was younger, I felt guilty about *sex desires*.
60. The worst thing I ever did was *joining the navy*.

Interpretative Summary: Has regrets about the past and seems mildly disturbed about his failure to contend with troubles.

Case No. 72   Rating: 0

Item

15. I would do anything to forget the time I *don't know*.
30. My greatest mistake was *leaving the army, I think*.
45. When I was younger, I felt guilty about *nothing*.
60. The worst thing I ever did was *to learn to think too hard*.

Interpretative Summary: Does not seem to be aware of any guilt feeling.

XII. ATTITUDE TOWARD OWN ABILITIES

Case No. 89   Rating: 2

Item

2. When the odds are against me *it's bad.*
17. I believe that I have the ability *to do nothing now.*
32. My greatest weakness is *disease.*
47. When luck turns against me *I feel sad.*

Interpretative Summary: Feels completely incompetent and hopeless.

Case No. 19   Rating: 1

Item

2. When the odds are against me *I keep on going.*
17. I believe that I have the ability to *teach.*
32. My greatest weakness is *fear.*
47. When luck turns against me *I get disgusted.*

Interpretative Summary: Feels he has specific ability and persistence, but tends to fear difficulties.

Case No. 98   Rating: 0

Item

2. When the odds are against me *I work harder.*
17. I believe that I have the ability to *overcome things against me.*
32. My greatest weakness is *making loans.*
47. When luck turns against me *I try harder.*

Interpretative Summary: Confident of his ability to overcome obstacles. Inspired by them to greater efforts.

XIII. ATTITUDE TOWARD PAST

Case No. 33   Rating: 2

Item

9. When I was a child *I was left to think for myself.*
24. Before the war *I was in the navy.*
39. If I were young again, *I would like my mother to be alive.*
54. My most vivid childhood memory *was the feeling of being no one.*

Interpretative Summary: Keenly felt lack of mother, rejected, emotionally isolated.

Case No. 11   Rating: 1

Item

9. When I was a child *I thought much.*
24. Before the war *I went to school.*
39. If I were young again *I'd do the same as I have done.*
54. My most vivid childhood memory *is a beating from my father.*

Interpretative Summary: Has some unpleasant memories, but does not seem to have been unduly traumatized.

Case No. 82   Rating: 0

Item

9. When I was a child *everything was swell.*
24. Before the war *I got along swell.*
39. If I were young again *I would work hard.*
54. My most vivid childhood memory is *graduating school.*

Interpretative Summary: Feels he was well adjusted. Positive feeling-tone. Memory of accomplishment.

XIV. ATTITUDE TOWARD FUTURE

Case No. 33   Rating: 2

Item

5. To me the future looks *black.*
20. I look forward to *cure.*
35. Someday I *shall be on the horse.*
50. When I am older *I shall be a bigger fool.*

Interpretative Summary: Pessimistic. No hope in his own resources for happiness or success.

Case No. 48   Rating: 1

Item

5. To me the future looks *uncertain.*
20. I look forward to *completing school.*
35. Someday I *hope to do much better.*
50. When I am older *I hope to have a comfortable home.*

Interpretative Summary: Unsure of himself, but generally optimistic.

Case No. 64   Rating: 0

Item

5. To me the future looks *good.*
20. I look forward to *work.*
35. Someday I'll *be in the money.*
50. When I am older *I'll do better.*

Interpret. Summary: Seems confident of achieving his materialistic goals.

XV. GOALS

Case No. 9   Rating: 2

Item

3. I always wanted to *kill someone.*
18. I could be perfectly happy if *I were alone.*
33. My secret ambition in life *is great.*
49. What I want most out of life *is everything.*

Interpretative Summary: Direct expression of hostility. Rejection of society. Extravagant, unrealistic.

Case No. 19   Rating: 1

Item

3. I always wanted to *be an artist.*
18. I could be perfectly happy if *I had wealth.*
33. My secret ambition in life is *to be rich.*
49. What I want most out of life is *happiness.*

Interpretative Summary: Seems to identify happiness with material success.

Case No. 79   Rating: 0

Item

3. I always wanted to *be happy.*
18. I could be perfectly happy if *I make enough money to support my family proper.*
33. My secret ambition in life is *to get somewhere in life.*
49. What I want most out of life is *good health.*

Interpretative Summary: Desires material things for family as well as self. Sees importance of health for happiness.

Illustrative Case.—The following responses, interpretative summary, and independent clinical impressions of the psychiatrist who treated the subject were obtained during the course of an experimental study of the SSCT by Sacks.

Subject No. 6   *Male*   *Age 19*   *Diagnosis: Psychoneurosis, mixed, severe*

I. ATTITUDE TOWARD MOTHER. *Rating: 2*

14. My mother *has been a problem to me.*
29. My mother and I *are closely tied together.*
44. I think that most mothers *love their children.*
59. I like my mother but *she has been a big problem to me.*

Interpretative Summary: Greatly concerned about emotional ties between mother and self and the problems involved in this relationship. (Clinical Impression: Ambivalent dependency with incestuous wishes and hostility.)

II. ATTITUDE TOWARD FATHER.   *Rating: 2*

    1. I feel that my father seldom *has shown affection towards me.*
16. If my father would only *act like a father.*
31. I wish my father *were more of a man.*
46. I feel that my father is *not much of a man.*

Interpretative Summary: Shows need of relationship with an adequate father-image. Feels that his own father fails to fulfill this role. (Clinical Impression: Father not a strong person. Can't identify with him.)

III. ATTITUDE TOWARD FAMILY UNIT.   *Rating: 2*

12. Compared with most families, mine *is more strict and European.*
27. My family treats me like *an intelligent person.*
42. Most families I know *are happy.*
47. When I was a child my family *didn't pay much attention to me.*

Interpretative Summary: Feels he was rejected by family in childhood, but that he is respected by them now. Feels he has been handicapped by parents' rigid attitudes and old-world ways. (Clinical Impression: Compulsive loyalty based on dependency.)

IV. ATTITUDE TOWARD WOMEN.   *Rating: 0*

10. My idea of a perfect woman *is one who is beautiful and smart.*
25. I think most girls *are looking for husbands.*
40. I believe most women *have good qualities.*
55. What I like least about women (no response)

Interpretative Summary: Favorable but timid. (Clinical Impression: Extreme libidinous impulses, which he fears.)

V. ATTITUDE TOWARD HETEROSEXUAL RELATIONSHIPS.   *Rating: 2*

11. When I see a man and a woman together *I envy them.*
26. My feeling about married life is *that it is swell.*
41. If I had sex relations *I'm not certain as to how I'll react.*
56. My sex life *has created feelings of guilt for me.*

Interpretative Summary: Lacks confidence in his sexual prowess or ability to enjoy relationship. Laden with guilt feelings. (Clinical Impression: Severe superego. Rigid upbringing.)

VI. ATTITUDE TOWARD FRIENDS AND ACQUAINTANCES. *Rating: 1*

    8. I feel that a real friend *would stick by me.*

    23. I don't like people who *are high and mighty.*

    38. The people I like best *are those who like me.*

    53. When I'm not around, my friends *talk about me.*

Interpretative Summary: Dependent and passive.
(Clinical Impression: Socializes well. Well liked.)

VII. ATTITUDE TOWARD SUPERIORS AT WORK OR SCHOOL. *Rating: 0*

    6. The men over me *are responsible men.*

    21. In school, my teachers *liked me.*

    36. When I see the boss coming *I continue with what I am doing.*

    51. People whom I consider my superiors *should be smarter than I.*

Interpretative Summary: Respects them and feels accepted by them.
(Clinical Impression: Dependency well controlled.)

VIII. ATTITUDE TOWARD PEOPLE SUPERVISED. *Rating: 2*

    4. If I were in charge *I would do my best to be a good leader.*

    19. If people work for me *I would let them off too easy.*

    34. The people who work for me *dislike me.*

    48. In giving orders to others, I *feel they will dislike me.*

Interpretative Summary: Fears he will not be able to handle hostility aroused by authority.
(Clinical Impression: Unknown.)

IX. ATTITUDE TOWARD COLLEAGUES AT WORK OR SCHOOL. *Rating: 0*

    13. At work I get along best with *everyone.*

    28. Those I work with are *good people.*

    43. I like working with people who *work with you and do their share.*

    58. People who work with me usually *like me.*

Interpretative Summary: Feels they are co-operative and well-disposed toward him.
(Clinical Impression: Co-operative, considerate.)

X. FEARS. *Rating: 2*

    7. I know it is silly but I am afraid of *being outstanding and rejected.*

    22. Most of my friends don't know that I am afraid of *being rejected and outstanding.*

37. I wish I could lose the fear of *letting myself go.*
52. My fears sometimes force me to *draw into my shell and even throw up.*

Interpretative Summary: Fear that any prominence on his part, rejection by others, causes him to withdraw or to take refuge in digestive symptoms.
(Clinical Impression: Libidinous impulses, hostility, seduction.)

XI. GUILT. *Rating: 2*

15. I would do anything to forget the time I *became hysterical.*
30. My greatest mistake was
45. When I was younger, I felt guilty about *all my sex feelings.*
60. The worst thing I ever did *was to keep myself from advancing to my fullest capacity.*

Interpretative Summary: Guilt involved in sex feelings has prevented development of his personality potentialities.
(Clinical Impression: Masturbation, libidinous feelings toward girls, mother, and sister.)

XII. ATTITUDE TOWARD OWN ABILITIES. *Rating: 1*

2. When the odds are against me *I get blue.*
17. I believe that I have the ability to *do anything I choose to do.*
32. My greatest weakness is *fear.*
47. When luck turns against me *I wait for it to change.*

Interpretative Summary: Feels he has high potentialities but is depressed when confronted by obstacles. Passive and frayed in dealing with them.
(Clinical Impression: Overambitious in relation to abilities. Would like to be more brilliant than he is.)

XIII. ATTITUDE TOWARD PAST. *Rating: 1*

9. When I was a child *I received little attention.*
24. Before the war, I *was happy.*
39. If I were young again *I'd probably get the same way as I have.*
54. My most vivid childhood memory *is my experience with a girl.*

Interpretative Summary: Felt rejected. Impressed by childhood sexual experience.
(Clinical Impression: Preoccupied with masturbation and with his illness.)

XIV. ATTITUDE TOWARD FUTURE. *Rating: o*

  5. To me the future looks *brighter.*
 20. I look forward to *when I'm well.*
 35. Some day I *will be truly happy.*
 50. When I am older *I will be wiser.*

Interpretative Summary: Optimistic with respect to health, happiness, and intellectual growth.
(Clinical Impression: No conflict. Feels able to do things he wants to do.)

XV. GOALS. *Rating: 1*

  3. I always wanted to *be outstanding.*
 18. I could be perfectly happy if *I had peace of mind.*
 33. My secret ambition in life *is to be famous.*
 49. What I want most out of life is *peace of mind, then I'll get all the rest.*

Interpretative Summary: Wants to be famous and outstanding despite fears previously mentioned. Goals seem somewhat vague.
(Clinical Impression: Wife, family, middle-class living.)

General Summary (Subject No. 6)

1. Principal areas of conflict and disturbance: Mother, father, family unit, heterosexual relationships, superiors, fears, and guilt feelings.

2. Interrelationships among the attitudes: Problem of close emotional tie with mother, lack of father-figure, and strict upbringing result in timidity toward women, lack of confidence in his sexual prowess, and strong guilt in his feelings with regard to sexual desires. Feeling of rejection in childhood and inadequate father-figure leave him with fear of handling hostility when he is in position of authority.

3. Personality Structure:

  (a) *Mode of response:* Responds primarily to inner impulses (x and xi).

  (b) *Emotional adjustment:* Emotionally constricted (37).

  (c) *Maturity:* Self-centered goals and lack of sexual adjustment reflect moderate immaturity.

  (d) *Reality level:* Tends to overevaluate his potentialities (17).

  (e) *Manner in which conflicts are expressed:* Need for recognition and acceptance (vi, viii, ix), conflicts with fear of hostility and rejection by others (x). Conflict expressed through withdrawal, passive dependency, and digestive disturbances.

REFERENCES

1. ALLPORT, G. W.: "The Study of Personality by the Intuitive Method," *Journal of Abnormal and Social Psychology*, Vol. 24 (1929), pp. 14–27.

2. ——: "Attitudes," in C. Murchison (ed.): *A Handbook of Social Psychology*. Worcester: Clark University Press; 1935.

3. ——: *The Use of Personal Documents in Psychological Science*. New York: Social Science Research Council; 1942.

4. BIJOU, S. W. (ed.): *The Psychological Program in AAF Convalescent Hospitals*. Army Air Forces Psychology Program Research Reports, Report No. 15. Washington: U. S. Government Printing Office; 1947.

5. CARTER, H. J.: "A Combined Projective and Psychogalvanic Response Technique for Investigating Certain Affective Processes," *J. Consult. Psychol.*, Vol. 5 (1947), pp. 270–5.

6. CATTELL, R. B.: "Projection and the Design of Projective Tests of Personality," *Character and Personality*, Vol. 12 (1944), pp. 175–94.

7. CLARKE, J., ROSENZWEIG, S., and FLEMING, E. E.: "The Reliability of the Scoring of the Rosenzweig Picture-Frustration Study," *Journal of Clinical Psychology*, Vol. 3 (1947), pp. 364–9.

8. COMBS, A. W.: "A Comparative Study in Motivations as Revealed in Thematic Apperception Stories and Autobiographies," *J. Clin. Psychol.*, Vol. 3 (1947), pp. 65–74.

9. DE MARTINO, F.: "The Similes Test as a Group Device," *J. Clin. Psychol.*, Vol. 3 (1947), pp. 164–8.

10. DOOB, L. W.: "The Behavior of Attitudes," *Psychological Review*, Vol. 54 (1947), pp. 135–56.

11. DUBIN, S. S.: "Verbal Attitude Scores from Responses Obtained in the Projective Technique," *Sociometry*, Vol. 3 (1940), pp. 24–8.

12. ECDAHL, O.: "Effect of Attitude on Free Word Association," *Genetic Psychology Monographs*, Vol. 5 (1929), No. 4.

13. ELLIS, A.: "A Comparison of the Use of Direct and Indirect Phrasing in Personality Questionnaires," *Psychol. Monogr.*, Vol. 61 (1947), No. 3.

14. FRANK, L. K.: "Projective Methods for the Study of Personality," *Journal of Psychology*, Vol. 8 (1939), pp. 389–413.

15. FRENKEL-BRUNSWICK, E.: "Mechanisms of Self-Deception," *Journal of Social Psychology*, Vol. 10 (1939), pp. 409–20.

16. GOODENOUGH, F. L.: "The Use of Free Association in the Objective Measurement of Personality," in Q. McNemar and

M. A. Merrill (eds.): *Studies in Personality*. New York: McGraw-Hill Book Co.; 1942.

17. GUILFORD, J. P.: *Psychometric Methods*. New York: McGraw-Hill Book Co.; 1936.

18. ——: *Fundamental Statistics in Psychology and Education*. New York: McGraw-Hill Book Co.; 1942.

19. HALL, G. S.: "Some Aspects of the Early Sense of Self," *American Journal of Psychology*, Vol. 9.

20. HANKS, L. M.: "Prediction from Case Material to Personality Test Data," *Archives of Psychology*, 1936, p. 207.

21. HANNA, J. V.: "Clinical Procedure as a Method of Validating a Measure of Psychoneurotic Tendency," *J. Abnorm. Soc. Psychol.*, Vol. 28 (1934), pp. 435–45.

22. HARRIS, D. B.: "The Woodworth-Matthews Questionnaire with Delinquent Boys," *J. Consult. Psychol.*, Vol. II (1947), pp. 151–2.

23. HARRISON, R.: "Studies in the Use and Validity of the TAT with Mentally Disordered Patients. II. A Quantitative Study," *Character and Pers.*, Vol. 9 (1940), pp. 122–33.

24. HARTSHORNE, H., and MAY, M. A.: "Testing the Knowledge of Right and Wrong," *Religious Education Association Monographs*, (1927), No. 1.

25. ——: *Studies in Deceit*. New York: Macmillan Co.; 1928.

26. HERTZ, M. R., ELLIS, A., and SYMONDS, P. M.: "Rorschach Methods and Other Projective Technics," *Review of Educational Research*, Vol. 17 (1947), pp. 78–100.

27. HOLLINGWORTH, H. K.: *Judging Human Character*. New York: D. Appleton-Century Co.; 1926.

28. HORST, P. (ed.): *The Prediction of Social Adjustment*. New York: Social Science Research Council; 1941.

29. HUSTON, P. E., SHAKOW, D., and ERICKSON, M. H.: "A Study of Hypnotically Inducted Complexes by Means of the Luria Technique," *Journal of General Psychology*, Vol 11 (1934), pp. 65–97.

30. HUTT, M. L.: "The Use of Projective Methods of Personality Measurement in Army Medical Installations," *J. Clin. Psychol.*, Vol. 1 (1945), pp. 123–40.

31. JONES, E. S.: "Subjective Evaluations of Personality," in J. McV. Hunt (ed.): *Personality and the Behavior Disorders*. New York: Ronald Press Co., 1944.

32. JUNG, C. G.: "The Association Method," *Am. J. Psychol.*, Vol. 21 (1910), pp. 219–69.

33. ——:*Studies in Word Association*. New York: Moffat, Yard & Co.; 1919.

34. KENT, G. H., and ROSANOFF, A. J.: "The Study of Association in Insanity," *American Journal of Insanity*, Vol. 67 (1910), pp. 37–96.

35. LEHNER, G.: "Projections of Men and Women to Items Referring to the Same and Opposite Sex on a Sentence Completion Test," *American Psychologist*, Vol. 2 (1947), p. 407. (Abstract.)

36. LEVINSON, D. J.: "Projective and Ability Tests," *Psychological Review*, Vol. 53 (1946), pp. 189–94.

37. ——: "Projective Questions in the Study of Personality and Ideology," *American Psychologist*, Vol. 2 (1947), p. 288. (Abstract.)

38. LORGE, I., and THORNDIKE, E. L.: "The Value of Responses in a Completion Test as Indications of Personality Traits," *Journal of Applied Psychology*, Vol. 25 (1941), pp. 191–9.

39. ——: "The Value of the Responses in a Free-Association Test as Indicators of Personal Traits," *J. Appl. Psychol.*, Vol. 25 (1941), pp. 200–1.

40. MACFARLANE, J. W.: "Problems of Validation Inherent in Projective Methods," *American Journal of Orthopsychiatry*, Vol. 12 (1942), pp. 405–12.

41. MALLER, J. B.: "Personality Tests," in J. McV. Hunt (ed.): *Personality and the Behavior Disorders*. New York: Ronald Press Co.; 1944.

42. MICHAEL, J. C., and BÜHLER, C.: "Experiences with Personality Testing in a Neuropsychiatric Department of a Public General Hospital," *Diseases of the Nervous System*, Vol. 6 (1945), pp. 205–11.

43. MURRAY, H. A., and MACKINNON, D. W.: "Assessment of OSS Personnel," *J. Consult. Psychol.*, Vol. 10 (1946), pp. 76–80.

44. PAYNE, A. F.: *Sentence Completions*. New York: New York Guidance Clinic; 1928.

45. PROSHANSKY, H. M.: "A Projection Method for the Study of Attitudes," *J. Abnorm. Soc. Psychol.*, Vol. 38 (1943), pp. 393–5.

46. RAPAPORT, D.: "Principles Underlying Projective Techniques," *Character and Pers.*, Vol. 10 (1942), pp. 213–19.

47. ——, and SCHAFER, R.: *Manual of Diagnostic Psychological Testing*, Vol. II, New York: Josiah Macy Jr. Foundation; 1946.

48. ROGERS, C. R.: "Some Observations on the Organization of Personality," *Amer. Psychologist*, Vol. 2 (1947), pp. 358–68.

49. ROHDE, A.: "Explorations in Personality by the Sentence Completion Method," *J. Appl. Psychol.*, Vol. 30 (1946), pp. 169–81.

50. ROTTER, J. B.: "Studies in the Use and Validity of the TAT with Mentally Disordered Patients. I. Method of Analysis and Clinical Problems," *Character and Pers.*, Vol. 9 (1940), pp. 18–34.

51. ——, and WILLERMAN, B.: "The Incomplete Sentence Test as a Method of Studying Personality," *J. Consult. Psychol.*, Vol. 11 (1947), pp. 43–8.

52. SARGENT, H.: "Projective Methods: Their Origins, Theory, and Applications in Personality Research," *Psychological Bulletin*, Vol. 42 (1945), pp. 257–93.

53. SEARS, R. R.: "Experimental Studies of Projection. I. Attribution of Traits," in S. Tomkins (ed.): *Contemporary Psychopathology*. Cambridge: Harvard University Press; 1943.

54. SHOR, J.: "Report on a Verbal Projective Technique," *J. Clin. Psychol.*, Vol. 2 (1946), pp. 279–82.

55. SPENCER, D.: "The Frankness of Subjects on Personality Measures," *Journal of Educational Psychology*, Vol. 29 (1938), pp. 26–35.

56. STEIN, M. I.: "The Use of a Sentence Completion Test For the Diagnosis of Personality," *J. Clin. Psychol.*, Vol. 3 (1947), pp. 47–56.

57. SYMONDS, P. M.: *Diagnosing Personality and Conduct*. New York: Century Co.; 1931.

58. ——: "The Sentence Completion Test as a Projective Technique," *J. Abnorm. Soc. Psychol.*, Vol. 42 (1947), pp. 320–9.

59. ——, and SAMUEL, E. A.: "Projective Methods in the Study of Personality," *Rev. Educ. Res.*, Vol. II (1941), pp. 80–93.

60. TENDLER, A. D.: "A Preliminary Report on a Test for Emotional Insight," *J. Appl. Psychol.*, Vol. 14 (1930), pp. 123–36.

61. TERMAN, L. M.: "The Measurement of Personality," *Science*, Vol. 40 (1934), pp. 605–8.

62. THORNDIKE, E. L.: *Psychology of Wants, Interests and Attitudes*. New York: D. Appleton-Century Co.; 1935.

63. THURSTONE, L.: "The Stimulus-Response Fallacy," *Psychol. Rev.*, Vol. 30 (1923), pp. 354–69.

64. VETTER, G. B.: "The Measurement of Social and Political Attitudes and the Related Personality Factors," *J. Abnorm. Soc. Psychol.*, Vol. 25 (1930), pp. 149–89.

65. WELLS, F. L., and RUESCH, J.: *Mental Examiner's Handbook*. New York: Psychological Corporation; 1945.

66. WHITE, R. W.: "Interpretation of Imaginative Productions," in J. McV. Hunt (ed.): *Personality and the Behavior Disorders.* New York: Ronald Press Co.; 1944.

67. WOODWORTH, R. S., and WELLS, F. L.: "Association Tests," *Psychol. Monogr.*, Vol. 13 (1911), No. 5.

▼

THIS final paper of Part II, on finger-painting, firmly establishes the right of this older technique to admission into the developing family of projective methods. Mrs. Asya Kadis has provided a useful and interesting treatment of the problems of administration, scoring, and interpretation of finger-painting productions. She makes it clear that this is one approach among many that may be employed in the long process of personality study and evaluation.

We feel that this offering should prove of use not alone to those clinicians who have had some reservations about using the method but also to the many clinical psychologists and psychotherapists who find it an appropriate avenue for approach to understanding their patients.

▼

Finger-Painting as a Projective Technique

Asya L. Kadis

INTRODUCTION

The Background of Finger-Painting.—The basic method of finger-painting, that of achieving graphic effects by direct manipulation of the paint with the fingers and hands, was repeatedly employed by artists prior to this century. The systematic application of finger-painting as a diagnostic, therapeutic, or educational tool, however, is a development of the past two decades.

A basic assumption in finger-painting is that it is a form of expressive behavior, the analysis of which will reveal significant characteristics of the individual. In this respect finger-painting is continuous with other forms of art expression, in that it permits a large measure of expressive behavior with a minimum of adaptation required.[1] We feel, thus, that it is a technique well

---

[1] I use the distinction proposed by G. W. Allport between adaptive and expressive aspects of behavior.

suited to the study and treatment of personality.

Miss Ruth F. Shaw [16, 17], the originator of modern finger-painting, adopted it as part of her many ingenious educational techniques. Finger-painting was developed in Rome for the purpose of overcoming a specific problem in her school. This school was the meeting-place for children of many nationalities, who spoke many languages, and finger-painting proved to be, as she had hoped, a satisfying common method of expression not dependent upon verbalization.[2]

Miss Shaw focused the attention of psychologists on her new educational technique when she observed that it was serving to release her young students from inhibitions, helping them to overcome fears, and strengthening their self-confidence. In juvenile life, she pointed out further, finger-painting had much in common with play in mud. Miss Shaw described the relationship aptly when she stated: "Finger-paintings are the direct descendants of mud pies—all I have done is to add the rainbow" [16].

Within the last decade many clinicians have come to recognize the many possibilities of this unique method of self-expression. In addition to being part of the general educational program, finger painting is being used today as a diagnostic projective technique [11, 12], as a means for stimulating free associations [10], as a part of psychotherapy [3] and play therapy [1], and by occupational therapists for the rehabilitation of spastic patients [13], the deaf [19], and the blind [5].

A number of investigators have reported on its diverse uses. Shaw and Lyle [9] have emphasized its power to elicit the fantasy expressions of children. Mosse [10] has stressed its utilization to evoke free associations, and Spring [18] has pointed out its values in relation to anal impulses. Its diagnostic uses have been elaborated by Rosenzweig and Durbin [15], who attempted to find personality correlates in the finger-paintings of psychotic patients in mental hospitals. Fleming [6], working with adult neurotics, attempted to relate content and painting behavior of her subjects to their personality characteristics. A comprehensive survey of the entire field relating to personality

---

[2] For a more detailed description of Miss Shaw's life and work, see Napoli [11].

diagnosis has been conducted by Napoli [11, 12], which was followed by a detailed report on the interpretative significance of the various painting categories [12]. In the earlier publication Napoli [11] isolated diagnostic criteria in finger-paintings of groups diagnosed to be paranoid and schizophrenic. Arlow and Kadis [3] conducted a project to evaluate the role of finger-painting in an integrated psychotherapeutic program.

Although finger-painting has been receiving increasing recognition, it has not been so thoroughly explored as have most other projective techniques. Finger-painting, nevertheless, promises to yield adequate criteria by which to arrive at certain basic characteristics of the individual. Many of the generalizations to be advanced in the present paper are based upon clinical experience with several hundred finger-paintings. They are suggested as tentative hypotheses and certainly require further verification.

Finger-Painting as a Projective Technique.—Perhaps more than any other current projective technique, finger-painting fulfills both the theoretical and the practical requirements for evoking an unrestrained projection of the personality. A good projective method, as Frank points out, must present the subject with the following points:

> A field with relatively little structure and cultural patterning so that the personality can project upon that plastic field his way of seeing life, his meanings, significances, patterns, and especially his feelings . . . that he can structuralize his life space. [7]

In devising a technique it must thus be the psychologist's aim to eliminate any factors that may inhibit the free flow of drives, emotions, and impulses. The major restrictive influences to be eliminated are mechanical motor limitations, cultural patterns, fear of social pressure, and age limitations.

Freedom from Motor Limitations.—Finger-painting makes minimal use of muscular co-ordination involving the finer muscle groups, thereby serving as a medium for the facile as well as for those handicapped in this respect. Other types of graphic creations, while usually very revealing, require a higher degree of muscular co-ordination and thus frequently tend to discourage the subject after a few unsuccessful atempts. In finger-painting, movements are sufficiently gross and bulky to decrease the probability of experience of failure. Clinical experience has demonstrated that there are few rejections in finger-painting, and this appears to be an advantage.

Physical limitations may in certain instances actually hamper or change to an unknown degree the amount of expressiveness. Because finger-painting is affected to a lesser extent by physical handicaps, it decreases such restrictions of expressiveness. Handicapped groups find many revealing sources of expression in finger-painting which compensate for their sensory limitations. There is great effectiveness in the finger-painting of blind, deaf, and spastic individuals.

Freedom from Cultural Influences.—Finger-painting involves a minimum of cultural values or trained precedents, so that responses are not so likely to be influenced by standards. There can be no particular style of finger-painting, as there is in handwriting; none that the subject might consider better or worse, accepted or unaccepted, right or wrong, in terms of his previous experience.

Perhaps of greater importance, finger-painting is a means of expression relatively unhampered by linguistic factors. Language is a primary carrier of culture and it frequently acts as a strong inhibiting agent in the expression of emotional processes. It is to be noted, however, that the very fact that verbal responses are no essential requirement makes *spontaneous* verbalizations only more valuable. They often endow the graphic creation with meaning to the observer.

Freedom from Social Pressure.—Social pressure may be thought of as the direct and personal aspect of culture, impinging upon the individual's freedom of self-expression. Finger-painting is a socially sanctioned "play in mud," which permits the individual to live out his aggressive impulses. It grants satisfaction to the destructive desires without being destructive and it enables the subject to defy taboos without fear of retaliation. In the finger-painting situation, with its play character, the subject's fear that he may reveal himself is minimized.

The finger-painting situation tends to foster a congenial relationship, the kind most favorable for eliciting spontaneous reactions in the subject. The relative lack of social pressure and freedom from experience of failure may well explain the very small number of rejections encountered with this technique. In this connection it may be noted that the introduction of finger-painting has been found effective when it has been discovered that it is difficult to establish rapport on a verbal level. The sequence of paintings (Figure 36 A, B, and C) offers an excellent illustration as to how finger-painting may be introduced when verbal rapport cannot be established by other means.

The Factor of Age.—Age factors constitute no limitation for the use of finger-painting. Personality patterns emerge from finger-paintings on almost all age levels. Diagnostic value is derived from the products obtained from three-year-olds as well as from subjects in old-age homes.

It is true that in the process of interpretation age factors must be considered. For example, in a three-year-old, his motility patterns are of greater importance diagnostically than his completed product. As we shall later see, color interpretation varies with age. But age as such never constitutes a limitation upon the use of the technique.

Process and Sequence Analyses.—Perhaps the most important advantage that finger-painting offers is that the administrator is given a view of the process by which the subject arrives at his finished product. Frank says [7] that the aim of projective methods is to represent personality as a *process* of organizing the individual's private world. In finger-painting the administrator can observe this process in the formation of concepts or growth of emotional expressions through the succession of color, lines, and motions employed during a single painting. In the analysis of finger-painting it is important to observe carefully the progressive changes in the subject's behavior. The observer must note, for example, not only what colors are chosen, but also how the subject changes his color choices from early to later stages in his painting. I shall refer to this type of analysis as process analysis.

Process analysis must be clearly distinguished from sequence analysis. Process analysis refers to intrapainting changes; sequence analysis refers to interpainting changes. Sequence analysis in finger-painting is made possible by the procedure that requires a number of paintings to be completed during one session or during several sessions. It is our practice to require three paintings in one session. Napoli suggests [11] that a total of eight paintings should be required, to give greater reliability. Sequence analysis may be used for purposes of reliability. It may also be used to determine to what extent the subject performs differently at different stages of diagnosis or therapy.

No Problem of Equivalent Form.—Another advantage of finger-painting is that there is no problem of equivalent forms when repeat paintings are required. Every finger-painting situation is a new and fascinating adventure to the subject, and each finger-painting seems to constitute a new test item or situation.

The Necessary Equipment.—1. *Paper.* The standard paper is a large rectangular sheet, 22 by 16 inches, with a glazed surface on the painting side and a dull back, which is used for identification, data, and other pertinent information. Smaller sheets are available, but larger sheets have been found to give the subject more ample space for self-expression. Once a certain size has been accepted, it is essential to keep the subject working on the same type of sheet. A greater uniformity of performance is thereby ensured.

2. *Paints.* Six basic colors are presented to the subject: blue, black, red, brown, green, and yellow. The paints come in jars, in the form of a resistant paste, and the subject must exert pressure and movements in order to start painting. Proper manipulation of paint and water (an emotionally stimulating process) will supply a smoothly working medium. The paints are not harmful if taken internally and they can be easily washed off all surfaces.

3. *Surface for painting.* Table height should fit the individual's need. A comfortable height corresponds to a point slightly below the subject's elbow when the subject is in a standing position. Enough space should surround the table to enable the subject to walk around it while he works. The surface of the table should be free from cracks, and for making it such materials as linoleum or plate glass are preferred. The surface must be larger than the designated paper size.

4. *Receptacles.* Standard equipment includes a large receptacle, about seventeen inches long, for wetting the sheet, a smaller pan for sprinkling and moistening, and a large pail for cleaning up. All these are desirable but not essential. A sink and an adequate table with ample space around it could suffice.

Administration of the Test.—A number of divergent methods are advocated for presenting finger-painting materials to the subject. The merit of these methods varies with the purpose of the examiner.

Shaw [16] and Napoli [11] applying finger-painting primarily in an educational framework, suggest that the examiner should introduce finger-painting by giving an initial trial demonstration. There is danger here, however, of destroying one of the major advantages of finger-painting—its freedom from trained standards. Illustration by the examiner would most likely set a precedent that might lead to imitation by the subject. Furthermore, any performance that appears superior to his own may inhibit the subject's performance. As a result a feeling of discouragement may destroy an initial advantage.

Mosse [10] advocates that the subject be left alone in the room for fifteen to twenty minutes, after which his production is used by the examiner to elicit free associations. It seems to me, however, that in this manner a whole series of valuable insights may be overlooked, for the examiner would be deprived of studying the subject's approach and his successive steps from initial to later performance. All advantages associated with process analysis would be lost. Mosse's objective, however, is really one of eliciting free associations. My experience has indicated that the point at which the subject is likely to yield the most significant free associations occurs during the painting process when painting activity has reached its maximum emotional tonus. At this point verbal associations are more genuine expressions of the subject than those that come out at any other time. Associations after completed performance might lack the desired freedom, since the subject would have had time to recover his constrictive mechanisms and rationalize and intellectualize his product.

For our purposes, in order to gain full advantage of process analysis, I deem it essential that the administrator be present throughout the painting situation and that a running record be kept of the subject's color, space utilization, and motions, as well as of his spontaneous verbalizations and approach.

On the basis of experience I have found the following procedure a good one. Prior to the subject's entering the painting room, the water receptacles have been filled, the paints have been opened, the sheet has been placed on the table. The subject is given these instructions: "Here are six basic colors, which may be used in any combination for any effect. We don't use brushes because we have ten fingers. Five are on one hand and five are on the other. That is much more than one brush. Do anything you want to do and tell me when you are finished." In the event that the subject has painted previously, it is sufficient to say: "Let us do another painting." If the subject should ask for further specific instructions, he is assured that he may paint anything he wants in any way he wants to paint it. He is given no time limit. The average performance is fifteen to twenty minutes. The range is from ten minutes to one hour. With various age groups there is considerable variation in the time consumed. After concluding his paintings the subject is asked to name each one, and then he is questioned as to whether or not he may relate it to his own life. Children are asked to make up stories in connection with the paintings.

DIAGNOSTIC CONSIDERATIONS IN FINGER-PAINTING

The Observation of General Behavior.—Clinicians are generally agreed on the diagnostic significance of certain aspects of the individual's general behavior in the clinical or test situation. The finger-painting situation, which resembles in many respects the play setting, affords an unusual opportunity to obtain behavioral data of interpretative significance.

The behavior before and during the actual finger-painting, which has been found to be significant, includes the subject's posture, his speed of movement, his rate of breathing, and spontaneous verbalizations. Significant factors unique to finger-painting are reactions to wetness and the tactile sensation of muddiness.

It is not easy to find a specific interpretative significance for each of such behavioral reactions. Rather, all behavioral reactions tend to form a configurational picture, usually representative of the general attitude or mood of the subject. The attitudes and moods to be inferred from the behavior characteristics can for convenience be summarized under the terms "distance" and "involvement."

In the finger-painting situation a subject may display two distinct tendencies. One of these shows the subject's desire to separate himself from his task; another indicates his inclination toward participation. The former we call distance, the latter involvement tendency. Both tendencies, that striving toward separation and that striving toward participation, are present in varying strength, although one or the other tends to predominate.

1. Distance. In the initial reaction to the finger-painting situation many subjects manifest behavior that suggests a predominant distance tendency. Such behavior may be classified as follows:

(a) Spatio-physical. This is shown in the manner in which the subject approaches the table or the paints. One subject may attempt to stay as far away as possible. Another may keep one of his hands behind his back, dip one finger into one jar or into the water with an outstretched arm, using the finger as a pencil or tool, as though it were not part of himself. In an extreme case all these behavioral manifestations may be present.

(b) Verbal. The subject may show verbal behavior indicative of distance tendency. He may give evidence of stalling. He may attempt to avoid independent action and try to place responsibility upon the examiner. He may ask such questions as "How shall I do it?" "What shall I paint?" "Who made these paints?" All these are inquiries designed to keep the subject from entering the situation.

(c) Nonverbal. A distance tendency may show itself in random arm movements, ease of distraction, or squirming. It may also be evidenced by an attempt at manipulations or an invoking of thoroughly planned, stereotyped behavior, such as persistence in the drawing of geometrical figures.

Distance in finger-painting may appear contradictory to an earlier statement that finger-painting fosters spontaneous participation and that instances of rejections are rare. The fact, however, is that distance behavior tends to decrease, once the subject has made any contact with the painting situation and whenever the situation is emotionally charged enough to break down any significant amount of distance.

A distance tendency may have varying underlying motivations. It may be motivated by infantile negativism, or by hostility, cautiousness, or by dissatisfaction. Cautiousness is most clearly seen in the anticipatory reaction to wetness or muddiness. It is at this point that distance frequently breaks down, for after contact with wetness or "dirt" has been established the subject may experience extreme satisfaction and a greater proportion of involvement behavior becomes evident.

2. *Involvement.* In contrast to those individuals whose behavior is marked by distance, there are subjects who immediately appear capable of establishing a close bodily relationship with the painting situation. Such behavior represents an involvement tendency. The subject may not merely paint with his fingers, but his entire body movements may be enlisted in the process. In his facial gestures there are expressions of enthusiasm or anger. Hands, arms, and back may join in rhythmical movements. Subjects may use paint to cover their bodies, children preferring particularly to smear the paint over their stomachs. Some subjects enjoy an excessive bathing of their hands in water. Behavior showing a predominant involvement tendency may best be described as "plunging into the task." Again, motivations underlying involvement behavior may be diverse. They may represent strivings for pleasure or satisfaction, particularly with reference to contact with water and muddiness, or they may be aggression or hostility.

In so far as an individual enters the finger-painting situation at all, some involvement must be present. Process analysis often reveals a change in the subject's general behavior in the direction of increasing involvement.

CHARACTERISTICS INHERENT IN THE FINGER-PAINTING TASK

1. *Time Elements.*—Three essential time elements may be observed. These are reaction time before beginning to paint, pauses during painting, and total time utilized for each separate production and all the paintings.

(a) *Initial reaction time.* This is another manifestation of the relative weights of the distance or involvement tendencies. Some subjects plunge into the task immediately; others stall, halt, or hesitate. Particularly long reaction time may reflect anticipatory anxiety associated with reactions to wetness or dryness.

(b) *Pauses during painting.* These are to be associated with unexpected emotional effects due to color combinations, or designs achieved in the painting which produce fear or anxiety. Confronted with a new color combination that in some way becomes meaningful to him, the subject may show verbal or facial expressions of horror or disgust, such as "Gee, that looks awful! Can I throw it away?" "Can I wipe it off?" "What can I do to make it whiter?" "I hate this color." The subject may even tear up the sheet and throw it away with violent gestures.

(c) *Total time.* The degree to which the subject allows himself to be involved in the painting as a whole is reflected by the total time used for finger-painting. Some subjects are incapable of separating themselves from the painting situation either because they have found great relief through the medium or because they strive for perfection. They may continue in their movements until the paper begins to tear. Others may separate themselves as quickly as possible, because the situation may have aroused in them feelings of anxiety.

2. *Space utilization and location.*—In finger-painting, most individuals tend to limit themselves to the white paper and to utilize the greater part of the entire sheet. For this reason deviations in the utilization of paper space become interpretively significant. Two major kinds of space deviations have been observed. These may be termed expansion and restriction.

(a) *Expansion.* This is obvious in individuals who tend to paint beyond the limits of the paper, the paints going onto the table surface. A person showing such behavior may sometimes manifest expansiveness in another manner. Although he may confine his work to the limits set by the paper, the organization of the pattern suggests expansiveness. He may sweep across the sheet with a strong line without beginning or end. Examples of expansion are shown in finger-painting in Figure 31. Such expansiveness in finger-painting may be said to represent relatively uncontrolled emotional reaction.

It has been found that children responding with expansion in finger-painting tend to display lack of inhibition or overaggressiveness. This behavior is found frequently among delinquents. It seems to be correlated with their lack of cognizance for authority and their insatiable drive for impulse gratification.

(b) *Restriction.* In this category only a small section of the painting sheet is used. It may be given an interpretation similar to that in drawing. The subject, refusing to use his space, gives evidence of self-restraint and withdrawing tendencies, particularly when the design is located in extreme corners of the sheet or is suspended in space. In such cases we find the reaction to be related to anxiety.

Space utilization in process analysis. When space utilization is subjected to process analysis it affords an excellent opportunity for viewing the growth of concept formation.

The subject may start by producing a peripheral pattern and then fill in details that are an integral part of the total design. This process is frequent among subjects who have an intense need to do something logical or to employ a security device. The subject may also first endow the sheet with a heavy black frame and then permit himself to proceed with his pattern.

On the other hand the individual may choose to begin with a central and nuclear pattern and then continue with accessory designs to cover the entire sheet. He may make a small house in the center and then proceed with a road, a tree, and the sun in the background. Thus in finger-painting, we can watch the growth of the concept because motor activity has become a substitute for thought processes.

3. *Color.*—The significance of color is similar in most projective techniques. Colors are direct expressions of our affect and emotional drives. They may be employed with strict adherence to the outline of the object or patterns represented, much like a Rorschach FC, or they may be shown in a diffused manner without strict boundaries, as in the painting of a flame or radiating sun in which the emotional impetus is given spontaneous expression.

But finger-painting tends to give color an enhanced emotional value. It is possible for the subject to choose his shades and to blend them in such a manner as to evoke a maximum of individual emotional reaction. This may be the result of a two-way reaction. The color choice will be made spontaneously or unconsciously, but, once confronted with the color on the sheet, the subject may react emotionally—a situation that in turn may serve as a stimulus for new color effects. That initial color selection may be quite spontaneous was testified by Arlow and Kadis [3] who found subjects reaching out for specific jars before they knew what they were going to do on the painting sheet.

(a) Specific colors identified with specific emotions. Whereas color may be said to represent the general emotional impulses, specific colors may in certain instances stand for specific emotional patterns. Much as in the Rorschach, observation has shown that the milder shades of blue and green stand for controlled behavior. Similarly Alschuler and Hattwick [2] in their presentation of easel painting (which may be applied to finger-painting), distinguish between cold and warm colors, the former being indicative of a higher degree of impulse control than the latter. Experience has also shown that black symbolizes a child's feeling of death, hostility, and aggression. Spring [18] says that black and brown tend to be color choices of subjects from refined homes; Mosse [10] reports that brown may be a color frequently produced by individuals with an anal character, although simultaneously he calls for caution against such generalizations.

Both Shaw [16] and Napoli [11] perceive well-defined male and female trends in color preferences. Although my experience does not confirm this observation, these investigators maintain that there is a distinct preference for blue and green among males and red and yellow among females. Females using male colors may be exhibiting masculine trends and vice versa. Shaw concludes from this observation that a boy who uses red predominantly tends to be "tied to his mother's apron strings." [3]

In addition to the general emotional values of various colors we have found them to have a personal and individual emotional value as well. To illustrate, one subject used color thus: light blue for the ship of success coming into port; green for the study of music and musical instruments, which she had hoped would bring her recognition; brown for the burial of a faithless friend; black for the bars that reminded her that living in an institution was like being a prisoner.[3]

The same color may actually stand for various aspects of the emotional life. Red may be used to express affection as well as aggression and hostility. The pouring of red in a scratching motion would suggest a feeling of hostility; a patting notion

---

[3] Shaw expressed this point of view at a lecture.

indicates affection. The personal meaning of a color is to be sought by a simultaneous consideration of the other categories.

(b) Color interpretation with different diagnostic groups. A number of observers have identified color preferences with various clinical syndromes. Rosenzweig and Durbin [15] maintain that manic depressives tend to choose more vivid colors, such as red and orange, while schizophrenics predominantly select green and yellow. Mosse [10] was unable to confirm Oberndorf's claim that yellow was linked to schizophrenics and red to manic states.

An excessive pouring of color and the lumping or overlaying of colors have been found to be characteristic of subjects with insufficient inhibitions or excessive aggression. Here we have a dramatic exemplification of the insatiable personality whose need for gratification knows no limits. The subject's behavior in diluting the colors excessively by overwetting the paper, and his applying of manifold layers of colors, have, in my experience, been associated with poor ego development.

Mixing and combining of colors can definitely be associated with higher intellectual functioning. A child who inquires: "How can I get purple?" demonstrates that he wants to explore, penetrate, and expand the immediate situation.

(c) Caution in the interpretation of color. Color usage is subject to educational and age factors, and these must always be taken into account.

Age. Small children employ red freely, whereas adults rarely use red in an initial painting. Youngsters from four to ten like to use several colors, usually primary ones, and they then employ them in striking combinations. As a rule they do not mix their colors to achieve intermediary tones. Older subjects prefer the use of a single mixture. For an intensive study in the interpretation of color at the preschool age level the reader is referred to the work of Alschuler and Hattwick [2], whose generalizations may be applied to finger-painting.

Age differences also account for different emotional reactions to color. Children show an immediate, impulsive, emotional response to color per se, independent of the pattern into which the color might have to be fitted. "Oh, wonderful, there is red" (or "green"), is not an uncommon remark. Sometimes the reaction is sufficiently strong to drive the child to pour the color over his own body, particularly in the stomach region. This may not be a reaction to color alone but may involve tactile stimulation.

Educational factors. These factors tend to be clearly reflected in the paintings of children up to the fourth grade. Here we find very rigid and realistic color representations; brown dogs, blue skies, green grass. In such cases color may be a reflection of the acceptance of social standards rather than more highly personalized emotional impulses. Individuality in color usage tends to decrease with increasing need for conformity. In the adult conformity to realistic shades may be likened to a high percentage of popular or animal responses in the Rorschach Test.

(b) Process and sequence analyses of color. Rigid conformity to realistic representation, just mentioned, is not, however, too serious a barrier to individual diagnosis. In most instances it does not persist over the entire finger-painting session. We may actually speak of a gradient of decreasing conformity. A subject who might start with stereotyped color representations couched in specific forms would often, through the excitement of the painting process, follow less and less the form to which the color was to be fitted. To exemplify, a change from an initial brown chair to purple or yellow flowers. This may best be described in Rorschach Test terms as a change from FC to CF.

4. *Shading.*—In finger-painting distinction can be made between shading effects that result from surface texture and those that result from depth or tridimensional concepts. (See Figure 31.)

The texture effect, comparable to Rorschach "c," is usually produced with patting or stroking motions and is indicative of intensified feeling. Figure 31 well exemplifies such texture effect. The dominant sensation for the subject was a tactile one and an interpretation of sensuousness was found to be valid. The depth element (Rorschach K factor) is the result of concept formation rather than tactile stimulation. A typical painting for portraying depth can be found in a spiral pattern or in the painting of Figure 32, a, b. Such depth effects frequently occur, but their interpretative significance is not clear from our experience.

5. *Strokes.*—By "strokes" is meant the final products of motions on the painting surface. The significance of strokes in finger-painting is akin to the significance of lines in drawing, and the findings of investigators in the field of drawing and

easel painting will be drawn upon in our discussion. In finger-painting, strokes may be considered to constitute an even more direct expression of the subject's inner dynamics, for they are a direct continuation of total bodily movements with no intervening tool to retard the momentum of expression.

In the interpretation of strokes attention should be focused upon repetition of attributes rather than on isolated instances. Furthermore, strokes can be understood only in terms of their total configuration. The meaning of a stroke is determined by its relation to other strokes. In their most general interpretative meaning, strokes may be said to be representative of emotional control. We may roughly differentiate the attributes of strokes into four major categories, as follows:

(a) The direction of strokes. The major direction of strokes may be horizontal or vertical. The former may be started at the left or at the right, the latter at the top or the bottom. The side at which the stroke starts varies with the handedness of the subject, which must be included in the consideration. Vertical lines have been identified by Alschuler and Hattwick [2] as representing assertive drives, horizontals to denote self-protective, fearful, overtly co-operative characteristics.

Some paintings of younger children and disorganized patients fail to show any definite direction tendency but merely produce a jumbled effect without system. With progressive emotional growth either through therapy or self-maturation, a more coherent structure frequently emerges from the disorganized jumble. Sometimes in one painting, through process analysis, we notice a "straightening-out" tendency, where direction is assumed by the subject after he has produced crisscross strokes for a while.

(b) Width, pressure, and multiplicity of strokes. Strokes may vary from fine and narrow, made by fingernails, to wide, heavy lines produced by the arm, palm, or elbow. The subject may exert varying degrees of pressure, which in extreme cases results in displacing all paints and leaving the line as a white surface on the painting sheet. Finally, strokes may also be produced as a single stroke with one finger or as double or triple parallel strokes by employing the corresponding number of fingers.

The pressure applied indicates the subject's energy level. Heavy pressure represents forcefulness and in other instances it is indicative of tension. Light strokes may represent timidity and fearfulness. A multiplicity of strokes is an indication of involvement; restriction to a single line symbolizes less involvement than a three-finger parallel stroke.

(c) Shape and continuity of strokes. Strokes may be angular or curved, continuous or discontinuous, closed or open. The angular tendency represents an aggressive conduct pattern, and if angular strokes are patterned in a zigzag direction they may reflect the subject's indecision toward his aggressive behavior. Long strokes represent controlled behavior; short strokes are characteristic of impulsive conduct. Discontinuous strokes can be identified with insecurity and anxiety.

By "closedness" is meant a stroke that represents a closed structure in itself, as in a circle or the figure 8. An open structure is exemplified in a crescent shape. Closedness represents a withdrawal factor. The degree of openness symbolizes the degree of willingness to communicate with the world. The significance of a closed line is illustrated in Figure 33.

(d) Texture of strokes. Another characteristic of finger-painting is the possibility of producing a two-way effect of strokes. A stroke may be made by a carving into the paint or by elevation of the surface through additional application of paint. The latter, producing an embossed effect, is frequently the result of "color excitation," and has already been shown to reflect insufficient inhibitory capacity. The significance of a carving line is related to that of scratching and other aggressive motion.

Another aspect of strokes that finger-painting facilitates is the utilization of figure and ground (foreground and background) strokes for the production of figure and ground content. The relationship between foreground and background strokes is important, although it has not as yet been clearly defined. The subject may attempt stark contrast figures or he may want to merge them imperceptibly into his background scene. The background strokes may suggest feeling tone about the figure, or the figure may be a reaction to background strokes. For example, the subject who is initially afraid to show his aggressive impulses may cover the entire sheet with soft-shaded strokes. Only then will he dare to place the central design that gives clear evidence of these impulses. In other instances a subject may be intensely perturbed about a central "bear" figure and may react with vigorous and heavy background strokes.

Obviously the possible combinations and configurations of strokes are endless. A vertical line may be the result of extension or flexion; it may be straight or wobbly; angular or curved; it may bear heavy or light pressure; it may stand isolated or supported by other lines. A more precise analysis of these combinations is not possible in this chapter. For further reference the reader is referred to the works of Werner Wolff [20] and Alschuler and Hattwick [2] which may be well applied to finger-painting with respect to strokes.

6. *Content.*—Content in finger-painting refers to (1) representations that are apparent to the observer, such as definite objects, figures, or abstract designs, and (2) verbalizations made about the paintings during or after the finger-painting process. The zero point of content may be defined as a painting in which the subject scribbles aimlessly and is also incapable of giving any verbal responses to it.

(a) Age levels and other factors influencing content production. Age levels are an important factor in the consideration of content. Random scribbling is perfectly normal for a child of three years whose expressiveness is centered in his motility pattern. In the early school years there is a predominance of outline representation—fruits, houses, trees. These stereotyped representations tend to break down quickly, often within one session, and thereafter more dynamic representations emerge. Again, among normal schoolchildren we have a gradient of disintegrating conformity much as we had in color.

Finger-painting material facilitates certain types of productions. For example, landscapes are easily produced, whereas there tends to be a marked resistance to representation of human figures. The highest frequency of content themes is in diverse modifications of landscape themes. Because of the relative infrequency of human representations it is difficult to assign a specific interpretative significance to human content per se.

(b) Organization of content. Organization of content is a significant diagnostic criterion. Napoli [11] has found the structuring of content to be important in differentiation of schizophrenics and paranoics. In the former group he reports that he observed two completely disconnected and independent layers or strata of representations. These tended to be accompanied by verbal expressions that bore no apparent relevance to the painting production. Arlow and Kadis observed [3], as will be elaborated later, that the relationship of content representation to verbalization is an important index of ego development in children.

In the painting of paranoics Napoli [11] found this characteristic organization: a central figure (symbolizing self-identification) sheltered and surrounded by a systematic arrangement of supporting figures (designed to safeguard the central figure against attack from all sides).

Patterson and Leightner [14] report that they found no actual content differences between mental deficients and normals, but that in the elaboration of content, normal subjects tended to fill out contours to a larger extent than did the mentally deficient, although the latter produced more patterned paintings.

(c) Further diagnostic uses of content. Content is given greater significance when it can be combined with other data known about the subject, particularly free associations and spontaneous verbalizations about the painting. As we shall see later, it is most effective when utilized concomitantly in the total therapeutic situation.

Content material frequently serves to portray an objectification of conflict. Figure 34, which shows two side figures flanking a boat, was spontaneously identified by the subject thus: "Two pirates are fighting for the possession of gold." Asked whether this reminded him of anything in his life, he replied, after a short pause and with a bitter smile: "Just like my parents fighting who will have me." Queried whether he had thought of this before he answered: "Not quite." Here we see that verbalization of content makes the latter more meaningful, not only for the examiner but to the subject as well. For this reason, asking children to make up a story after they have painted, has proved to be an effective procedure.

(d) Process and sequence analyses of content. The greatest value is derived from content when it is observed as a series of recurrent themes. The succession of themes and symbolic substitutions makes the finger-painting process analogous to the dream process. It actually affords the observer a graphic view of the dream process that is well termed a "graphic dream" [3].

In the course of a single painting, for example, a subject shifted from the painting of an animal and converted it into a little boy. The symbolic substitution, equating the two figures, provided an understanding of the subject's defenses [3].

The graphic dream may also give us a glimpse of what is being concealed by the defenses. In a case of Harry, aged ten, reported by Arlow and Kadis [3], the subject had strong feelings of inadequacy because of small genitals and undeveloped testicles. Over a series of sessions he produced repeatedly simple, large objects that this little boy wanted badly—a football, a pipe, and the like. During a time when his feelings of inadequacy were particularly strong he painted a huge football; when in the playroom he modeled a human figure of clay and then made a large penis, which he placed in the appropriate position. Here is an illustration of the emergence of an unexpressed unconscious wish in the content of a finger-painting.

A final word of caution should be said about content analysis. It varies with the particular theoretical school to which the observer belongs. It is certainly the least defined and the most intuitive aspect of finger-painting. Therefore it is necessary to draw upon complementary data as a check upon conjectures. Symbolism should not be held significant after a single occurrence. Subjects, particularly children, may be easily affected by their daily experiences and they also tend to project these experiences with ease. We must observe a constant recurrent aspect in the content, consistent with the total diagnostic picture, in order to draw valid inferences from it.

7. *Movements and motions.*—Movements and motions are behavioral categories and we thus refer to body movements only and not to movements or motions projected on the finished product. Movement and motion concepts refer essentially to the reactions of the hands or fingers, but they may spread to the entire body when there is a greater amount of involvement. Movement refers to direction of reaction—that is, either away from or toward the subject—flexor or extensor. Motions are specific actions independent of direction.

(a) Motions. Motions usually represent a clear and overt expression of an immediate feeling. There is nearly a one-to-one relationship between a specific motion and the emotion that it represents. Motions reflecting aggressive impulses are shown by manifestations of pulling, slapping, scratching, scrubbing, or tearing. The motions associated with sensuous feelings are patting, smearing, and wallowing. Wallowing in particular represents strong pleasure feelings. It can be described as a bathing of the palms on a thoroughly wetted sheet, often after generous amounts of paint have been poured on the paper. The motions are gentle, circular, and smooth, frequently accompanied by verbal expressions such as "delicious." [4]

The grouping of motions into "sensuous and aggressive" is of course completely inadequate. Actually, each motion represents a very specific feeling which is best conveyed by the naming of the concept. Its name conveys more than does a detailed verbal elaboration.

Motions may undergo relatively frequent changes, for they are direct expressions of immediate feelings and definite moods. For example, a subject may begin his painting with pleasurable feelings, by patting the sheet as if it were a beloved object, and then through a sudden, frustrating experience change his motion to a violent scratching of the surface which nearly tears the paper.

Motions sometimes appear with greater consistency in a subject, possibly representing a corresponding personality disposition. Ambivalence as to the use of opposing motions, such as patting and scrubbing, may be indicative of conflicting feelings and attitudes.

(b) Movement. Movement may take two basic directions: away from the subject or toward the subject. It persists with relatively greater constancy in a subject's painting behavior than do motions. We may have a variety of motions employed by a subject while he maintains a constant movement. By analysis of the painting process we may distinguish the extreme movements when they are reflected in the formation of a painting. In painting a tree, for example, a subject may start from the root, with movements toward the branches and widening crown, or he may start with a limited top shrinking toward the root. To be sure, these are only the extremes of basic movements; most instances involve a modification and merging of the extremes, as exemplified by horizontal movements.

One may hypothesize that the basic direction of movement

---

[4] For a more complete description of motions see Napoli [11].

corresponds to the "Erlebnistypus" in the Rorschach Test. The mode of movement may reflect the individual's basic method of impulse gratification. I have observed some subjects who shifted from crisscrossing to an extreme in-going movement and accompanied this shift by expressions of pleasure and satisfaction, as if they had found their particular mode of expression.

8. *Rhythm.*—Rhythm consists in the recurrent use of patterns or themes in a sequence. It may be the attribute of all previous categories—color, strokes, motion, and the like—and, as we shall see, finds expression even in the rhythmic presentation of numbers. Rhythmic arrangement may be studied both in the behavior of a subject and in his completed product.

In the completed product we can observe a rhythmic arrangement. For example, the subject's preference for choosing a succession of interweaving straight strokes and curved strokes may be shown in a scheme of contrasting relationships. This rhythm may be reflected in a preference for extreme contrast or soft blending. (See Figures 32a and b.)

Behavioral rhythm can be detected from the moment of the subject's initial contacts with the paint. Certain motions may recur or may be executed in a specific time sequence.[5] The subject's posture and even his breathing may follow in the rhythmic arrangement.

There tends to be considerable agreement in the rhythm of one subject as displayed in the various categories. The same characteristic rhythm may be reflected in any one or more of the categories. The examination of this rhythm may reveal his characteristic mode of approaching a task. The concept of rhythm, because of this relatively consistent tendency, may thus be extended to refer to a subject's characteristic mode of approaching a task.

To illustrate, the rhythm of a compulsive individual may be complex but rigid. It may contain intricate lines and shades, but we can predict their recurrence, since the subject is compelled to repeat his pattern again and again. On the other hand we have the clumsy and monotonous rhythm of the retarded sub-

---

[5] Napoli *[11]* claims to have observed definite sex differences in the timing of motions.

ject—the same color, the same movements. There is also a wholesome rhythm of spontaneous variation. Here we have a constant, harmonious theme around which the subject is continuously building and trying to expand. The perception of this rhythm, of course, depends upon the keen judgment of the observer. Rhythm may be much more highly individualized and thus cannot be described in rigid categories. Rhythm, if we consider it as a characteristic mode of approaching a task, may give the observer a view of the subject's style of life.[6]

Rhythm of numbers. I have noted a striking consistency in number usages in finger-paintings. This number consistency persists throughout most categories. We may find the same number of objects represented, the same number of strokes produced for a given pattern, or the same number of motions employed. The content or appearance of paintings over a sequence may change considerably, but a given number may persist. We may speak of this as a "personal number" consistency. Furthermore, there may also be a marked consistency in the subdivision of this personal number. For example, a "four consistency" may appear in a three-and-one or in a two-and-two form.

I have found that this "personal number" corresponds to the number of members in the subject's family and that his subdivisions correspond to the feeling-tone that he maintains toward the various members of his family, including himself. (For illustration, see Figures 32a and b.) The subdivision may be affected by the employment of any of the categories. Thus, a subject may portray four forms by painting three in red and the remaining one in black; similarly, three straight strokes and one wavering stroke. Usually such grouping reflects varying degrees of affection or hostility. This diagnostic concept of number rhythm grants the clinician a view of the subject's unconscious experiencing of his family constellation.[7]

---

[6] Cf. the works of Alfred Adler, who introduced and developed this term. See particularly *Understanding Human Nature* (New York: Greenberg; 1927), *Problems of Neurosis* (New York: Cosmopolitan Book Corporation; 1930), *Study of Organ Inferiority and Its Psychical Compensation* (New York: Nervous and Mental Disease Publishing Co.; 1917).

[7] Kadis, A. L., and Lazarsfeld, S.: "The Respective Roles of Earliest Recollections and Images," *American Journal of Psychotherapy*, Vol. 2 (1948), pp. 250–5.

THERAPEUTIC ASPECTS OF FINGER-PAINTING

From a therapeutic standpoint the individual's subjective experience of his finger-painting is of greater importance than what he actually produces. For this reason increased emphasis will be given in this section to the subject's experience of his finger-painting situation.

In a clinical situation no clear-cut division between diagnosis and therapy can be made. Finger-painting may involve the living and "painting out" of problems for the subject, while at the same time this "painting out" becomes apparent to the observant therapist. Thus, finger-painting is diagnostic while it is therapeutic, and therapeutic while being diagnostic.

In the course of therapy the painting situation yields a source of communication with the inner self that the subject is unable to express in verbal terms. By communication Beach [4] means: "The degree to which the painting expresses for painter and to the onlooker the experience—physical, kinesthetic, intellectual, and emotional—that has been set down in color and space. It represents an integration of inner feelings and external experience. The more deeply felt the experience, the closer the communication achieved." It seems that it is exactly this type of communication which finger-painting accomplishes and which the therapist needs to establish with his subject so as to integrate finger-painting effectively as part of the total therapeutic situation.

Finger-painting has the therapeutic function of aiding in the emotional preparation for a verbal and intellectual acceptance of insight. Language is a most powerful therapeutic tool, but it is effective only if the subject can avail himself both of its denotative and connotative meanings. Finger-painting permits an acting out of concealed material that evokes emotional experiences. That is, the "acting out" or "painting out" paves the way for a "verbal working through" of the subject's problem.

This process is well exemplified by the following case of B. R., an adult female, aged twenty-seven.

B. R. came to the clinic with somatic symptoms: inability to swallow solid foods, nausea, stiff neck, insomnia. During therapy it developed that her vocational adjustment was one aspect of her problem. She was a pianist, and being dissatisfied with her own performance, she had discontinued her playing. The thera-

FIGURE 30. Uninhibited, Free-floating Drives in a Finger-Painting

Made by an adolescent delinquent girl, fifteen years old. These paintings exemplify uninhibited "expansion," limitless, free-floating drives.

FIGURE 31. Shading Effect Through Depth Impression
above

Made by an adult female aged twenty-seven years, exemplifying shading effect through depth impression.

FIGURE 32. Rhythm of Color and Strokes
opposite

These paintings were made by an adult female twenty-five years of age. They exemplify rhythm of color and of strokes, each presented in a contrasting arrangement, that is, contrast through alternating straight and curved lines and contrast of color patterns. Picture *B* was painted several weeks after painting *A*, during which interval the subject underwent therapy. The sequence *A-B* also exemplifies growth process. Growth is shown by a reduction in the contrast element, that is, by the dominance of curved lines over straight ones, and by the blending of colors rather than by the simple contrast of them. This is a variation on a theme, but the basic theme does persist.

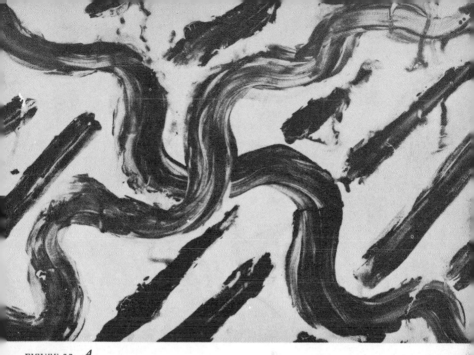

FIGURE 32. A

FIGURE 32. B

FIGURE 33. Rhythm of Numbers

Exemplifies the rhythm of numbers. Made by a male aged twenty-one years, shows a four-consistency. Here the family constellation was four. The subdivision of the number concept should also be noted. Only three of the pillars are held firmly together by the three-bar line at the top. The fourth pillar has almost broken off. An interview revealed that this corresponded to the subject's experience with his family group.

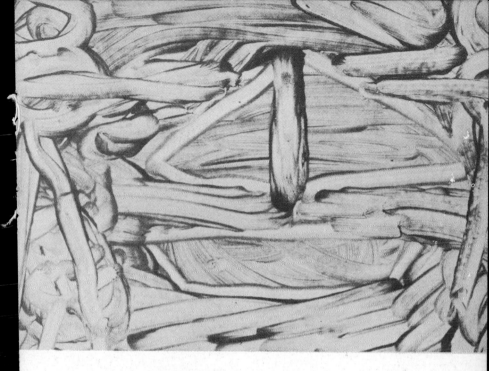

FIGURE 34. Objectification of Conflict

Exemplifies objectification of conflict. Made by an adolescent male aged fourteen years. Spontaneously, the subject verbalized, "Two pirates fighting for possession of gold." Having been asked for associations, the subject replied, "Just like my parents fighting, who will have me."

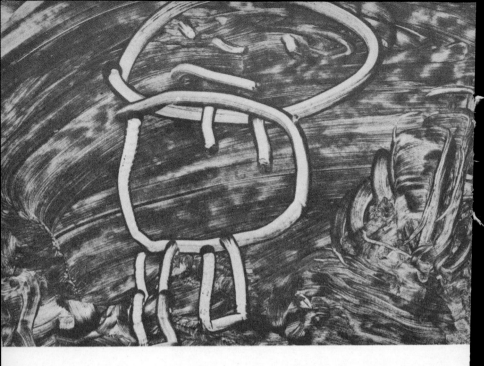

FIGURE 35. Sequence Analysis in Three Therapeutic Sessions

These paintings illustrate the sequence analysis developed by means of five therapeutic sessions that took place at the rate of one each week. The subject, an infantile, six-year-old boy who suffered from delayed speech, had attended a speech clinic for one and a half years without making any progress. His negativism and determination not to talk were readily apparent.

above depicts a human figure of primitive structure, without hands, on a black background.

opposite top produced during the third session, maintains the black background. In this picture, which includes a mailbox at one side, the figure is depicted as jumping a rope and enjoying it. The function of a mailbox as an element of communication was mentioned, as also that the boy had hands and that he was using them as a means for obtaining pleasure.

opposite bottom made during the fifth session, again depicts the boy with a mailbox. In this painting the figure is better proportioned, its balance is better, and the foundation is more stable. The mailbox again appears as a symbol of communication. At this session the subject asked to play with blocks and other material, thus establishing mutual rapport. Because his negativism had now receded, speech training could proceed from this point onward. No other means of play therapy was used.

RESUME: During the five sessions, the subject's speech and general adjustment process began to show definite improvement. both at home and on the block.

FIGURE 36. Finger-Painting Exemplifying Resistance Breaking

pist recognized that many of the subject's fears were evoked by actions that she knew her mother might disapprove of. Her mother, whom she admired as a very efficient woman, attempted to imbue her with a strong sense of perfectionism. Her fear of failure to reach perfection was the source of her vocational difficulties.

While her sense of failure was at its height, she produced a picture containing three abstract forms and then painted a determined, wide, heavy stroke separating one from the other two. After that stroke she showed signs of released tension. She engaged in pleasurable patting motions which yielded soft strokes. When asked what two and one meant (see rhythm of numbers), she pointed to the single design to the left and said it was her mother. The other two she designated as her father and herself.

In this painting, as was revealed later, she began to face her desire to rid herself of her mother's restrictive influence, although this was not verbalized during the actual painting situation. Subsequent interviews made it possible to work through this problem and she was then ready to accept the above interpretations. Her ability to free herself from the restrictive influences relieved her from her psychosomatic symptoms.

Prior to the painting the therapist attempted to channel the discussion so as to bring out the possible relationship, but the subject was completely unwilling to recognize it as pertinent. She could not accept it. In the course of her finger-painting, however, she was able to confront herself and to act out some of those personal emotional problems that she had previously been unable to face. The problem had reached the "speech-ripe" level at the completion of the painting.[8] Having accepted the emotional content, she was ready to extend the content into her verbal awareness.

Another function in the therapeutic process which finger-painting may play is that of catharsis. Oftentimes the process allows the subject to act out or paint out his hostilities in the painting situation.

Resistance, commonly encountered as the therapy progresses,

---

[8] For a discussion of the "speech-ripe level" see Froeschels [8].

may manifest itself as inability by the subject to produce material, such as dreams, free associations, and fantasies. Finger-painting can play a helpful role in providing a way for the patient to overcome his resistance. (See Figure number 35.)

In a like manner finger-painting has been used successfully as a barometer of therapeutic success, assisting the therapist in the timing of his interpretations and helping him develop his therapeutic tactics.

SUMMARY AND EVALUATION

It was not the purpose of this chapter to set finger-painting above other techniques. It does seem to me, however, that finger-painting, in addition to being a diagnostic complement to other projective techniques, yields specific data that are helpful from a therapeutic viewpoint. As a dynamic instrument it has the outstanding advantage that it can be employed concomitantly as a part of therapy. A few of the major advantages and characteristics that were cited may now be summed up and a few others briefly mentioned.

A. *Finger-painting permits a most genuine projection of the personality.*—As a task relatively free from motor limitations and social pressure, finger-painting involves little experience of failure. It is fun to do and conducive to the establishment of rapport. Complete rejections are rare.

As a performance technique finger-painting is not dependent upon language factors. It tends to elicit strong emotions and makes for spontaneous verbalizations, which give easy rise to the production of fantasy material, all permitting a genuine projection of personality upon a plastic field.

B. *Finger-painting is a very flexible diagnostic technique.*— Through the technique of process analysis, observing every step the subject takes, leading to the final product, the administrator is enabled to have an understanding of the subject's concept formation and his changes in emotion or symbolic substitution of content.

Making recurrent use of finger-painting over longer periods of time—finger-painting is sufficiently sensitive to yield indices of emotional growth—is particularly helpful when the method is used in connection with therapy. Any number of paintings can be obtained from one subject; there is no problem of equivalent forms.

In the interpretation of various categories, such as space utilization, color, or strokes, finger-painting is much akin to other projective techniques, such as drawing or Rorschach.

In the subject's motions we have a direct expression of his immediate feelings. In the concept of rhythm, finger-painting gives a truly individualized picture of the subject's characteristic approach to his task, which may help us to understand his style of life. In the rhythmic arrangement of numbers finger-painting may give clinicians a graphic view of the subjective experience of the individual's family constellation.

C. *Finger-painting is an effective tool when used as part of a therapeutic situation.*—The painting situation permits easy moving from therapy to diagnosis and vice versa. The task involves a unique experience for the subject which may elicit and permit an emotional "painting out" of previously concealed material. This frequently enables a subject to integrate insights into his verbal awareness that he had previously been unable to face. In some cases the graphic dream may enable the subject to gain an immediate perception of his own problem; he may experience his own resistance and the reasons for this resistance. This may open the way for a further fruitful continuation of therapeutic work.

In this chapter we have considered only one of the approaches to personality that are included under the heading of projective techniques. These techniques are based on similar fundamental assumptions, and in some instances employ similar concepts and terminologies.

I have attempted in many instances to relate observations on finger-painting to those made in connection with other techniques. It is an important task to determine further the relationships existing among the various kinds of data obtained with different projective techniques. To the extent that agreement can be found, the projective hypothesis may be further substantiated. To the extent that we have observed in finger-painting certain agreement with observations from other techniques, particularly with regard to the diagnostic categories, to that extent finger-painting has given strength to the rationale underlying projective methods as a whole.

REFERENCES

1. ALLEN, F. H.: *Psychotherapy with Children.* New York: W. W. Norton & Co.; 1942.

2. ALSCHULER, R. H., and HATTWICK, L. B. W.: *Painting and Personality.* Chicago: University of Chicago Press; 1947.

3. ARLOW, J. A., and KADIS, A.: Finger-Painting in the Psychotherapy of Children," *American Journal of Orthopsychiatry,* Vol. 16 (1946), pp. 134–46.

4. BEACH, V.: "Phases in the Development of Children's Paintings," *Journal of Experimental Education,* Vol. 13 (1944), pp. 1–4.

5. CAIRNS, J.: "Finger-Painting at Perkins Institute," *Teachers Forum for Instruction of Blind Children,* Vol. 8 (1935), pp. 6–7.

6. FLEMING, J.: "Observation in the Use of Finger-Painting in the Treatment of Adult Patients with Personality Disorders," *Character and Personality,* Vol. 8 (1940), pp. 301–10.

7. FRANK, L. K.: "Projective Methods for the Study of Personality," *Journal of Psychology,* Vol. 8 (1939), pp. 389–413.

8. FROESCHELS, E.: *The Human Race.* New York: Philosophical Library; 1947.

9. LYLE, B., and SHAW, R. F.: "Encouraging Children to Express Their Phantasies," *Bulletin of the Menninger Clinic,* Vol. 3 (1937), pp. 78–86.

10. MOSSE, E.: "Painting Analyses in the Treatment of Neurosis," *Psychoanalytic Review,* Vol. 27 (1947), pp. 65–81.

11. NAPOLI, P. J.: "Finger-Painting and Personality Diagnosis," *Genetic Psychology Monographs,* Vol. 34 (1946), pp. 192–230.

12. ———: "The Interpretative Aspects of Finger-Painting," *J. Psychol.,* Vol. 23 (1947), pp. 93–132.

13. OBROOK, I.: "The Therapeutic Value of Fingerpainting," *Crippled Child,* Vol. 13 (1935), p. 172.

14. PATTERSON, R. M., and LEIGHTNER, M. A.: "A Comparative Study of Spontaneous Paintings of Normal and Mentally Deficient Children of the Same Mental Age," *American Journal of Mental Deficency,* Vol. 48 (1944), pp. 345–53.

15. ROSENZWEIG, L. G., and DURBIN, L. A.: "Fingerpainting as an Investigative Approach to Therapeutic Technique," *Occupational Therapy,* Vol. 24 (1945), pp. 1–12.

16. SHAW, R. F.: *Fingerpainting*. Boston: Little, Brown & Co.; 1934.
17. ——: "Out of the Mouths of Babes," *Atlantic Monthly*, 1934.
18. SPRING, W. J.: "Words and Masses," *Psychoanalytic Quarterly*, 1936, pp. 244–58.
19. STEVENS, K. H.: "Fingerpainting for Little Deaf Children," *Volta Review*, Vol. 48 (1946), pp. 445–7.
20. WOLFF, W.: *Personality of the Pre-School Child*. New York: Grune & Stratton; 1946.

Projective Tests in Nonclinical Areas

▼

Projective Tests in Nonclinical Areas

INTRODUCTION

A SURVEY of the recent psychological literature provides convincing evidence that projective tests enjoy wide application outside the clinical area. Indeed, projective methods are being increasingly employed in a wide variety of situations in which inquiry into personality is an essential consideration. This section of the book stresses some of the contributions that the projective techniques are making in business and industry and in action research. In each of these areas psychologists who have become acquainted with projective methods have felt that these newer techniques offer a fruitful and rewarding means of resolving certain of the troublesome issues that research workers in the areas have constantly had to face.

The fact that projective methods have entered the fields of social and industrial psychology is evidence of the profound changes that have taken place in recent years in the entire field of psychology, movements that reflect a change in focus from "segmental man" to "total man." This interest in the whole human being is a far advance over the time when Spranger's types and a psychology of personality based on traits divorced social behavior from motivation and the rest of the dynamics of personality.

In a similar manner, industrial psychology not too long ago was concerned primarily with the measurement of efficiency and of aptitudes among workers in a highly circumscribed way. Largely as the result of forces from outside the area, the emphasis has shifted from an exclusive attention to such conditions as lighting and seating arrangements and even to programs of motivation like the premium incentive to the interpersonal relationship of the worker to his supervisors, equals, and subordinates. In this new frame of reference, feelings of insecurity among workers, the character structure of executives and administrators, and group dynamics have become important considerations. Thus it is that projective techniques are moving to the fore, capable of providing information on the complex matrix of biological, psychological, and social determinants that make up man as a *zoon politicon.*

IN THEIR paper Dr. Daniel Brower and Dr. Arthur Weider report on the ways in which psychologists who serve business and industry have in recent years utilized various projective techniques. The authors stress the point that the usefulness of psychology to business and industry has been greatly enlarged through the introduction of the procedures. In examining the material that follows, the reader will find it helpful to refer also to the section of Harrower's chapter in Part II which deals with the application of the Rorschach Test in the industrial setting.

Spurred on by the recent war, projective methods are likely to find ever wider application in personnel work, in employee and industrial relations, and in allied areas of business and industry.

▼

Projective Techniques in Business and Industry

Daniel Brower and Arthur Weider

THE recent emergence of the clinical point of view in the activities of psychologists in business and industry has resulted in many attempts to introduce projective techniques as part of the evaluation programs. Traditionally psychologists in these fields have concentrated their efforts upon selection and placement procedures [17, 23, 34], appraisal for promotion [11], job evaluation and merit rating [12, 14], training of supervisors [24, 26], accident reduction [10], measurement and improvement of morale [15], evaluation of departmental efficiency, [2, 3, 20], marketing and advertising research [9, 13, 35], and the like. These contributions have been of great value to many business organizations. All of these operations have depended upon nonprojective methods in the main and have been characterized by two shortcomings:

1. The evaluation of personality in terms of traits alone.
2. The failure to consider manifestations of unconscious motivation.

Thus as a consequence these traditional procedures have

yielded a partial picture of temperament and the personality patterns of the subjects tested, but have fostered several abuses in the employment of testing devices in industry. Not the least of these is the deliberate misrepresentation of himself by a testee in order to appear in a more favorable light; for example, concealing antisocial tendencies, marked emotional instability, and so on. On the other hand, the apparently simpler nature of the inventory and rating techniques in the hands of the tester has resulted in widespread oversimplification and misinterpretation of test findings, however unwitting this may have been.

It has become evident in recent years that projective devices for the evaluation of personality serve to lessen the deficiencies of the inventory and rating scale techniques. This may be understood in terms of the ambiguity of the stimulus, the wider latitude of response possibility, and the necessary training with which to interpret properly the data obtained. These techniques are bound to be helpful where the nonprojective methods failed since they consider personality in terms of patterns and not in terms of generic traits or divorced entities such as self-sufficiency, confidence, dominance.

The central thesis of projective techniques is that the major part of personality structure, as tested in the industrial context, comprises material that is either withheld or repressed for reasons motivated by the immediate job situation or by virtue of a habit pattern acquired in previous job adjustments. On the other hand, the inventory and rating scale methods tap only those layers of the personality which are not unduly affected by repression or conscious concealment.

The first effective projective techniques, such as the Rorschach and Thematic Apperception Test, did not lend themselves to large-scale adoption because of time and cost. Newer projective methods, however, have been developed and older ones modified toward the end of making them more practicable for diagnostic or screening purposes. These briefer methods have been found valuable as supplements to testing batteries consisting of intelligence, aptitude, interest, and personality questionnaires.

It has become obvious even to nonprofessional personnel in industry that these traditional methods do not provide data from which *potentialities* of job behavior may be determined.

Manifest behavior, conscious wishes, and self-evaluation, which are ascertained by means of these older methods, tend to give a distorted picture as well as an inadequate one, thus making *prediction* of future job adjustments very difficult, if not impossible.

METHODS

1. *The Cornell Word Form (CWF)*.

The Cornell Word Form [*16, 27, 33*] was devised to effect the differentiation of "normals" from those with neuropsychiatric and psychosomatic disorders in a manner not apparent to the subject. This test has both quantitative and qualitative usefulness for industrial situations.

The subject is presented with a list of stimulus words, each of which is followed by two response words. He is asked to encircle whichever of the two words seems to him to be related to the stimulus word. Some of the choices are comparatively obvious in their implication; for example, SLEEP—comfort, restlessness. Others are not; for example, MOTHER—mine, woman. Stimuli of the latter type are in the majority. Although many items are of the obvious type, this point is often unwittingly overlooked and the subject may give informative responses in spite of a desire to falsify.

While this modification of the word-association techniques has been dictated by the exigencies of quick group methods applied to large-scale testing, some of its projective qualities have been maintained in its present forced-choice form. The total score affords a method of comparison with norms established in various standardizations, while an examination of "wrong" responses adds qualitative cues for clinical interviews.

In a large Midwestern industrial plant this test was part of a battery; another instrument for the appraisal of emotional factors was more direct in its methodology, and the two best complemented each other satisfactorily. When the direct questionnaire [Cornell Index [*16, 27, 29, 31, 33*]] pointed up symptoms that were known to the subject, the CWF would indicate the extent, the depth, and the intensity of these symptoms. Invariably, when the Cornell Index uncovered many symptoms and the CWF revealed but few, the nature of these symptoms was either superficial, situational, not severe, or of short duration. The

Cornell Word Form is used in business and industrial situations as a pre-employment tool, prior to upgrading, and for diagnostic purposes prior to counseling [28, 30].

High scores indicating faulty associations occurred infrequently in pre-employment testing, but when the scores reached above norm levels the subject was interviewed in order to ascertain the nature and the extent of psychological disturbances.

In the precounseling testing of a twenty-two-year-old married clerk referred because of "depression, loss of interest in work, and a falling-off of efficiency," the following italicized responses were given:

THROAT	*lump*	neck	DISEASE	*die*	doctor
BOY	*trouble*	pal	THOUGHTS	*miserable*	happy
HEALTH	*worry*	good	NERVES	steady	*nervous*
MOUTH	*dry*	taste	NIGHT	sleep	*shaky*
SLEEP	comfort	*restless*	HEART	*beat fast*	good

Subsequent diagnostic testing and clinical interview revealed a severely maladjusted young man with much depression and conflicts produced by a confusion concerning his sexual role. In addition to his depression, there was marked suspiciousness with preschizoid emotional blunting; there was also a history of hypertension in the army, which was diagnosed as being psychosomatic in nature.

A perusal of his associations offers the following qualitative nuances by confirming his depression (DISEASE—die, THOUGHTS —miserable, HEALTH—worry, SLEEP—restless); preschizoid status (BROTHER—my brother, WATER—to drink it, MESSAGE—mysterious); latent homosexuality (BOY—trouble, MAN—hate); psychosomatic, hypochondriacal, and psychoneurotic symptoms (in addition to those already mentioned): THROAT—lump, HEALTH —worry, PERSON—nervous, NERVES—nervous, MOUTH—dry, NIGHT —shaky, SLEEP—restless, HEART—beat fast, DOCTOR—die). Several of these responses above offer qualitative cues and do not enter into the quantitative score.

The effectiveness of this tool in industry can be measured in terms of the following:

1. It has simplicity of administration and scoring (requires but five minutes).

2. It is a screening device for production workers when a more extensive personality battery is not feasible.

3. Its qualitative material can be derived without any formalized scoring procedure.

4. It is a point of departure in the employee counseling situation.

5. It lends itself to group administration with no time minimum limit, thus making it practically self-administering.

2. *Draw-a-Person.*

In its industrial application, this technique lends itself to group administration as a screening device. While certain clinical cues that might be gained from observing the individual's performance are not obtained, it has been found that sufficient insight may be achieved by the examiner in this group form to warrant its use. These psychomotor expressive productions reveal all components in the personality that revolve around the body-image; for example, acceptance of sexual role, anxiety or depressiveness in the sphere of interpersonal relations, anxiety relating to bodily processes or structures, relative degree of rigidity or flexibility of the personality, tendency to withdraw from reality, low sense of self-esteem or inferiority complex, indication of structural brain damage.

Specifically, some of the most revealing features that emerge are the following:

1. Existence of such severe interpersonal disturbances as to warrant further exploration in the pre-employment situation.

2. Since the degree of maleness and femaleness on both the biological and psychological levels is a subtle but influential determinant of job behavior, it is most helpful to obtain a dynamic picture of the degree of acceptance of one's sexual role in the light of one's relations to subordinates and superiors. There are cases known of job maladjustment traceable to such conflicts.

3. Extreme inclinations toward either a passive-dependent job relationship or an expansive-aggressive pattern. The former drawing pattern may be manifested in overconscientiousness, perfectionism, compulsive behavior, and an inability to accept higher-level responsibility involving the issuance of orders. The aggressive drawing pattern may be manifested in an antiauthoritarian or autocratic tendency, depending upon the echelon of the job.

4. Evidence of marked emotional immaturity or disintegrative patterns in the involutional periods.

While a full discussion of the interpretation of this test is left to be presented in another chapter, it is suggested that the following are among the more important differentiæ of emotional stability for the purposes of the psychologist in industry:

1. Degree of deviation from center of the page for the placement of the drawing.

2. Absolute size of drawings.

3. Relative size of drawing of man compared with that of woman.

4. Degree of pressure exerted upon the page.

5. Variability in pressure exerted.

6. Degree of connectedness of major regions of body—head, neck, truck, and limbs.

7. Position of figure drawn—*en face*, profile, or back.

8. Area of preoccupation with detail.

9. Number of dimensions of body indicated—unidimensional, "stick-figure"; bidimensional; shown in depth.

10. Evidence of alteration or erasure.

11. Degree of nudity of drawings and any indication of genitalia.

12. Posture and degree of muscular tension drawn.

13. Resemblance of figures to animal forms.

14. Omission of, or preoccupation with, special part of the body.

15. Number of colors and apparent fluidity with which these are used.

The use of a set of colored pencils makes the test more flexible and permits the subject to shift his orientation from one color to another. It has been found thus far on several hundred cases that the more constricted individuals use fewer colors while the more effervescent or dissociated types tend to shift rapidly from one color to the next. Furthermore, depressed individuals apparently select the black and brown while aggressive ones select bright colors. The added use of colors in this technique apparently serves to accentuate some of the cues which may be derived from an examination of the formal aspects of the drawings.

This is one of the few expressive projective methods which

combine the advantages of minimal cost and time, can be administered in groups without the presence of a psychologist, and yet penetrate to the deeper subsemantic levels of the personality without the masking effect of verbalization. In addition to the diagnostic cues gleaned from this technique, the authors have found this method useful in inducing a more relaxed and informal atmosphere which facilitates the development of rapport.

3. *Sentence Completion Test (SCT).*

The Sentence Completion Test has recently been reintroduced into the armamentarium of the clinical psychologist [*19, 21, 25*]. Each investigator has worked with his own improvised series of incomplete phrases, and for the most part the interpretation has been primarily subjective. More recently some attempts have been made to establish norms by standardizing the administration and scoring, which may increase the test's usefulness and extend its application [*18*].

In its present forms the instructions on most revisions have been standardized to encourage freedom and spontaneity of response. This projective technique allows much latitude in expressing underlying inhibited drives, emotions, sentiments, and complexes that the subject is unwilling or unable to admit. In writing his responses the subject may inadvertently reveal these covert tendencies by completing the phrases that stimulate free associations.

Some examples of this technique classified into clinical categories follow:

A. Feelings of inadequacy:
  My worst . . .
  My hardest job . . .
  The only trouble . . .

B. Suppressed wishes:
  I secretly . . .
  I hate . . .
  If only . . .

C. Level of aspiration:
  My greatest hope . . .
  The future . . .
  I want to know . . .

E. Interpersonal relations:
  If only my boss . . .
  Most supervisors . . .
  The men under him . . .

F. Familial situations:
  My father used to . . .
  If my mother . . .
  My family never . . .

G. Psychosexuality:
  Most girls . . .
  A wife . . .
  Other men . . .

D. Self-evaluation:
    I impress people as . . .
    I feel . . .
    I am best when . . .

H. Aggression problems:
    All minorities . . .
    I hate . . .
    The most dangerous . . .

    I. Inner conflicts:
        I cannot understand what makes me . . .
        My mind . . .
        I worry . . .

The list above is suggestive and not definitive since the ramifications and interrelations of data yielded can be interpreted in several ways, depending upon the circumstances necessitating the testing in the first place.

For example, a forty-eight-year-old clerk, employed by his company seventeen years, was referred by his supervisor because of "worrisomeness, over-conscientiousness, run-down physical condition ('hypertensive'), and a sudden loss of interest in his work." The psychodiagnostic test battery was administered, including a Sentence Completion form, before clinical interviews were instituted. Some of the more illustrative responses that reveal the nature of his emotional difficulties were:

1. *I feel* a little tired at present—stayed up a little late.
2. *What annoys me* injustices—intolerance.
3. *If my mother* in better health could live with someone congenial.
4. *What puzzles me* is why people in positions of authority and control are so many times absolutely dumb.
5. *If I had my way* I would put men in high places with brains and tolerance.
6. *My ambition is to* give or create a lasting idea for humanity.
7. *When I was a child* I was always nervous but idealistic.
8. *I suffer* an inferior complex with some people some places.
9. *My father used to* have a wonderful but weak personality—was a good executive in shop.
10. *A wife* should be intelligent and happy and co-operative partner.
11. *I failed* to take responsibility when it seems that I should have.
12. *My most important decision was* to get married and leave home.
13. *I object* to being driven or to anyone losing their right to free thought and action.

A summary of the subject's entire Sentence Completion Test responses indicates strong inferiority concerning the lack of education and strong mother fixation resulting in conflict with his wife. He identifies himself with his father, whom he characterizes as having a "wonderful but weak personality." The subject loses his patience with a supervisor who lacks intelligence. He feels that his wife is not co-operative and he is having much difficulty in deciding how to be a good husband and a good son simultaneously. This is indicated by his remark: "My most important decision was to get married and leave home." The subject never really left home since he is still under the strong influence of his mother. He feels very strongly about "being driven" and objects to anyone's "losing his right to free thought and action." He has lost his freedom, however! He attributes early childhood nervousness to idealism, which as an adult he has translated into strict conformance to society. While he identifies himself with his father, who was a "wonderful but weak personality," but "was a good executive in shop," the subject rationalizes that people with authority and position, his supervisors in particular, are "dumb" and stupid. He envies such people, but because he feels inadequate and cannot hold a position of responsibility, he is harboring much resentment, which, together with his marital problems, is the basis of his psychosomatic complaints and symptoms.

4. *Thematic Apperception Test (TAT)*.

This device has the great advantage in the industrial field of being self-administering while also being a penetrating clinical instrument. It is best used for further diagnostic determinations beyond the data derived from the Sentence Completion Test and other abbreviated devices. Clinical hunches derived from the shorter screening techniques may be confirmed through the use of the TAT. Specific situational complexes revealed by other methods may be more completely explored in dynamic and genetic terms through the TAT. After revealing himself as a maladjusted person in the briefer devices, a testee will more readily express his difficulty when confronted with ten Thematic cards. Not only does this follow from the very nature of the Thematic Test stimuli, but the retest situation in which the testee is called back for the TAT after having taken an entire battery certainly serves to raise the anxiety level. Since too many subjects take psychological tests in the industrial context under conditions of compulsion and with consequent evasive inclinations, it has been our experience that a moderate degree of anxiety increment serves to portray more of the personality structure and dynamics than do conditions of complete relaxation. The TAT has the most to offer when used as a supplementary test in this connection.

In the TAT, as with the Sentence Completion method, there is some tendency for recent events, the residues of which lie more or less in consciousness, to overshadow the content of the responses a subject gives. It cannot be overemphasized that such recent experiences function merely as vehicles for the inevitable emergence of the personality of the testee and can be clearly differentiated by the experienced clinician. In other words, the subject's recent experiences are the verbalized manifestations of his more underlying and latent mental processes.

Specifically, the psychologist in industry can use the TAT to determine the employee's interpersonal tendencies against the background of his fundamental parental and sibling experiences and the still active residues thereof. Thus, the reaction tendencies of an individual toward his superior may be determined from his Thematic projections in relation to father-figures, while his most likely behavior toward contemporaries would be more readily gleaned from his Thematic productions about sibling-figures. While a highly skilled clinician, staking a great deal on clinical intuition, can obtain these data from The Sentence Completion Test and other devices, such data may be more reliably obtained from the TAT and also derived more in their natural setting of the whole personality.

In examining candidates for executive training and other positions of responsibility, the TAT provides the most dependable yardstick for level of aspiration which has yet been devised. While it is true that other test and interview techniques may supply data in this area, such findings are spotty if not integrated in terms of motivational and emotional factors underlying one's level of aspiration, largely unconscious in nature. The TAT also offers some clue to the threshold of limitation beyond which a candidate for a responsible position will not be likely to exert his intellectual and aptitudinal resources.

Further applications of the TAT in business and industry lie in the confirmation of marked neurotic trends revealed by other devices, and some indication of the testee's degree of insight. The latter will be found most important in selecting individuals for personnel work. For an individual who is psychologically sophisticated or has become "test-wise" through frequent exposure to psychometric devices, it is well to administer the TAT at the outset in preference to more easily slanted instruments. Suspicions of possible psychopathic deviation may be confirmed or ruled out through the TAT, which should therefore be used in all cases where a serious degree of responsibility is to be placed in an individual's hands; for example, treasurer or other top-management executives.

Finally, the TAT is an instrument of profound revelation of the latent forces of aggression that lie within the individual, the relative degree of emphasis upon internalization or externalization thereof, and the likely directions and intensity of manifestation of aggression on the job.

The following Thematic productions are intended to illustrate some of the points alluded to above:

Male, 22 years of age. 7 BM. "This is youth consulting with the experience of age. This is the young college student consulting with a professor whom he admires, respects, and trusts.

"The student is attempting to set his course in life and he has come to talk it over. His manner shows a burning desire and a deep concern, a seriousness of purpose, and a willingness to be open-minded toward the advice of others.

"They, the young and the old, will find a solution and the student will go forward and the professor will find the deep satisfaction of having been at least a small part responsible for it all."

High level of aspiration. Respects advice of experienced supervisors. Evidence of doubt as to vocational goals.

Male, 36 years of age. 7 BM "The young man in the picture has been working a long time at the job the older man gave him and found out after a lot of work that he could not do the job assigned to him and now wonders if the work could have been done better by someone else. The older man is questioning his helper to try to learn what went wrong with the work and is trying to find out if it will pay to continue the work."

Feels insecure in his job situation. Doubts his ability for his pres-

ent position and wonders if his employer is contemplating dismissal.

Male, 31 years of age. 18 BM "The man is drunk. He is being supported by friends who are taking him home."

Claimed he indulged in social drinking only on rare occasions and that he never experienced any emotional difficulty as a result of drinking. His attendance and work record attested to chronic intoxication necessitating psychological evaluation.

5. The Rorschach Technique.

The individually administered Rorschach still provides the most penetrating and integrated profile of an individual's personality structure, far more completely than any of the briefer techniques. The psychologist in industry, however, does not usually need such a penetrating and complete picture for routine selection and classification of personnel [1, 22, 32]. For these purposes a battery of briefer methods generally provides sufficient material. In cases where there is still reasonable doubt, the TAT, which has the advantage of being self-administering, usually serves the purpose of clarifying the individual's personality dynamics. It must be stressed in this connection, however, that any one of the briefer techniques in and by itself cannot fulfill the needs of industrial psychology.

It has been found that it is best to reserve the individual form of the Rorschach for clinical diagnosis of those who appear to be markedly disturbed, malingering, or prepsychotic or for prognostication of special problem cases. For example, many highly intelligent but markedly disturbed employees will often succeed in being thoroughly evasive and noncommittal through all other projective devices described in this chapter out of fear of demotion or dismissal. The careful psychologist will generally recognize evidence of such evasiveness and will subject these persons to the individual Rorschach. His recommendations to management will then be based, in part, upon a clear awareness of the predominant needs of such persons to be evasive.

Management frequently refers an employee, generally a member of the higher echelons, who has been exhibiting some serious maladjustment in the recent past after having served the company very adequately for a number of years. The problem may be that of absenteeism, alcoholism, dishonesty, or a general decline in efficiency. It is, of course, desirable to subject this employee to an extensive battery of tests of intelligence, relevant aptitudes, temperament, and interests. An interview with the psychologist will often clinch the nature of the difficulty. Unless one is in a position to conduct many interviews, however, which is very rare, it will be rather difficult to prognosticate the course that might be expected from such a person without the benefit of the Rorschach. Thus a progressive-minded employer may be willing to spend company funds on psychotherapy to help the employee gain insight into and overcome some personal difficulty, the effects of which are being manifested in his job performance. The psychologist then has the obligation of estimating the degree of remediability of the difficulty with reference to the amount of patience and expenditure the employer is inclined to offer. The Rorschach enables the psychologist to make the most equitable statement of diagnosis and prognosis for both employee and employer.

6. *Tomkins-Horn Picture Arrangement Test (PAT).*

This test was designed by Tomkins and Horn[1] for the purpose of exploring an individual's reaction tendencies to work situations, to frustrations incurred at work, to accidents at work, to supervisors and co-workers. Figure 37 illustrates the format of this test, which consists of twenty-five situations arranged in the manner indicated in the sample situation that appears in this figure. For highly specialized or rough screening purposes, shortened forms have also been used rather successfully; these consist of six or even three situations. The format tries to eliminate the element of suggestion as to which order the testee should use to organize his responses. This is accomplished through the use of symbols instead of numbers or letters and by requiring the subject to turn the page to see each item.

Thus far the interpretation has been purely clinical and qualitative, since no norms have yet been prepared. The interpretation is accomplished in three ways:

1. Analysis of the sequence of items in each situation.

———

[1] We are grateful to Dr. S. S. Tomkins and Dr. D. Horn for the opportunity of being among the first to experiment with this technique. Thus far we have used it on over 2,500 applicants and employees in industry.

INSTRUCTIONS - This is a test to see how well you can arrange pictures so as to tell a story that makes sense. Each page contains a set of three pictures Each of the three pictures has a mark at the bottom of the picture; one is marked △ another is marked ☐ and another is marked ○

Your job is to put one of these marks on each of the three lines at the bottom of the page in the order which makes the best sense. Following each mark write one sentence which tells the story.

You will have to turn the booklet around to see the different pictures

PLEASE USE INK

Example:

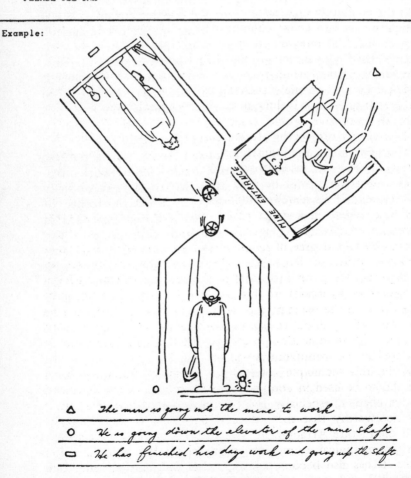

△ The man is going into the mine to work

○ He is going down the elevator of the mine shaft

☐ He has finished his days work and going up the shaft

FIGURE 37. Format of the Tomkins-Horn Picture Arrangement Test

2. Analysis of content of each response, together with the quantity of verbal production.

3. Observation of significant perseveration or other trends that seem to recur over the course of many of the situations.

The basic assumption in this technique is that the testee identifies himself with the worker appearing in the figures. Since this worker is portrayed in terms of manual labor, one might assume that clerical, managerial, and executive personnel would not reveal their interpersonal work attitudes. However, the larger part of our experience with this instrument thus far has been with "white collar," semiprofessional, and executive personnel, and it is apparent that all testees do reveal work attitudes with the exception of top-management or higher executives. In the latter group there is a conscious, let alone unconscious, tendency to view such figures with great distance and even disdain. Here it is difficult to obtain a clear picture of how a higher executive would react to his fellow staff members. They tend to project highly stereotyped responses, which are clear repetitions of the industrial mores as to how a higher-level person *should* react instead of how he feels like reacting.

This instrument must be used with considerable caution, not only because of its novelty, but because of certain special problems that inhere in a given office, plant, or industry. For example, in an advertising agency one is expected to show the highest possible degree of initiative and self-reliance; in a manufacturing plant of large size one is expected to report all mechanical defects or difficulties to the repair mechanic. Therefore in those situations of this test which portray an apparent breakdown in the machine (see Figures 38 and 39), it would be a sign of lack of initiative for an advertising-agency applicant to respond with an indication of calling for aid where this would be expected in the manufacturing plant.

While this technique cannot yet be solely depended upon and should be used in conjunction with other devices described in this chapter, especially the Sentence Completion Test, it is still noteworthy that the industrial psychologist finds it easier with the Picture Arrangment Test to translate some of his findings from clinical terms into more applicable work-situation terms. It has also become apparent that these stimuli are more structured and concretized than such techniques as Draw-a-

Person and the Sentence Completion Test and therefore permit interpretations more directly in terms of work adjustment.

Some of the specific interpersonal dynamics that emerge most frequently in this technique are:

1. Tendency to express aggression toward the superior.

2. Tendency to assume or shun leadership; in other words, the way in which the testee views himself in the matter of influencing opinions of others.

3. Regressive tendencies, such as alcoholic, hysterical, and psychosomatic resolution of conflicts on the job.

4. Reaction to illness and physical injury as relating to work.

5. Degree of independence or dependence upon supervisor for guidance in expediting the work.

6. Obsessive-compulsive traits revealed in orderliness and perfectionism.

7. Apathy, ineptitude, or confusion in the face of an obstacle.

8. Degree of persistence and consistency of work habits.

9. Apparent degree of flexibility in shifting the set from one task to another.

10. Reaction to criticism.

It must be stressed that very little can be gleaned from one situation or even a few and that the entire interpretation must be viewed against the background of sex, age, amount of work experience, and the job under consideration.

The following examples have been taken from actual PAT protocols:

Figure 38:

○ The man is working and the machine breaks down.
△ He begins to take the machine apart to repair it.
□ The machine is all apart and he realizes he can't fix it, after all.

△ The man is in the process of repairing a lathe.
□ All the parts are out on the table.
○ He has put the lathe together successfully and is now working on it.

△ He is taking it apart.
□ He has it apart.
○ He has it together and it won't go.

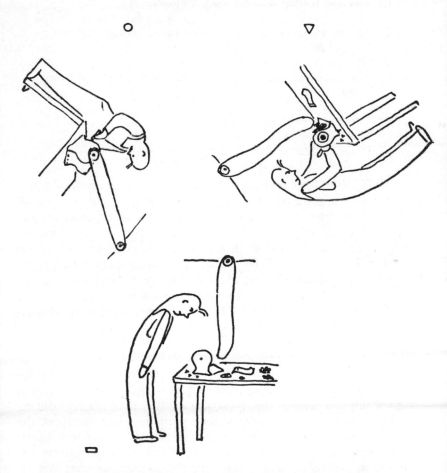

FIGURE 38. Situation One of the Picture Arrangement Test

□ The man has the parts of the motor ready to assemble.

△ The man has started to assemble the motor.

○ The man has the motor assembled and is operating it.

Figure 39:

△ The foreman introduces the new worker to his work bench.

□ He gives the worker a word of encouragement on starting his job.

○ The new worker does his job with gusto.

○ The man is working and something goes wrong with the machine.

△ He calls the repair man to fix it.

□ The machine is fixed and the repair man says, "Don't feel so bad, it wasn't your fault."

○ The man is working at his machine.

△ The foreman comes over to inspect the work.

□ He praises the worker for a job well done.

7. *Mirror-Drawing Technique.*

This method has recently been developed as an easily administered test of adjustment to stress *[4, 5, 6, 7, 8]*. It is a visuo-motor expressive technique which functions as a projective device. The subject is asked to trace a line or path by observing his movements in a mirror while his direct vision of the task is obstructed by a plate. The record is scored quantitatively for time and qualitatively for clinical cues that yield evidence of erratic performance, impulsiveness, cautiousness, depressiveness, and marked anxiety states. These categories have been empirically established by research on 300 college students, 75 hospitalized patients in a psychiatric hospital, and over 3,800 employees and applicants in industry.

In the industrial and personnel fields the mirror-drawing device lends itself to ease of administration and portability, and it does not necessitate the presence of the psychologist during administration. Yet nonprofessional people cannot interpret the results, thus providing a measure of protection against abuse. Furthermore, this device is nonverbal and it samples overt expressive behavior under experimental conditions that are at sharp variance with early acquired visuo-motor habits.

The following are the more essential factors that can be

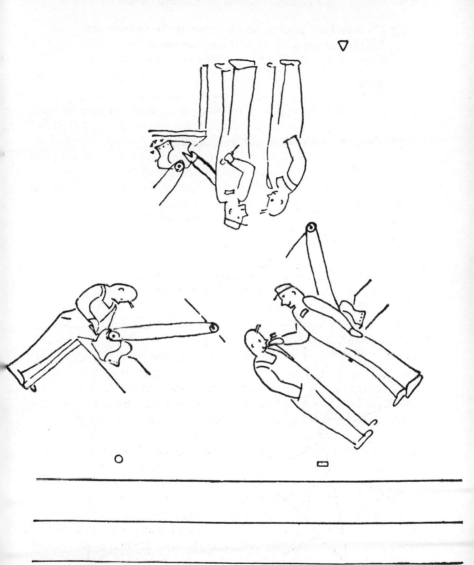

FIGURE 39. Situation Six on the Picture Arrangement Test

partially measured and tapped by this device:

1. Relative emphasis on speed and accuracy of performance.
2. Marked agitation and disorientation.
3. Degree of endurance under stress and adaptability to novel situations.

The interpretation must be made, of course, in the light of the subject's age and sex and the requirements of the job under consideration. Integrated with the rest of the aptitudinal, interest, and temperament battery, this method serves as a useful adjunct to indicate, in expressive nonverbal terms, the individual's adjustment to stress resulting from experimentally induced conflict. Examples of mirror drawings are presented in Figures 40, 41, and 42.

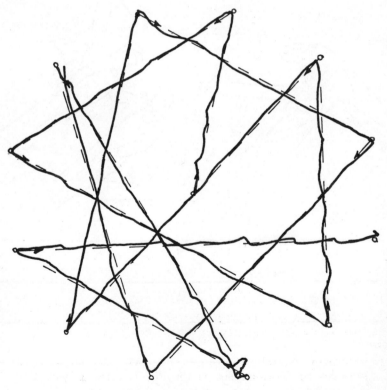

FIGURE 40. Mirror Drawing of a Very Stable Subject

CONCLUSION

These devices, while still insufficiently validated, lend themselves as highly flexible instruments which, in skilled hands, can be applied to a wide variety of situations in business and industry.

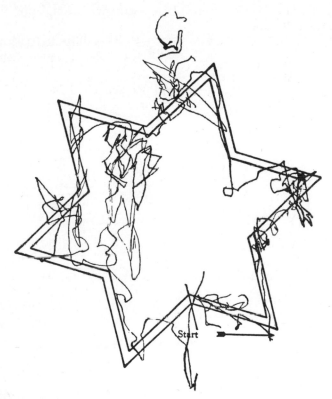

FIGURE 41. Mirror Drawing of an Individual in Acute Anxiety State

They make the test situation more lifelike and less artificial. Yet it is essential for the psychologist to translate the data of projective techniques into readily intelligible terms for management.

In conclusion, the following *modus operandi* for temperament-testing in industry is suggested:

1. Use of the Cornell Word Form, in conjunction with self-appraisal (questionnaire and self-rating) devices, for large-scale

screening of applicants and candidates for promotion. This is effective for pre-employment testing and identifying supervisory potential among the employees in a given plant.

2. Administration of a battery of temperament tests to those who clear through the initial screening. This may consist of the Picture Arrangement Test, Sentence Completion Test and Draw-a-Person.

3. Use of mirror-drawing as a test of ability to withstand stress after a testee has passed the basic temperament battery described above.

4. Reservation of the TAT and Rorschach Test for evaluation of higher-level personnel and for diagnosis and prognosis of difficult cases.

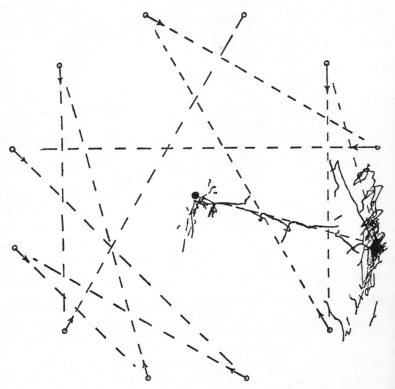

FIGURE 42. Mirror Drawing of Deeply Depressed Patient

REFERENCES

1. BALINSKY, B.: "Note on Use of the Rorschach in the Selection of Supervisory Personnel," *Rorschach Research Exchange,* Vol. 8 (1944), pp. 184–8.

2. BILLS, A. G.: *Psychology of Efficiency.* New York: Harper & Brothers; 1943.

3. BILLS, M. A.: "A Method for Classifying Jobs and Rating Efficiency," *Journal of Personnel Research,* Vol. 1 (1922), pp. 384–93.

4. BROWER, D.: "The Relations of Visuo-motor Conflict to Personality Traits and Cardiovascular Activity," *Journal of General Psychology,* Vol. 38 (1948), pp. 69–99.

5. ——: "Respiration and Blood Pressure in Sensory Motor Conflict," *J. Gen. Psychol.,* Vol. 34 (1946), pp. 47–58.

6. ——: "The Relation between Certain Rorschach Factors and Cardio-vascular Activity before and after Visuo-motor Conflict," *J. Gen. Psychol.,* Vol. 37 (1947), pp. 93–5.

7. ——: "The Relations between Minnesota Multiphasic Personality Inventory Scores and Cardio-vascular Measures before and after Experimentally Induced Visuo-motor Conflict," *Journal of Social Psychology,* Vol. 26 (1947), pp. 55–60.

8. ——: "The Relation between Intelligence and Cardio-vascular Activity before and after Visuo-motor Conflict," *Journal of Genetic Psychology,* Vol. 70 (1947), pp. 233–5.

9. BURTT, H. E.: *Psychology of Advertising.* Boston: Houghton Mifflin Co.; 1938.

10. DRAKE, C. A.: "Testing for Accident-Proneness." A paper presented before the American Association of Applied and Professional Psychology, University of Minnesota, August 31, 1937.

11. FILE, Q. W., and REMMERS, H. H.: "Studies in Supervisory Evaluation," *Journal of Applied Psychology,* Vol. 30 (1946), pp. 421–5.

12. FREYD, M.: "Merit System Research," *Personnel Journal,* Vol. 18 (1939), pp. 27–35, 61–6.

13. HEPNER, H. W.: *Effective Advertising.* New York: McGraw-Hill Book Co.; 1941.

14. LAWSHE, C. H., and SATTER, G. A.: "Studies in Job Evaluation," *J. Appl. Psychol.,* Vol. 28 (1944), pp. 189–98; Vol. 29 (1945), pp. 177–84.

15. MATHEWSON, S. B.: "A Survey of Personnel Management in 195 Concerns," *Person. J.,* Vol. 10 (1931), pp. 225–31.

16. MITTELMANN, B., and BRODMAN, K.: "The Cornell Indices and the Cornell Word Form: I. Construction and Standardization," *Annals of New York Academy of Science,* Vol. 46 (1946), pp. 573–8.

17. MOORE, H.: *Experience with Employment Tests.* Studies in Personnel Policy No. 32, National Industrial Conference Board; 1941.

18. ROHDE, A. R.: *Sentence Completion Tests (Manual).* New York: A. R. Rohde; 1947.

19. ROTTER, J. B. and WILLERMAN, B.: "The Incomplete Sentences Test as a Method of Studying Personality," *J. Clin. Psychol.,* Vol. 2 (1947), pp. 43–8.

20. RYAN, T. A.: *Work and Effort.* New York: Ronald Press Co.; 1947.

21. STEIN, M. I.: "The Use of a Sentence Completion Test for the Diagnosis of Personality," *Journal of Clinical Psychology,* Vol. 3 (1947), pp. 47–56.

22. STEINER, M. E.: "Use of the Rorschach Method in Industry," *Rorschach Res. Exch.,* Vol. II (1947), pp. 46–52.

23. STRANG, R.: "The Technique of the Interview," *J. Consult. Psychol.,* Vol. 3 (1939). pp. 90–2.

24. SUTERMEISTER, R. A.: "Training Foremen in Human Relations," *Personnel,* 1943.

25. TENDLER, A. D.: "A Preliminary Report on a Test for Emotional Insight," *J. Appl. Psychol.,* Vol. 14 (1930), pp. 123–36.

26. TURNER, G. C.: "Executive Training," *Advanced Management,* Vol. 4 (1939), pp. 87–93.

27. WEIDER, A., and WECHSLER, D.: "The Cornell Indices and the Cornell Word Form: II. Results." *Ann. N. Y. Acad. Sci.,* Vol. 46 (1946), pp. 579–88.

28. WEIDER, A., and MITTELMANN, B.: "Personality and Psychosomatic Disturbances among Industrial Personnel," *American Journal Orthopsychiatry,* Vol. 18 (1946), pp. 631–9.

29. WEIDER, A., et al.: "The Cornell Index: a Method for Quickly Assaying Personality and Psychosomatic Disturbances, to be Used as an Adjunct to Interview," *Psychosomatic Medicine,* Vol. 8 (1946), pp. 411–13.

30. WEIDER, A.: "Mental Hygiene in Industry: a Clinical Psychologist's Contribution," *J. Clin. Psychol.,* Vol. 3 (1947), pp. 309–20.

31. WEIDER, A., *et al.: Cornell Index (Manual).* New York: Psychological Corporation; 1948.

32. WILLIAMS, G.: "Possibilities of the Rorschach Technique in Industry," *Personnel*, Vol. 24 (1947), pp. 224–30.

33. WOLFF, H. G.: "The Cornell Indices and the Cornell Word Form: III. Application," *Ann. N. Y. Acad. Sci.*, Vol. 46 (1946), pp. 589–92.

34. WOOD, W. F.: "A New Method for Grading the Employment Questionnaire," *J. Appl. Psychol.*, Vol. 31 (1947), pp. 9–17.

35. WULFECK, W. H.: "The Role of the Psychologist in Market and Advertising Research," *J. Appl. Psychol.*, Vol. 29 (1945), pp. 95–102.

ADDITIONAL REFERENCES

BELLAK, L.: "The Concept of Projection: an Experimental Investigation and Study of the Concept," *Psychiatry*, Vol. 7 (1944), pp. 353–70.

MURRAY, H. A.: *Explorations in Presonality.* New York: Oxford University Press; 1938.

——: *Manual for the Thematic Apperception Test.* Cambridge: Harvard University Press; 1943.

TOMKINS, S.: *Thematic Apperception Test.* New York: Grune & Stratton: 1947.

▼

UNDER the sponsorship of the Commission on Community Interrelationships, and guided by the genius of the late Kurt Lewin, the field of action research has come into its own in recent years. As a unique approach to the study of social psychological problems, action research is concerned constantly with the role of personality in the study of problems of group tension, morale, conflict, and prejudice. As Harold Proshansky's chapter ably indicates, projective methods have found significant application in this new area.

The results obtained from using the techniques have amply justified the faith of social psychologists who turned to them as methods for enriching their inquiries and for providing data which often could not otherwise be obtained. There is every reason to believe that in the period ahead the projective hypothesis will find further expression in inspiring and guiding the design of crucial studies in this new sector of social psychology. Proshansky has pointed the way for the accomplishment of important experimental studies that utilize projective methods.

▼

Projective Techniques in Action Research: Disguised Diagnosis and Measurement [1]

Harold M. Proshansky

INTRODUCTION

THERE is a growing tendency for civic-minded leaders, educators, directors of industrial organizations, and other individuals interested in or responsible for the welfare of large social groups to look to social science for assistance in solving the complex social problems with which they are confronted. Quite eager to be of service to these individuals, the social scientist soon discovered that concerning himself with complex social problems was not simply a matter of turning his weapons in a new direc-

[1] I wish to express my gratitude to Dr. Isidor Chein of the Commission on Community Interrelations of the American Jewish Congress for his valuable guidance in preparing this chapter.

tion. The atmosphere of a community, labor organization, or un-affiliated boys' club presented him with a twofold challenge: first, he had to deal with large and complex heterogeneous groups that were not amenable to the ordinary academic labo-ratory procedures; second, his research efforts had to have social significance as well as theoretical importance.

Science is often defined in terms of its objectives—namely, predicting and controlling natural events. Social scientists have not agreed on the implications of this definition as applied to social events, and as a result they have tended to fall into one of two groups, depending upon whether they regard prediction or control as the more important aspect of the definition. In one group we find those social scientists who emphasize the acquisi-tion of a systematic body of principles concerning group be-havior by means of unbiased investigations. In the other group we find those social scientists who insist that their task is to control social events for the benefit of mankind. The first group lays stress on predictions based upon disinterested investigation, the second on the need for social change.

Partly in response to the challenge of dealing with complex heterogeneous groups, and partly to transcend this artificial dichotomy of "two types" of social scientist, there has devel-oped a new field in social psychology, especially associated with the name of Kurt Lewin and appropriately designated as *Action Research*. Action research simply is the application of scientific procedures to real social problems. More specifically, it concerns itself not merely with discovering the causes of these problems, but also with finding the means for dealing with them and ap-plying these means as the most effective methods of bringing about change. In a recent article by Chein, Cook, and Harding [3], action research is described as "a field which developed to satisfy the needs of the sociopolitical individual who recognizes that, in science, he can find the most reliable guide to effective action, and the needs of the scientist who wants his labors to be of maximal social utility as well as of theoretical significance."

Interested on the one hand in bringing about social change, and on the other in deriving principles for the understanding of human behavior, the action researcher finds himself confronted with a host of new problems. Some of these problems emerge from the fact that he must structure and organize his research plans with the basic long-range view of bringing about change. It may easily be argued at this point that the ordinary applied social scientist is faced with the same problems. Yet this is not so, for while the applied social scientist is interested in change, this is a result toward which he hopes, but does little to assure, that his research efforts will lead. Ordinarily he is given an assignment or commission to investigate some very specific and limited problem, which he may choose to accept or reject, depending on his own needs and interests. He concerns himself with providing information and even with measuring change, but not with seeing that his efforts actually lead to change. The action researcher, on the other hand, is not content with simply discovering but also wants to make certain that what he discovers is properly applied. His research program includes not only methods and techniques designed to accumulate facts but also methods and techniques designed to bring about social change on the basis of these facts.

Equally interested in making theoretical contributions as in socially meaningful ones, the action researcher finds himself confronted with other problems. Concerned with real social groups as they occur in everyday life, he is unable to dominate his subjects and secure their co-operation with the ease that is so characteristic of research in the academic laboratory or hospital clinic. The emotionally disturbed individual who comes to the clinic for some kind of psychiatric aid often stands ready to participate in whatever research programs the clinician may suggest. In the laboratory situation the needs and interest of the "theoretical" investigator determine the organization of his research efforts. The problems he selects are not only those which are of interest to him, but also those which are amenable to maximally controlled scientific procedures. He deliberately makes use of college sophomore populations because he can manipulate them as he desires, but also because, as relatively homogeneous groups, they present him with fewer variables with which to contend.

In the community situation the relation between investigator and his subjects changes completely. Whether it is an entire community, a labor union, or some particular religious group, the research program of the action researcher set up within the framework of a group desiring significant social action must be guided closely by the needs and interests of the group in order to bring about this change. Thus from the moment he enters the community the action researcher must focus his attention upon what the community regards as significant. His role in the community is a subordinate one, and his own interests and needs are of little consequence. Since his research program must be established within the framework of the existing social setting, he is confronted with problems of experimental design that are unknown to the academic investigator. He is faced with different problems from those of the applied social scientist because he is interested not merely in immediate and practical results but also in developing general laws of behavior. For the action researcher there is an integral relationship between scientific inquiry and social action. Chein, Cook, and Harding [3] summarize the difficulties of the action researcher very adequately when they state:

"To summarize, the action researcher interacts with the community in which he is working and finds special limitations imposed at every level of his work from the choice of problem areas, the specific formulation of the problem, the selection of procedures, the presentation of his findings, on through to their application. . . ."

The brief discussion of action research up to this point has been offered in order to crystallize some basic facts about this relatively new field and to facilitate the subsequent discussion on diagnosis and measurement. One can find a more thoroughgoing analysis of action research in the article quoted above, as well as in another paper by the same authors entitled "The Use of Research in Social Therapy" [2].

The specific problems that are of interest to us here are those of diagnosis and measurement as they relate to action research, with special emphasis on projective techniques. In the discussion to follow I shall not attempt to distinguish between diagnosis and measurement, since in actual practice they are interdependent. Data obtained with objective and standardized measuring procedures may be valuable in making a specific diagnosis, and information obtained for diagnosis from techniques designed to yield qualitative information (projective tests and others) may also be utilized for purposes of measurement by the application of some method of scaling or quantification.

From the standpoint of obtaining useful data for diagnosis and measurement in the community setting, it is essential that the social scientist utilize disguised techniques. The setting of an unaffiliated boys' club, labor union, or housing project is not the congenial atmosphere that one finds in the laboratory setting. Individuals in these situations are apt to react with suspicion and antagonism to the investigator who inquires about such crucial and controversial issues as their attitudes toward minorities, their political beliefs, and so on. In most cases the investigator must give serious consideration to disguising his techniques for measurement and diagnosis in order to avoid alienating his group, an eventuality that may well lead to a breakdown of the research program.

Furthermore, assuming for the sake of discussion that the members of the group are quite willing to voice their opinions and attitudes, the investigator may be confronted with the problem of individuals who are unable to articulate these opinions and attitudes. The ease with which college students are able to respond to questionnaires, interviews, and other techniques for obtaining data tends to give the highly experienced academic researcher a false sense of security when he first enters the community setting. This is not to assert pretentiously that only individuals in the university can articulate their attitudes and opinions, but rather that in community research one must be prepared to deal with individuals who differ considerably in their ability to express themselves. The use of indirect methods of measurement and diagnosis serves to avoid the distortion that may be introduced into the data by this variable.

Even in those rare situations in which a group is willing to co-operate and is also quite capable of articulating its attitudes and opinions, the investigator may still find it necessary to use disguised measurement and diagnostic techniques. An individual may possess mutually contradictory attitudes, and which of the two attitudes appears at the level of awareness depends to a great extent on the characteristics of the immediate situation. In other instances an individual may be quite unaware that he possesses certain attitudes; that is, they may appear at the behavioral level but not at the verbal level. For example, an individual may always give a white woman his seat in a train and be quite unaware that he does not extend this courtesy to a Negro woman in the same situation. Even when the individual attempts to co-operate maximally it may be impossible to reveal attitudes of this type.

The needs for disguised techniques of measurement and diagnosis in community research are obvious. In actual practice the investigator is almost always faced with hostile individuals who, even if they are in a position to co-operate, are unable to express their attitudes and opinions without some distortion. The degree to which these problems arise in the natural social setting depends upon the particular group, the circumstances surrounding the request for the investigator's assistance, the particular social problems being investigated, and other factors. These factors give some indication not only of how disguised the researcher's techniques must be but also of what techniques, if any, can be used. In a highly tense industrial organization where there have been verbal skirmishes among various racial and religious groups, it may be impossible for the investigator to utilize direct methods of diagnosis and measurement. Participant observation may have to be used, or if this is not possible, perhaps only an inspection of the personnel records of the employees. For action research, where the important goal is to bring about change, the entire experimental design will depend on the characteristics of the group setting.

Since the problems of measurement are especially acute in the data-gathering processes of action research, investigators have given considerable attention to the development of new techniques and the modifications of old techniques originally designed for laboratory use. Considerable emphasis has been given to projective tests because of the success with which these methods have been used for diagnosing and measuring personality. Where direct methods have failed to provide information about the individual's basic personality structure, such tests as the Rorschach and the Thematic Apperception Test have proved to be especially useful. In community research it is usually essential that the techniques of diagnosis and measurement be disguised. Since not all projective techniques are disguised and not all disguised techniques are projective, community investigators have also made use of such methods as observation, sociometry, personal and public records, and interviews. When properly disguised these methods have been especially useful in those community situations in which the investigator has encountered considerable resistance from group members in his efforts to accumulate data by means of specific testing situations. In other instances, however, where testing was possible and the respondents varied considerably in their ability to articulate, investigators have found projective tests extremely valuable. While it would be worth while to discuss all these techniques, it is not possible to do so within the scope of this paper. For this reason I shall confine our discussion to the use of projective techniques in action research. For a fairly comprehensive survey of methods designed for or appropriate to the investigation of complex social problems in the community setting, the reader is referred to a recent article by Deri, Dinnerstein, Harding, and Pepitone *[4]*.

With the realization that individuals often cannot or will not reveal their attitudes and opinions, social scientists have turned to using projective techniques, among others, for obtaining such information. The essential feature of a projective test is that the individual's responses are not accepted with the meaning with which he gave them, but are interpreted in terms of some pre-established psychological conceptualization of what his responses to the specific test situations mean. The subject may be required to interpret a situation, answer a question, or tell a story about a picture, while he remains unaware of the way in which his responses will be used. Since the basic requirement of the projective techniques is that the data be interpreted projectively[2]—that is, according to some pre-established theory—any one of the standard psychological methods (interviews, questionnaires, etc.) may be used as projective tests.

The degree to which the test is structured determines what areas of freedom the individual will have in imposing his meanings and organizations on the stimulus material, but the degree of test structurization does not necessarily determine whether or not a test is projective. A highly structured test may provide a great deal of information about the individual, but the information obtained is usually limited by the particular characteristics

---

[2] This definition of a projective test was first given in the article cited above by Deri, Dinnerstein, Harding, and Pepitone. Defining the method in terms of what is done with the data—i.e., in operational terms—tends to avoid many of the difficulties involved in the use of the term "projection."

of the test stimuli. In the Rorschach Test we obtain information about many different aspects of the individual's personality. If, however, we require the individual to recite a poem (a highly structured situation), it may be possible to obtain information about the individual's personality from the tone of his voice, the distribution of emphasis, the nature of his errors, and the speed with which he reads. In both instances the tests are projective, but with the Rorschach a more extensive picture of the individual's personality is obtained.

If we accept the individual's lack of awareness as the defining characteristic of a projective test, then different projective tests can be distinguished in terms of the extent to which the individual remains unaware of the real meaning of his reactions. In a situation in which the individual is not even aware that he is being tested, all the subject's reactions may be interpreted projectively, and consequently one may regard such a technique as maximally projective. In this category one can include all those techniques used for collecting data on the individual as he behaves in his normal environment. One may, for example, projectively interpret data that have been obtained by a participant observer.

Techniques used for collecting data which are projectively interpreted, and in which the individual is aware he is being tested but unaware of *how* he is being tested, may be regarded as less projective than those described above. In these situations the individual is aware of the presence of the investigator, but he is unaware of the nature of the medium being used for testing him. To a certain extent the individual may repress or deliberately suppress many of his reactions. In this category may be included data obtained by means of the psychodramatic technique. Here the subject acts out a certain situation as he might act it out in everyday life. His behavior in this special situation is recorded and interpreted projectively.

While the techniques described above may be considered more projective, in that the individual is more unaware, in actual practice specific test situations are used in preference to these methods. The less restricted or more natural situations described above have a number of difficulties involved in their use which make them less valuable as projective tests. In most cases, though they provide an abundance of data that can be used for projective interpretation, these data are often difficult to organize for that purpose.

On the whole, most of the investigations utilizing the projective method for analyzing attitudes or opinions that the individual cannot or will not reveal have used specific test situations for this purpose. Primarily interested in the operation of these attitudes and opinions under given realistic conditions, investigators use test stimuli that are sufficiently structured to produce data bearing directly upon the problems being investigated. Subjects are required to tell a story about an ambiguous picture, fill in or complete pictures or sentences, recall pictures or stories, reply to open-ended questions, and so forth.

Studies reported in which one or more of these techniques were used consist of (a) attitude or opinion investigations of noncollege populations, (b) attitude or opinion investigations of college populations, and (c) investigations specifically aimed at studying general personality problems. Since there are as yet no detailed published accounts on the use of projective tests in an action-research project, it seems desirable to discuss a few studies in each of these categories in order to achieve some insight into the problems involved in using projective tests in action research.

A very early attempt was made by Fromme [7] to study opinions on preventing war. The subjects were individuals from many walks of life living in New York City or in the surrounding areas. One of the techniques was a cartoon test consisting of a series of five political cartoons from which the original captions had been removed. Four other captions were provided for each cartoon. The subject was required to select the caption that he regarded as being most appropriate, and his choice served as a rough measure of his opinion. The discussion provoked by the selection of captions provided diagnostic data for projective interpretation. Fromme also employed a procedure adapted from Murray's Thematic Apperception Test. Five ambiguous pictures were used that the investigator believed would provide data relevant to opinions on preventing war. The subjects were required to tell a story about each picture, and the material was then interpreted projectively.

J. F. Brown [1] recently reported a preliminary attempt to

study the nature and basis of racial attitudes by means of a modification of the Rosenzweig Picture-Frustration Test. Twenty-four pictures were used, six of which were taken directly from the Rosenzweig series for purposes of disguise. The other eighteen pictures consisted of situations in which (a) Negroes or Jews frustrate whites or gentiles, (b) whites and gentiles frustrate Negroes or Jews. In one case, for example, an older man is saying to a younger "Jewish-looking" individual: "You damn Jew—trying to marry my daughter!" In some pictures the subject is required to supply a response for the individual against whom the aggression is directed, and in others for the individual in the role of the aggressor in the picture. The test was used as an individual test and was also administered to groups. In the individual situation it was utilized as part of a routine clinical interview. In these interviews the subject was required to expand his replies, and the material was interpreted projectively. In the group situation the technique was projective in that the subjects were required (a) to tell what the individual in the picture would say, (b) to tell what they would say in a similar situation, and (c) to tell what they would like to say.

In its present form Brown's technique may not be very effective in many community settings. It is not sufficiently disguised and where individuals are likely to react with suspicion to discussions about their racial and religious attitudes the technique may readily alienate the group. A possible solution to this problem may lie in the addition of other neutral pictures and the use of more subtle ways to identify the individuals in the pictures. Both of these precautions would tend to conceal the purpose of the test and perhaps allow its use with unsophisticated respondents.

Saenger and Gordon [12] attempted to determine to what extent majority and minority groups in America accept or reject the basic American philosophy that success in this country lies within the grasp of all those who desire it and have the ability to achieve it.

Horowitz and Horowitz [10] employed pictures for studying the social attitudes of white schoolchildren in a small rural community in the South. The investigation represents an early attempt to study attitudes in the community setting. The investigators formulated their problems on the basis of data they obtained as participant observers in the community. In describing their approach the authors state that ". . . the community defined the problems for the research workers, and methods of investigation were developed as a function of both the problems and the community. Tests were developed as based upon the particular group and standardized for it."

No attempt was made to interpret the data obtained from the picture tests projectively; the tests, however, could be adapted for this purpose. In one case, for example, the children were shown a picture of a "group of three boys huddled about a Negro lad who was kneeling." While the investigators do not indicate what questions were asked about this picture, it is not too difficult to think of questions that would provoke diagnostic data for projective interpretation. Simply asking the children to tell a story about the picture may provide this kind of data.

There have been a number of studies undertaken for the purpose of investigating attitudes and opinions among college populations by means of one or another of the projective methods, and the study of Proshansky [1] utilized an adaptation of the Thematic Apperception Test as a means of determining specific attitudes toward labor.

Hartley [9] attempted to determine the relationship between basic personality traits and tolerance among college students. The subjects were presented with a list of topics that had to be covered in the process of writing a detailed personality sketch of themselves. Some of the topics included questions which produced material that was interpreted projectively. Such questions as "When are you happiest?" and "If you had a magic wishing wand and could wish for absolutely anything, what might you wish for?" provided imaginative material which was analyzed for what it revealed about the individuals' basic personality traits. The topics also included likes and dislikes, interests, skills, etc., and combined with the information elicited by the less structured questions it provided the investigator with data that he could use to construct a fairly comprehensive picture of the individual's personality. Basic personality traits were related to tolerance scores obtained from a social-distance scale.

Frenkel-Brunswik and Sanford [5] used four thematic pictures for analyzing the personality factors in anti-Semitic college women. The subjects were told that they were being given an imagination test and were required to write a story about each picture. The content of each picture was of such a nature that the investigators were relatively sure of obtaining material related to the racial attitudes of the respondents. One picture showed a number of "Jewish-looking" people in a lower-class section, another a Negro woman with a Negro boy, and so on. The stories were analyzed with the intent of determining the types of attitudes these respondents had toward minority groups, and also how these attitudes functioned in different kinds of personalities.

Worth mentioning briefly are a number of relatively new projective techniques which were originally designed for studying personality, but which can easily be adapted for use in the community setting.

Temple and Amen [15] designed a novel picture technique for studying personality problems in young children. The face of the central character in each of twelve pictures was omitted, and the child's task was to select either a happy face or a sad face to complete the picture, and then give his reasons for his selection. The central character in each picture, a small child of ambiguous sex, was shown in a variety of situations. The technique provided data that revealed many different anxiety areas in the experience of small children. By using pictures related to this problem the method can be adapted for studying racial and religious attitudes in young children.

Shor [14] describes a sentence completion technique designed for studying general personality problems. The subject is required to complete the beginning of sentences that touch upon such areas as feeling tones, and qualities of attitudes. Incomplete sentences such as "What puzzles me . . ." and "My greatest fear . . ." yielded an abundance of diagnostic material. One can easily envisage this technique's being adapted for research on complex social problems. Incomplete sentences, for example, such as "The boss is . . ." and "The best workers . . ." may easily be applied to the study of labor-management relations.

Haggard [8] employed comic-strip characters in designing a projective test for studying the personality of young children. The children were required to select their favorite from among many comic-strip characters. They were also asked to describe what was happening in the comic strip, and following this they had to be the "author" and make up a story about the comic-strip hero. By using pictures of Negro athletes familiar to young children—for example, Joe Louis, Jackie Robinson—social psychologists may find the test useful for studying racial attitudes in young children.

The discussion of projective tests, while not exhaustive, does shed some light on the way in which projective methods may be used for studying social problems. At the present time many studies in which projective tests are employed are undoubtedly being carried on by research agencies. Since these projects are time-consuming and since they usually extend over a period of years, the reader must wait for more extensive accounts of the use of projective tests in community research.

Two outstanding problems face the action researcher when he attempts to collect data in the community situation for purposes of diagnosis and measurement. First, he can usually anticipate only a minimum of co-operation from the members of the group at which his research efforts are being directed, and therefore he finds himself confronted with the obligation of using test methods that will serve to establish more positive relations between himself and the group; second, since he usually is concerned with large population segments consisting of individuals who vary in their ability to articulate their opinions and attitudes, he must use test techniques that do not depend too heavily upon direct probing of the individual for eliciting this information. With regard to both these problems projective techniques have a special usefulness and are therefore important possibilities for action research.

The action researcher often receives a lukewarm welcome into the social group around which his research plans are being organized. The problems he has been requested to study are usually of a controversial nature, and for that reason members of the group exhibit little enthusiasm about revealing their opinions and beliefs to an outsider. In many instances he also faces this same cool reception from group leaders and administrators. Resistance may sometimes reach a maximum when the investigator indicates a need for testing the members of the group. Where, however, the action researcher can demonstrate, by the use of disguised projective tests, that his diagnostic and measurement techniques are innocent enough and that they will not disrupt the normal behavior of the group, he may expect a more cooperative attitude from those responsible for group supervision. The use of a harmless picture test, or a questionnaire made up of seemingly harmless items, or some other projective technique can go a long way toward establishing positive relations between the investigator and group members and leaders.

Projective techniques may be useful in securing the co-operation of community members and leaders in action as well as in collecting data for a description of the situation. To be more specific, Chein, Cook, and Harding [3], among others, discuss an approach to social therapy which they have designated as the "participant approach." Underlying this approach is the belief that the probability of securing social change will be greater if the individuals who are to take action—that is, community members and administrators—are themselves involved in the research process. The authors point out "that diagnoses and recommendations frequently do not lead to action, and that one of the principal difficulties in securing a change in social relations stems from insufficient involvement of group members." For this reason group members actually serve on the research staff and with the guidance of the trained social scientist they interview, test, etc. Not only do they function in the data-gathering process of the investigation, but they also aid in planning activities that may lead to change.

The action researcher has no guarantee, even when using the participant approach, that the changes he suggests or recommends will be used by the group members, that they will lead to action. Where community members and leaders are serving as collaborators in the research program, however, it may often be desirable to use disguised projective tests that have some face validity. For example, if the problem being investigated is racial and religious prejudice among schoolchildren, it may be desirable to use a projective test that consists of pictures depicting children in various intergroup relationships. The advantage of this procedure lies in the fact that the collaborators (teachers) in the process of accumulating data will to some extent be able to understand and appreciate what the test data mean. Consequently it is reasonable to expect that because of their involvement in the research program in this way, they will be more likely to co-operate in whatever action programs the social scientist may suggest. In other words, where collaboration is possible, the employment of a projective test with face validity increases the probability that the group administrators—that is, the research collaborators—will realize the need for the recommendations for change made by the action researcher.

Projective techniques may be valuable in securing co-operation in action as well as in diagnosis. It should be pointed out, however, that the use of projective techniques in this way is restricted to research programs with limited objectives. In more extensive investigations the research requirements are usually of such a nature that the action researcher must forgo the use of simplified test techniques, and in this respect he cannot employ nonscientific personnel (collaborators) in his research programs. Chein, Cook, and Harding [3] point out that "There are obvious limitations upon the capacity of lay people to participate in scientific research, and the needs for action may often conflict with certain research requirements."

Even more significant for action research is the fact that projective techniques can be used effectively for diagnosing and measuring attitudes and opinions of community members who vary in their ability to articulate. This, perhaps, is one of the most serious problems for the action researcher. In most cases he is dealing with large groups of individuals who are inexperienced and often unable to express themselves on highly "intimidating" issues. It is quite true that individuals in labor unions, army battalions, or housing projects may often discuss vital issues among themselves. But this is altogether different from those situations in which they must express their own concrete ideas in response to concrete questions. Some individuals may be expressing their opinions and attitudes as nearly as possible as they really are, while others may be expressing attitudes and opinions that have been created momentarily to meet the need of making some kind of response to a stranger. The problem facing the action researcher is a complex one in that it involves individuals who may be co-operative but who unknowingly distort their responses because they are either unable to express themselves or unaware of what their real attitudes and opinions are.

The use of some projective picture test in which the individual simply has to tell a story or describe what he sees tends to retain at least some of the spontaneity necessary to get at what the individual really thinks. Attempting to ascertain what white workers in a factory think about working with Negroes is a delicate task. In some instances individuals may be insecure about lower-paid Negro competition and yet may not possess basic anti-Negro attitudes. In other individuals there may be strong anti-Negro attitudes and no particular fear of competition for their jobs from Negroes. The attempt to tease out such differences by probing the workers directly represents an almost impossible task, even if they are willing to co-operate. A sufficiently disguised projective test, however, using pictures involving whites and Negroes in different relationships in factory and nonfactory situations may go a long way in revealing these differences.

The importance of obtaining such subtle information cannot be stressed too much. If the action researcher is going to participate in bringing about change, he must recognize the complexity of prejudice and other social problems. In order to achieve action these problems must be closely scrutinized. They vary greatly in intensity and technique from situation to situation. Prejudice toward Negroes may occur in one factory setup and not in another. The factors that determine these variations depend on group relationship patterns, economic and social positions of Negroes and whites, the presence or absence of other minorities, and so on.

While projective techniques may be extremely useful instruments in action research, there are nevertheless many pitfalls involved in their use which have to be viewed realistically. Some of these problems are general ones (reliability, validity), which have to be met in using projective tests for any kind of research. Others, however, are quite specific to their use in action research. Let us briefly discuss each of these two types of problem in the order given.

The data obtained from projective tests can be viewed in two ways. On the one hand the data present the investigator with a variety and an abundance of material that seems to have a limitless potentiality for diagnosing attitudes and opinions in the individual; on the other hand they also present him with many difficulties with respect to the scientific treatment of his data. In terms of treating his data scientifically, the investigator faces many insurmountable difficulties. It is quite difficult, for example, to apply the usual methods for determining the reliability and validity of a test to one that is projective. While the material it provides is very rich with respect to possible interpretations, these interpretations can be subject to serious error. In most cases investigators will check on the reliability of their technique by having a number of individuals make independent interpretations. This, however, eliminates only one source of chance factors—that is, that the interpretation depends upon who is doing the interpretation. It does not provide a check on the problem of whether the interpretations will vary on repeated tests of the same individual. Whether one can use the usual split-half techniques or correlations between repetitions of the same test or between alternate forms depends on the method of interpretation. In most cases the obtained data are analyzed qualitatively and as such are not subject to such rigorous experimental checks. If the data have been quantified by means of some scaling method, however, such statistical checks are possible.

One of the crucial requirements of a projective test is that the interpretation of its data be based upon a valid theory. The usual methods of validating a test—correspondence with other criteria, internal consistency, etc.—must undergo some modification in order to be applied to projective tests. Validating these tests by means of inter-consistency checks is a somewhat different process from what is usually implied when this method is applied to attitude scales, personality inventories, and the like. Sargent [13], in describing some of the methodological problems involved in the use of projective techniques, indicates that the agreement found between the results of various projective tests administered to the same subjects constitutes the measure of internal consistency for these techniques. She points out that the weakness in this procedure lies in the fact "that true validity cannot be established through correspondence between measures which are not themselves validated."

Other investigators have attempted to validate projective tests by means of establishing their agreement with other criteria. This requires, however, that the data be categorized or quantified in order to be able to apply the usual statistical procedures. For example, in the study by Proshansky [11] cited earlier, the respondents' stories were rated by judges, and a final "attitude toward labor" score was obtained for each subject. These scores were then correlated with their scores on a standard attitude scale. The weakness of this procedure lies in the fact that it depends on the adequacy of the standard selected—in this particular case, an attitude scale. Furthermore, it should be remembered that projective methods are usually selected for studying attitudes with the view in mind of acquiring information ordinarily not revealed by attitude scales.

Investigators have also employed predictive success as a means of validating projective tests. There are some difficulties involved in this procedure, however, which have made its use somewhat limited. A summary of these difficulties is given in the article by Sargent [13] cited earlier.

For use in action research the investigator has to consider a number of other specifications in the selection or design of his projective test. He cannot assume that simply because a test is projective it is automatically endowed with the characteristics necesary for its use with community populations. On the contrary, since many projective techniques have been developed in the academic or clinical setting, they probably fail to meet the necessary specifications. If the action researcher takes it upon himself to modify these projective tests, he has two types of specification to consider: first, general requirements that are essential for the use of projective tests in almost any kind of social setting; second, requirements that are specific to the particular social group being studied, the circumstances surrounding the investigation, the problem being studied, and so on.

Whether projective tests are to be employed, or for that matter any other kind of test, it is the specific requirements that make diagnosis and measurement procedures especially difficult for action research. The investigator is in most cases unable to bring his projective tests to the particular social setting being studied. In general he is aware of what they will have to be like, but beyond this he cannot commit himself to any particular type of projective test. He can determine the exact specifications of his technique only after he has made a preliminary survey of the total situation (the group, the problem, etc.). In a sense his tests must be "tailor-made." His problems do not end here, however, because it is more than likely that as his research program progresses, changes will occur in the total situation which may necessitate the development of new techniques or the modification of the ones being used.

Although he is unable to indicate the specific characteristics of his projective test, the action researcher is well aware of the general lines along which it will have to be designed in order to be applicable for use in the community setting. As indicated earlier, projective techniques have considerable value for action research because they may permit the testing of individuals who vary in their ability to articulate. This does not mean, however, that any test which is projective is automatically acceptable for use with these kinds of populations. In general these tests have to be so designed that the individual is not required to verbalize to a degree or in a manner to which he is unaccustomed. The open-end projective question, for example, especially the kind that requires the respondent to verbalize in an abstract fashion, may frequently be rejected by less literate individuals in the community. The projective question: "What moments are embarrassing?" employed by Frenkel-Brunswik, Levinson, and Sanford [6] in their study of anti-minority attitudes, though applicable to college students, may not be accepted so readily by noncollege respondents. A question of this sort assumes not only that the respondent possesses some facility for verbal expression but also that he understands the question.

This criticism not only applies to projective questions but can also be made with respect to picture tests. The picture test suggested earlier for analyzing anti-Negro prejudice among white factory employees may not be applicable if some members of the factory are not educated to the extent of being able to make up stories. Asking less literate individuals to tell a story may easily invoke feelings of insecurity in the respondents which may cause them to reject the test completely.

In the clinic the psychologist's task with respect to his use of projective tests is defined in terms of obtaining a full description of the individual. When he employs the Rorschach Test, for example, it is with the idea in mind of providing himself with as complete a picture as possible of the patient's personality structure. It is quite possible, however, that while the information he acquires from all his patients with this test is along the same general lines, the quality and quantity of information he obtains may vary from patient to patient. Anyone who has used the Rorschach in the clinical situation will bear out the statement that there is a difference in the quality and quantity of material obtained from a 35-response record and a 100-response record. This is not to assert that the clinician is unable to make a diagnosis or gain insight into the personality of the person giving the 35-response record, but rather that the 100-response record is much richer and, in that sense, provides a more detailed picture of the individual's personality. In any event the clinician is not disturbed by these differences since he sees his problem in terms of learning all about each individual patient. Whatever information he derives from the Rorschach is valuable if it helps him in this respect. He is quite capable of shifting from a scanty record to a rich one without being any less effective in his role, since he is usually not concerned with combining or comparing his test results. In almost all cases where he feels doubtful as to what the test tells him about the individual, he will use other tests to supplement his findings on the Rorschach.

In contrast to this picture we find the action researcher using projective tests with a very different idea in mind. Like the clinician he is interested in discovering things about the individual, but not for the purpose of studying him directly. His interest in the individual is secondary, in that he is primarily concerned with diagnosing and measuring the behavior of the group to which the individual belongs. The action researcher uses projective tests for the purpose of providing himself with information relevant to the characteristics of the group that interests him. In some instances he may desire accurate measurements expressed in statistical terms, and in others meaningful diagnoses expressed in qualitative terms. In either case it is essential that the projective tests he uses provide him with data that he can combine for purposes of group description. To be of service in this way it is essential that his projective test provide him with the same kind of data about each member of the group. It is unimportant whether or not the test contributes to his understanding of the individual group member. What is important is that it provide him with data scientifically useful for a description of the group to which the individual belongs. For this reason the action researcher is interested in designing projective techniques which will transcend not only the problem of differences in the ability to articulate but also other problems that may serve to distort his data.

CONCLUSION

Throughout this chapter I have stressed the importance of disguised testing in action research. Furthermore, I have indicated how valuable disguised projective techniques may be in securing the co-operation of community or group administrators in carrying out testing programs designed to secure data on crucial and controversial issues. Properly disguising projective techniques is important not only in terms of assisting the action researcher to interact with the community, but also in terms of obtaining scientifically useful data. One of the essential requirements of the testing situation involving a projective technique is that the individual be spontaneous. How relaxed and how spontaneous he will be will depend upon how well the particular social problem being investigated is hidden from the individual. The problem facing the researcher who desires to develop special projective tests for use in the community is in finding the optimum degree of ambiguity of his test stimuli. His stimuli must be structured to the extent that he gets data relevant to the attitudes and opinions being studied and yet sufficiently disguised so that he can be assured of a fairly high degree of spontaneity.

As indicated earlier in our discussion, not all projective tests are disguised, and for that reason the investigator must give considerable attention to modifying these tests so that they will be applicable for use in the community. In their present form the techniques used by Proshansky [11] and Brown [1] would not be altogether suitable for action research since they suffer from a lack of concealment. These tests may possibly be disguised (a) by the use of a number of additional neutral items, and (b) by presenting the tests in a context that will be accepted by the respondent. Where the investigator attempts to disguise his test by means of additional neutral items, he is confronted with the problem of striking a balance between making his test too long, on the one hand, and using too few items and thus reducing the reliability of his crucial items, on the other.

In many respects it may be said that for action research it is more important that a test be disguised than that it be projective. Yet there is no denying that when they are properly disguised, projective tests can play an important role in the diagnostic aspects of community studies. Perhaps the one question that remains to be answered is where and when these techniques can be most effective in the community setting. When should they be used, and when should other disguised methods be employed—for example, observation? In order to answer this question we have to consider once again what the action researcher is striving for when he studies group behavior. The reader will recall that the action researcher is interested in bringing about social change by means of research efforts organized within the framework of the social group he is studying. For this reason the needs and interests of the group will determine what his particular role in the community will be and what methods and procedures he will have to use in order to fulfill this role.

It would appear, then, that where and when projective techniques can be most effective will depend upon the particular social setting in which the action researcher must function. Since social settings vary from place to place and perhaps from time to time, it is not possible to specify or indicate when projective techniques can best be used. In the academic atmosphere the investigator can select his test techniques on the basis of his own needs and interests. In the community setting the investigator has to consider not only the problem he has been called into study but also all the factors that are involved in his interaction with the social group. His selection of tests, for example, can be determined by such factors as how much cooperation he will receive, how much time he has for his investigation, how many people are on his staff, how much money he has at his disposal, what freedom he is given in the community setting, any special groups he will have to work with or whether he will have to make his own populations. Furthermore, it must be remembered that the action researcher is primarily interested in bringing about change. In certain situations it may be desirable to forgo testing altogether and concentrate on action.

REFERENCES

1. BROWN, J. F.: "A Modification of the Rosenzweig Picture-Frustration Test to Study Hostile Interracial Attitudes," *Journal of Psychology*, Vol. 24 (1947), pp. 247–72.
2. CHEIN, I., COOK, S. W., and HARDING, J.: "The Use of Research in Social Therapy." (To be published in *Human Relations*.)
3. ——: "The Field of Action Research," *American Psychol.*, Vol. 3 (1948), pp. 43–50.
4. DERI, S., DINNERSTEIN, D., HARDING, J., and PEPITONE, A. D.: "Techniques for the Diagnosis and Measurement of Intergroup Attitudes and Behavior," *Psychological Bulletin*, Vol. 45 (1948), pp. 248–71.
5. FRENKEL-BRUNSWIK, E., and SANFORD, R. N.: "Personality Factors in Anti-Semitism," *J. Psychol.*, Vol. 13 (1945), pp. 425–59.
6. FRENKEL-BRUNSWIK, E., LEVINSON, D. J., and SANFORD, R. N.: "The Antidemocratic Personality," in T. M. Newcomb and E. L. Hartley (eds.): *Readings in Social Psychology*. New York: Henry Holt & Co.; 1947.
7. FROMME, A.: "On the Use of Certain Qualitative Methods of Attitude Research," *Journal of Social Psychology*, Vol. 13 (1941), pp. 425–59.
8. HAGGARD, E. A.: "A Projective Technique Using Comic Strip Characters," *Character and Personality*, Vol. 10 (1942), pp. 289–95.
9. HARTLEY, E. L.: *Problems in Prejudice*. New York: King's Crown Press; 1946.
10. HOROWITZ, E. L., and HOROWITZ, R. E.: "Development of Social Attitudes in Children," *Sociometry*, Vol. 1 (1938), pp. 301–38.
11. PROSHANSKY, H. M.: "A Projective Method for the Study of Attitudes," *Journal of Abnormal and Social Psychology*, Vol. 38 (1943), pp. 393–5.
12. SAENGER, G., and GORDON, N.: *Patterns of Discrimination*. New York: Commission on Community Interrelations; 1948.
13. SARGENT, H.: "Projective Methods: Their Origins, Theory, and Application in Personality Research," *Psychol. Bull.*, Vol. 42 (1945), pp. 257–93.

14. SHOR, J.: "Report on a Verbal Projective Technique," *Journal of Clinical Psychology*, Vol. 2 (1946), pp. 279–82.

15. TEMPLE, R., and AMEN, E. W.: "A Study of Anxiety Reactions in Young Children by Means of a Projective Technique," *Genetic Psychology Monographs*, Vol. 30 (1944), pp. 61–113.

Index of Names

Index of Subjects